D0236349

This Land

OWEN JONES

This Land

The Story of a Movement

ALLEN LANE
an imprint of
PENGUIN BOOKS

ALLEN LANE

UK | USA | Canada | Ireland | Australia
India | New Zealand | South Africa

Penguin Books is part of the Penguin Random House group of companies whose addresses can be found at global.penguinrandomhouse.com.

First published by Allen Lane 2020
001

Set in 10.5/14pt Sabon LT Std
Typeset by Jouve (UK), Milton Keynes
Printed and bound in Great Britain by Clays Ltd, Elcograf S.p.A.

A CIP catalogue record for this book is available from the British Library

ISBN: 978–0–241–47094–7

www.greenpenguin.co.uk

To Keir and Rickman,
two beloved feline companions,
who got me through the double trauma
of a pandemic and writing this book

This land is your land and this land is my land
This land was made for you and me

– Woody Guthrie

We've captured the top of the Labour Party by mistake.

– Ash Sarkar

Why do you want to just walk away and pass the title deeds of this great party over to someone like Jeremy Corbyn? I don't want to, I resent it, and I work every day in some small way to bring forward the end of his tenure in office. Something, however small it may be – an email, a phone call or a meeting I convene – every day I try to do something to save the Labour Party from his leadership.

– Peter Mandelson

Contents

Introduction – A Nation in Turmoil 1

PART I

Rise

1 Before Corbyn 13

2 From the Ashes 39

3 'It's Gonna Be Brutal': The War Within 62

4 Dysfunction 91

5 How to Run a Campaign 126

PART II

Fall

6 The Brexit Bandersnatch 165

7 The Antisemitism Crisis 210

8 'A Blizzard of Lies and Excuses' 257

9 Things Fall Apart 282

Conclusion – The Centre Cannot Hold 307

Notes 321

Acknowledgements 335

Introduction – A Nation in Turmoil

'This is going to be a fantastic year for Britain.' So proclaimed Boris Johnson's Twitter account two days into 2020, accompanied by a picture of the British prime minister, thumbs up, suited and booted, conveying an air of workmanlike determination, ready to forge a new buccaneering post-Brexit Britain. Four months later, thousands of Britons were dead, the nation was in lockdown, the economy in collapse, unprecedented social upheaval beckoned, and Johnson was in intensive care. Amid such trauma, the recent past quickly becomes distant; it might, too, feel trivial, somehow detached from our new age of pandemic. But it should not be forgotten that, in the previous half decade, Britain had suffered its worst political turmoil since the last world war, a period of bitter division and stifled hope. The lessons we learn from this era will not just help determine the future of this profoundly troubled nation, but may have consequences far beyond Britain's borders too.

It seems hard to believe now, but when, back in 2019 – in what seems another age – the Conservatives crushed Jeremy Corbyn's Labour Party in a general election, stability of a sort appeared to beckon, albeit on terms millions resented. But as coronavirus triggered an unparalleled combined public health crisis, economic crisis and social crisis, those five years, it transpired, were just the warm-up act, the hors d'oeuvre of chaos.

This is the story of the political consequences of both the 2008 financial crash and the slash-and-burn cuts that followed over the next ten years and more, inflicted by Conservative governments bent on enacting the endgame of an ideologically driven attack on the state and society that had started some four decades earlier, with

Margaret Thatcher's ascent to power. During this period, Britain's workers suffered the longest squeeze in wages since the Napoleonic War, a slide in living standards surpassed in the industrialized world only by calamity-stricken Greece. Public sector workers – nurses, firefighters, teachers among them – endured real terms pay cuts which shrank their wage packets by up to 14 per cent in just seven years.[1] Up to £37 billion was cut from the welfare state, hacking away support for low-paid workers and the disabled in particular.[2] While the fortunes of the 1,000 wealthiest families more than doubled during the first half of the 2010s, hundreds of thousands of people were driven to food banks to satisfy one of the most fundamental human needs: to eat. No aspect of public life was immune from this sustained economic assault, which we know by the name of austerity: there were cuts to spending on school pupils – an act of vandalism against their futures, and the future of Britain itself – libraries, museums, leisure centres, parks, and arts and culture, to name but a few.[3]

What are the political consequences of stripping away both security and optimism from millions of citizens in a prosperous nation? This was the British experiment of the 2010s: a time of riots, protests, strikes and, most divisive and damaging of all, the protracted Brexit saga, whose culture wars would bitterly divide families, communities and the nation as a whole. In fact, it would drag Britain's political system to the very precipice.

At the mid-point of this period of political bedlam, Britain witnessed an audacious political revolution. On 3 June 2015, a scruffy, amiable Labour Party backbencher whose name – Jeremy Corbyn – was little known outside of left-wing circles, declared his intention to run for the party leadership. His initial odds of winning were rated at 200–1, and he seemed unlikely to gather enough nominations from his fellow Labour MPs even to appear on the ballot paper. When he cleared that threshold, his team's ambition was to avoid coming last, to achieve up to 20 per cent of the vote, and to place a brake on the party's rightward drift to embracing pro-austerity, anti-welfare and anti-immigration positions. That summer, Corbyn and his supporters pushed against a door they thought was made of reinforced steel; as things proved, it was made of cardboard. And so began an unprecedented political experiment in British democratic history, whereby the new, radical leadership of a major political party attempted to assert a transformative political programme – which, if successful, would have changed the very nature of Britain – in a hostile political environment determined to crush it, and whose fervid support from its grassroots membership was matched by embittered opposition from politicians within its own party. Ultimately, it failed, spectacularly so. Following the wreckage of Labour's calamitous 2019 election result, the standard narrative of the Corbyn years now goes like this. Here was a man demonstrably unsuitable for high office, his leadership sustained only by the deluded infatuation of an ideologically crazed political cult. Midwife to Brexit, morally disgraced by the evil of antisemitism, intolerant of dissent, Jeremy Corbyn offered a policy prospectus which was self-evidently too extreme and otherworldly for the sensibilities of the British public. This era – so the narrative goes – was a tragic aberration, to be remembered only as a salutary lesson in where political radicalism and self-indulgence lead: to electoral ruin.

There is another narrative, its polar opposite. This contends that Corbyn and his project were wrecked solely by a deliberate campaign of internal sabotage within the Labour Party itself, wedded to a vicious and unrelenting onslaught from an overwhelmingly antagonistic establishment media. Corbyn, a decent and genuine man, was politically destroyed by a smear campaign on a scale without precedent, coordinated not just by the right, but by the liberal 'centre'. Both these narratives need correcting; I'll do so in this book.

Though Corbynism emerged out of a fractured British political landscape, it was also part of a global phenomenon. Around the world, the aftershocks of the 2008 financial crash had had many impacts. One was the global growth of the far right, who typically blamed Muslims, migrants, refugees and other oppressed and marginalized minorities for growing social trauma. This helped to spawn Donald Trump in America; the resurgence of France's National Front (now, National Rally); the German AfD; Britain's UKIP and Brexit Party; Spain's Vox party; Italy's Lega Nord; Austria's Freedom Party. This era also saw the ascendancy of left movements which, rather than blaming social crises on the most vulnerable, realized that responsibility lay instead with elite vested interests, and championed a radical redistribution of wealth and power. So rose the Bernie Sanders movement in the United States; the anti-austerity Podemos party in Spain; Syriza in Greece; the Left Bloc in Portugal; La France Insoumise (loosely translated as 'France Unbowed'); Ireland's Sinn Fein; and, of course, Corbynism. The Corbyn insurrection, then, was just one manifestation of a broader wave of political unrest across the Western world – albeit a very British one.

Corbynism was also symptomatic of another global phenomenon: the crisis of social democracy. By the early 2010s, the centrist-led parties who had triumphed in the 1990s – from Blair's Labour to the Spanish Socialists and German Social Democrats – had entered a long slow decline. As they fell apart – their mantras of free trade and trickle-down prosperity no longer workable in an era of rampant inequality, deprivation, economic and environmental crises – so their support polarized. At the time of writing, there is not a single majority social-democratic government in the Western world.

Corbynism, as we'll see, was woven together from many disparate strands: from people who marched against the Iraq War in 2003 to a new generation whose hopes and ambitions were hit hard by the Conservative–Liberal Democrats' trebling of college tuition fees in 2010; the millions aggravated by the Conservatives' failure to fund essential services while the wealthy got ever richer; and the millions more frightened by a looming climate emergency which posed a threat to human existence itself. What all these people lacked was a political voice, a magnetic force which could bring them all together. In 2015, Corbyn provided that focus. Yet that strength also proved a weakness: Corbynism itself was an unstable coalition of older political activists and younger supporters radicalized by student, anti-austerity, climate and tax justice movements – movements much more resistant to hierarchy and discipline.

As I'll explore, Corbynism largely overlapped with the age of Brexit, something which, for a time, worked to its advantage. The party offered a compromise solution – to leave the EU but with a close new relationship – while focusing on popular domestic policies such as taxing the rich, public investment, scrapping tuition fees and establishing public ownership, attracting Remain and Leave voters alike. Yet as the middle ground on Brexit collapsed, this compromise offer appealed to an ever-declining constituency. A constitutional split over Britain's relationship with the EU escalated into a full-blown culture war that proved deadly to a political project founded on the idea that the real divide that mattered was between the people and the establishment. As Brexit sucked the oxygen out of all political discourse, Labour was slow to define its position, and Corbyn's own primary advantage – that of being a man of principle who spoke out of conviction, whether you agreed with him or not – was obliterated as the party desperately tried to reconcile its political reality: that it needed to keep its majority Remain flank on board, but could not win power without its Leave supporters.

Was Corbynism always doomed to fail? Did it carry within it the seeds of its own destruction? When Corbyn assumed the Labour leadership, the left had been consigned to irrelevance for over a generation. The fragments that remained defined themselves by what they were against rather than what they were for: a coherent vision of what society should look like was largely missing in action. Corbyn had few skilled strategists, communicators or managers to draw on – which especially mattered given that, from the get-go, Corbynism found itself under savage assault, both from enemies outside and inside the Labour Party.

The impact of this onslaught should not be underestimated. Most British newspapers are owned by wealthy moguls fundamentally hostile to even the most modest redistribution of wealth and power. The top echelons of the broadcast media, too, are institutionally ideologically opposed to the aims and ambitions of the Corbyn project. New Labour's concordat with Thatcherism, meanwhile, had entrenched contempt for even mild social democracy among some of the party's MPs and much of the party machinery; they deployed a scorched earth attack against their own elected leadership. Corbyn himself was subjected to a character assassination campaign unprecedented in British political history. The consequences were devastating.

But the Corbyn project also shot itself repeatedly in the foot. It's important to make this point – and I will, throughout this book – because not to do so would lead to a fatalistic conclusion that any radical political project will inevitably be destroyed by entrenched establishment opposition. There was, it was true, a lack of experience in the Corbyn leadership. But there was also a disastrous failure in strategy, compounded by hubris after the 2017 election, and, ultimately, divisions within the leadership paralysed Corbynism from the top down. Damningly, there was no serious attempt to turn around what were, in the end, catastrophic personal ratings for Corbyn himself that deterred many from voting for the party he led. There were other profound mistakes too. Although antisemitism was abhorred by most of the Labour membership, and although some of Corbyn's bitterest opponents seized upon the issue in a cynical manner, there was a disastrous failure to face down this racism from the start, or to reach out to a Jewish minority who felt understandable collective trauma from two millennia of persecution and, within living memory, an attempt at total extermination.

These were harrowing years for those involved in the Corbyn project. Most were driven by a sense of idealism and a burning rejection of injustice (nobody committed to socialist principles prior to 2015 did so because they believed it would be beneficial for their political careers). Many paid a significant personal price. Being under relentless siege – in some cases, singled out for personal vilification with little means to defend yourself – takes its toll. Mental health was damaged, and relationships were torn apart.

Which brings us back to the coronavirus crisis. The pandemic has acted as a flare, exposing existing injustices, but also as an accelerant. It has driven home to us all what our society has become: how millions are always just one paypacket away from extreme hardship; how key workers, whose astonishing sacrifice and bravery were acknowledged by applause every Thursday evening, are underpaid and undervalued in real terms, often toiling in underfunded services; how health and social care are badly under-resourced; how many self-employed and gig economy workers live in desperate precariousness; how our welfare state is woefully inadequate.

We were told coronavirus is a great social leveller, that it affects rich and poor just the same. This has been proven grimly untrue, with fatality rates among poorer people and minorities significantly higher – terrible statistics that underline profound pre-existing inequalities. Unemployment was projected to hit low-paid workers hardest,[4] and food bank use jumped 326 per cent.[5] While those on poverty wages had little choice but to risk their health and indeed their lives, middle-class professionals could work safely from home; some even enjoyed increases in their savings as outgoings on pre-coronavirus leisure activities – restaurants, theatres, holidays – stopped. According to the Office for National Statistics, by June 2020 coronavirus had killed 1 in every 1,701 people in England's least deprived areas; in the most deprived areas, that figure was 1 in 779.[6]

That the Conservative government responded to the pandemic with the greatest expansion of the state in peacetime history, including paying the wages of millions of workers and securing the incomes of self-employed people, proves one thing: the state can intervene on a colossal scale for the social good, if the will is there. It also reveals the decade and more of punishing austerity – austerity which killed thousands and wrecked the hopes and dreams of unnumbered thousands more – for what it was: an ideological sham that should never have happened, and worse, that never needed to happen. Back in 2017, Prime Minister Theresa May told a nurse who hadn't received a pay rise for eight years that 'there is no magic money tree that we can shake that suddenly provides for everything that people want.' Turns out, there was after all.

The fact is, however, that this change of direction is an unnatural one for a Conservative Party in thrall to vested interests which prioritize economic considerations over human lives. In most respects, its approach to the coronavirus has been catastrophic, leading to the avoidable deaths of tens of thousands. On 5 March 2020, as the first British death from coronavirus was reported, Boris Johnson publicly declared that government advice was 'wash your hands and business as usual'. A decade of Conservative austerity meant there was not enough personal protective equipment to ensure the safety of front-line workers; lockdown was delayed in pursuit of a hideous policy of 'herd immunity'; social care was left chronically underfunded and underprepared; testing capacity was not invested in. As Professor Neil Ferguson – one of the country's most renowned epidemiologists and a former government adviser – put it in June, if lockdown had been introduced a week earlier, at least half of Britain's deaths could have been avoided.[7] Former Chief Scientific Adviser Sir David King goes even further: lockdown a week earlier could have limited Britain's death toll to 10,000.[8] A state hollowed out by austerity and market dogma is, in large part, to blame: it cannot be stressed enough that it is mostly because of these ideologically driven failures that Britain has been – is – one of the worst-hit countries on Earth.

In the interests of transparency, I should say that I write this book both as observer and participant. Socialism and Labourism are, for me, a family tradition which stretches back generations. My great-grandfather, a railwayman in the West Country, had his wages docked after downing his tools in solidarity with the miners in the 1926 General Strike; my great-uncle was a Welsh Methodist lay preacher and socialist who, in the 1930s, played for the Independent Labour Party's football team in Liverpool. My grandfather joined the Communist Party as an apprentice Portsmouth dockworker following the Nazi invasion of the Soviet Union in 1941 before becoming a Labour member; my grandmother was a Labour councillor whose proudest achievement was saving a family from eviction by a private landlord at Christmas. My parents met while canvassing for the Labour Party in a snowstorm outside Tooting Bec station in 1969. I was babysat by striking miners in South Yorkshire and strapped to my dad's chest at rallies in which the voice of miners' leader Arthur Scargill would boom defiantly; as a five-year-old I marched with my family against Thatcher's hated poll tax. My dad was a senior shop steward who helped lead an unsuccessful struggle to defend hundreds of jobs at Sheffield City Council in the mid-1990s. If there's anything I've learned from my family's decades of political commitment, it's that history is not linear, a tale of victories followed by successes and yet more victories, but often defeats, setbacks, followed by victories, then more defeats and setbacks. Finally, you might get somewhere approximating to where you're aiming for. It's called a struggle for a reason.

After I left university in 2005, I worked for three years for a then little-known left-wing backbencher named John McDonnell, and helped run his doomed bid to replace Tony Blair as Labour leader. Frustrated by the constraints of Parliament, I took to writing to try to highlight social injustices and promote movements which sought to overcome them; that was the aim, at least, of my books, articles and

TV appearances. When Jeremy Corbyn stood for leader in 2015, I had no hesitation in campaigning for him. Although I voted for him again in 2016, I had a period of disillusionment before the general election – something which still riles his most ardent supporters. Since then, aware that most of the British media were not just aggressively hostile to Corbynism, but regarded it as fundamentally, dangerously illegitimate, I used my position as one of his few sympathizers with a platform to try to rebut a relentless onslaught, while voicing criticism whenever I dissented. This book is based on the experiences of those who served in the Corbyn leadership, as well as the wider labour movement: many are friends and comrades, some of whom I've known most of my adult life. Their words and insights speak for themselves.

A note on this book's sources. I've interviewed dozens of people involved in this story – including the key figures behind the Corbyn project – at great length. But this was an extremely polarized period, both in British politics as a whole and within the febrile confines of the Labour Party. Many spoke on the condition that they would not be publicly identified. They may still be contractually forbidden from speaking to journalists; they may fear professional or personal consequences if they publicly say uncomfortable things about erstwhile colleagues. Their anonymity does not make what they are saying any less heartfelt or true to them, nor does it mean that they are driven to comment by anything other than the wish to learn lessons from a terrible political defeat.

This is a period of political and personal trauma, and different people often have conflicting but good faith interpretations of the same events. 'This is my truth, now tell me yours,' as the British Labour politician Aneurin Bevin put it. I have done everything I can to reconcile those different perspectives.

Everything I write is intended – in the very limited capacity that any writer has – to support struggles against injustice, and this book is no exception. As I show, these five years underline the lengths much of the establishment will go to in order to destroy any movement which challenges concentrations of wealth and power. The book also aims to provide a clear-eyed assessment of the many failures and mistakes of the Corbyn era. This will upset some, but it is necessary.

There is no future for any emancipatory project that does not learn from its errors. We live in disturbing times. Social and economic convulsion that few of us have experienced in our lifetimes beckons – yet Labour's rout in 2019 has been used to suppress the political imagination of those aspiring for a better world: to curtail dramatically what is seen as politically possible.

Yet this is no time for despair. In our age of upheaval, imagining what might be possible is more important than ever. 'A revolutionary moment in the world's history is a time for revolutions, not for patching,' declared William Beveridge in 1942 as he laid the foundations of the welfare state. Beveridge was no radical; he was a Liberal reformer who understood that tinkering was no answer in an age of tumult and crisis. We can build a world free of injustice, oppression, exploitation, bigotry, racism and violence, but if our time is to come, then we must learn from our past.

PART I

Rise

I
Before Corbyn

Let me take you back to May 1997. The scene: the interior of 10 Downing Street, the elegant Westminster residence of the British prime minister. Just weeks after his party's May 1997 landslide over an imploding Conservative Party, Tony Blair, the prime minister of Britain's shiny new Labour government, was enjoying an extended honeymoon. With him was Rupert Murdoch, the right-wing media mogul whose newspapers had over the previous decade and more systematically smeared his political opponents – the left, trade unions, LGBT people, immigrants, dead Liverpool fans, you name it – walking down a corridor arm in arm with Anji Hunter, one of Blair's closest aides. Also inside Number 10 that day was Mark Seddon, then editor of the iconic Labour-supporting magazine *Tribune*. 'I was told,' Seddon recalls in his well-spoken, staccato accent, ' "you must never tell people what you see".'

It was all over for the Labour left – or so it seemed. At this moment, free-market capitalism looked unassailable. As Labour's new leader, the telegenic rightwinger Blair had succeeded in banishing the party's historic commitment to public ownership, enshrined in Clause IV of its constitution. Not long after the party adopted new wording – with vacuous motherhood-and-apple-pie type talk of 'opportunity' being 'in the hands of the many, not the few' – Seddon was in Millbank Tower, then Labour's London HQ, when he bumped into the political editor of the *Mail on Sunday*, Simon Walters, who told him: 'In five years' time, you'll all be gone.' It was tongue in cheek. Partly. 'They wanted to get rid of all of us really, didn't they?' says Seddon, rueful even now.

The political party fronted up by Tony Blair had come a long way from its origins. Labour had been founded at the dawn of the twentieth century by Britain's trade union movement to give working people political representation. As it evolved, however, the party had become a coalition between modest reformers, who believed in humanizing the existing system, and those who wanted to transcend it in favour of a new society which prioritized human needs over the search for profit. This latter faction was known as the Labour left. In the 1950s, its figurehead was the Welshman Nye Bevan, a former miner and the founder of Britain's National Health Service; two decades on, its flag-bearer was the pipe-puffing, tea-drinking cabinet minister Tony Benn, who had famously renounced his unwanted hereditary peerage, confounding the stereotype of politicians growing more conservative with age. During the 1970s, Benn became known for his barnstorming speeches, for making cups of tea for striking workers, and for his emphasis on democracy, for which he established five tests: 'What power have you got? Where did you get it from? In whose interests do you exercise it? To whom are you accountable? How can we get rid of you?'

Benn's embrace of workers and socialism saw him become a hate figure for the right-wing media, to whom he was, variously, 'Bolshevik Benn', 'Commissar Wedgie' and 'The Most Dangerous Man in Britain Today'.[1] But Benn was no Marxist ideologue: he was not an avid book reader, rather forming his opinions through his lived experiences. 'In the years up to 1968 I was just a career politician,' he later wrote. It was his experience of power – which all too often numbed the radicalism of politicians – that convinced him of the need for more far-reaching political change.[2]

But by the mid-1990s, with Blair at his blazing zenith, Labour's radical left had all but evaporated. 'You really don't have to worry about Jeremy Corbyn suddenly taking over,' quipped Blair to a journalist in 1996 about the nonconformist left-wing backbencher, then best known for his unkempt beard, home-knitted jumpers and support for campaigns spanning opposition to apartheid and to the Gulf War. The journalist in question never printed the quote because, in his own words, 'Jeremy Corbyn was such a marginal figure at the time that the idea of him taking over anything sounded ridiculous.'[3] The shift in Labour's political centre had been seismic.

*

Some two decades before the coming of Tony Blair, the Labour left had optimistically believed the direction of history could well be on its side. In 1974, the party edged into power with perhaps the most radical manifesto it had ever put before the British electorate, promising to bring about 'a fundamental and irreversible shift in the balance of power and wealth in favour of working people and their families'.[4]

It was not to be. As a global oil-price shock helped plunge the British economy into crisis, the Labour government had two possible ways to stimulate the stagnant economy and combat spiralling inflation. One approach was the interventionist 'alternative economic strategy', pioneered by the radical left-wing politician Tony Benn, which proposed hiking taxes on the rich, control of the banks and a 'vigorous micro-investment programme'. In practice, this involved taking several leading companies into direct public ownership, and imposing compulsory planning agreements on other privately run businesses. Instead, the government chose a different path.

Now chief of staff of Unite, the UK's second largest union with somewhat over a million members, and a key figure in the Labour left, Andrew Murray cut his teeth in political activism as a teenager in the late 1970s. He remembers a country trembling on the brink of an uncertain transition. The left was then institutionally stronger, more entrenched in civil society because of the strength of the trade union movement, but to Murray there was no real sense of it being in the political ascendancy, despite the incumbent Labour government.

'The beginning of "neo-liberalism" in Britain wasn't when Thatcher came to power in 1979,' Murray tells me, tilting back in his office chair in Unite's headquarters in Holborn, the central London skyline forming a backdrop behind him. Murray has an unflappable air about him; he speaks with seriousness and precision, carefully weighing each word before offering it up. 'It was when Labour Prime Minister Jim Callaghan and his chancellor, Denis Healey, rejected Benn's proposals and embraced a "monetarist" agenda including a squeeze on real wages and very savage cuts in public spending.'

Labour's radical activists felt bitterly betrayed by the economic policies their party had embraced in government – a memory that endured through Margaret Thatcher's rise to power in 1979 and the economic blitz of her first two years in office. They also resented their party's top-down aversion to democracy. 'It was a campaign about democracy as far as I was concerned,' says the chirpy, well-spoken former Labour MP Chris Mullin, a leading figure on Labour's left in the 1980s. 'There was quite a lot of evidence of a widening gulf between the party in Parliament and the party in the country in the 1960s and 70s' and, he recalls, 'lots of idle, useless MPs in safe seats'. None more so, in his view, than the MP in the south London constituency of Vauxhall, where he then lived. Astonishingly, the local MP, George Strauss, had been the party's candidate since 1924. With Labour's rules making it difficult to unseat incumbents, the local party was moribund – and it did its best to keep newcomers out. 'The party had died for all practical purposes in that constituency,' says Mullin, 'so you didn't have to be a "Trot" to see something wrong with this arrangement.'

When, in 1981, Tony Benn made a bid to become the party's deputy leader, he did so as a representative of the radical left, tapping into activists' angry disillusionment with Labour's recent record in office. 'If you look at the defeat of the Labour government in May 1979,' declared Benn a year and half after the election, 'the more I think about it, the more I think it was a surrender rather than a defeat . . . One could argue that Mrs Thatcher and the Conservative Party won last year with very little opposition to the ideas that she preached.'[5]

Before Benn, the Labour left had been more of a parliamentary bloc than a popular movement. His deputy leadership campaign sought to change that, energizing grassroots activists, but his narrow loss – thanks to the opposition of fellow Labour MPs, and in spite of the membership, over 81 per cent of whom voted for him – would be a high-water mark for the left over the next quarter-century. After another failed challenge for the leadership, in the following years and decades Benn himself changed: no longer a figurehead for a movement seriously aspiring to power, he became more of a moral conscience, a comfort to the defeated fragments of the left. This was the iteration of Tony Benn I was familiar with. Growing up in the age of 'The End of History' – the title of political scientist Francis Fukuyama's 1989 landmark essay, which argued that free-market liberal democracy was the endpoint of human development – I found him a reassuringly defiant, but isolated, voice challenging the neoliberal dogma of 'There is no alternative'. In his final years, we spoke together at meetings and rallies, and I got to know him; his warmth, optimism, tea-drinking and pipe-smoking were undimmed. At a public event in central London attended by his adoring supporters, a few months before he died in April 2014, I put it to him that he had gone from being 'the most dangerous man in Britain' to a national treasure, a kindly, harmless old gentleman. Smiling, he responded to rapturous applause: 'I may be old, I may be kindly, I may be a gentleman but I am not harmless!' Nonetheless the ascent of this left-wing radical to national treasure status had come with the neutering of the politics he espoused. His politics had long ceased to represent a threat – and so, consequently, neither did he. A man who had once spooked the political establishment was now an endearing curiosity to be indulged.

In the 1980s and early 90s, as Thatcher's government set about transforming Britain, Labour collapsed into civil war between its left and right flanks; a sizeable chunk of the latter left to form the Social Democratic Party, thereby fatally splitting the anti-Tory vote. Labour's leader, the intellectual, unworldly Michael Foot, was no match for Thatcher's tub-thumping demagoguery. In the general election of 1983, the hitherto profoundly unpopular Thatcher government, surfing the wave of national jingoism born of victory over Argentina in the Falklands War the previous year, inflicted a catastrophic landslide defeat on a divided Labour Party, which the party's right and its media allies blamed squarely on the Labour left. From this point on, the party's direction of travel was encapsulated in its new, post-election leader, Neil Kinnock: originally from the left, he abandoned the party's more radical policies, and tacked right.

In 1985, the most seismic industrial struggle in post-war British history – the miners' strike – ended in devastating defeat for the miners. Thatcherism had aspired to create a new political consensus of privatization, deregulation, toothless trade unions, and low taxes for big business and the wealthy. With the crushing of the miners, it had succeeded. The victory seemed to be total. 'It marked the end of the twentieth-century British left,' shrugs Murray.

A cowed Labour Party simply adjusted to the new political weather, jettisoning dearly held commitments such as nationalization and high taxes on the rich. Local councils, the last bastions of the Labour left, were stripped of their powers by Thatcher's government and demonized by a compliant media as 'loony left' – drawing attention in particular to left policies of challenging racism and supporting gay and lesbian people – an early attempt by the right to stoke the fires of culture war. In 1986 the Greater London Council, under the leadership of the Labour left, was abolished altogether. Meanwhile, trade unions, on the back foot in the aftermath of the miners' strike, increasingly abandoned a strategy of industrial action in favour of what was termed a 'new realism': a defensive attempt to strike partnership deals with employers. Murray remembers the *Daily Mail* in the late 1980s crowing that the spectre of socialism had been lifted from Britain. 'We didn't have a convincing rebuttal,' he says, 'other than a sense that history would turn at some point.' In these dark moments, it was only this faint hope that sustained the left: where neoliberals, convinced of the permanence of their triumph, talked of the end of history, the left clung to the idea that history had a habit of coming back. But, in the early 1990s, it didn't look likely any time soon. A new consensus had been forged, one defined by the late cultural theorist Mark Fisher as 'capitalist realism', or 'the widespread sense that not only is capitalism the only viable political and economic system, but also that it is now impossible even to imagine a coherent alternative to it'.[6]

Len McCluskey, a thick-set Scouser whose rectangular spectacles give him the air of an intellectual bouncer, is the most influential trade union leader of modern times. His platform speeches – which range from cold fury and icy denunciation to sing-song optimism to brutal wit – are met with rapturous applause from his followers. McCluskey is a self-described 'child of the 60s', who remembers a time when 'there was revolution in the air'. He's also a man obsessed with strategy. As I take a seat facing him in Unite's offices, a glass table separates us; the only object on it is an ornamental chess set.

As we talk, McCluskey tells me of his eleven years working on Liverpool's docks, 'perhaps the happiest years of my life, amongst fabulous people, solidarity, community, sticking together, fighting your cause – that's what I learned down there'. After the Soviet Union invaded Czechoslovakia in 1968 to crush the so-called 'Prague Spring' – an attempt by the Communist state to introduce political freedoms and civil liberties – he was permanently inoculated about Stalinism and, two years later, on hearing Benn speak – 'I liked this guy, he captured me' – he became a Labour member. Then, three months before Thatcher's assumption of power, McCluskey became a full-time union official. 'The rest is history,' he tells me. 'Merseyside was decimated by Thatcherism.' He recalls how the labour movement slid to the right after the debacle of the miners' strike. 'I remember being very, very pessimistic and almost defeated in the late 90s.'

As if this weren't enough, Labour faced another existential challenge. When the party was founded in the early 1900s, most working-class people toiled in industrial occupations: mines, steelworks, docks and factories. Entire communities were built around such workplaces. This is not an era to glorify: these were often back-breaking jobs in dangerous conditions. Meanwhile, many women not only worked in factories or as domestic servants, where the conditions were often worse and the pay generally lower, but were at the same time compelled to do vast amounts of unpaid labour – cleaning, cooking, child-rearing – at home.

Yet such industrial occupations – often with densely concentrated workplaces – produced an organic sense of solidarity. Workers in these industries often believed they were bound together by the same class interests – and, in turn, believed that Labour existed as a party to advance those interests, thereby providing Labour with a bulwark of support. By the end of the twentieth century, however, many of these jobs and the communities that were forged around them were long gone.

Working-class people are now far more likely to work in supermarkets, call centres, shop floors and offices, and though that is truer today than ever, it was a process that was well underway by the 1990s. Unionization in the service sector is low: in retail only around 12 per cent are union members.[7] Turnover levels are high: overall, 15 per cent of workers shift jobs each year, but in call centres, for example, the rate is over a quarter.[8] The rise of zero-hour contracts from the 1990s onwards, along with increased numbers of temporary and agency workers, and reluctant part-time workers, has produced a more precarious, individualized workforce, particularly among younger workers. A more fragmented working-class has meant less of a sense of collective identity – or of a class with a common purpose, which could pool its strength to extract concessions from bosses. This in turn fuelled a feeling that class politics no longer served a practical purpose for many people: it was out of date, the relic of a bygone age, pointless. This belief would prove a fundamental pillar of capitalist realism – and few clung to it more fiercely than New Labour, the party remoulded in the image of its leader, Tony Blair.

When Blair became leader in 1994, the Labour left had been more or less extinguished, along with the politics it espoused. The Blairites 'wanted Year Zero: they wanted to change the party for ever', says former *Tribune* editor Mark Seddon. Under Blair's leadership, the party moved to accept the fundamental assumptions of Thatcher's new political consensus – or, as Blair put it, 'I always thought my job was to build on some of the things she had done rather than reverse it.'[9] For some of New Labour's leading lights, embracing 'some of the things' – privatization, lower taxes on wealthy individuals and corporate Britain, and reduced workers' rights – was a matter of conviction. At the 2001 Labour Party Conference, Tony Blair recounted an encounter with a former colleague, who had implored him to 'drop all this New Labour and do what we believe in'. Blair – as he recalled with relish – replied: 'It's worse than you think. I really do believe in it.'[10] Others in the Labour Party, less messianic than Blair, drifted right out of a sense of political pessimism, a belief that to accept the Thatcherite status quo was the only way to gain and retain power. As the Blair years progressed, however, the initial exuberance among Labour's grassroots at ending eighteen years of Tory rule gave way to disappointment and anger. After a decade of Labour government, well over half the members had left, bringing the membership to its lowest level since the party was founded, down to 176,891 – compared to over half a million by the end of the 2010s.[11] The diminished remnants of the Labour left, meanwhile, were consigned to poorly attended and often grouchy conferences. 'The meetings were just the same bunch of us, in the same room in London's

Conway Hall, on a wet Saturday afternoon,' recalls Seddon, adding with a laugh: 'With the same speech from Jeremy [Corbyn] as now!' As far as the mainstream of the party was concerned, Labour's left became an irrelevant political fringe, an embarrassing relative whose occasional irascible interventions at family gatherings had to be endured with an eye-rolling silence, but could by and large be safely ignored. 'We were reduced, I suppose, to a moral critique of capitalism,' says Andrew Murray. 'There was a general assumption that the wheel of history would turn and capitalism would dig itself back into crisis some way or other.'

Although Blair's government attempted to humanize Thatcherism – introducing a minimum wage, hiking public investment and scrapping anti-gay laws, for example – it accelerated the intrusion of the private sector into public services, slashed taxes on big business and allied with Republican President George W. Bush in the catastrophic 2003 invasion of Iraq. The remaining true believers were sustained by a belief that another sudden political sea change, this time in the left's favour, was just around the corner – but in truth, it seemed to be all over. 'It was a live debate for most of the early to late 2000s about whether it was actually worth socialists staying in the Labour Party,' says Andrew Fisher, Corbyn's thoughtful former policy chief. 'It was a live debate even within the Labour left. It was that bad. The Iraq War intensified that: for a lot of people, it was a pivotal moment.'

By the mid-2000s, the key figure in the ruins of the Labour left was John McDonnell. Grey-haired, besuited, softly spoken, slightly built, with the whiff of the avuncular bank manager about him, he didn't seem your typical left-wing firebrand. But McDonnell had a plan.

McDonnell chaired the Socialist Campaign Group of Labour MPs, a ragtag collection of some twenty-five rebels and mavericks. Originally founded by allies of Tony Benn in the early 1980s to coordinate left-wing strategy in the House of Commons, two decades on it was severely depleted: a mere 7 per cent of the parliamentary party, huddling together for political warmth. Only a handful of MPs showed up to weekly meetings – and even this marginalized caucus was riven with ideological, strategic and personal divisions: proper People's Front of Judaea against the Judean People's Front.

In the summer of 2005, I graduated from university with a history degree and little idea what to do with my life. As I spent months pulling pints in a Manchester bar and toyed with the thought of moving abroad to teach English, I emailed my CV to every Labour MP who had voted against the Iraq War. After a shower of rejections, an envelope dropped onto the doormat. Inside was a handwritten note from John McDonnell, suggesting he might have an opportunity. After a nervy, sleepless night, I arrived in that den of mischief for politicians, staffers and lobby hacks commonly known as 'the Westminster Village'. Walking into Parliament's Portcullis House – all glass, concrete and gun-toting security – I was met in the atrium by a bald, rosy-faced man with a gothic cross hanging from his left earlobe: Simeon Andrews, McDonnell's right-hand man. So began my association with Labour's beleaguered left flank. I could hardly have guessed at the tumultuous fifteen years that beckoned.

That November, I began work in McDonnell's cramped office off an obscure corridor in Norman Shaw South, a red- and white-brick Victorian building which once housed the Metropolitan Police but had long since been absorbed by the Parliamentary Estate. (Parliamentary offices are in the gift of the party whips, who were charged with enforcing discipline, and they apparently did not feel generous when it came to rebels: this was exile in Parliamentary Siberia.) My colleague and office mate was Andrew Fisher, an intimidatingly competent and fresh-faced researcher. Despite its vanishingly small presence in Parliament, McDonnell's operation helped coordinate backbench rebellions against particularly pernicious New Labour policies. When, days after I joined McDonnell's team, Blair sought to introduce ninety days' detention without charge for suspected terrorists – an egregious attack on civil liberties – we duly leaped into action, lobbying Labour MPs across the party's political spectrum to defy the party leadership. On 9 November, thanks to a backbench rebellion, New Labour suffered its first ever parliamentary defeat: ninety days' detention was dead.[12]

Such triumphs, though, were rare. Although many MPs professed themselves sympathetic to McDonnell's aims, they were unwilling to risk the wrath of the Labour leadership by acting on their avowed principles. When, in 2007, New Labour put forward legislation to privatize the nation's probation service, one of McDonnell's fellow backbenchers took up the fight: organizing meetings with ministers, putting down parliamentary motions, leading a parliamentary debate. When it came to the vote, the same MP voted in line with government ministers. Why? Because the whips told him that a defeat for the government would prove embarrassing on the eve of local elections. 'Without any flicker of conscience Labour MPs trotted dutifully through the lobbies to vote for this handing over of yet another section of our welfare state,' McDonnell angrily wrote of the New Labour loyalists at the time.[13] Such supine behaviour helped forge McDonnell's lasting contempt towards many of his colleagues – and he did not shrink from expressing that disdain.

As career-minded MPs worked the parliamentary tea rooms and bars, trying to charm their peers, McDonnell had other plans. Attempting to provide a parliamentary platform for otherwise marginalized campaigns, struggles and movements, he set up parliamentary groups to lobby for left-wing trade unions on issues ranging from pensions to workers' rights to government legislation. He also brought together an advisory panel of experts to advance an alternative left-wing economic vision, and – in an attempt to reinvigorate the grassroots left – refounded the Labour Representation Committee, which took its name from the historic pressure group established in 1900 that would eventually become the Labour Party. The committee's mission statement was updated to reflect the 2000s: that New Labour's betrayals had produced a crisis of working-class political representation which needed an answer. The freshness quickly faded, however; soon, the committee had become little more than a refuge for the ageing remnants of the old Labour left. Its conferences were predictable and dull, lacking in dynamism, and had no apparent agenda other than a heartfelt combination of anger, frustration and disappointment at what the party had become.

Without drastic action, the Labour left was going to die. By summer 2006 McDonnell had decided that, with Blair's departure as Labour leader fast approaching, he would stand as the left's candidate to be his successor. Yet even on the left, like-minded MPs believed it a doomed enterprise – and, at one meeting that July, told McDonnell so, to his face. Undeterred, the next day McDonnell marched over to

College Green and, in front of the waiting news cameras, declared his intention to stand. His likely sole rival would be Gordon Brown, chancellor of the exchequer, co-founder of New Labour and – despite their tempestuous personal relationship – Blair's anointed successor.

With few in the media taking McDonnell seriously – his chances of even getting nominated by the requisite 12.5 per cent of the Parliamentary Labour Party, or forty-five MPs, to appear on the ballot paper were remote – the press coverage of his campaign was minimal. In the face of a media blackout we – McDonnell's team – did the only thing we could: present this as a David versus Goliath, against-all-the-odds campaign aimed at building as much grassroots support as possible, so that (we hoped) MPs would feel morally obliged to nominate him, simply in order to facilitate a debate within the parliamentary party.

McDonnell's team was – well – Andrew Fisher and me. We did most of the practical work. Before the age of mass social media, McDonnell became one of the first MPs to set up a blog and a Facebook profile. We launched a website, compiled a database of supporters' emails, organized meetings and rallies of activists across Britain, courted trade unions and sympathetic journalists. The latter were virtually non-existent. One notable exception was Seumas Milne, then head of the *Guardian*'s Comment section.

McDonnell himself, meanwhile, proved an exceptionally polished performer. In one public debate, Brown was visibly flustered as McDonnell outperformed expectations. Looking on, one of Brown's senior aides at the time recalls watching McDonnell's performance with appalled admiration. McDonnell, he concluded, would shine in a campaign and therefore he had to be stopped. McDonnell skewered Brown on cuts to English-language courses for migrants. After the debate, the aide recalls, Brown stormed backstage, bellowing to his apprehensive team: 'I didn't know that would come up!' He was genuinely concerned about McDonnell getting on the ballot paper. Nick Brown – then chief whip and no relation – assured him it wouldn't happen. Concerned that McDonnell's inclusion in the contest would indeed fulfil his aim of shifting the political debate and the Labour Party leftwards, Brown's camp informed MPs in no uncertain terms that their future careers in the party depended on having nothing to do with McDonnell. Brown duly secured his coronation; Labour's left seemed simply irrelevant.

By mid-2007 McDonnell was more isolated than ever, but he had one ally: a bearded Labour backbencher who carried his socialist principles with an air of dishevelled good humour. 'Jeremy Corbyn is my best friend in Parliament,' McDonnell would say (on one occasion I recall his wife, Cynthia Pinto, swiftly correcting him: 'Your only friend!'). The pair dovetailed nicely: where McDonnell focused on domestic issues, Corbyn's entire political career had been devoted to foreign affairs. He was seen as the left's 'foreign secretary', championing the Stop The War movement, which emerged out of the widespread popular opposition to the 2003 invasion of Iraq; and solidarity campaigns with oppressed peoples, including the Kurdish, Palestinian and Chagos Islanders' struggles for self-determination. While MPs resented McDonnell – 'they saw him as an unlikeable, hard left dogmatist, I suppose,' Andrew Fisher muses – they took to Corbyn, at least on a personal level: a jovial and unassuming presence in the corridors of Parliament with no airs or pretences and often, unthreateningly, on his own. 'I've always liked him as long as I've known him,' says Chris Mullin, who first met Corbyn in the late 1970s but did not support him in either leadership contest. 'He's a thoroughly decent human being, almost a saintly man.' Though he refused to toe the party line on many things, Corbyn displayed a reassuring lack of political ambition and – a side effect of his independent-mindedness – was clearly lacking in organization, as those close to him candidly acknowledged. 'He's a complete nightmare to work for from a diary point of view,' says Cat Smith, now Labour MP for Lancaster and Fleetwood. 'He doesn't do what he's told. Anyone who works for an MP wants them electronically tagged and to do what you want them to do, when you want them to do it. But Jeremy didn't, and frequently lost his mobile phone. I'd be ringing his number, then he'd walk in, saying: "I think I left my mobile in a café in Finsbury Park."' He was chaotic, but also extraordinarily busy. His diary would overflow with often impossibly overlapping events, a situation he just about managed to control with an indefatigable energy.

Corbyn was the long-standing MP for Islington North, in a multicultural borough long associated with 'champagne socialism', but in reality scarred with huge injustices: nearly half of Islington's children grow up in poverty.[14] Corbyn did his politics out of the spotlight. One of his researchers remembers taking a call from Corbyn one night: he had got talking to a homeless man in his constituency and, learning the man had no accommodation that night, was trying to find him somewhere to sleep. Britain's housing crisis – particularly acute in inner London constituencies such as Corbyn's – would remain one of his greatest passions; so, too, were his constituents. Advice surgeries would begin at 2 p.m. on Saturdays in Islington's Old Fire Station; they would end whenever the last person left, sometimes around midnight.

If Corbyn and McDonnell represented the old thinking and strategies of the Labour left, they were also deeply involved with extra-parliamentary movements for, respectively, social justice and peace. Given that these campaigns were often deeply hostile to New Labour because of its failure to roll back Thatcherism at home and its support for military escapades abroad, it was hardly a surprise that most Labour parliamentarians kept their distance from the pair and their activities. McDonnell and Corbyn were frequently seen on picket lines, at trade union conferences, on protest marches and rallies, and even supporting peaceful civil disobedience. Many trade unionists, marginalized and patronized under New Labour, came to see both men as their champions in Parliament. Corbyn in particular would commit to every meeting going, which often meant his appearances were late and brief. 'Jeremy Corbyn is the most orgasmic MP ever,' Alan Simpson, a left-wing former Labour MP, would often joke. The joke had a groan-worthy punchline: 'It doesn't matter what meeting you're at, whatever event you're at, he's always coming.'

McDonnell and Corbyn's association with radical, often marginalized movements was frequently cited as evidence that they belonged to a different political age (sneeringly referred to as 'the seventies'), or at least the extreme political fringe. For all this, their commitment to solidarity bestowed upon them an authenticity and credibility with grassroots activists who were otherwise profoundly suspicious of, or even hostile towards, Labour politicians. It was this authenticity, and their symbiotic relationship to those who were profoundly disillusioned with mainstream politics – climate and peace activists, radical trade unionists, campaigners against tax avoidance and student tuition fees – that were to give them their chance.

In the first decade of the new millennium, a new political constituency was quietly forged on Britain's streets. Movements emerged against economic injustice, war, austerity, student debt, tax avoidance, the climate emergency and the onslaught against workers' living standards; together, they helped give a voice to hundreds of thousands of British citizens who felt increasingly unrepresented by an ever more remote political class in Westminster. Younger people were at the forefront, and little wonder: theirs was a generation robbed of the optimism which had been an article of faith for those who came before them, that a better lot in life than their parents' beckoned. The financial crash that followed the collapse of Lehman Brothers in September 2008 proved a searing experience for many younger people. In an instant, their futures seemed to be snatched away: by 2011, youth unemployment surpassed a million. As they were expected to pick up the tab for the financial calamity, their living standards fell more acutely than in any industrialized country other than Greece.[15] Home-ownership plummeted among the young – between the mid-1990s and the mid-2010s, it was cut by more than half among young, middle-income adults[16] – and the failure to replace lost council housing stock meant the only other option was a rip-off, poorly regulated private rental sector.

Youth services were butchered[17] – and cuts to social security impacted badly on poorer young citizens in particular. The free-market revolution, driven by Thatcher and embraced by New Labour, had promised to liberate the aspirational go-getter from the deadweight of the state and collectivism, their ambitions buoyed up by an apparently ever-expanding bubble of cheap credit. But in the wake of the financial crisis, that bubble popped, the economy collapsed and people found that the lived experience of that 'freedom' was financial insecurity, which is no freedom at all. For the young, in particular, all that had seemed solid really had turned into air. The eternal sunshine of neo-liberalism was exposed for what it was: a sham. As people realized this, they turned again to politics and history, and started to protest.

By this point, the veneer had long since come off the shiny surfaces of the Blair government and similar centrist administrations around the world, with their implied mantra of 'The End of History'. At the close of the twentieth century, the term 'anti-capitalism' had started to creep into mainstream news bulletins, along with coverage of mass worldwide protests from Prague to Seattle, Genoa to Gothenburg. The political establishment saw these demonstrations as a futile howl against 'globalization', the system that was now here to stay. The protesters saw it differently. They took to the streets because this system nakedly prioritized financial profit over the needs of the vast majority of people. Their protests centred on global institutions – the World Bank, the International Monetary Fund and the World Trade Organization – which they accused of fostering policies of privatization and deregulation, of favouring the interests of capital over labour, of forcing poorer markets open to multinational corporations at the expense of domestic industries, and of destroying the environment – making the lives of billions immeasurably poorer in the process. Their placards and banners summed it up: 'Our Resistance Is As Global As Their Capital'; 'Say No To The WTO'; and most enduringly – in a defiant, desperately hopeful rejection of capitalist realism – 'Another World Is Possible'.

These movements were diffuse and disconnected and, without the ability to build a coherent alternative to the established order, their moment soon passed. Nonetheless, they revealed a deep well of discontent with the established order, and new radical voices – Naomi Klein's *No Logo*, a *cri de coeur* against modern consumer capitalism, became the defining book of a generation – found a mass audience. These movements were, in retrospect, the first concerted attempt to throw off the suffocating blanket of market triumphalism.

Then came the atrocity of 9/11. In the following months and years, the anti-capitalist movement was knocked off course. The US administration of George W. Bush, followed closely by a supine Blair government, saw its opportunity to reorder the world according to its desires and, in 2003, invaded Iraq. Around the world, millions were appalled by this illegal act of naked aggression. In Britain, a new anti-war movement, Stop The War, launched days after 9/11, quickly found a mass audience among an anxious British public – and, particularly, among Labour's membership.[18]

In the last months of 2002, during the build-up to war, Britain saw a series of protests and peaceful civil disobedience. On Halloween, anti-war slogans were projected on to Parliament, and protesters dressed as witches and ghouls shut down Whitehall. Present among the speakers was the scruffy, passionate figure of Jeremy Corbyn.[19]

'Corbyn was very prominent in the anti-war movement,' recalls Unite's Andrew Murray. 'It burst him out of the confines of being a radical London MP to being a national figure.' Perhaps this was only the case if you were on the left, but it was true that, while Corbyn remained little known among the wider public, he won admiration beyond the capital's radical milieus. Veterans of the movement all say the same: Corbyn put in the hours, attending meetings and rallies across the country. He found Stop The War an office located in the same building as his own, and would go on to chair the movement for four years, its mass meetings, rallies and protests foreshadowing his own leadership campaign more than a decade later. 'What the anti-war movement told me was that it was possible to build a mass movement on the left,' says James Meadway, an activist and adviser to John McDonnell. 'It showed that, on our side, the left can stop squabbling and do something halfway useful.'

On a bright, frosty day in February 2003, London was the stage for the biggest protest in British history: two million people marched against the impending invasion of Iraq. Millions more demonstrated across the globe. The mass mobilizations of the anti-capitalist movements had reinvigorated protest as a political tactic, and had created networks of activists with the know-how and experience to build demonstrations with significant numbers. But the attendance far exceeded the organizers' expectations. So many protested, waving placards ranging from 'Not In My Name' to 'Make Tea Not War', that it was more of a giant shuffle than a march. Yet it was ignored by politicians in Westminster and, in the following weeks, disillusionment rapidly set in. As bombs dropped on Iraq, this vast demonstration – for many, their first experience of active protest – seemed to have achieved precisely nothing. For some, the march's failure was the failure of an outmoded style of protest: the placard-waving 'A to B' march through city streets, listening to some tub-thumping speakers, then going home. A drastic new strategy was needed. It emerged in the aftermath of the disastrous financial crash of 2008.

The 2008 crash ushered in another age. New Labour's political model had relied on taking the tax revenues from an economy increasingly powered by the financial sector to invest in public services. Now, with the part-nationalization of the ailing British banking sector, that paradigm was apparently destroyed. Until 2008, the opposition Conservatives had backed the Labour government's spending plans pound for pound.[20] But in the aftermath of the crash, history was revised. The Conservative shadow chancellor, George Osborne, argued that the real proximate cause of Britain's crisis was Labour's lavish overspending, that Britain's rulers had failed to 'fix the roof when the sun is shining'.[21] This critique pointed in one direction: the post-crash financial deficit would be eliminated through drastic spending cuts. With Labour and the Lib Dems eagerly embracing this idea – later, Labour would commit to cuts which were 'deeper and tougher' than those of Thatcher,[22] while Lib Dem leader Nick Clegg promised 'savage' spending cuts[23] – people who craved a break with a broken system had nowhere to turn, as far as mainstream politics was concerned. They had no choice but to take to the streets.

One of the first significant expressions of this new form of protest came in the late 2000s with the 'Camp for Climate Change', or 'Climate Camp' as it became more commonly known. A loose, media-savvy network of some two to three thousand activists, it launched high-profile direct actions designed to capture media attention and generate headlines – which they duly did. In 2008, it targeted Heathrow Airport which, already Europe's busiest airport, was planning to build a third runway, a development that would add significantly to the UK's carbon emissions, as well as generating extra pollution in England's overcrowded Southeast. Heathrow was located in John McDonnell's constituency of Hayes and Harlington. McDonnell was himself an active participant in the movement. As Simeon Andrews put it in football terms, 'the lad who jumped the fences'. He would sit among the activists and listen, approach the police on their behalf, and even launched his own direct action in the House of Commons itself. During a debate over the airport's expansion, he picked up the parliamentary mace – a breach of protocol that had the Westminster establishment collectively clutching its pearls – in protest at the government's plans to ride roughshod over the opposition of the local community. 'It's a disgrace to the democracy of this country!' he thundered.[24] This expression of solidarity with the protesters earned McDonnell a five-day suspension from Parliament; it also gained him lasting trust and respect among activists.

More camps followed. In spring 2009, months after the global financial crash, London hosted the G20 summit of the world's major leaders: an unmissable opportunity for demonstrators, who laid on a carnival of protest. This centred not on a march, but a new form of direct action – or, rather, a new form with ancient origins: occupying space. (With a nice nod to history, one of the sites they held was Blackheath, assembly point for the Peasants' Revolt back in 1381.) They also set up a 'Camp in the City', in London's Bishopsgate, epicentre of the capital's financial sector. The area was transformed into a sea of tents featuring workshops, meetings and high-profile speakers, and the mood was peaceful – until it got dark. At this point, police began to kettle – or encircle and trap – activists; then, as soon as the media packed up and went home, officers charged the camp. The protesters put their hands up and chanted: 'This is not a riot.'[25] Such peaceful resistance did not deter the police, who aimed their truncheons at the skulls and backs of activists, some of whom were dragged away and arrested. One bystander, 47-year-old homeless newspaper vendor Ian Tomlinson, collapsed and died after being batoned by a police officer.

Though Climate Camp would formally disband itself less than two years later, through its audacious protests it had succeeded in focusing establishment attention on the growing climate emergency. As much as anything, the movement's significance lay in the form that protest had taken: occupying sites rather than marching, and accompanying strategies. But while direct action remained a crucial tactic, the movement's closing declaration also suggested a willingness to evolve and to cooperate. Now, they declared, came the chance to link up with other progressive movements, and 'play a crucial role in the revolutionary times ahead'.[26] The times were indeed changing. The general election of May 2010 brought to power a new

Conservative-led government – putting the Tories back in government for the first time in thirteen years. They wasted no time in picking up where Thatcher left off, with a fresh ideologically charged onslaught to drive back the frontiers of the British state and to remould society in favour of the wealthy and powerful.

Many voters who would never dream of voting Conservative but felt alienated by Labour ended up turning to the Liberal Democrats, a so-called 'centrist' party which had positioned itself as an insurgent challenge to a failed political duopoly. They appealed especially to young first-time voters. Turnout surged among the under-25s – albeit from a derisory 37 per cent to 44 per cent – and at the 10 p.m. deadline overwhelmed polling stations turned away angry citizens who had queued for hours.[27] From a commitment to abolish tuition fees to a pledge not to increase the regressive Value Added Tax, the Lib Dems beckoned seductively to the disillusioned. In one party political broadcast, their doe-eyed leader, Nick Clegg, wandered around the streets of London, the broken promises of Labour and the Tories fluttering around him. Like so many Liberal Democrat statements, it would prove ironic.

The Lib Dems, in the role of powerbroker, facilitated a new Conservative-led coalition government, which quickly proved united in its commitment to slash-and-burn cuts to the welfare state. Soon after the election, the new Conservative chancellor, George Osborne, unveiled a battery of cuts in his first Spending Review, including £7 billion slashed from the welfare state, unleashing Britain's age of austerity. This marked a seismic moment. Instead of blaming reckless financial entities for the runaway speculation and short selling that had triggered the crisis, the Conservative-led government saw an opportunity to turn its fire on those who had nothing whatsoever to do with the crash – particularly disabled people, single parents, public sector workers and the low-paid – but who would now be compelled to pay for it. Dearly, as it would turn out.

Tom Costello, a veteran of Climate Camp, is a self-assured, boyish-looking man with a mischievous sense of humour. Months after the 2010 general election, he came across a piece in *Private Eye* magazine about a sweetheart deal between the British tax authorities and mobile phone giant Vodafone, allegedly worth £6 billion of unpaid tax. The corporation aggressively disputed the figure, but *Private Eye* journalist Richard Brooks later suggested to me that it was, if anything, an underestimate. In any case, Costello was convinced that many more companies were violating the spirit of the law to avoid paying billions annually – a claim vindicated by the House of Commons Public Accounts Committee a year later.[28] He discussed it with fellow activist Stephen Reid; the pair decided they had struck political gold.

What Costello liked about focusing on the issue of tax avoidance was how exposing it undermined both of the big lies that successive British governments had hammered home to their citizens, especially since the crash of 2008. If those who could more than afford to cough up were avoiding paying billions in taxes, it didn't say much about the Conservatives' claims that, when economic disaster struck, 'We Are All In This Together' – that everybody, rich and poor, would be affected the same. Likewise, government claims that the kitty was now empty, that the money was not there to sustain public spending or the welfare state, strained credulity. As they wondered how to protest, Reid had a lightbulb moment: why not occupy Vodafone's shops? Though Costello worried that such a move would 'piss off punters', the pair ultimately agreed: they had to make noise to have an impact.

Contacting his network of activists, Costello – a pioneer of Twitter, then still in its early days – was overwhelmed by the positive response. The movement's first action was set for 27 October 2010, a Wednesday, but, he stressed, 'the target and the action are designed to be repeatable. The idea,' he continued, 'is that Wednesday sets the model, and then the secret team making it happen dissolves and the ownership of the protest passes to you guys and whoever else.' He was full of optimism. 'If this works,' he predicted, 'there will be shockwaves.' He was right.

On 27 October, around seventy protesters marched down a drizzly Oxford Street to Vodafone's flagship store. There, they staged a mass sit-in, refusing to move. Chanting 'Pay your taxes Vodafone!', they brandished giant banners proclaiming 'Vodafone's unpaid tax bill: £6bn. Cuts to welfare: £7bn' and 'We just called to say you owe us

£6bn'. The police were summoned; their first response was to start dragging protesters out of the shop, the activists yelling 'Shame on you!' A social media hashtag to mark the protest started trending on Twitter: '#UKUncut'. Here was an early use of social media to bypass largely hostile mainstream media outlets in raising support for a campaign challenging the status quo; many others would soon follow. The hashtag swiftly became the name of a new movement: UKUncut would go on to occupy the shops of other high-profile alleged tax avoiders, such as Philip Green's Topshop and Topman – an allegation denied by Green. Its occupations were inventive, funny, quirky: protesters turned up dressed as nurses, converting shop interiors into pretend hospitals to highlight looming cuts to Britain's beloved NHS. What was more, the protests were attracting a new, very different kind of activist: people who had never protested before, especially families with kids.

'Having done climate change stuff, we were used to getting reactions from the public of "Fuck off! Get a job!",' says Costello. This was totally different. Shoppers would come up to the activists, start conversations, shower them with support. After all, people had to pay their taxes, and they resented big corporations for whom different rules apparently applied, especially in this new age of economic winter, with the effects of Conservative cuts beginning to bite.

Suddenly tax avoidance was all over the news and a hot political issue. The protesters had devised an accessible, easily comprehensible message for their cause, one with which large swathes of the public could readily identify. And, critically, they brought together a new generation of activists.

As UKUncut emerged into the light, another movement was being born. The first decade of the new millennium had seen a deepening sense among Britons that the future looked bleak. The prospects for millennials appeared especially rocky: punished on the one hand by the slashing of social provisions and services, and on the other by a job market increasingly dominated by low-paid and insecure work, which they would enter saddled with debt from increasingly expensive university courses. Given that, by the end of the 2010s, over half of school leavers were enrolling at universities, this scenario played a major role in shifting their generation leftwards.

One of the Liberal Democrats' most eye-catching policies, touted during their 2010 general election campaign, had been a commitment to abolish student fees. But as they joined forces with the Conservatives in power, it was a pledge they quickly and spectacularly tossed overboard, Liberal Democrat leader Nick Clegg instead committing his party's support for a trebling of tuition fees. The student protesters' objections were prescient: by 2019, graduates carried an average of £50,000 worth of debt.[29] Claims of a new age of financial sustainability for higher education proved anything but as university staff's real-term pay fell by 20 per cent during the 2010s[30] and a quarter of English universities were in deficit by the end of the decade.[31] Teaching suffered as staff numbers failed to rise at the same rate as student numbers, and student accommodation rents soared by a third.[32] With some poetic justice, it was Clegg, with his crocodile-teared remorse, who became the face of the coalition government's onslaught on public services and higher education in particular. His party's betrayal inadvertently played a critical role in forging the political consciousness of hundreds of thousands of young people – and the biggest student movement since the 1960s.

On 10 November 2010, some 52,000 people, mostly students, marched through the central London streets with handmade placards and banners. I marched with them, under the red-and-gold banner of the Labour Representation Committee that I held with Andrew Fisher, the two of us among the few representatives of the Labour left. Undoubtedly, very few of the marchers saw Labour – newly in opposition – as a potential instrument of political salvation: for them it was the party of foreign wars and pro-market dogma. A sizeable proportion of these students had voted for the Liberal Democrats just six months earlier, which made their contempt for and disillusionment with the Conservatives' coalition partners all the rawer. The vast majority, too, had never been on a demonstration before, being too young to have participated in – perhaps even to remember – the anti-Iraq War marches of seven years earlier. Many were taken aback by a sense of collective power they had never before experienced.

Though the turnout was impressive, the protest resembled precisely one of those traditional, boring marches that the protest planners, students bursting with energy and immersed in the new activism, had been so keen to avoid. The march culminated in one of those predictably choreographed rallies, in Parliament Square. Bored, the protesters drifted away.

As thousands of students passed Millbank Tower, a huge glass building housing the Conservative Party's campaign headquarters, the mood changed. Around the entrance, pink-bibbed NUS stewards desperately tried to move on crowds of young demonstrators to prevent the building becoming a target for protest. But, overwhelmed by the tide of protesters, the stewards soon gave up. The occupation was spontaneous. As hundreds of students marched into the building, the atmosphere was charged. There was a kerfuffle with security officers, and then the sound of glass breaking.

This wasn't the organized radical left, many of whom stood outside watching the unfolding chaos in perplexed fascination. Most of those seizing the tower were not only engaged in their first act of civil disobedience, but their very first protest too. A few months earlier, they had been voting Lib Dem. Now they were smashing windows – and making front-page news.

A political detonator, the Millbank occupation catalysed a wave of nationwide protest that autumn. Across the UK, some eighty universities were occupied by their own students. These campuses became focal points of a new movement. Radical politicians came to speak, John McDonnell among them; there were guest teach-ins by supportive academics and campaigners; and trade unionists turned up in a show of solidarity, one reciprocated by students attending picket lines for striking transport workers. Notably, none of these occupations had clear leaders; they were all, in the activist term, 'horizontal', with decisions made by consensus.

The media and government response predictably sought to portray student protesters as mindless thugs: 'DISGRACE OF THE STUDENT HOOLIGANS', 'THUGGISH AND DISGRACEFUL', 'BRAINLESS', brayed various purple-faced headlines. It was also instructive. For years, young people had been ridiculed as apathetic, more interested in daytime TV, drinking and mobile phones than politics. Now they were proving to be anything but – and, unsurprisingly, the UK establishment didn't like it very much. Organizing in huge numbers, they were met with police brutality: some students suffered serious injuries;[33] many were kettled, trapped by police officers, often in freezing conditions and without access to toilets, for hours on end, a repressive form of crowd control that stoked rather than defused tensions. As the Labour MP David Lammy put it in Parliament: 'Is not the point of a kettle that it brings things to the boil?'[34] The outcome was so predictable that it almost seemed as if the police wanted it that way.[35]

Despite the determination of the students in the face of the heavy-handed policing, the government was deaf to the protests. On 9 December, as police confronted crowds of enraged students outside the Houses of Parliament, MPs voted to treble tuition fees. In the vote's aftermath, the student movement began to evaporate.

Yet those heady weeks left their mark. The students' mass mobilization, from the campus to the street, coming so soon after a coalition welded together by austerity had assumed power, had broken a widespread feeling of resigned apathy, and had inspired others to follow their lead. The students' initiative had put trade unions 'on the spot', admitted Unite's general secretary, Len McCluskey, both exposing their supine response to the financial crash and showing them a way forward.[36] The unions, accordingly, took up the baton. A year later, in November 2011, they organized the biggest coordinated industrial action since the 1926 General Strike. In 2013, a coalition spanning trade unions and single-issue campaign groups launched the People's Assembly Against Austerity, with mass rallies and protests against the government taking place across the country. Other campaigns emerged, such as Disabled People Against the Cuts: demonstrators in wheelchairs shutting down roads in protest at devastating government cuts to social security.

For many British citizens, and especially for the new generation for whom the events of the 1980s were the stuff of history books, these protests served as a mass political education. Those drawn into them started to understand politics – and the impact of politics on their own lives and those of their families and friends – for the first time. They understood that it was necessary to interrogate and confront the prevailing social order, rather than simply opposing the government of the day, whether Labour or Conservative.

In a sense, too, the temporary defeats of these campaigns and mobilizations didn't matter: it was the participation that counted. Irrespective of the outcome, the activists were like radical spores, who went back to their communities, workplaces, schools, universities, taking their new politics with them. From the anti-war movement of the early 2000s to the student and anti-austerity movements of the early 2010s, a mass political constituency was starting to form, below the radar, one which understood that the various discrete injustices against which they had campaigned were all in fact linked; and, moreover, that it wasn't simply the incumbent government that had to be held responsible, but the entire system. They were no longer under the spell of capitalist realism, that imagination-crushing sense that the way society was organized might be unjust, but that there was fundamentally no viable alternative. As James Schneider, later one of Corbyn's communications heads, recalled, 'each cycle of struggle and resistance' built up the capacity of activists. But while there had emerged a broad grassroots constituency thirsting for radical change, that constituency lacked both organized political representation and leadership. That was about to change.

2
From the Ashes

When the result of the 2015 general election was called in the early hours of 8 May that year, it was difficult to recall a greater moment of political despondency – if, that was, you had pinned your hopes on Labour. In dribbling rain, the media had set up camp on College Green, opposite the Gothic bulk of Parliament. The final polling had been tight. There was a suggestion that, with a slight edge, Ed Miliband's Labour Party might even pull off a narrow win; most felt that the election would result in a hung Parliament, with no one party claiming an overall majority. Nevertheless, there was a sense of anticipation – that the Tory-led coalition, having presided over devastating cuts and a protracted squeeze in living standards over the last five years, would collapse, for a different kind of government to emerge. It would, but not in the way most had imagined.

As voting came to an end on the evening of the 7th, an exit poll had overturned most pundits' projections, placing the Tories far ahead of Labour as the largest single party: 316 seats to Labour's 239. When the projection flashed up on a screen at ITV's King's Cross studios, where I was settling in for an evening of live political analysis, the mood changed. For me, it felt like being at a funeral, surrounded by Tory supporters at a wedding. On air, the presenter turned to me and remarked: 'Your face went green when the exit poll flashed up.'

On College Green a few hours later, as I wandered across to a BBC radio presenter beckoning me to a microphone, the scale of the disaster was becoming apparent. The exit poll was wrong: the Tories had done even better than projected and had snatched an overall majority. Five years of austerity, of stagnating living standards, of devastating cuts to social security – and still the Tories had achieved electoral vindication. As I contemplated the miserable prospect of another half-decade of Conservative rule ahead, the radio presenter welcomed another guest down the line. It was Iain Duncan Smith, a Tory cabinet minister notorious for a punitive benefit regime that effectively disadvantaged disabled people; I had once confronted him on national television with the names of benefit claimants who had died after being mistakenly found fit for work. The presenter introduced him, quipped that it was 'fair to say' I hadn't been his biggest fan. A triumphant Duncan Smith gently cackled into the microphone.

Nearly five years earlier, after Labour's 2010 general election defeat, Gordon Brown had resigned and, in the leadership contest that followed, Ed Miliband had narrowly beaten his older brother, David, to become leader of the Labour Party. The sons of preeminent Marxist intellectual and Jewish refugee Ralph Miliband, both had become special advisers at the heart of the New Labour project before being parachuted into safe northern parliamentary seats. There, the political similarities ended.

While the older Miliband had become the acknowledged torchbearer of the Blairite flame, Ed flatly declared New Labour 'dead', lambasting its failure to properly address inequality. It was, he stated, 'plain wrong to think that we can build a stronger society when we are relaxed about bankers being paid 200 times that of their cleaners'[1] and he denounced 'brutish US-style capitalism'. In all this, Ed Miliband had been inspired by a profoundly influential book by the epidemiologists Richard Wilkinson and Kate Pickett, *The Spirit Level,* which produced evidence to show that societies with less inequality have fewer social problems, from crime to physical and mental health to child wellbeing. In his campaign, Miliband attracted the decisive support of major trade unions – notably the most politically powerful, Unite – on the left of the party, a factor which would fuel bitterness on the Blairite Labour right.

But if those on the Labour left hoped that Miliband would prove the Messiah who would lead the party back to its roots, they were to be disappointed. As leader, Ed Miliband was politically tortured, torn between his father's radicalism and his own political upbringing in New Labour, and this manifested itself most evidently in a hopeless indecision. Tom Baldwin – Miliband's former director of communications and strategy – is in reflective mood over a cup of tea at my kitchen table. If Miliband's leadership was going to work, he reflected, he needed to be himself – but his lack of self-confidence had prevented him from doing so. Instead, Baldwin recalls, he would do 'a bad Bobby Kennedy impression' or, ruefully, 'a rather bad David Miliband impression sometimes'. This is harsh. In truth, Ed Miliband was a genuine, well-motivated politician with sincere progressive instincts, who felt imprisoned by a hostile environment both within the Labour Party – the political centre of gravity among parliamentarians still tended towards Blairism – and in wider society. But ultimately, it was fair. While Miliband's shadow chancellor, Ed Balls, had once made an impressive speech against austerity as a solution to the economic crisis,[2] he soon tacked predictably rightwards, embracing the dominant policy of cuts to government spending and public services pursued across Europe, albeit more slowly and less drastically than those of the Tory-led coalition had been. 'Austerity lite' became the de facto Labour mantra. 'Like the Tories, but a bit less' was hardly a compelling message to win over an electorate still bitterly disillusioned with what Labour had become.

Miliband and Balls didn't see eye to eye politically and, increasingly, personally. By the time the 2015 general election came round, they were barely on speaking terms. Yet Miliband had long since surrendered to Balls's lukewarm critique of government policy. Although Miliband was more or less the most left-wing member in his own shadow cabinet – with the exception of Jon Trickett, the gruff northern shadow minister without portfolio – he didn't have the courage of his own convictions. Averse to what he regarded as factionalism, he triangulated between Labour's soft left and right, in the process satisfying no one. Part of Miliband's problem, summed up one of his advisers, Simon Fletcher, was the dynamic of the debate around him: 'But he didn't create the apparatus around him because he didn't have the confidence of his own politics. So the actual apparatus around him was to his right.'

So, while during the Blair years Labour had a zealous neoliberal vision, under Miliband the party lacked a coherent vision at all. This became strikingly apparent in a sequence of convoluted policy initiatives: chin-stroking analyses of things that were wrong that Miliband's own team found hard to grasp, never mind the wider public. A bold, optimistic vision of how society would be transformed for the better under Labour was notable by its absence.

It's a political truism that if you do not define yourself, you will be defined by your opponents. This became devastatingly true with Miliband, who, laudable though his impulses were, was seen as wonkish, remote and out of touch with the British public. He was unjustly crucified by a hostile press, most notoriously over his calamitous attempt to eat a bacon sandwich in front of the assembled ranks of the national media; the image of Miliband trying and failing to negotiate this national breakfast summed up his campaign. A year before the election, Labour hired the US political guru David Axelrod. On his first day, surrounded by Miliband's advisers, he suddenly piped up: 'I've been hearing a lot from all of you today, but Ed, can you tell me why you want to be prime minister?' The room fell completely, uncomfortably, silent. Then Miliband launched into a twelve-minute answer explaining why he stood against his brother for the leadership. After a long pause, Axelrod said: 'You just told me why you ran against David. You didn't tell me why you're running for Downing Street.'

And yet. For all the disjunction of Miliband's leadership, it would – as he himself later put it – serve as a bridge between New Labour and the call for radical change that was becoming ever louder in the grassroots Labour Party, and in the nation as a whole. When, in 2011, Miliband committed to challenging business 'predators' and the economic consensus, he was met with vitriolic Tory condemnation and internal Blairite contempt.[3] When Miliband announced that, under Labour, the state would intervene to freeze energy bills, Conservative Prime Minister David Cameron denounced the policy as 'Marxist' (ironically, his successor, Theresa May, later raided the policy); his commitment to scrap private rent increases was vilified by the Conservatives and their many media cheerleaders as 'Venezuelan-style' rent controls. Since the late 1980s, Thatcherism had established a consensus which saw state intervention as beyond the political pale; that Miliband was, however tentatively, suggesting a modest revival of social democracy was enough of a threat to provoke a violent reaction from the political establishment. If not exactly a rupture, Milibandism represented a tear in the fabric.

Yet his timidity during the 2015 general election campaign allowed the gleeful Conservatives to set the terms of political debate, claiming that Britain had been plunged into disaster after 2008 not by global financial collapse, but rather by chaotic overspending by the previous New Labour government. Astonishingly – or perhaps not so much, given where they saw themselves politically – Blairites embraced this narrative, including the former prime minister himself. Blair went on the record as owning this failure – though, characteristically, he took the opportunity for a swipe at his successor as Labour leader: in his memoirs, he declared that his government should have reduced spending from 2005 onwards, and blamed Gordon Brown for not doing so.[4]

Labour's failure to rebut this outright deception during the 2010 election campaign left the party's economic credibility shattered; now in opposition, its record in power was seen through a prism of disastrously wasteful extravagance. As they had done before the 2010 election, the Tories relentlessly pushed a narrative that this alleged lavish waste of public funds was supposedly frittered away on the undeserving poor. The claim that a bloated welfare state was generously handing out hard-earned taxpayers' money to the idle and workshy further bolstered public acquiescence. Tory austerity was justified as 'clearing up Labour's mess', a phrase deployed constantly by the Conservative government, to devastating effect. For fully five years, polls showed the public blamed Labour for the cuts more than the subsequent coalition government that had implemented them.[5] This was a tragic case study of what happens when a social democratic party surrenders to the narrative crafted by the right.

So, even though people in Britain had endured five years of crippling austerity under the coalition government, with the prospect of worse to come, by 2015 Labour was still hopelessly adrift. One Miliband aide recalled, extraordinarily, how the party was taken by surprise at the Conservative election tactics: 'we were shocked that the Tories majored on Labour spending too much money because we never dealt with it properly in the last four years. It was down to different factions. Down to Ed Balls, who was extraordinarily lazy as shadow chancellor and sort of patronizing towards Ed.' But, he concluded damningly, 'it was also down to Ed's indecisiveness'.

As if all this weren't enough, in the run-up to the 2015 general election, Labour was rocked by a political disaster. In the 2014 referendum on Scottish independence, Labour had allied with the Tories in a Remain (in the UK) campaign that dripped with establishment scaremongering. For many Scottish Labour supporters, already profoundly disillusioned with the era of Tony Blair, it was the last straw. In disgust, they defected *en masse* to the Scottish National Party (SNP), a party devoted to the creation of a sovereign Scotland independent of the UK, which presented itself as a more progressive alternative. With its Scottish heartland – traditionally a Labour bulwark – lost, there seemed no way Labour could win an outright majority; its hope of forming a government rested instead on the support of the SNP. This was catnip to the Conservative campaign. Picturing a hapless Miliband in the pocket of SNP leaders, the Tory campaign painted an apocalyptic scenario of a minority Labour government committing to the break-up of Britain in exchange for the support of a Scottish party to keep it in power.

In 2015, the average British voter had no sense of Labour's vision, or how that vision might benefit them, their family and community. 'We just weren't being different enough, it was far too timid a campaign,' explains Nancy Platts, who was narrowly defeated as Labour's candidate in Brighton Kemptown in 2015. 'Labour lived in the shadow of fear that if it was too radical, people won't vote for us. But it was *because* we weren't being radical enough, not offering hope, not being different enough. We spectacularly failed to have any kind of narrative that would make people think they would vote Labour because it'll change my life.' On the doorstep, disillusioned voters spoke about how nothing in politics ever made a difference to them. Labour's support was crumbling in all directions: to the xenophobic right of UKIP, the civic nationalists of the SNP and the anti-austerity left of the Green Party.

Unsurprisingly, following his disastrous election campaign, Miliband resigned. In that late spring of 2015, as the dust settled, Labour announced elections for a new leader, someone capable of imposing a new vision on the now moribund party. Meanwhile, in a protracted post-mortem, Miliband's failings were picked apart.

The dominant narrative that emerged – from within the Labour Party itself – was that it had been Miliband's left-wing policies, rather than his political timidity, that had cost Labour the election. In other words, it wasn't that he had been insufficiently distinct from the Conservatives; rather, he hadn't been enough like them. He hadn't understood where voters were on the economy, immigration and social security – and what people wanted (or so the noises coming out of the Labour Party now concluded) was more austerity, less migration, more cuts to social security. If Labour sought political success, so this view held, it would have to pivot to the right, towards the Shangri-la of some mythical centre ground, where there were rich electoral pickings to be had. Vocal proponents of this idea were especially to be found on the Labour right: the new shadow chancellor, Chris Leslie, condemned Miliband's Labour for being too statist, too interventionist, too anti-business, and for demonizing private landlords.[6]

That May, as the party started its search for a new leader, several MPs threw their hats in the leadership ring, including the patrician historian Tristram Hunt, the career-minded political shapeshifter Chuka Umunna and Wakefield MP Mary Creagh, privately dubbed 'Sweary Mary' because of her penchant for fruity language. They all withdrew, leaving three MPs standing: Liz Kendall, representing the New Labour right; Yvette Cooper, a technocrat; and Andy Burnham, who as shadow health secretary pitched for the left-wing vote, including the crucial support of the unions. Even Burnham, though, had drunk the mainstream Kool-Aid. Castigating Miliband's Labour for supposedly being anti-business, he launched his campaign in the headquarters of Ernst & Young, an accountancy firm notorious for facilitating industrial-scale tax avoidance, and refused to take any money from the unions, surrounding himself, in Len McCluskey's pithy phrase, 'with people who want to have a go at us'.

The mood on the Labour left, meanwhile, was one of despair. 'This is the darkest hour that socialists in Britain have faced since the fall of the Attlee government in 1951,' wrote John McDonnell.[7] With Britain enduring the most severe crisis of capitalism since the Great

Depression, there should have been a natural opening for left ideas on social justice and the redistribution of wealth. Yet here were senior party figures parroting the line in the media that the way to win was being more pro-business, more anti-welfare, more anti-immigration. Despondent, I recorded a video for the *Guardian* newspaper titled 'What's the point in the Labour party now?'[8]

Looking at the developing leadership contest with horror, figures on the left searched desperately for a candidate. To make it on to the ballot paper, a prospective leader had to be nominated by 15 per cent of the parliamentary party, or thirty-five MPs, a higher hurdle than John McDonnell and Diane Abbott had fallen at back in 2007 and 2010 respectively. Various names were bandied about. I threw one possibility into the ether, or rather Twitter: the Wigan MP, Lisa Nandy, who had been privately critical of Miliband's political tentativeness, but had no interest in the job at the time; others called for the candidacy of Jon Trickett, who had been Miliband's left-wing conscience in the shadow cabinet. Trickett decided against it. Instead, that summer, he and I planned to go on tour across the country to argue for radical policies, hoping to exert pressure on the successful leadership candidate and rebuild a Labour left movement.

But as the deadline for leadership nominations loomed, few thought further than actually finding a candidate who might scrape together the requisite nominations. For the left, this was about little more than political survival. If the mainstream narrative – that Labour had lost the general election because it was too left-wing – was allowed to stick, the left's voice would be effectively extinguished in Labour, and the party really would have ripped itself up by the roots. 'The debate was veering off to the right at a pace of knots,' Simon Fletcher explains. 'Even just to have a candidate to pull the debate back a bit and organize the left for future things would be a victory.'

Eventually, the quest for that candidate settled on the most unlikely of politicians. Gently spoken, unkempt, profoundly unconventional Jeremy Corbyn was detached from the usual run of party politics. After all, his main passions lay with championing the oppressed abroad, such as the Kurds and the Palestinians. Outside the activist left, he was practically unknown. Thanks to the left's exile from political life for more than a generation, he'd never held a frontbench role or run an organization; moreover, he was no great orator in any conventional sense. Corbyn was, unquestionably, an implausible leader. But he had his advantages. While John McDonnell and much of the Parliamentary Labour Party had a profound mutual antipathy, Corbyn had no personal enemies. Everyone liked him. Relentlessly cheerful, endlessly generous with his opponents, he exuded integrity. Now in his mid-sixties, he had consistently – mulishly, some might say – stuck to his politics throughout his three decades as a backbench Labour MP.

With the leadership contest already under way, at a meeting of left-wing MPs, McDonnell ruled himself out of the running and expressed his scepticism about any left-wing candidate putting themselves forward: whoever did so, he opined, would get hammered. Privately, however, Corbyn was seriously contemplating doing so – pushed hard by his loyal, long-standing office manager, Nicolette Petersen. McDonnell was taken aback. After the meeting, he and Corbyn went for a cup of tea. When the division bell rang, calling MPs in to vote on some legislation, Corbyn drained his mug and asked: 'You'll run my campaign, won't you?' 'It'll be a mistake,' McDonnell shot back. 'We'll be annihilated and be out for a generation.'

McDonnell recalls phoning me as I got off a train at Paddington station. I shared his concerns, fearing the left would secure a derisory vote, leaving it permanently marginalized and discredited. From McDonnell's point of view, the one thing worse than not getting on the ballot paper would be to appear on the ballot paper and get smashed. As it turned out, Corbyn had got the idea in his head, and wouldn't be dissuaded – at which point, McDonnell pledged to back him. 'I think it's a mistake,' he told his friend, 'but you've made your mind up.'

The caucus of supportive left-wing Labour MPs included some new faces who had won seats in the recent election: Richard Burgon; a telegenic former soldier turned BBC journalist, Clive Lewis; Corbyn's youthful former long-standing parliamentary researcher, Cat Smith. Then there was the old guard, chief among them Corbyn, McDonnell and Diane Abbott. They met on 3 June, when McDonnell stagily announced that Corbyn would run for leader – but there was widespread scepticism among those present. Cat Smith, who had worked for Corbyn for years, was worried for him. 'Do you want this?' she asked gently. Not only was she concerned about her former boss, but also, privately, like most, she didn't think he'd get on the ballot. But she did see advantages, in that 'it'd be a chance to talk about our socialist politics, raise issues, drag the debate to the left, talk about topics like public ownership.' In response to fears that the trouncing Corbyn would inevitably receive would make the left look weak, Lewis shrugged. 'Well, we are weak,' he shot back, 'but we look even weaker if we don't have a candidate.'

Finally, unanimous agreement was reached, although Smith was insistent that her former boss would have to trim his beard and smarten up. Making their way out to the House of Commons Terrace overlooking the Thames, where Labour colleagues were drinking and socializing, the group discreetly began sounding out potential support, which was, if noncommittal, at least not negative; some were even sympathetic to the idea of nominating Corbyn in order to broaden the political debate. Corbyn was well liked, after all – and no one took the prospect of him actually becoming leader in any way seriously.

For me, it had all come full circle. I had begun my working life in McDonnell's office, but never really embraced Parliament, which seemed politically barren. Leaving its stultifying confines, I felt, offered better prospects for radical politics, and I used my media platform to make a public argument for previously marginalized ideas. But now I was suddenly back with the old band in a desperate attempt to stop Labour hurtling off to the right.

That June, out on the road – I was then in Milton Keynes, talking to an anti-cuts meeting – I was finding the public mood surprisingly receptive. I had feared that Labour's general election loss would cause mass demoralization among grassroots supporters and that nobody would turn up to meetings. But in fact they were packed, turning into rallying points for those who, feeling unrepresented and voiceless, were desperate for the hope and radical change which for decades Labour had so manifestly failed to offer. Rather than despondency at the prospect of another five years of punishing Conservative rule, there was a sense of defiance and fury. Now, people who had lived through events from the Iraq War to the financial crash to austerity had had enough. They didn't just want to protest. They demanded a political voice – inside Parliament.

Shortly before the Milton Keynes rally started, my phone rang. It was McDonnell again, fresh from endorsing Corbyn's bid for the leadership. He got straight to the point: would I help build a social media campaign to get Labour MPs to nominate Corbyn? Given that I'd spent my entire adult life arguing for Labour to demand an unapologetic break with the current political order, my answer was yes. Whatever reservations I might have privately felt, there was no point in half-measures. If Corbyn were to stand, his vote share had to be maximized; the more votes he received, the stronger the left's presence in the party. Not that he was going to win; that was unthinkable. The next morning, I wrote the first pro-Corbyn column to appear in the mainstream media: a *Guardian* piece headlined 'Jeremy Corbyn is in the Labour leadership race. The real debate starts here.'

Through social media, Labour supporters and members were encouraged to bombard MPs – politely – in support of Corbyn. Meanwhile, left-wing politicians, key activists, trade unionists and commentators – myself included – all lobbied MPs. Our point was the simple, familiar one: Corbyn needed to be on the ballot to ensure as wide a debate as possible about the Labour Party's future direction. It was this argument that bore fruit. After all, few would have nominated him if they actually thought he stood a chance of winning. Some on the party's right, indeed, were prepared to nominate Corbyn to teach the left a lesson. Corbyn's performance in the leadership election would be so dismal, they believed, that it would drive home to the left once and for all exactly what a tiny and irrelevant minority they really were.[9]

With a deadline of 15 June, Corbyn had just twelve days to amass thirty-five nominations. There were some tight moments. One left-wing MP, Graeme Morris, had nominated Burnham, but suddenly aware of Corbyn's candidature, he asked his office manager, Karie Murphy, to get his nomination back, which controversially she did after a furious argument with an official in the whips' office. Social media played a pivotal role, with Corbyn supporters using Twitter and Facebook to encourage Labour members to bombard MPs demanding they nominate Corbyn to allow a democratic debate over the party's future direction. But despite herculean efforts, two days before the election nominations had ground to a virtual standstill at eighteen. 'We decided the numbers weren't there,' recalled Corbyn's parliamentary assistant Jack Bond, 'and we were a bit depressed.'

With forty-eight hours to go, Corbyn had what one senior ally recalls as 'what I can only describe as what I thought was a nervous breakdown': friends found him extremely agitated and speaking incoherently. Protective of his closest friend in politics, and believing he had been pressured into standing, McDonnell declared it was time to give up. 'It's not fair on Jeremy to use him like this,' he told allies. Refusing to pick up the phone to potential supporters, Corbyn himself went to ground, attending a meeting in his Islington constituency in support of refugees.[10] MPs who had said that if Corbyn rang them personally they would consider nominating him, heard nothing.

Less than forty-eight hours before the deadline, Jon Lansman, a veteran of the Labour left, turned up at Corbyn's house. Lansman, a silver-haired, goateed, bespectacled man with a penchant for colourful shirts, had played a leading role in Benn's deputy leadership campaign in 1981. Corbyn wouldn't speak to him about the campaign, and changed the subject; he was, he said, thinking of writing a book. Lansman came away from the meeting convinced that it was time to throw in the towel.

Yet, as the weekend came to a close, things started to shift: Rushanara Ali, who was standing for the deputy leadership, offered her nomination in exchange for two from Corbyn supporters. Monday 15 June was dramatic. With Mary Creagh standing down her doomed campaign the previous Friday, the nine MPs who nominated her shopped around again: two lent Corbyn their nominations. Corbyn himself had emerged from his melancholy, telling journalists that it would be nice to appear on the ballot paper.[11] Yet, with an hour to go, he was still nine backers short. Suddenly, Margaret Beckett – a left-wing firebrand turned Blair loyalist who was then conducting a review into Labour's election defeat – marched into Corbyn's office to nominate him without even being asked. An election for Labour's London mayoral candidate was running in parallel, and it was in the interests of the candidates to win over party members by being seen to allow a contest for leader. While Sadiq Khan – the eventual winner – Gareth Thomas and David Lammy did not share Corbyn's politics, all nominated him. Fifteen minutes before the noon deadline, Corbyn was still two short. McDonnell resorted to – literally – tearfully begging MPs on his knees for nominations. With minutes to go, Corbyn had scraped on to the ballot with thirty-six nominations. 'You better make fucking sure I don't get elected,' Corbyn told Lansman, in possibly the only recorded instance of a Corbyn expletive at that point.

As the campaign got under way, the odds of Corbyn becoming leader started at 200–1. The other three contenders had been preparing their campaigns long before the general election. Corbyn's operation had no staff, no headquarters, no press operation, no messaging and no clarity on whether Labour's main trade union affiliates would be supportive. The day after Corbyn got on the ballot paper, a group of us met in Jon Trickett's office to try to sketch out some policies, messages and strategies. 'It wasn't really a campaign,' recalls Andrew Fisher, who was seconded from his job as policy officer at the Public and Commercial Services union. 'It was very disorganized.' As we discussed what a good result for Corbyn might look like, our aims were modest. 'I just didn't want him to come last!' Fisher recalls, echoing my own thoughts at the time. 'Coming third would be a result, to defeat Liz Kendall.' Beating the Blairite candidate would be a result, of sorts.

Corbyn himself was plunged in at the deep end, starting on Wednesday 17th, with his first national televised leadership debate on the BBC. It was to be held in Nuneaton, a bellwether seat in the recent general election – which Labour lost. Worried about Corbyn's lack of media experience, I rushed into Parliament to pluck him from Prime Minister's Questions. As I fired questions at him, trying to emulate an inquisitorial TV interviewer, Corbyn suddenly stopped answering and went off on one of his characteristic tangents. 'If we win 20 to 25 per cent, that'll be a success, won't it?' he mused.

That evening, the Nuneaton debate unfolded in front of a studio audience comprising former Labour voters who had abandoned the party in the recent general election. Burnham, Cooper and Kendall all stuck monotonously to scripts they would follow slavishly in the coming weeks. There was a lot of striving for effect: when Burnham said 'the party should come first', Kendall jabbed back with 'country should come first', a line lapped up by pundits but met with groans from the audience.

Then, as Corbyn got going, people started to sit up. He spoke off the cuff about housing, about the failures of privatization, about jobs. 'He spoke in terms of needs and wants in a genuine unscripted way,' says Andrew Fisher, who had done his best to brief Corbyn and was watching backstage. Afterwards, in an untelevised straw poll of the audience, 40 per cent opted for Corbyn in a four-horse race. Charlie Falconer, a former cabinet minister and one-time flatmate of Tony Blair who was working on Burnham's campaign, wandered up to Andrew Fisher. 'Your man won there,' he muttered. 'He did really well.' Some on Corbyn's team started to dream.

In the following days, Corbyn's campaign assembled. Unions began to swing behind him. Despite Unite's early flirtation with Burnham, it was a no-brainer for McCluskey to back Corbyn as soon as he announced; now, the nation's largest trade union pumped its money and resources into the campaign. Strikingly, even Unison – long considered the most 'moderate' of the major unions – endorsed him. 'That made him seem like a serious contender,' says Anneliese Midgeley, a Unite official seconded to Corbyn's campaign team. 'It put him on the map.' As campaigns director, Simon Fletcher brought a wealth of experience from his role as chief of staff to London's former mayor Ken Livingstone. By day eleven of the campaign, 1,500 volunteers had signed up online, and the first volunteering event was hugely oversubscribed.

Corbyn's stated aim was to draw a thick red line under the failures of two recent Labour eras: first, New Labour, with its perceived triangulation and spinning, most damningly in the run-up to the 2003 Iraq War; and second, the tortured timidity of the recent Miliband leadership. 'We wanted a campaign that was full of energy, open and inclusive,' Midgeley explained. Contact was made with existing activist organizations on the left and a network of local organizers put together; a volunteer-staffed phone banking operation was set up, together with a digital strategy including a canvassing app. John McDonnell, meanwhile, was the strategic linchpin, overseeing messaging, linking together the separate wings of the campaign, smoothing out conflicts, and negotiating with the party apparatus.

The sense of something happening around Corbyn gained momentum with his leadership rallies. Traditionally, Labour leadership events were small, stage-managed, with audiences packed full of wonks and ambitious political hacks. Corbyn's leadership rallies were entirely different. In Birkenhead in early July, hundreds of people turned up. And, says northerner Alex Halligan, a burly young trade union official, the Wirral wasn't the kind of place where people turned up to listen to politicians – not for generations. 'I knew there was something very unusual about what was happening.' A few weeks later, a huge crowd crammed into Liverpool's Adelphi Hotel. On a burning hot day at the Durham Miners' Gala, Britain's biggest annual celebration of working-class culture, I watched in the wings as Corbyn took to the stage. There was euphoria in the air: a crowd who had waited over a generation for a moment that they had long come to believe they would never see. It was relief as much as anything else.

Speaking at pro-Corbyn rallies around the country, I could sense a palpable change. The crowds grew bigger, more enthusiastic by the day – and these were people who normally wouldn't have touched Westminster politics with a bargepole. In early August, at a mass rally in London's Camden Centre, it struck me that I was witnessing an unprecedented political phenomenon unfolding. 'Hundreds and hundreds of people are queuing around the block in King's Cross to see Jeremy Corbyn speak,' I tweeted. 'It is incredible.' Speakers had to rotate around spillover rooms, and then address a large crowd which couldn't make it through the door. It produced one of the iconic photographs of the campaign: three teenage boys who had clambered on to a windowsill to watch what was happening.

And people seemed to love Corbyn. While other contenders refused to give direct answers to questions, and were caught squirming between their principles and their political compromises, he spoke with immediacy – sometimes rambling, always authentic, always passionate. When other contenders refused to commit to scrapping the Tory-imposed cap on benefits, Corbyn answered directly that he would do so. He came across as a plain speaker who stuck to his principles; this would become Corbyn's defining advantage in the leadership election campaign. Local Labour parties – including those not even on the radar as possible wins – began to nominate him in droves. 'Those nominations,' recalls Fletcher, reliving the moment, 'were extraordinary.'

What was more, those rallies were translating into concrete support. People were joining the Labour Party – to vote for Corbyn. That they were able to do so was down to recent wholesale reforms in Labour's electoral system, pushed through by Ed Miliband during his time as leader. Miliband had abolished Labour's electoral college, which, equally divided into three sections – MPs, trade unionists and Labour Party members – had had the responsibility of choosing the party's leader. The move was opposed by left-wingers such as Jon Lansman, on the grounds that it would dilute the trade unions' power within the party; indeed, supporters certainly saw it like that. But Miliband was nonetheless a genuine believer in a new 'one member, one vote system', as were key advisers, including his left-wing union liaison officer, Simon Fletcher. Now, anyone who paid a £3 fee to join the Labour Party could have a vote in leadership elections. Those on the right of the party saw an opportunity. Their theory went like this. Party members and trade union activists were significantly to the left of public opinion. If members of the public had a say, their voice would anchor a future leadership contest in a supposed 'centre ground', rather than depending on the whims of supposedly out-of-touch party members. In the days before Corbyn's confirmation on the leadership ballot, one Kendall ally told *The Times*: 'We will get hundreds of thousands of new supporters. Social media has changed how we communicate in a way we can't grasp and it has blown open this leadership contest too.'[12]

Kendall was right, but not in the way she expected. The £3 scheme mobilized a rather different new support base. Many people, politicized by the political and economic crises and activist movements of the preceding years, now flooded into the party. They weren't joining to vote for Liz Kendall. As it turned out, the leadership electoral reforms would prove the biggest self-own in British electoral history.

The Corbyn campaign organized mass sign-ups, but had to tread carefully not to do anything which could call into question the whole process and lead to the election being re-run with less helpful rules. Burnham's potty-mouthed campaign manager, Michael Dugher, who had a particular loathing for the left, kicked up a huge fuss over the thousands of new members, who were portrayed as Trotskyist 'entryists' previously hostile to Labour. In response, Corbyn's team did all they could to ingratiate themselves with the party's apparatus and show they were on message. When the media tried to whip up a storm over sign-ups, Corbyn visited a Labour Party office in the Northeast charged with processing membership and thanked the staff for their professionalism.

A core strategy of Corbyn's campaign was to target those Labour supporters who over the decades had become progressively disillusioned with the party. 'If you're about to join, welcome,' announced one full-page *Guardian* advert. 'If you're coming back, welcome home.' Thousands signed up off the back of it. While his rivals had a dearth of ideas, Corbyn offered a ten-point plan which might as well have been a love letter to those both disenchanted by the Blair era and angered by Tory policies, not least those attracted to the movements of the 2010s: an end to austerity, a national investment bank, tax justice, reducing the social security bill by creating properly paid jobs and a mass housebuilding programme, public ownership, the abolition of tuition fees and an end to illegal wars. The brains behind this bold policy agenda was the meticulous Andrew Fisher, foreshadowing his role as architect of Labour's later manifestos.

The campaign's energy and inventiveness matched its insurgent politics, in the process drawing on the energy of movements earlier in the decade, such as UKUncut. 'We injected politics with a bit of fun,' Midgeley recalls. Envelopes were sent to members imprinted with: 'WARNING: NEW TYPE OF POLITICS'. 'We don't just want to stick things in envelopes,' Simon Fletcher told staff. 'Always think: "How can we make this the best thing ever?" ' With the other campaigns rooted in a fetishization of safety-first politics, the difference was marked. Then there was Corbyn himself, whose affability and visceral objection to injustice had found its moment. That he was a dogged, decades-long campaigner on behalf of apparently lost causes, rather than a former party apparatchik, gave him a zeal and purpose his opponents could not match. Where rival campaign videos consisted of a candidate speaking contrived over-rehearsed messages to camera, Corbyn's showed packed rallies and tub-thumping speeches. Social media played a pivotal role. Online outriders used Twitter and Facebook to spread campaign messages, encourage people to sign up to vote for Corbyn, rebut attacks from rival candidates and bypass a media largely hostile to Corbyn's social democratic manifesto.

The other campaigns, increasingly panicked, briefed that their data showed Corbyn pulling ahead. And, as Corbyn's team printed out their own now extensive data, 'We thought fuck me, we could win,' recalls veteran activist Jon Lansman. 'We didn't want to tell anyone, it didn't seem plausible. We looked at our methodology, and spent days agonizing over it.' Corbyn was shown the data. 'Oh!' he exclaimed, his eyes looking like they might pop out of his skull.

All of which prompted growing horror in the Labour Party establishment – including among those MPs who had nominated him to widen the debate, but certainly not to hand him the leadership. Clive Lewis recalls how one such MP wrote a letter to Corbyn's team saying that they had made their point and it was now time for their man to stand down. The MP approached Lewis himself, telling him: 'Stop this now.' 'What do you mean?' Lewis asked blandly. 'It'll end badly,' was the MP's response. 'Jeremy is a nice man, but some of the people around him aren't, it'll get nasty.' 'Worse than neoliberals in charge of the party?' Lewis retorted. 'I'm my own man. I'll make my own mistakes, it'll be about democratizing the party, handing power back to the membership and opposing austerity, why wouldn't I back it?' The pair agreed to differ.

As Corbyn hurtled towards victory, the existence of an organized grassroots movement in his campaign was crucial. When Tony Blair had won the Labour leadership back in 1994, his supporters founded 'Progress', an organization dedicated to promoting his agenda within the party. Corbyn needed one, too: to bolster his political agenda against the inevitable backlash from within the party; to get supportive candidates selected as Members of Parliament and local councillors; and to bypass an anaemic and unimaginative party hierarchy, in order to mobilize what was now a rapidly expanding membership. Besides which, there was another significant task. In weeks, the Corbyn campaign had managed to bring together disparate factions of the left, groups with wildly divergent views: old and young; veterans of Tony Benn's campaigns of the 1970s and 80s; younger activists involved in the various movements of the 2000s, from Climate Camp and UK Uncut to the student-led protests against education fees; hardened trade unionists, and others wary of them; anarchists, Trotskyists, Communists.

What united these different demographics was a previous, and profound, antipathy towards the Labour Party. 'I wasn't a party member until he ran,' says Faduma Hassan, a young activist who knew Corbyn from the anti-war and anti-austerity movements, and who would end up working in Labour's hierarchy. 'If you told me I'd be heavily involved in working in Labour,' she smiled, 'I'd have laughed at you.' Having brought them together, somehow the Corbyn campaign had to keep them united, under one new umbrella grassroots movement.

One sunny July afternoon in Parliament, I sat in a room with Jon Lansman and other activists to come up with a name for the nascent organization. Originally, this new organization was, for Lansman, the whole point of the leadership campaign. While Corbyn was unlikely to win, the campaign would revitalize the Labour left, and a movement was needed to organize its supporters – now, whatever happened in the forthcoming election, that opportunity had emphatically presented itself. Representatives from an advertising agency – the campaign had reached that point by now – had written various keywords on a board: things like 'Swarm' and 'Straight Talking'. One by one, we shouted out the ones we objected to; one by one they were erased. One of the few suggestions which remained summed up the mood of the summer: 'Momentum'. It would quickly become one of the most recognizable names in British politics, and a *bête noire* of Britain's media and the Parliamentary Labour Party.

What happened in those manic months, overturning the long-established rules of British politics, was reflected in turbulent currents far beyond Britain's shores. Across the globe, as social democrats abandoned their core values and precepts – state-led investment, public ownership of utilities, a universal welfare state, even public spending – new political forces were filling the vacuum they had created. This included the formation of Spain's Podemos, which had itself emerged in the aftermath of an activist movement, the *Indignados*;

and the astonishing rise of Greece's radical left party, Syriza. In Britain, those who believed in social democracy now clung to Corbynism as to a life raft.

The Labour Party establishment tended to see their relationship with the grassroots membership as akin to a world-weary parent telling hard truths to a naively idealistic child; acquainting a delusional activist base with electoral reality – or, as Kendall put it, telling them to 'eat your greens'. Now, Kendall's ally Chuka Umunna likened the rebellious membership to 'a petulant child who has been told you can't have the sweeties in the sweetshop', and starts 'running around stamping' their feet.[13] Blair himself sneered that if people's hearts were with Corbyn, then they should 'get a transplant',[14] a characteristically tin-eared and counterproductive intervention, which only served to fuel Corbyn's campaign. After the former prime minister's comments, a media scrum assembled outside the Royal College of Nursing in Bloomsbury, where Corbyn was launching his economic agenda with McDonnell, hoping for a public spat. 'I don't do personal,' Corbyn told them calmly. 'He's entitled to his opinions, but let's have a debate about politics.' Even Corbyn's way of doing politics seemed different, more honest: where they went low, to use Michelle Obama's phrase, he went high.

Corbyn tapped into 'something that was already there', as Halligan put it – and as the Labour establishment, in their own curious way, knew all too well. 'There was already a large number of people with that thinking,' Halligan added, 'they just weren't very organized.' In that summer of 2015, Corbyn proved to be the focus people needed.

With Corbyn's campaign surging into a runaway lead, the now desperate party machine turned to implicit threats, trying to persuade Labour MPs to surrender what grassroots activists regarded as their principles for the sake of their careers. In the midst of the contest, the Conservatives presented a welfare bill slashing £12 billion from social security, including tax credits which low-paid workers depended on. Labour's acting leader, Harriet Harman, provoked horror among the grassroots when she instructed her MPs to abstain; some Labour politicians even stood up at the weekly Parliamentary Labour Party meeting to urge their colleagues to support it. A party founded to represent the interests of the working class was effectively filing for political and moral bankruptcy. Clive Lewis was hauled into the whips' office, and told by Chief Whip Rosie Winterton: 'Clive, I know you want to do what's right,' before urging him to 'prove your detractors wrong'. Lewis was perplexed about who his detractors were – presumably those who believed he was a dangerous left-winger – but felt that he was essentially being told, as he put it, to 'suck up your morals, suck up your politics, suck up your backbone, take the king's shilling'. Richard Burgon was rung up by Phil Wilson – Blair's successor in the constituency of Sedgefield – who told him: 'I know you don't like it, sometimes there are things I don't like, but we have to do it, you vote the way the Labour leader wants, that's the way it is.'

At a drinks meeting for the new parliamentary intake, Harriet Harman told MPs dismissively: 'It pains me to think some of you would come down on trains and buses to vote against the whip. You don't need to be here.' For the most part, among MPs, the concerted tactic worked: just forty-eight Labour MPs ended up voting against the bill. Of the leadership candidates, only Corbyn voted against, despite later protestations of regret from Burnham and Cooper. The episode impressed upon the grassroots the necessity to break decisively from the party's past; and indeed, Labour MPs across the spectrum credit this moment for making a decisive Corbyn triumph all but inevitable.

By the end of July, it was clear that Corbyn was going to win – and by a landslide. The rival campaigns collapsed into panic. There was vague talk about putting up a unity 'Stop Corbyn' candidate, which was a waste of time, given that the electoral system allowed voters to rank candidates by preference. Aware of their impending rout, no other candidate even bothered to prepare a transition plan for assuming the leadership. That September, as leadership election day neared, I was sitting in Parliament's Portcullis House with John McDonnell and his team when a resignedly cheerful Andy Burnham walked past, clutching a couple of coffees. 'Is that the new shadow cabinet meeting, then?' he quipped sardonically.

Among the Tories and their media outriders, meanwhile, there was jubilation. Like many on the Labour right, they firmly believed Labour had lost the 2015 election because they were too left-wing;

now, it appeared that they were doubling down on the reasons for their own failure. 'How you can help Jeremy Corbyn – and destroy the Labour Party,' sneered the Tory-supporting *Telegraph* newspaper, encouraging its readers to join the party to vote for Corbyn.[15] The right-wing journalist Toby Young likewise backed Corbyn's campaign, arguing that 'With Corbyn at the helm, Labour's loss will be so catastrophic – so decisively humiliating – that the Left of the party might finally be silenced for good . . . We might even see a bit less of Owen Jones on the telly.'[16]

But there were other, savvier right-wing voices. 'A Corbyn victory in the Labour leadership battle would be a disaster,' declared the *Telegraph* deputy editor Allister Heath. Socialism was supposed to have been long defeated, he wrote, but 'left-wing ideas have since made a return, to the great regret of commentators such as myself'. Corbyn's victory would be 'disastrous' because it 'would become acceptable again to call for nationalising vast swathes of industry, for massively hiking tax and for demonising business. The centre-ground would move inexorably towards a more statist position.'[17] Another prominent Conservative activist, Oliver Cooper, echoed this fear, believing it would 'shift the entire political debate to the left' and give 'credibility to the far-left's rejection of reality', fearing Corbyn's 'brand of socialism would poison the groundwater of British politics for a generation: influencing people, particularly young people, across the political spectrum'.[18] It proved a prophetic warning.

As voting closed on 10 September, hundreds crammed into the Union Chapel in Corbyn's Islington constituency, clutching red-and-white placards proclaiming 'I VOTED FOR A NEW KIND OF POLITICS'. That night, I was Corbyn's warm-up man. As I introduced him, rapturous applause echoed from the walls. For my own part, I tried to suppress a rising sense of trepidation. A political hurricane was about to hit.

Two days later, I stood with colleagues from the *Guardian* in the Queen Elizabeth II Centre, an ugly grey building just across from the House of Commons, as the results were announced to ecstatic cheers. Nearly six out of ten eligible voters had opted for Corbyn; the nearest competitor, Burnham, who had attempted to veer left in the final desperate weeks, won less than a fifth of the vote. Outside, a triumphant crowd cheered, then packed out nearby pubs to celebrate. Tears streamed down the faces of some supporters. Inside, members of the rival campaign teams wandered around, wondering what had happened.

Corbyn and his team were equally, but ecstatically, bewildered. Months before, he could barely scrape together enough votes for his nomination. Now, against overwhelming odds, Jeremy Corbyn was leader of Britain's Labour Party.

The celebrations, though, were tinged with apprehension. Events chief Kat Fletcher had told her parents back in Sheffield that she was taking a job in the new leadership, but 'it'll be bloody miserable, that I don't know if I'll last three months or three years, that I know it'll be a horrendous job in lots of ways, but I've got to join, no alternative, it's an amazing moment in history'. Full of excitement, she presumed there would be 'grownups' planning for what came next. The path lay open to a tumultuous new political era for Labour – but it was a challenge for which the new leadership was almost completely unprepared. The party's establishment was stunned, enraged and frightened – but, as everyone felt, they would fight back. 'There was this huge intimidating feeling,' says Joss MacDonald, Corbyn's youthful parliamentary researcher. 'It was: "Fuck, none of us have ever been near the leadership of the Labour Party before. What do we do now?" '

3
'It's Gonna Be Brutal': The War Within

Entering Parliament in September 2015, Jeremy Corbyn's new leadership team literally crashed through the doors. In normal circumstances, a handover process from the outgoing team would be expected, but Corbyn's predecessor as Labour leader, Ed Miliband, had resigned in the immediate aftermath of the party's clobbering at the polls four months earlier. To the frustration of Corbyn's advisers, desperate to get going, there was no one from his operation to give the newcomers a guided tour of the office: here are the computer passwords, here are the printers, there's where important files are kept. Worse still, they couldn't even get into the opposition leader's office.

'The parliamentary keys are set in such a way that if you attempted to open a door that the key isn't registered to, it'll block the whole key and you have to go to security and get it sorted,' says Angie Williams. She and Simon Fletcher were the only two Miliband staffers to take up a post in Corbyn's new team; no other staff member even had a parliamentary pass. Williams had learned a trick in the Miliband years: one of the doors could be opened without a key if it was bumped hard enough. This time, it didn't work. The parliamentary authorities had clearly done a security check and fixed the quirk. Not wanting to lose face in front of Corbyn's campaign staff, Williams threw herself against the door until it broke open, splinters and metal everywhere. In they walked.

No leader of any major British political party has assumed office with odds so stacked against them while simultaneously being so unprepared as Jeremy Corbyn in September 2015. In normal times, here's what happens. An aspiring leader is someone who has spent years, decades even, casting their sights on the top job. They have long prepared for this moment – some, since their early teens, pacing in front of bathroom mirrors practising future conference speeches. They enjoy the backing of a significant portion of their parliamentary party, and can count on the loyalty and support of its officials. Corbyn had none of this. Not only had he never harboured any ambitions of leadership, he had never held even the most junior ministerial role, nor had he stood at a parliamentary dispatch box, making speeches in front of a rowdy and often aggressive Parliament. Then there was the media. Anybody who knows anything about the British press knows that it is almost unique in the Western world for its level of commitment to aggressively defending and furthering right-wing partisan politics. Some sections of the press, moreover, behave as overtly partisan extensions of the Conservative media operation. Unsurprisingly, then, attacking Labour leaders is a blood sport for the British press, the one striking exception, of course, being Tony Blair, whose Faustian pact with the Murdoch empire was founded on a commitment not to challenge the social order or undo the new Thatcherite consensus. 'I always thought my job was to build on some of the things she had done rather than reverse them,' as Blair put it when Thatcher died. Corbyn was about as far from Blair as it was possible to get – and the media onslaught that greeted his leadership win in 2015 was as predictable as it was unrelentingly hostile.

With most voters switching on to politics for only brief moments in their lives, there are three key windows for an opposition leader to make an impression: when they assume the leadership, at their annual party conferences and at general elections. The first impression is likely to be lasting, or at least difficult to dislodge, so the early weeks are crucial. Accordingly, in Corbyn's first few weeks, the right-wing press machine systematically attempted to shape his image in the public imagination: crudely, negatively and often deceitfully. 'CORBYN: ABOLISH THE ARMY', was the *Sun*'s front page splash two days after his leadership victory – a piece based on a comment Corbyn had made three years previously about wishing that one day every country on earth would abolish their own army.[1] On Remembrance Day 2015, the same newspaper accused Jeremy Corbyn of failing to bow his head in memory of Britain's fallen at the Cenotaph.

'SNUB ON POPPY DAY', screamed the paper, along with 'Pacifist Corbyn refuses to bow' and 'NOD IN MY NAME'. Again, this was blatantly untrue: video footage showed Corbyn quite clearly bowing his head. Dishonestly trashing Corbyn over Remembrance Day etiquette became an annual tradition. The following year, the *Sun* and Mail Online were forced to take down stories which falsely suggested that Corbyn had danced his way down Downing Street on the way to the commemorations.[2] The actual disrespect to Britain's fallen, surely, lay in right-wing newspapers hijacking a day dedicated to mourning their deaths, in order to deceitfully hound the Leader of the Opposition.

In 2016, a group of academics at the London School of Economics compiled a report examining a period of media coverage that spanned Corbyn's first few weeks as leader. Their findings, they wrote, illustrated 'the ways in which the British press systematically delegitimised Jeremy Corbyn as a political leader' through a 'process of vilification that went beyond the normal limits of fair debate and disagreement in a democracy'. They found that 57 per cent of news articles – which are supposed to be objective – had a critical or antagonistic tone: 'scathing, disingenuous, insulting or mocking'. According to their analysis, 30 per cent of 'news stories, editorials, commentaries, features or letters to the editor mock the leader of the opposition or scoff at his ideas, policies, history, his personal life – and, alarmingly, even his looks'. Over half of all articles failed to include Corbyn's own views; another 22 per cent stripped them of context or distorted them. He was depicted by turns as a comic caricature, referred to repeatedly as the 'Jezster' or as 'Mr Corbean', a reference to the slapstick sitcom character Mr Bean; the Grinch (Jeremy Corbyn 'cancels Christmas' and 'refuses to issue festive message', declared the *Daily Telegraph*, four days after Corbyn had written a Christmas message for the *Daily Mirror*); Chairman Mao (on the grounds that his fairly bog-standard bike looked – according to *The Times's* news section, no less – like something the Great Leader might ride[3]) and a terrorist sympathizer. He had 'suspicious ties to terror groups', announced the *Daily Express*, while the *Sun* called him a supporter of the IRA and 'any heavily bearded jihadi mentals who long for the destruction of the West'.[4] And so it went on.

Corbyn was also met with profound hostility from within the publicly funded, professedly impartial BBC, perhaps unsurprisingly for a public broadcaster described to me by one of its own senior presenters as broadly 'Blairite', and a number of whose senior staff – including the then head of the corporation's political programming output, Robbie Gibb – went on to work for the Conservative Party (Theresa May, David Cameron, George Osborne and Boris Johnson all recruited their spin doctors from the BBC). Six months later, after Corbyn's election as leader, Sir Michael Lyons – former chair of the BBC Trust – declared there had been 'some quite extraordinary attacks on the elected leader of the Labour Party. I can understand why people are worried about whether some of the most senior editorial voices in the BBC have lost their impartiality on this. All I'm voicing is the anxiety that has been expressed publicly by others.'[5]

But Corbyn's Labour was not just under assault from the outside. There was also an enemy within. The vast majority of the Parliamentary Labour Party not only did not support Corbyn, they regarded his elevation to the leadership with horror, as a dystopian nightmare which must be brought to an abrupt end; many believed it would all be over by Christmas. Even before Corbyn's team had broken the Westminster door down, political opponents inside the Labour Party were at work on a scorched earth assault on the leadership. It would never let up.

For most of this period – except for a brief spell at the red-brick Brewers' Green offices near St James's Park – the party's officials responsible for its day-to-day operation were based in an unlovely generic glass office building called Southside on Victoria Street, a twelve-minute walk from the Houses of Parliament. These officials were Labour's equivalent of the civil service; they were expected to serve whoever the membership had elected with strict, rigorous impartiality. Instead, they acted as a hostile political faction, conspiring and plotting not only to bring down their leadership, but even wishing ill on the party's own electoral prospects.

It is impossible to overstate the political hostility of these bureaucrats. Staff at the Labour Party HQ reportedly used a messaging service, conversations on which allegedly expose systematic efforts by a number of figures to undermine the Corbyn leadership.[6] These messages suggest a dysfunctional and toxic culture within the party's headquarters. (I put these quotes from the leaked report to Labour HQ for comment: but at the time, the party had commissioned an inquiry, headed by a barrister, Martin Forde QC, and therefore chose not to comment until it was finalized. A statement from the current Labour leader, Keir Starmer, and his deputy, Angela Rayner, asked 'everyone concerned to refrain from drawing conclusions before the investigation is complete'. The inquiry itself had three mandates: to examine 'the background and circumstances in which the report was commissioned', to look at 'the contents and wider culture and practices referred to in the report', and to look at 'the circumstances in which the report was put in the public domain'.)

To be fair, this cabal didn't just shower invective on the left; prominent members of their own political factions – broadly speaking, Blairites and Brownites – were not spared. A week after Labour lost the 2015 general election, the leadership contest to replace Ed Miliband was under way (though it would be some three weeks before Corbyn entered the race). Staffers shared their despair at the candidates. '[Chuka] Umunna must be stopped,' declared one. 'And [Yvette] Cooper and [Andy] Burnham.' 'They are all dreadful,' concurred another. 'Liz Kendall is nuts as well,' they added in a swipe against the Blairite candidate. 'Seriously is there nobody? And Tom Watson for deputy would be the end of the party. I've never felt so bleak about the future of the party.' 'We are fucked,' the first staffer shot back. They gossiped about refuted and defamatory accusations, including suggesting that Chuka dropped out of the leadership race 'as [the] *Mail* were sniffing around gay stories . . .' 'Yes, apparently they had an ex-male lover willing to testify re gay and cocaine,' chipped in another staffer breathlessly. 'Wonder why they didn't run it? Maybe saving it for his next leadership bid.' When it was suggested that Burnham would win the leadership contest 'by a mile', yet another staffer worried 'that he will get found out as the stupid person that he is and if that is the case I can only hope we finally get the courage to gut a leader before the full term and put someone new in'. This was how they saw their own. How they dealt with Corbyn would prove to be on an entirely new level.

On 15 June 2015 – the deadline day for prospective leadership candidates to receive sufficient nominations from MPs to get on the ballot paper – one staffer messaged a colleague that 'anyone who nominates Corbyn "to widen the debate" deserves to be taken out and shot'. The colleague agreed: 'Quite. If the left can't get on the ballot, it shows they're moribund . . . putting them on there only validates their views.' Shooting proved a recurring fantasy among the staffers. After Corbyn had won the leadership, one opined that a staff member who had 'whooped' at his victory speech 'should be shot'.

'Trot', an abbreviation for 'Trotskyist', was used with absurd and wild abandon. When a staffer described a Labour MP as 'such a Trot', another replied: 'Yep. Like most of the PLP [Parliamentary Labour Party] it seems.' As the leadership election advanced, a staff member suggested Corbyn's first wife left him because 'he was such a boring Trot', another declared that they felt 'physically sick about JC'. Yet another warned that there would be 'rampaging Trots' at Labour's annual conference, and 'stewards [will] need pepper spray' or 'body armour'. Conceding the fact that 'Trot' was a label applied to anyone with the mildest leftish inclinations, one staff member admitted: 'everyone here considers anyone left of [Gordon] Brown to be a Trot'. Ed Miliband, meanwhile, was 'pathetic' and 'probably secretly loves Jeremy'.

That summer, as Corbyn's once unthinkable triumph acquired an air of inevitability, the panicked staffers discussed postponing or cancelling the leadership election. When one asked: 'Where do you think Iain [McNicol, the party's general secretary] and Mike [Creighton, director of risk and auditing] are on delay?' the reply came: 'Finely balanced . . . I am now of the view that the three other candidates could just drop out next week and the whole thing would have to be halted.' 'That would be ace' and 'great idea' were the enquirer's enthusiastic replies. 'The party is about to be taken over by complete nut-jobs,' complained another a few days later. 'We need to finish him [Corbyn],' said one on 13 August 2015. Someone else, showing an unwonted caution, declared that 'hanging and burning does seem like overkill', another adding, as if in clarification: 'We can figuratively do that but not literally.'

When Corbyn first visited the party's headquarters shortly after his election triumph in September 2015 to meet staff and deliver a speech, one staffer complained that 'he should have maybe addressed the massive elephant in the room that we all kind of hate him. But I'm not sure how he could have done that without making me hate him more.' They complained about policies from rail nationalization – 'all it looks like is Trots doing what Trots do' – to John McDonnell, now the shadow chancellor, committing to increase corporation tax: 'you're kidding me . . . I can't quite believe it.' In April 2016, one staff member shared a link from the website of the Manchester Conservatives which declared 'Higher tax rates do not necessarily yield more revenues because they reduce incentives to work. What Corbyn fails to understand is that the UK is actually becoming more equal.' 'Indeed, very true', responded a staffer from the policy unit.

If this burning animosity towards the left was ubiquitous among the staffers, they reserved their worst vitriol for BAME politicians, using language that was particularly disturbing and cruel. The Corbyn-supporting MP Clive Lewis was referred to as 'the biggest cunt of the lot'. When Diane Abbott – a politician on the receiving end of relentless misogyny and racism – appeared on BBC's *Question Time* in early 2017, one staffer denounced her as 'a very angry woman'; later that year, another called her 'truly repulsive'. When a staff member bragged that Abbott had been 'found crying in the loos', another suggested they give the story to Channel 4's political reporter Michael Crick (who had himself once tweeted 'London cabbie: You couldn't vote for that Corbyn, could you? Not for anyone that's messed around with that Diane Abbott.'). Yet another replied 'Already have.'

The abuse of Corbyn's chief of staff, Karie Murphy, and political secretary, Katy Clark, was laced with misogyny: terms of disapprobation included 'Medusa', a 'fuckwit', 'Lady Macbeth', 'pube head', 'fat', 'smelly cow', 'crazy snake head lady' and 'crazy woman'. Neither was mental health off limits. In February 2017, they discussed a young Labour activist who, they acknowledged, had 'mental health issues'. That did not stop one staffer declaring that they hoped 'he dies in a fire', another quipping: 'That's a very bad wish . . . But if he does I wouldn't piss on him to put him out.' The first staffer replied: 'Wish there was a petrol can emoji.'

They didn't like me very much either. At the 2015 Labour

conference – the first of the Corbyn leadership – I'd been invited to speak at a Young Labour fringe meeting. One staffer declared that I was 'an arsehole' and demanded that I be removed from the panel. 'Young Labour need not to be Trots,' they added. Pointing out, in a rare spasm of rationality, that 'us thinking he's an arse isn't a legitimate reason to remove him from a panel', another nevertheless reassured their interlocutor that a colleague is 'going to speak to you about Trot purge'.

'Trot purge' referred to the staffers' obsessive attempts to remove left-wing supporters from the Labour Party. (This always seemed like a sport to them: one described a colleague as loving 'Tory bashing second only to Trot bashing'.) 'Trot hunting' included trawling through the social media accounts of prospective Labour Party members – or 'stalking', as they put it – looking for any excuse possible to kick them out. Those purged as 'Trots' included anyone who had retweeted the Green Party or National Health Action Party on issues they agreed with, or liked their Facebook pages. The party's 'Government and Legal Unit' searched through the Twitter feeds for abuse against Labour MPs – but only, it must be noted, their favoured MPs. They included not a single MP who backed Corbyn, or even the shadow cabinet, let alone the leader himself or Diane Abbott, who received a staggering volume of abuse.[7]

Constantly the staffers willed Labour MPs to remove Corbyn from the leadership and for Labour to fail. They discussed working to prevent 'Trots' from winning positions on party boards and the executives of the Welsh and Scottish Labour Party. When one suggested emulating the Social Democratic Party's breakaway from Labour in 1981, another responded: 'Ha, nah we all have to stay and fight. It's gonna be brutal and take for ever, but it's the only option.' Just after Corbyn's victory, rather than discuss how they could make his leadership a success, they spoke about the possibility of Welsh First Minister Carwyn Jones going 'on broadcast and slag [off] JC', adding, 'I hope it happens.' They openly prayed for an opinion poll putting the party 'like 20 points behind'. When the Corbyn-inspired grassroots movement Momentum was formed in October 2015, a staffer declared that Labour MPs 'have to get rid of him in the next couple of months or the Trots will embed themselves'. And, while they were busy doing all this, they deliberately failed to carry out the work they were employed to do, thereby effectively running down Labour's machinery and the left of the UK's main opposition party. They even talked about pretending to look hard at work when they were anything but. Joking about 'hardly working', they suggested using the private messaging service so 'tap tap tapping away will make us look v busy'. Some did the bare minimum, leaving the office at 4 p.m. for the pub.

For those seconded to Southside from the Corbyn movement, none of this is surprising. Like many young people, Georgie Robertson was inspired by Labour's leftward shift. She had worked as a volunteer on Corbyn's second leadership campaign and then as a Momentum press officer, before being seconded to Labour HQ a week after Theresa May called the 2017 general election. 'It felt as though you were in the room with the enemy, with the Tories,' she tells me. 'There was constant sabotage, leaking and briefing.' When Robertson asked Southside officials repeatedly for crucial attack material relating to Tory candidates – information which Robertson was reliably told they had in their possession – it was never granted. 'Many Labour staff were incredibly hostile and nasty,' she tells me. 'They would heckle Jeremy when he was on TV, they would shout and talk down to us, especially to young women.' One reduced a fellow left-wing staffer to tears at the party's manifesto launch. 'It felt very difficult. If we had to get information from anyone at work, it was like drawing blood from a stone.'

There were many things deficient with Corbyn's operation, and I will examine them. Upon Corbyn's election by the membership as leader, the role of Labour Party staff was to ease the transition, to support the operation from the early rocky stages onwards, to ensure its decisions were faithfully implemented, and to do all they could to ensure their party succeeded. Instead, their all-encompassing hatred towards Labour's elected leadership was so intense they relished every potential setback and defeat and felt nothing but despair at success. Rather than serving as a loyal bureaucracy, here was a wrecking operation by a hostile political faction. There are many reasons why the Corbyn project failed. This is one of them.

But Corbynism faced a far more formidable internal threat even than this. Its sole base within the Labour Party was the mass membership, hugely inflated in number because of Corbyn's victory. The parliamentary party, on the other hand, mostly believed that Corbynism was a hideous aberration which needed to be brought to a swift termination. They did all they could to bring that day closer, whatever the cost.

Andy McDonald is a gently spoken man; every word he utters in his strong northeastern lilt seems carefully considered. 'Growing up I didn't have an overtly political heritage,' he tells me. The catalyst for his shift to the left was an unusual one. 'People always say, who inspired you? Attlee, Gandhi? And I always say no, it was Margaret Thatcher, and I do mark it at that moment.' This was what could be called reverse inspiration: it was his revulsion at her policy agenda which politicized him. It was a proud moment when, in 2012, he was elected as an MP to represent a constituency in his native Middlesbrough, an opportunity to fight for some of the burning issues close to his heart. He became a diligent campaigner against the so-called 'bedroom tax' – a pernicious Conservative policy that penalized poorer citizens living in rented social housing who were deemed to have a spare room in their accommodation – and the privatization of the East Coast rail line, a vital national artery. In the 2015 leadership election, McDonald backed Andy Burnham – 'I felt that he represented the best shot for us in terms of democratic socialism.' Like many, he believed Corbyn's leadership bid was doomed. Though he knew and liked Corbyn, 'quite frankly, I thought, this is pointless, it's not going to happen, let's be realistic and pragmatic about it. There's never going to be a huge swathe of support behind Corbyn. How wrong was I!'

McDonald wasn't a dyed-in-the-wool Corbynite, he just believed that Labour MPs had a duty to accept the democratic mandate of an elected leader and to help them succeed. Neither was McDonald an ambitious man, in terms of his party career at least. He'd only ever wished to be a dedicated constituency MP and had no aspirations to join the frontbench. The approach of many of his colleagues towards Corbyn's leadership, however, has scarred him. 'I've been involved in politics since the 1970s and I can honestly say I've never been involved in anything so unpleasant and bitter in my whole life,' he says. 'It was personally distressing, it tore me apart, it challenged my mental health fundamentally. I've never seen such unpleasantness from what I thought were my comrades'. He concludes, emphatically: 'The way in which Jeremy was treated was just quite frankly appalling.'

One notorious location for the acting out of this intra-party conflict was Committee Room 14 in the House of Commons. Every Monday at 6 p.m., Labour MPs would assemble in this long room decorated with grand paintings and chandeliers, for the weekly Parliamentary Labour Party meeting. Many of us are familiar with the bearpit of the House of Commons, as government and opposition face off against each other: the braying, bellowing, guffawing, the hectoring, heckling, sniping and abuse and, occasionally, truly bizarre noises evocative of a busy farmyard. But, away from the watchful gaze of television cameras, the Parliamentary Labour Party meetings during Corbyn's tenure were even nastier, and its participants were all supposed to be on the same side.

Traditionally, a leader's arrival in the room would be met with roars of approval and a general drumming on tables and floor. Not so under Corbyn. 'It was vile, and it was vile for a very long time,' McDonald says. He would walk through Central Lobby to the Committee Room with a sinking feeling. By the time Corbyn appeared, 'the atmosphere was toxic', McDonald recalls. MPs 'vilified him and abused him and shouted at him'. One time, during an attempt to remove Steve Rotheram – then Corbyn's private parliamentary secretary – from the party's National Executive Committee, McDonald was himself on the receiving end. As he stood to defend Rotheram, a roar of protest went up from across the room, one of his colleagues yelling: 'Oh, here comes thicko!' Along with other MPs loyal to the leadership, McDonald would find himself shunned, colleagues either blanking him, or staring him down. Other MPs were treated much the same: Richard Burgon, who would serve as justice secretary, remembers one MP screaming in his face that he was a 'cunt'. Rarely, if ever, did anybody step in to denounce this behaviour. As McDonald points out, such behaviour would not be tolerated in normal workplaces. At her first PLP meeting, Corbyn's events chief, Kat Fletcher, recalls cowering in the corner as MPs raged. Across the room, Tristram Hunt – a lanky, blue-eyed Blairite – was staring at her, clearly trying to work out if she was a newly elected MP. He sauntered over and, without saying anything, grabbed the parliamentary pass hanging on a lanyard around her neck. Seeing she worked for Corbyn, Hunt dropped the pass, sneered and stormed off. 'I thought, "this place is vile",' recalls Fletcher. 'I don't know how Jeremy does it standing up there being as calm as he always was. You do understand how the bunker mentality – not just for him, but his staff – developed.'

Then there was the constant undertow of plotting against Corbyn's leadership, which began before he was even elected. At the end of July 2015, shadow cabinet sources were briefing the right-wing *Telegraph* newspaper that a coup could be launched within days of the result. 'We will have to decide whether he should be removed immediately, or whether it would be better to give him a year or two of being a disaster and get rid of him by 2018,' one anonymous informant pronounced. The Labour MP John Mann, firmly on the right of the party, demanded that the leadership contest itself be halted, alleging 'Trotskyist infiltration'.[8] A couple of weeks afterwards, Simon Danczuk – another Labour right-winger who would later be suspended from the party for allegedly sending graphic text messages to a seventeen-year-old job applicant – was asked whether attempts to remove the leader would begin on day one. 'Yeah, if not before,' was his brazen response. 'As soon as the result comes out. Am I going to put up with some crazy left-wing policies that he is putting forward and traipse through the voting lobby to support him? It's not going to happen, is it? So I would give him about twelve months if he does become leader.'[9] Shortly after, Labour MPs briefed the *Guardian* that as soon as Corbyn assumed the leadership twelve MPs would instantly resign from the party – and that, in any case, a coup attempt would soon follow.[10]

Corbyn's support among the 232 Labour MPs that then made up the parliamentary party was derisory. While thirty-five MPs had nominated him, many did so only to 'widen the debate' in the Labour Party and some would end up ranking among Corbyn's bitterest opponents. One such was Neil Coyle, a London MP who became notorious for his tired and emotional late-night Twitter tirades against the leadership.

The fact was that a good number of the MPs who nominated Corbyn had done so hoping that he would be utterly humiliated in the bright lights of the leadership election, which would thereby confirm the marginalization of the left. 'I would never underestimate the ruthlessness and effectiveness of the PLP and media establishment linking hands to turn victory into an opportunity for organizational and ideological destruction of the left,' left-wing Labour MP Richard Burgon told me during the contest. I wrote in an article at the time: 'Hostile MPs will obsessively leak to the media; they will cite Corbyn's rebellious record as justification to refuse to toe the line; their strategy will be to bleed a Corbyn leadership to death.'[11]

Machinations began as soon as Corbyn's team walked into the leader's office. Midway through Corbyn's victory speech on 12 September, Jamie Reed, a little-known shadow health minister, resigned and his obscurity did not stop much of the media from bigging the episode up. Aiming to head off accusations of political sectarianism, Corbyn's first shadow cabinet represented the broad ideological spectrum of the Labour Party. Even though the Labour right had been overwhelmingly defeated in the leadership election – and though many refused to serve, making the process of forming the cabinet fraught and protracted – they were given a strong presence at the top table. By contrast, few Corbyn allies were handed shadow cabinet positions. While the new leader insisted on John McDonnell as his shadow chancellor, his only other key allies were Diane Abbott in international development, a relatively junior position, and Jon Trickett in communities and local government. From the outset, the narrative peddled by hostile MPs was that Corbynism was politically intolerant, had collapsed Labour's broad church, and confined its opponents to political exile. Yet almost the entire shadow cabinet appointed by Corbyn had campaigned to stop him from becoming leader. Four days later, one of these new shadow cabinet ministers hid behind anonymity to brief a *Channel 4 News* reporter that the inevitable climactic bust-up 'will have to be brutal, putting the left in a box for thirty years or out of [the] party'.[12]

With so few sympathizers in the shadow cabinet, the Corbyn project was stymied in its infancy, its ability to promote an ambitious political programme held back. When thousands of jobs at the Port

Talbot Tata steelworks were threatened in the spring of 2016, Corbyn's allies wanted to call for its nationalization. Polls showed that 62 per cent of voters backed such a move, with only 17 per cent opposed; even most Tory supporters agreed. But Angela Eagle – then shadow secretary of state for business, innovation and skills – privately pushed back against the policy, until, that was, the Tory business minister Anna Soubry suggested it was an option, when it suddenly appeared to become acceptable to Eagle.[13] Shadow Health Secretary Heidi Alexander opposed Labour officially supporting a strike by junior doctors – even though polling showed most of the British public backed them[14] – and called on her colleagues not to attend picket lines. Shadow Work and Pensions Secretary Owen Smith backed the Tories' arbitrary and punitive cap on benefits. With Labour's top team opposed to even mild social democratic politics, the prospects of putting forward a genuinely transformative agenda seemed non-existent.

If the leadership was isolated within its own shadow cabinet, it was nothing in comparison to the situation among Labour MPs in general. Some within Corbyn's operation believed that Labour MPs would swing behind them, given that they were hierarchically minded and would do anything to get jobs. But this, acknowledged Joss MacDonald, was 'total naivety about the PLP and party and the extent to which we were interlopers'.

When Corbyn became leader, 'the mood in the Parliamentary Labour Party was shock, fear, was just incredulous', recalls Jonathan Ashworth, a self-described 'left-wing Brownite' who supported Yvette Cooper yet served in Corbyn's shadow cabinet throughout. He recalls the tearoom and bar chat that autumn of 2015 – that it wouldn't last until Christmas. Following the death of the veteran MP Michael Meacher, a by-election was called for 3 December in his constituency of Oldham West and Royton. MPs privately expected that there would be a significant dent in Labour's vote – if, that was, it wasn't completely smashed. In fact, to most MPs' bewilderment, the party's share of the vote increased. 'MPs couldn't quite understand what was going on,' Ashworth tells me. 'All their instincts about political campaigning, what Corbyn was and what he stood for; they thought he'd just jar with voters.'

Yet while most of the PLP seemed to think they were trapped in the Upside Down – the dystopian parallel universe in the iconic science fiction drama Stranger Things – they had no strategy to escape it. A rational plan – if you were that way inclined – might have been to try to win over the grassroots membership who had catapulted Corbyn into the leadership. That was their only route back. Many MPs, though, were not so democratically inclined. Their contempt for the membership oozed out, merely solidifying support behind Corbyn.

The foreign policy fights picked by Corbyn's most entrenched opponents underlined ideological commitments which strongly jarred with what most members thought. When the Conservative government unveiled plans to bomb Syria at the end of 2015, Shadow Foreign Secretary Hilary Benn, along with a significant chunk of the shadow cabinet and the PLP, swung behind it at a tense party meeting. One dissenting voice was Clive Lewis, a former soldier who had been deployed to Afghanistan, and who stood up to make his case: 'I've seen what Allied bombs do to people, I've seen what it does to civilians, I'm not signing up to this. Why's our first reaction always to bomb somewhere?'

In Parliament, Benn made a passionate, widely acclaimed speech in favour of dropping British bombs on the war-torn Middle Eastern nation, then resumed his seat alongside the Labour leader, who sat, ashen faced, arms folded, in obvious discomfort as Conservative MPs roared their approval and clapped. The pro-war Labour MPs won plaudits from the Conservatives and the right-wing press, who delighted in a Labour schism and the undermining of the party's leadership. 'Jeremy Corbyn faces humiliation as more than 100 Labour MPs plan to defy leader over Syria strikes', declared the *Telegraph*.[15]

To Clive Lewis, the pro-war MPs seemed to give more thought to political point-scoring against Corbyn than to the prospect of heaping more misery on the already traumatized Syria. 'Benn and others saw it as an opportunity to prove they were right, that Jeremy was wrong,' he says, recalling the decade and more of Labour infighting over Blair's catastrophic participation in the US invasion of Iraq – in which, ultimately, Corbyn's anti-war position had been spectacularly vindicated. 'It was a sense of: "there were things we did right in Iraq, and you can't have history all your own way" . . . It was about not letting Jeremy have the last word on Iraq.' In other words, the old guard saw the Syria vote as a means to revive the principle of Western intervention which had been so discredited by the calamity of Iraq, and even more so by the election of an anti-war leader. For many of his internal critics, indeed, Corbyn's opposition to Western military intervention was the central plank of their opposition to his leadership.

There could have been no worse strategy for winning over the membership, many of whom had been drawn to Corbyn because of his firm anti-war stance. In the following weeks and months, pro-war Labour MPs came under fire on social media from aggrieved members. At Andrew Fisher's suggestion, the leadership did its own survey among the membership, asking whether or not they supported a bombing campaign. The result was unsurprising: the membership proved emphatically opposed. It was a result from which the leadership took heart.

'What did keep us buoyed was we felt that we had the strength of the movement behind us,' says Joss MacDonald, then in charge of Corbyn's personal correspondence. Whatever the hostility of the parliamentary party, 'we knew that the membership supported us, that most of the unions supported us in our position. We still had the triumphalism of 2015, the energy with us, we never doubted ourselves.' This would be a recurring theme. Though many members did have moments of profound and repeated disillusionment with the leadership, brazenly antagonistic behaviour by hostile Labour MPs would lead them to cast their misgivings to one side.

For all that, the Syria vote set a precedent. It was the first clear evidence that when it came to key parliamentary votes, Corbyn could not expect the support of his own party, who, whatever the importance of the issue at stake, would use such votes to try to destabilize the leadership. Ten months later, over a hundred Labour MPs refused to back Corbyn's call for a UN investigation into alleged Saudi war crimes in Yemen.[16] And each time Labour MPs rebelled in this way, often while flaunting parodically reactionary politics (you hardly needed to be a revolutionary socialist to oppose the murderous actions of Saudi Arabia's theocratic dictatorship), it prompted an equal but unintentionally opposite reaction, driving the membership further into the arms of Corbynism.

When in July 2016 Corbyn stood up in Parliament to respond to the Chilcot Inquiry into the Iraq War – with its damning findings on Tony Blair's role – right-wing then-Labour MP Ian Austin shouted at him to 'shut up' and yelled 'you're a disgrace'. Later that year, 150 Labour MPs voted against a new investigation into whether Blair misled Parliament in the run-up to the Iraq War.[17] Backing war, indulging anti-immigration sentiments, favouring the interests of big business over those of the country: time and time again, Labour MPs adopted stances which alienated members, leading them to rally still further behind the leadership.

Some of Corbyn's opponents were savvier than this. They knew that the one issue that united them with the membership was a passionate commitment to Britain's continued membership of the European Union. In the aftermath of the 23 June 2016 referendum result – 52 per cent to 48 per cent in favour of Leave and Brexit – many Labour MPs were genuinely distressed, but they also saw an opportunity to move against Corbyn. Their rationale was as follows. According to the generally reliable polling company YouGov, shortly before the referendum 72 per cent of Labour members thought Corbyn was doing well and 27 per cent thought he was doing badly. The days after the referendum saw a dramatic shift: just 51 per cent thought he was doing well, but 48 per cent thought badly. Only 47 per cent thought he'd done well in the referendum, while 52 per cent believed he had done badly.[18] It was a moment of genuine grassroots disillusionment with the leadership that anti-Corbyn Labour MPs were determined to exploit.

It is worth emphasizing that there was a 'good faith' element to the parliamentary party's post-referendum breakdown. Having failed to win the referendum he had called, pro-EU Conservative Prime Minister David Cameron resigned. Washing his hands of the whole thing, he retired to a specially built £25,000 shed in his Oxfordshire garden to write his memoirs. Many MPs feared his successor would call a general election and the pro-Brexit Tories would sweep across traditional Labour areas which had voted Leave. 'It was absolute meltdown,' says Jonathan Ashworth. 'MPs were absolutely despondent. They felt that because of these huge Leave votes in traditional Labour areas, the new Tory prime minister would come in, immediately have a general election and we'd lose fifty seats. Panic set in. They were saying, "We can't go into a general election with Jeremy, we're going to get destroyed." And that was absolute panic, absolute panic.' At the shadow cabinet meeting, a mood of despondency hung around the table and Corbyn himself seemed exhausted. Some shadow cabinet ministers were furious that, hours after the referendum result, Corbyn had publicly called for Article 50 to be triggered, thereby beginning the process of withdrawal from the EU, with a maximum two-year deadline. 'The British people have made their decision,' Corbyn declared. 'We must respect that result and Article 50 has to be invoked now so that we negotiate an exit from the European Union.' In the eyes of many, Corbyn's statement – demanding that Article 50 be invoked before any democratic discussion of what Britain's terms of exit might be – was a gaffe, and revealed his true political colours. Whatever the case, Corbyn's pronouncement on Article 50 was, said Jonathan Ashworth, 'the catalyst for a coup against him'.

For some, this was the opportunity for which they had been waiting and planning. Within forty-eight hours of the referendum result, the coup was under way. It was triggered by the shadow foreign secretary, Hilary Benn, of Syria-bombing fame, who called shadow cabinet ministers one by one, canvassing support for a leadership challenge. When Corbyn was tipped off, he phoned Benn in the early hours of Sunday 26 June. The shadow foreign secretary expressed his lack of confidence in the Labour leader and was duly sacked from the Labour frontbench. This act of political martyrdom was what Benn had likely been seeking. The coming days saw rolling waves of front bench resignations. Astonishingly, in the thirty-six hours after the Benn incident, twenty-three out of thirty-one shadow cabinet ministers tendered their resignations. In part, this was coordinated to maximize the pressure on the leadership, a hard core of anti-Corbynites calculating that their actions would force the hand of others more reluctant to resign. One senior aide, though, dismisses the idea that there was some grand masterplan. 'I think saying the coup was planned gives the Parliamentary Labour Party too much credit, they're fucking idiots, look how incompetent they are,' the aide tells me off the record. 'I heard this from the leader's office all the time, about how the PLP have masterminded this or that – but they're really just not that smart.' Nonetheless, at a time of national crisis, when the focus should have been on the turmoil enveloping a rudderless and divided Conservative government, the opposition had plunged itself into civil war.

Every year, Corbyn's senior adviser Andrew Fisher went on a trip – or 'annual pilgrimage' as he puts it – with a group of friends to the West Sussex Downs. It was there he got the news of Benn's resignation early on Sunday 26 June. That morning, searching for decent mobile reception, he ended up in a car park in the historic market town of Arundel, on a conference call with Corbyn, McDonnell, Seumas Milne, Karie Murphy and political secretary Katy Clark. 'We thought: tough it out, no other thought than that,' Fisher tells me. 'We were pretty resilient, we realized this would be a series of resignations. Once it started happening, we cottoned on quickly to how it would play out'. They agreed to get on the phone to any shadow ministers who might be wavering. Later that day, there were discussions about which MPs could be called upon to replace those resigning from the shadow cabinet to keep it all afloat.

The day after the referendum, two arch-critics of the leadership – Margaret Hodge and Ann Coffey, the Stockport MP who would later defect to the new and short-lived centrist party Change UK – had tabled a vote of no confidence in Corbyn. Four days later, the slew of resignations having happened in the meantime, the rebel MPs won, 172 to 40. While the motion itself had no constitutional weight, the numbers looked damning. In 'normal' circumstances, the position of a 'normal' Labour leader would be completely and utterly unsustainable, and they would have to resign.

But Corbyn was no normal leader. Corbynism rejected the parliamentary focus of traditional Labourism; it existed primarily as an extra-parliamentary movement, one which drew its legitimacy from the mass membership, not from MPs. The net consequence of the no-confidence result was to firm up battle lines between the PLP and the membership. And that was not a battle Labour MPs could win.

The atmosphere in Parliament was darkening. In the previous nine months of Corbyn's leadership, staffers reported reasonably cordial relations with the party's right. They had built some bridges, getting to know anti-Corbyn MPs and their aides and – though they weren't, could never be, close – were on decent enough terms to stop and have friendly chats in the parliamentary corridors and lobbies. (It cut both ways, of course. Mike Hatchett, who joined Corbyn's operation at the outset, recalls shadow ministers' political advisers trying to take him under their wing, 'telling me why Jeremy was shit and we needed a different leader'.) Now, post-no confidence vote, it was back to square one – or, rather, worse. 'It was basically a bullying campaign to get Corbyn to resign without having the guts to have another leadership contest,' Andrew Fisher tells me. 'They weren't confident they could beat him in an election, so their strategy was not to have a proper leadership challenge.'

All of which led Corbyn loyalists to label the rebellion the 'chicken coup', a phrase swiftly popularized by social media. Humour was one thing but, among Corbyn's staff, the doubts – fuelled by Labour shadow ministers marching into the leader's office practically every hour with resignation letters – were real. As McDonnell aide Rory Macqueen put it: 'I think, genuinely, initially we were all wondering whether Corbyn could survive.'

Junior staffers in particular, worrying that the Labour Party would really break apart, came to feel there would be no choice but for Corbyn to stand aside. 'There was this feeling – because I was someone from the Labour left, and genuinely did care about the Labour Party as an institution – of "Oh shit, it's not working under Jeremy" ,' a staff member tells me. 'I started to doubt myself: maybe we should have a soft left candidate now who can unite the whole party?'

In desperation at this apparently unresolvable mess and at the lack of information coming from the circle around Corbyn, he walked into John McDonnell's office, and asked the shadow chancellor: 'What's the plan? What are we doing? It feels like the last days of Rome, we need a plan to get out of this and save the Labour Party.' McDonnell told him there was a plan, but then wouldn't say what it was. The aide recounted this to Andrew Fisher, hoping for more details, but all Fisher would say was: 'Don't worry, we're holding our nerve. And you've got to do it, too.'

What was going through Corbyn's mind? There are conflicting accounts. Some claim he was contemplating resignation. 'There was a point where it really did feel that Jeremy was going to go.' Others insist that he held firm, remembering how he strolled through his office and its visibly nervous staff, and calmly told Seumas Milne: 'They seem very wobbly in there, have they never been in a fight before?' Perhaps, too, his famous zen nature kicked in. Another Labour aide says: 'Jeremy comes across as quite detached from what is going on, whether it's resilience or emotional detachment from everyday life.'

Whatever the case, there is no question that most politicians simply could not have withstood the amount of pressure that Corbyn was now under. It came from every direction, even from the front page of the Labour loyalist Daily Mirror, which on 27 June 2016 splashed Corbyn's face alongside the headline: 'Britain is in crisis and now, more than ever, we need a strong & united Labour Party. So today we send this heartfelt message to Jeremy Corbyn. You are a decent man. But for the sake of your party . . . and for the sake of your country . . . GO NOW.'

With everything seemingly disintegrating, Unite General Secretary Len McCluskey arrived in Parliament to meet with the deputy Labour leader, his former flatmate Tom Watson; John Cryer, chair of the Parliamentary Labour Party; and Chief Whip Rosie Winterton. In order to avoid a leadership challenge, McCluskey proposed a deal. Corbyn should be given a chance and be granted a new probation period of two years, with a committee appointed to examine the electoral evidence, including assessing where the polls were at and how Labour's support was holding up in key constituencies. After that they would revisit whether the leader should stay. McCluskey then put the same offer to Corbyn. Watson suggested another meeting in a couple of days' time in Brighton, near where he would be celebrating his father's birthday. Driving down on that day, McCluskey heard on his car radio a news presenter announcing that Watson, who had evidently changed his mind, had pulled out of the talks. McCluskey turned his car around and headed back. 'He never told me', says McCluskey. 'We have never spoken since that day.'

In the circumstances, Corbyn's office did the only thing it could: turn again to the membership that had voted Corbyn in so spectacularly the previous September and had stayed solidly loyal ever since. In the early hours of 24 June, one Corbyn aide was crawling up a tree at Glastonbury music festival, high on illicit substances, when a friend, after checking the news on their phone, told him that Britain had voted to leave the EU. 'It was one of the only times in my life I nearly had a panic attack,' he told me, 'because I knew exactly what that meant for the next six months, that they'd come for Jeremy, it was all planned.'

Emerging from his narcotic cloud, he left the festival a day early. On the train back to London, he used Facebook and WhatsApp to help organize a 'Keep Corbyn' rally to be held in Trafalgar Square on Monday 27 June, the day before the Labour MPs' confidence vote. On the day of the rally, Corbyn stood at the dispatch box in the House of Commons, spelling out the reality of the situation to gasps and jeers from MPs on all sides: 'Our country is divided and the country will thank neither the benches in front of me, nor those behind, for indulging in internal factional manoeuvring at this time.' Just up the road in Trafalgar Square, a massive crowd of ten thousand gathered. On that heady, sunny evening, they chanted 'Jez We Can', clutching make-do placards, as speakers railed against the coup, standing on the back of a fire engine supplied by the Fire Brigades Union.

There could be no greater contrast with the goings-on in Committee Room 14 a few hours after the Labour leader's appearance at the dispatch box. Corbyn stood at the front of a room rammed with enraged Labour MPs and Labour Lords who took it in turn to flay the Labour leader. 'You are not fit to be prime minister,' declared one. Another spat: 'You are a critical threat to the future of the Labour Party.' The furious statements were thick and fast, punctured only by applause and baying. 'You've got to go!' 'Even now, Jeremy, you and your team have failed to learn the lessons from the catastrophic result.' When another claimed his staff had been subjected to 'intimidation' by supporters of the pro-Corbyn grassroots organization Momentum, some MPs bellowed: 'Scumbags!' When an MP was reprimanded by the PLP chair John Cryer for interrupting the Labour leader, he simply replied: 'I'll keep doing it!' Barry Gardiner, a softly spoken, mild-mannered Labour MP, spoke up to ask colleagues to be quiet and let their leader speak, but a Labour MP yelled at him to 'shut up and sit down'. Some of the MPs who walked out of the committee room were candid about the atmosphere inside as they passed waiting journalists – although whether they were boasting or expressing regret is unclear. 'That was brutal,' said one. 'A bloodbath, the worst I've ever seen,' said another. 'Like being in a pressure cooker' was the conclusion of Aberavon Labour MP Stephen Kinnock.[19] Diane Abbott would write a couple of days later: 'A non-Corbynista MP told me afterwards that he had never seen anything so horrible and he had felt himself reduced to tears. Nobody talked about Jeremy Corbyn's politics. There was only one intention: to break him as a man.'[20]

The two scenes were a metaphor for the Labour civil war: a membership which formed the leadership's praetorian guard ranged against an overwhelmingly hostile parliamentary party. Such a moment lacked any precedent in the history of British democracy. As Corbyn marched out of Parliament with his aides – who knows, the angry denunciations still ringing in his ears – he received an ecstatic response from the waiting crowds. His speech was vintage Corbyn: a rather meandering structure, but passionate, and the crowds lapped it up. 'Stay together, strong and united for the kind of world we want to live' he bellowed.[21] His aides are adamant that this show of strength played a key role in stiffening Corbyn's resolve.

That week proved critical. One afternoon, Tom Watson rang Karie Murphy, formerly his office manager, now working for Corbyn as director of the leader's office and charged with liaising with his deputy's operation. 'I'm phoning you to tell you on a personal level that it's over', Watson told her calmly. 'Your newly appointed shadow cabinet are about to resign. Andy Burnham is bringing a delegation to see Jeremy. I just want you to know.' A meeting with Burnham had indeed been entered in the diary, but had not been signed off by Murphy personally. She promptly cancelled the meeting and told Corbyn's staff that no one was going to enter. She then contacted those expected to be in the delegation individually, persuading them against resigning, promising that things would improve. As she left the office she confronted one member of the delegation: 'You're coming to resign, how fucking dare you!' It should, however, be noted that Burnham did not resign during this time, a period in which the pressure on non-Corbynite members of the frontbench to do so became excruciating. Jonathan Ashworth, meanwhile, was bombarded with furious messages demanding to know why he wasn't resigning. 'In the end,' he says, 'I just put my phone on to flight mode to get people to stop sending me texts and calls and avoided talking to anyone.'

As Corbyn's beleaguered team tried to stem the flow, leading figures rallied to their support. An all-staff meeting was called on the afternoon of Wednesday 29 June. Corbyn, having had a heart-to-heart with John McDonnell, marched in looking visibly upset. 'John had convinced him he wasn't going to quit and to stay,' says one leader's staff member. 'A lot of the staff felt like that; it was all hanging by a thread.' After Corbyn delivered a fairly restrained common-or-garden stump speech – he hated talking about himself, and he suspected some of the assembled staff privately thought he should go – it was the two figures of McDonnell and Karie Murphy who fired everyone up. During this time Murphy was, as Clive Lewis puts it, like a 'sergeant major' – and former soldier Lewis would know one when he saw one. Murphy was, he says, 'a proper character, pretty brutal'. On one occasion, a shadow cabinet minister turned up at the leader's office complaining about his stressed state and poor mental health. Murphy shook him and said something along the lines of: 'Are you a man or a mouse? Go get those Blairites!' 'All right,' mumbled the shadow minister in reply.

Corbyn's big challenge was restocking the frontbench. More than two dozen shadow cabinet members had resigned, along with many junior ministers. Every resignation placed more pressure on those who had decided to stay. 'You could sense the tension of the ever diminishing group of MPs trying to hang on,' recalls Andy McDonald. 'And,' he admits, 'I have to say my resolve was challenged: I was on the absolute brink of saying I can't do this any more, this is too vile, it's going to fall, and I hung on by my fingernails. It was the most difficult time I've ever experienced in politics, perhaps in life. It was dreadful.' Campaigns director Niall Sookoo was taking a respite from the chaos, enjoying the sun near his home in Chiswick, west London, dressed in shorts, T-shirt and flip-flops when Seumas Milne phoned to ask him to collect Corbyn from his Islington home. When Corbyn's aides arrived, it was carnage there: dozens of cameras flashing and throngs of yelling journalists. They negotiated their way through the crowd and drove to Parliament, where Seumas Milne and John McDonnell were waiting. There they tried to construct a frontbench. There were moments of farce. Corbyn allies would yell: 'There's no one on the frontbench, we need to get someone on the frontbench!' But they compared the crisis-stricken operation to a young person's first car, a jalopy, their grandfather's old car: some chewing gum stuck on this or that bit, don't hit a bump or it'll fall apart like the Wacky Races. But somehow, it never did.

The whole thing, indeed, felt knocked up in somebody's shed. Some were doing two jobs at the same time: Emily Thornberry was both shadow foreign secretary and shadow Brexit secretary; Dave Anderson – an MP in northeast England – was shadow Scottish and Northern Ireland secretary; Paul Flynn was both shadow leader of the House of Commons and shadow Welsh secretary. MPs who had been elected only a year earlier – like Clive Lewis and Rebecca Long-Bailey – were now expected to stand at the dispatch box, in front of hundreds of baying Tory MPs, shadowing entire government departments. 'I remember [the political secretary] Katy Clark phoning me,' Lewis recalls. 'I knew what it was about, and to my eternal shame I turned my phone off. I didn't want to go into the shadow cabinet.' In the end, he felt he had little choice but to do so. The real test, though, was yet to come.

Corbyn's opponents had failed in their strategy of driving him off the road, of leaving him with no alternative but to resign. It was now time for Plan B. They had long believed that, if he refused to stand down, they would call a new leadership contest and prevent him from getting on the ballot paper. Under the party's rules, a challenger needed nominations from 20 per cent of Labour MPs or Members of the European Parliament to trigger a contest automatically. The leadership argued that, as the incumbent, Corbyn should automatically appear on the ballot; those ranged against him declared that he must once again seek parliamentary nominations – a process that, now, would make the 2015 nominations process seem like a walk in the park. This was quite unlike a year earlier, when the incumbent leader had resigned and automatically triggered a contest: it was therefore up to the party's ruling body, the National Executive Committee, or NEC, to adjudicate. Because Corbyn could not count on MPs lending him a nomination to widen the political debate this time round, his prospects were doomed unless his place on the ballot was automatically granted – something those opposed to him were determined to block. On Tuesday 12 July, the party's National Executive Committee – composed of representatives of party members, trade unions and other affiliates, councillors and the parliamentary party – met behind closed doors in Southside. When a majority voted that the nominations process would be decided via a secret ballot, it seemed all over for Corbyn: surely this was simply to provide cover for those voting to exclude the leader. The leader's office was wracked with anxiety. Everything looked about to fall apart.

Corbyn's detractors claimed that the meeting took place amid a suffocating atmosphere of intimidation. One NEC member later tearfully told a *Channel 4 News* reporter: 'A prominent journalist was texting members of the NEC, saying they had to vote for Jeremy, a union general secretary was phoning round members of the NEC telling them they had to vote for Jeremy. It is intimidation and he endorsed it.' But all this was simply untrue. And I should know as I'm the journalist she's referring to, while the union general secretary in question, the GMB's Tim Roache, wasn't a Corbyn supporter. The day before the NEC convened, I had politely suggested to them that the party would collapse if Corbyn was excluded from the ballot, and urged Roache to contact NEC members. As for my text messages, they hardly constituted intimidation. I suggested simply and politely that Corbyn's non-inclusion on the ballot paper would trigger a Labour Party civil war, disillusion a young generation and turn the Labour Party into a byword for stitch-ups by and for a political elite, not to mention leaving the next leader (whoever they might be) without authority. 'Whatever the flaws in Jeremy's leadership,' I concluded, he had to be on the ballot.

In no way could this be construed as bullying or intimidation, and indeed one NEC member, Alice Perry, publicly declared she 'really appreciated [my] support – it was in no way threatening!'[22] These were serious accusations that should always be treated seriously and never casually bandied about to advance factional interests, yet they were frequently and cynically used by Corbyn's opponents to feed a narrative of the leadership as a vicious and intolerant cult.

That evening, as deeply anxious staffers crammed into the leader's office in the House of Commons, Karie Murphy received a phone call: the NEC had voted 18–14 to place Corbyn automatically on the ballot paper. There was an explosion of joy, like fans celebrating a goal at a football match. Despite an unsuccessful attempt by the wealthy businessman and Labour donor Michael Foster to reverse the decision – taking his own party to court in the process – Corbyn's place on the ballot paper was assured.

Two candidates put themselves forward, both with supposedly unimpeachable 'soft left' credentials: Angela Eagle, the softly spoken MP for Wallasey, and Owen Smith, a short, Welsh, bespectacled former special adviser. Much of the Blairite right coalesced around Eagle, confirmation of which came when former 'prince of darkness' Peter Mandelson was spotted leaving her office. Originally Smith had told Len McCluskey – the most powerful trade union leader in the history of the Labour Party, and therefore a crucial powerbroker – that he would not run, but in early July he met the general secretary at the union's Holborn headquarters to declare his intention to stand. 'I think you're making a huge mistake, but if I can't persuade you not to run, don't attack Jeremy,' declared McCluskey. Smith responded that his platform would be based on agreeing with Corbyn on policy, but presenting himself as a competent alternative. And with Eagle lagging behind him in nominations, Smith duly became the standard-bearer of the anti-Corbyn resistance.

With a significant number of Corbyn's supporters disillusioned after the Brexit referendum result and the subsequent goings-on, Smith's team were confident. Smith was further boosted by a High Court ruling that 130,000 new members, who had almost certainly overwhelmingly joined the Labour Party to vote for Corbyn, were ineligible to cast any votes unless their membership exceeded six months. Here was a victory for Iain McNicol and his allies at Southside, all of whom regarded Corbyn's leadership as an aberrant nightmare that needed to be terminated as soon as possible. But Smith's campaign crashed. Framing the leadership election as a contest between the membership and the Parliamentary Labour Party, Corbyn's campaign loudly reminded the grassroots of episodes ranging from the Conservatives' Welfare Reform Bill – which slashed in-work benefits for low-paid workers, and on which Smith had abstained – to the Syria vote – in which Smith had voted against bombing, but many of his prominent supporters had not. They were also quick to call members' attention to the fact that Smith had once served as a corporate lobbyist for pharmaceutical company Pfizer, and had advocated against the NHS being able to use cheaper drugs, on the grounds that it reduced economic incentives for research and development.[23]

That alone shot his credibility with almost any Corbyn supporter – but Smith also possessed an unerring ability to shoot himself in the foot. His campaign was marred by gaffe after gaffe. After declaring that he wanted to 'smash' Tory Prime Minister Theresa May 'back on her heels', he was forced to apologize for blatantly sexist language. Other apologies followed: for comments he had made about the Lib Dems' coalition agreement with the Tories ('Surely, the Liberals will file for divorce as soon as the bruises start to show through the make-up?'), and for a tweet in which he had 'joked' about gobstoppers being the perfect present for Scottish National Party Leader Nicola Sturgeon. He bizarrely told a television presenter that he had never needed to use Viagra, one of Pfizer's most famous brands, and joked at a campaign event that he had a 29-inch penis. (Smith's 29-inch penis joke was denied. It was said on his behalf that he was referring to his inside leg measurement.)[24]

Whatever the reason, the size of the crowds at his events was small. Smith had promised to retain Corbyn's policy agenda, and the membership didn't believe him; his supposed advantage, of 'competence', quickly disintegrated. Whatever frustrations members had with Corbyn, they believed his loss would lead to a restoration of the old party order, that the left would be smashed or purged, that support for foreign wars and triangulation on economic policies would return and that the party would still lose. By the end, many of Smith's nominal backers despaired; some couldn't even bring themselves to privately vote for him.

But in fairness to Smith, any prospective candidate would have lost to Corbyn at that point. The contest seemed to resuscitate Corbyn, whose principal skill and passion lay in campaigning. According to

YouGov polling a month before Corbyn's re-election, over three quarters of Labour members thought he was principled, nearly two thirds felt he was honest, and 6 out of 10 believed he 'shares my political outlook'. That didn't mean there were not huge doubts: just 35 per cent associated 'competent' with Corbyn, and only 33 per cent believed he was 'likely to lead Labour to victory at the next general election'. But Smith's ratings were simply dire: members were even less likely to believe he was competent, a derisory 18 per cent believed he was principled and just 17 per cent felt he was honest.[25]

Though his supporters came to see it differently, the coup paradoxically helped Corbyn in a number of ways. Crucially, it galvanized Corbyn's base and fired up his increasingly disillusioned supporters. 'I thought the leadership operation was utterly dysfunctional,' Jon Lansman admits to me, but the Labour right completely messed up their planned coup. 'They fucked it up so much in so many ways: not having a plan, then being ludicrously over the top and alienating all the people who'd voted for Corbyn and become disappointed with him. The coup delivered them back to us. Many felt alienated by the appalling way the coup's instigators behaved.' Another senior aide who worked on Corbyn's second leadership campaign puts it even more brutally. 'Before the coup began,' he says, Corbyn's organization was a mess 'and Jeremy was crumbling under pressure as leader, not stepping up to the mark. Then it turned into the best PR Jeremy could possibly get.'

Liberated from a hostile shadow cabinet, the frontbench crammed with his own loyalists, Corbyn could now push the ambitious radical policies that he had always wanted to champion. At a post-contest meeting on 20 September, the policy pledges of Corbyn's leadership campaign – such as public ownership, a progressive tax system, a National Educational System and rent controls – received unanimous support from the party's executive council. 'The effect of the whole coup and Jeremy's re-election was to strengthen his leadership,' recalls one senior adviser, 'and gave us more authority to make changes.' There was an understanding, too, that this was a second chance, that things at the top really did have to change. The problem was, they didn't.

4
Dysfunction

Amid the euphoria of Corbyn's barely believable victory in Labour's leadership election, a number of his key advisers gathered together to organize a 'war room' to plot a way through what they knew would be an overwhelming first week. Hopelessly unprepared, Corbyn's team was also deeply inexperienced – though they knew enough to realize that, from the outset, they would be under relentless internal and external attack. Having launched the leadership campaign just three months earlier with third place their most optimistic ambition, they had no clear plan, no 'first 100 days' blueprint.

Around the table were Corbyn's new chief of staff, Simon Fletcher; his deputy, Anneliese Midgeley; and Neale Coleman, the new policy chief. Veterans of Ken Livingstone's London mayoralty, they all had at least some management experience. Sensibly, they kept things simple. The upcoming week would be focused on trumpeting rail renationalization, a key Corbyn policy which, polls consistently showed, had overwhelming public support; and developing a media strategy, including penning articles for newspapers in order to try to get some sort of grip on the narrative around the new leadership. Then, the new leader blew a hole in the plan.

From the moment of Corbyn's victory speech on 12 September, surrounded by triumphant supporters at the Queen Elizabeth II Centre applauding his success, it was clear that he had to learn on the job, and learn fast. The speech was his first big opportunity to introduce and define himself to the wider country. But it wasn't very good. There was no structure, no obvious key takeaway message for a puzzled, uncomprehending nation to digest. As he always had done, Corbyn refused to use an autocue, instead relying on scrawled bullet points, and it showed, in a sprawling and digressive address. His speech to the Trades Union Congress three days later – also broadcast to the nation – was even more rambling. After he'd finished, the Unite chief of staff, Andrew Murray, told a Corbyn aide in no uncertain terms that the speech was terrible. 'We need to give the guy a break,' came the response. An understandable reaction, it was also entirely wrong. Corbyn wasn't going to get a break from anybody outside his operation.

The inexperience soon started to show. The evening after his victory, Sky News journalists pursued Corbyn over Westminster Bridge. His shadow cabinet had been announced a few hours previously. As they yelled questions at him about the lack of women in top posts, he ignored them, marching onward in stony and increasingly agonizing silence. It is, still, an excruciating watch, all two minutes and forty-three seconds of it, culminating in the new leader yelling querulously at his youngest son: 'Tommy, there's people bothering me', before jumping into a taxi back to his Islington home.[1] It wasn't a good start with the media, to put it mildly. Irritating and invasive as the media can be, and as blatantly politically motivated as their actions all too often are, such a performance could only leave the average punter with a deeply negative image of the new Labour leader. Obviously, Corbyn should have fallen back on cheerful patter or banter. More to the point, the leader of the Labour Party should not have been casually walking around Westminster, prey to its concentration of political hacks. An experienced team would have arranged for a car to pick him up from New Palace Yard, where politicians are typically whisked discreetly away from Parliament. But the bigger problem was that this wasn't a one-off response. As time went on, Corbyn managed to learn on the job; and some of his media interventions became assured, relaxed even. But his sometimes transparent impatience with the media, combined with a dysfunctional communications operation, ill served this audacious political project.

On Tuesday 15 September, in the first week of his leadership, Corbyn attended his first ceremonial event, a memorial service at St Paul's Cathedral to mark the anniversary of the Battle of Britain. An occasion more suited to allowing him to demonstrate his leaderly gravitas to a massive TV audience could hardly be imagined. He was accompanied by a young Welsh aide, Gavin Sibthorpe, who talked Corbyn through the etiquette, from the appropriate dress code, to how he should walk into the cathedral. It all seemed to be going to plan – until the congregation rose for the national anthem. As all around bellowed out 'God Save the Queen', Corbyn – TV cameras trained on him – kept his mouth firmly shut. A ravenous media looking for excuses to savage a left-wing Labour leader had been tossed ample cuts of red meat. Days of hostile coverage followed, drowning out any potential message from the party. Labour MPs across the party's spectrum report, even to this day, that this one moment cut through on the doorstep in the worst possible way.

The memorial service at St Paul's was a striking example of a left-wing backbencher, long condemned to the fringes, now having to abide by rules and expectations he resented. As it happens, 'God Save the Queen' is a miserable dirge of a national anthem. You don't have to be a republican to find a national song that venerates only the monarch, with nothing to say about the country itself, rather depressing – compared to, say, the 'unofficial' English anthem of 'Jerusalem', in Sir Hubert Parry's rousing musical setting of William Blake's radical poem. Nonetheless, the vast majority of the public would reasonably expect the Leader of the Opposition to sing the national anthem at an event celebrating the Royal Air Force's triumph in what was to be the first stage of a potential Nazi conquest of Britain. Given that Corbyn was being smeared – falsely – by the Conservatives and the media as a Britain-hating extremist, it was a deeply unwise slip on his part. The new Labour leadership had many worthwhile battles to fight, such as pushing a transformative economic agenda, or a new foreign policy based on peace and justice. This was not one of them. From the start, Corbyn's behaviour contrasted markedly with that of John McDonnell, who had red lines that could not be crossed – an economic vision based on public ownership, tax justice and investment – but who would avoid pointless controversies which delivered no political gains and only damaged the project. After the St Paul's fiasco, McDonnell assumed the role of firefighter, touring the studios, claiming Corbyn's silence was down to the new leader being so moved by the service. 'I know it wasn't the worst thing ever to have happened,' says Anneliese Midgeley of Corbyn's *faux pas*, 'but it kind of symbolized something which never went away: like when you start pulling at a thread.'

Corbyn's resentment at having to 'play the game' in his new role was crashingly apparent the following month when, during a state visit to Britain by China's President Xi Jinping, he was invited to a white tie state banquet at Buckingham Palace. His policy chief, Neale Coleman, talked Corbyn through how it would work: here's how it will look; here's how the table is set; there's a bowl on the table – don't put your money and keys in it – and so on. Coleman's first headache was Corbyn's mulish refusal to wear white tie. Desperate, Coleman googled pictures of Martin McGuinness, the iconic Irish Republican leader, in white tie. 'Even Martin McGuinness, enemy of the British state, wore this for the Queen!' he pleaded. Midgeley, the product of a proudly working-class Scouse family, chimed in: 'Jeremy, this is a middle-class affectation. Working-class people aren't going to understand you going to the state banquet and you wearing your cord hat and your Harrington jacket. It's about respect. You wouldn't turn up to a funeral with your jeans on, it's all very hippy-ish.' Finally, Corbyn relented.

Other efforts to impose Corbyn's own style on official etiquette were endearingly reminiscent of the classic 2000s political satire *The Thick of It*. April 2016 saw the Queen's ninetieth birthday, and – much to Corbyn's irritation – his team met to discuss how to mark it. It was impressed upon him how crucial it was not to mess up, given anthem-gate. 'Why not give her jam from your allotment?' piped up one aide. Corbyn's mood changed. 'Great idea!' he responded warmly. 'I'll bring in some apple and blackberry jam.' The next day, he did exactly that, looking pleased as punch when he placed the jam on the table. It had been scooped into an old Kenco jar with a label half peeled off, but a red plastic bow had been wrapped around it, showing at least some effort. 'That's a *Daily Mail* front page right there,' said one press officer.

A bewildered Labour aide was ordered to pick up a few jars, but returned with some actual jam from Sainsbury's, which was no good. Another aide was sent to House of Fraser, and brought back a gingham basket and a nice jar, which was promptly sterilized. But when a Labour aide opened up Corbyn's jam to decant it, he noticed some evident mould covering the top, which he simply scooped away before pouring the rest into the jar. 'What if the Queen dies?' he fretted – and continued to fret as Corbyn's parliamentary assistant Joss MacDonald was dispatched on his bike to deliver the jam by hand to Buckingham Palace. Fortunately, the monarch lived on, writing a letter in her distinctive handwriting thanking the Labour leader for his kind present.

The instinctive reactions of Corbyn and his team to the relentless political and media bombardment they were under were defence and suspicion. This quickly calcified into a *modus operandi*. In response to internal threats, a 'ring of steel' was thrown up around Corbyn; over time, rather than being dismantled as he grew into the job, it tightened. If his enemies were shut out, then so too were important sympathetic voices – including, in time, some of his closest allies. Meanwhile, appointments were often made based on loyalty to the machine, rather than talent. Demoralization, evident from the get-go, permeated Corbyn's operation, and the mental toll on those within it was often severe. And, from the start, his team made many mistakes.

In the first phase of Corbyn's leadership, his old friend and ally John McDonnell loomed large. McDonnell, who had been deputy leader of the Greater London Council and chief executive of the Association of London Authorities, possessed the kind of administrative expertise that was badly needed in Corbyn's team. His appointment as shadow chancellor had faced stiff opposition from trade unions, many of which believed his uncompromising demeanour would be like a red rag to a bull, as far as the Parliamentary Labour Party was concerned. (Shortly before Corbyn's leadership triumph, an official from the powerful Unite union had instead put forward Owen Smith – who would later stand against Corbyn for the Labour leadership – as its choice for shadow chancellor.) But in those early months, McDonnell, effectively Corbyn's second-in-command, provided stability to an otherwise chaotic operation.

Mike Hatchett, who abandoned a well-paid secure post in the civil service to take a job in Corbyn's office, was interviewed by Neale Coleman and John McDonnell. Afterwards, McDonnell pulled

Hatchett, soon to be the leader's office head of economic policy, aside: 'Just so you know, it's really fucking hard working here. We're really under the shit. It's tough. You need to be up for that.' Hatchett respected the honesty of the sales pitch. But nobody had told him quite how shambolic Corbyn's operation was. From the moment he walked through the doors of the leader's office, 'What the fuck have I done?' Hatchett thought to himself. 'I had a perfectly good civil service career up to that point, I'd been a diplomat, a senior policy adviser doing tedious things in the Treasury but doing absolutely fine.' He was notionally put in charge of policy, but nobody in the office seemed to understand what policy was for. 'What is your politics if you don't have policies to back them up?' he wondered.

Rory Macqueen, an economics PhD student and socialist Labour activist, was keen to offer his services to the new leadership. Attending Corbyn's first Labour Party Conference in September 2015, he bumped into John McDonnell in an Indian restaurant with Mark Serwotka, leader of the civil servants' union, and asked: 'Do you need an economist?' McDonnell, who had barely any experts to draw on, leapt at the suggestion. Macqueen duly took three months off his PhD. 'It was absolute carnage,' he recalls. 'We didn't make any announcements, didn't advance left-wing policy in any way because we were literally just trying to be there until tomorrow,' he tells me. It was a daily battle for political survival.

The chaos partly stemmed from a lack of resources. Labour headquarters did not provide enough funds to sustain a team anywhere near as big as that of Corbyn's predecessor, Ed Miliband. But it went further than that. Job titles and roles were unclear. Junior members of staff in particular often had little idea about what they were doing. Although most were new to an operation of this size and scale, it soon became clear that it was not working. Unsuitable hires and the politically inexperienced rubbed shoulders with others who had political worldviews diametrically opposed to those of Corbyn and his project. Destabilizing leaks to the media were a near daily occurrence.

Corbyn himself was no natural manager – something that would have come as no revelation to anybody acquainted with his frenetic parliamentary office as a backbencher. During the leadership campaign, some of those closest to Corbyn begged his senior allies to take control over appointments away from him, warning how several past members of staff had exploited his goodwill.

Indeed, many of Corbyn's key strengths could also prove to be weaknesses. What attracted so many to this strikingly unconventional leader – apart from his politics – was a sense of decency and integrity. The flipside was that Corbyn was strongly averse to conflict – a problem, given that taking difficult and controversial decisions and facing down opposition are fundamental components of leadership. 'His weakness is he's too nice. He's a pacifist in every sense of his life, which is sometimes not a positive,' says Frankie Leach, a young Mancunian who worked as an aide in the events team. 'We had office dramas in which he would never get involved. He didn't want to engage in what were often menial spats. He always wanted to avoid conflict. When a decision needed to be made, he'd make it, but he wanted everyone on side. If there was an argument about policy or a decision, he'd put it off, put it off – he just wouldn't want to choose.' He struggled to chair shadow cabinet meetings, which often lacked structure or focus, and he had the same aversion to taking decisions that might cause disputes. He would turn up late to meetings, then would go off on evasive tangents, avoid saying what he thought, or clam up. Other times, he wouldn't turn up at all, disappearing off the map and switching his phone off so he couldn't be contacted. 'His office was a shambles,' says one shadow cabinet ally. 'And it was a shambles because of his personality: he just doesn't know how to say no.'

Corbyn's stubbornness, too, exasperated his team. His big weakness, says one former press officer, was his consistent refusal to deal with the mainstream media. 'He refused to play the game, refused to do media trainings. He just felt it'd be selling out, that he wanted to be himself.' When he did appear on television's major political programmes, such as BBC's *Andrew Marr Show*, he would time and time again fail to deliver the key news line crafted by his team. 'Jeremy's performances have a very large standard deviation,' says his former spokesperson and head of strategic communications, James Schneider. 'His highs are very high, but his lows can be low. He's not a polished politician, and,' Schneider added understatedly, 'that can give you both things.'

*

One area in which Corbyn's operation was acutely lacking from the start was media experience. There were few socialists embedded in as politically hostile an institution as the British media, and those who were, were reluctant to take a job with the new leadership. Including me. A few weeks before Corbyn assumed the top job, *Guardian* journalist Seumas Milne and I were invited to a meeting at a St Pancras station bar with Simon Fletcher, Anneliese Midgeley and Andrew Murray. Then and there, Fletcher offered us both a job. I immediately rejected it, not least because I was unconvinced that I had the skillset. (Shortly after Corbyn's victory, McDonnell suggested I come in once a week or two as an unofficial adviser, but that struck me as a violation of journalistic ethics.) Milne, though, accepted, taking unpaid leave from the *Guardian* before leaving the newspaper in early 2017.

In October 2015, Milne arrived in his new position of director of strategy and communications. By all accounts, Milne felt a sense of obligation to get involved. He knew the new leadership lacked infrastructure, and was aware of the internal hostility it faced within the Labour Party. He arrived with no pretences about his own suitability for the role – who else was there? – but his genuine political commitment and his inside knowledge of the British media.

There is a striking mismatch between the relentless media portrayal of Milne as a dour, ideologically crazed Stalinist, and the actual reality. Milne follows in a long British tradition of anti-establishment rebels born in the heart of the establishment itself. His father was director-general of the BBC, and Milne was educated at the prestigious public school Winchester College, where he stood as a Maoist candidate in a mock election. He began his journalistic career editing the radical *Straight Left* magazine and, even as British and global politics shifted right, stayed true to his beliefs. A stint as the *Guardian*'s labour correspondent in the 1990s deepened his already strong trade union links, and his appointment as comment editor in 2001 provoked furious consternation among New Labour-aligned columnists. According to iconic Canadian writer Naomi Klein, the paper's comment section under Seumas Milne became a 'truly global debating forum', with even Conservative politician Daniel Hannan lauding him for taking 'full advantage of the *Guardian*'s comment pages' and 'making them the most thought-provoking opinion in

Britain'. For me, as a teenager growing up in a suffocating political environment – the age of 'The End of History' – Milne was, along with other dissenting writers such as Gary Younge and Klein, a political life raft, a rare example of someone who used their media platform to challenge vociferously the prevailing political consensus. When I joined the *Guardian* in 2014, he was an ally and a mentor.

Even after the searing experience of the five-year Corbyn project, Milne's angular cheekbones and elven looks make him appear much younger than a man in his early sixties. Despite an apparently insatiable appetite for pastries, he remains irritatingly lithe. He is also unflinchingly polite, genuinely interested in people, and has a mischievous, witty charm of a very English-public-school kind. When its full beam is trained on you, you feel like the most important person in the room. Milne rubbed plenty of people up the wrong way. Some believed he was, as one shadow cabinet minister put it, 'a bit of an intellectual snob. You have to be able to be intellectually toe to toe with him, to be as sharp as him.' His charm, though, made it difficult to stay angry with him for long. On one occasion, Corbyn's private secretary, Laura Parker, lost her temper with him, declaring, in tears, 'I could punch that posh idiot in the face.' Then he walked into the room and asked, full of warmth, how she was. Instantly she replied, 'Yes, fine, thanks for asking.'

Although Milne anticipated a hostile media, nobody could be prepared for the firestorm which ensued. Newspapers trawled through every aspect of his life, dragging in his family and children. He was regularly abused in the streets, while shopping, while travelling. At one point, the media was camped outside his house for a week; journalists knocked on the doors of all his neighbours, showing them pictures of Milne.

When he took up his post, Milne's reputation among Corbyn's team was very good indeed: he was something of a celebrity in left-wing circles, after all. Very smart, exceptionally well read, he was also an accomplished writer and had a visceral sense of political loyalty. Crucially, Corbyn hugely rated and trusted him.

Corbyn's primary interests lay in international affairs; the same was true for Milne. Their shared political interest springs from what can be called the anti-imperialist tradition. This correctly understands that colonialism was based on the violent subjugation of a lot of the planet by Western nations who accumulated much of their wealth by plundering the resources of their victims – from India, where millions are believed to have died as a result of British imperial policies, to the Belgian Congo, where up to ten million perished. It also rightly understands that the end of formal colonialism did not mean the end of Western domination, and that the foreign policies of the United States, as the global hegemon, and its allies are overwhelmingly driven by economic and strategic self-interest. Often, these policies involve war, support for brutal dictatorships, Western-backed coups and even terror groups. But there is a danger that this way of thinking can also lead to the whitewashing of murderous regimes deemed to have fallen foul of Western interests.

Corbyn displayed huge deference towards Milne. 'This is Seumas Milne, he does our thinking for us,' would be how Corbyn sometimes introduced him, while his communications director grinned self-effacingly. Accordingly, Milne became known as the Labour leader's brain. 'Jeremy trusted him for everything,' says ex-speechwriter Joss MacDonald. 'One of the first questions he'd ask when we'd written a speech was, "Has Seumas seen this? Has he OKed it?" He'd want Seumas's approval for everything he did.' Milne was Corbyn's intellectual lodestone; the leader would refer to him as 'The Great Milne', sometimes abbreviated to TGM. For some, this had everything to do with the Labour leader's own sense of self-doubt. 'What Seumas capitalized on,' as one left-wing former shadow cabinet member puts it, 'is Jeremy's intellectual insecurity, because Jeremy has no university degree.'

Milne had a strict rule he told press officers to abide by: never lie. He worked exceptionally hard – often twelve-hour days – and was notably calm and collected under pressure and at crucial moments. 'It's worth noting that he barely took time off, and worked a full seven-day week,' says his deputy Anjula Singh. 'Whenever he edited something it was inevitably better than its original. Although – given Brexit and the divisions in the Parliamentary Labour Party – he couldn't translate the politics into a deliverable strategy which he was seen to lead, his intellect is undeniable.' He was creative: when media officers were struggling with writing lines, he would intervene in important and morale-boosting ways. To his defenders, Milne was instrumental in keeping the leadership on track with its political agenda. 'Seumas was obviously the messaging guy; he's the guy who always keeps the politics exactly right,' says one senior aide. At key moments, too, he made judgement calls which were controversial but were subsequently vindicated. After the horror of the Manchester bombings in 2017, Milne was among the loudest voices calling for Labour to link the hiked risk of terrorism with British foreign policy, a position which, it turned out, chimed with the British public. And, although he was an avowed left-wing Eurosceptic, Milne's assessment of electoral reality – about the importance of winning round Leave voters concentrated in marginal seats – was sound. On this, asserts Milne's deputy James Schneider, Milne was 'more right than anybody else'. It's an opinion with which Milne himself undoubtedly agrees.

What was more, at the outset at least, there weren't the resources to give Milne a team. Efforts to impose message discipline – for politicians to say the same thing over and over again until it pierces the public consciousness, like the Tories and 'Get Brexit Done' – were complicated by the fact that leading Labour politicians refused to stick to agreed lines, including Corbyn himself.

But in other ways, Milne was sadly lacking. He was used to writing a weekly newspaper column, not to managing the strategy and communications of a political party. 'He was not somebody that understood the 24/7 news cycle,' says one former aide. 'He wrote a column on issues he wanted to talk about rather than issues that were present in the news agenda of the day, what was on people's minds. He doesn't do deadlines, can't think far in advance, isn't very proactive, and doesn't understand protocol and etiquette and how things should run, I guess.' It was an offhandedly damning litany.

One of the recurring complaints from those who worked with Milne was his evasiveness. They found it almost impossible to get him to sign off press releases, speeches or other public interventions. This apparent non-engagement would frequently bring the entire operation to a grinding halt. 'Getting stuff signed off became a joke,' says one former aide. 'We'd have to laugh about it. We didn't know what was going on.' Though Milne insisted everything went through him, which was needlessly inefficient, he often simply wasn't physically present, which led to a perpetual vacuum of leadership. 'I'd describe his management style as "absent father vibe",' says another aide. 'He'd turn up to birthdays late, but he was largely absent for the rest of the year.'

Milne would turn up to strategy meetings late and would waltz in and out, often munching on food, much to other participants' irritation. Top-level senior management team meetings would frequently start hours late as they awaited his arrival (or Corbyn's, whose own tardiness was legendary). 'I'd regard him as very ephemeral; he was engaged in things on the level of ideas rather than the level of practicalities,' says an aide. The planning for Corbyn's first ever speech to the Confederation of British Industry – the bosses' organization – in November 2016 was a case in point. In general, junior members of the team started planning for such occasions a few weeks in advance: organizing Corbyn's arrival, who he'd meet, the format, how the question and answer session would work, achieving consensus to get everyone at the same place. Milne attended none of these meetings. Then, on the morning of the speech – one which would be delivered to an exceptionally sceptical audience and attract huge media attention – he enquired why they had to turn up so early. His alternative suggestion, that they should rock up half an hour before, caused widespread frustration and resentment.

Milne was a poor correspondent, answering WhatsApp messages only infrequently; emails rarely received replies. Moreover, he picked and chose his topics, showing little interest in anything which didn't involve international affairs or Brexit.

'He had a complete disregard for organization, he never turned up on time and often wouldn't turn up at all,' says another former aide. 'He never replied to emails. I think he responded to one email to me in the four years, and that's when I went to his desk and replied to my own email, saying the idea was signed off. It was debilitating for the organization.' Collective deadlines were disregarded. Meetings became a farce, because, after they had finished, Milne could undo decisions by privately whispering in Corbyn's ear. Those pushing to reverse collectively agreed outcomes knew this and would make a beeline for Milne when meetings broke up.

Some suspected Milne withheld signing off decisions until the last-minute for political reasons. 'I'd check my emails so I could see what he'd changed,' recalls Corbyn's senior policy adviser Andrew Fisher, about speeches which had been written, 'but he wouldn't highlight what he'd changed, so I'd have to read through the script, then have a last-minute row – which didn't benefit Jeremy.'

Neither was Milne immune to errors of judgement. In one of the most serious early examples, in the spring of 2016, he agreed to allow Vice Media to film a behind-the-scenes documentary. Now, politics is like making sausages: you don't necessarily want to see the process before you eat the product. In this case, the sausage factory wasn't even given the chance to make itself presentable. One day, Anneliese Midgeley walked into the office to find a camera shoved in her face. When she protested, the crew explained who they were and that Milne had OKed it – but he hadn't consulted the rest of Corbyn's team. Milne then claimed that Corbyn's office would be given editorial sign-off, which proved not in fact to be the case. Simon Fletcher and Milne sharply disagreed about the documentary but the contract had already been signed. Even in a well-functioning operation, this project would have been a serious mistake with nothing to be gained. This was not a well-functioning operation and one under internal and external siege. When senior staff members refused to take part, some junior colleagues tried to busk it. In one notorious moment in the documentary, Corbyn's head of events, Gavin Sibthorpe, told the videographer: 'The best thing to do would be wait and let Jeremy fail on his own. I don't think he will. But fail in his own time, you know.' Sibthorpe's comment – a well-meaning but badly worded observation on the counterproductive tactics of Labour rebels – went viral, and was dubbed by Corbynsceptics the 'Sibthorpe Doctrine'. Sibthorpe kicked himself, but it was hardly his fault. He was a former NHS administration worker finding his feet in an alien environment, with little support or training. Besides, he reasonably pointed out, 'It was always going to be a piss take, because it's Vice.' The only person who seemed not to realize that this would be the case was Milne. The documentary led to widespread ridicule and derision.

Ultimately, what really riled many people about Milne was a lack of professionalism. 'As a manager, and a manager in a role that demands communication, dissemination of information, quick decision-making,' said the same aide – speaking on condition of anonymity – 'I'm afraid he sadly falls woefully short. It really pains me to say that. I would defend Seumas to anybody, particularly fiercely to people who think they know him and think they know what he's about. But it does pain me to say he was not a good manager.'

It wasn't just the managerial skills. The Corbyn project was glaring in its lack of strategy – and given Milne was executive director of communications and strategy, the buck stopped with him. Only it didn't. 'We struggled and battled to get a sense of direction, to get access into what's in Seumas's head,' said the same aide. 'Just the general process: things take so long, things don't happen because they go into a black hole and disappear.'

'Seumas has many strengths, not least his serious politics,' says Joss MacDonald. 'Despite our portrayal as zealous Marxists, he was one of the few people in LOTO [leader of the opposition]'s office that you could actually discuss socialist theory with. His weakness is he's never around. People are always looking for him, but he's an elusive figure. He doesn't do his job. That's a big weakness as executive director of strategy. We were never shown a strategy document. He never showed us a strategy. He never made proactive decisions, he'd agree or disagree with people's decisions. He'd never sit down and talk through what was needed.'

For those charged with implementing a strategy, therefore, there was little to work from or with. 'There wasn't any strategic direction coming from Corbyn's office,' says one of the comms team. 'Seumas never provided us with a strategic direction or a brief to work towards.' He never ran morning press meetings, surely crucial in any organization to plan the day's strategy. 'The idea that the executive director not only wouldn't be chairing meetings, but wouldn't be absolutely driving that meeting is just unfathomable.' Large volumes of polling and focus groups were commissioned, but they weren't turned into plans that could be acted on; work submitted by press officers was seemingly ignored.

Internal communications were poor. Southside media officers would never know why certain decisions were being made but were expected to implement them anyway. Decisions would be made based on snatched conversations in Milne's office during his rare appearances. 'The operation was a lot of people blindly trying to pin things into the wall, or like throwing darts at a board half blindfolded,' says one strategy officer, 'and people without power or people feeling they didn't have the power to do things.' A functioning operation would have set out short-, medium- and long-term strategies, assigned particular work streams to different press and strategy teams, and set out how the leader of the opposition's office could best work with party headquarters to achieve certain objectives with a clear division of labour, but this was desperately missing.

There should, for instance, have been a properly worked out 'Grid' – a day-to-day, week-to-week calendar setting out plans – plotted six months ahead, populated with stories Labour wanted to run. Instead, there was a phone call each morning in which a senior Labour press officer would go through the day's news stories and suggest comments on them. Long-term work was done on an ad hoc basis, often because press officers used their initiative to carve out space on areas of personal interest: for one, it was climate change, for another, international issues. The Grid, such as it was, was a 'mess', says one press officer. 'It was more a random diary of what was happening rather than a strategic grid with an aim or objective.'

The problem was structural. Subordinating strategy to communications was a mistake: strategy should emerge from the party's electoral aims, the key demographics being targeted, the organizing on the ground, the policy positions and indeed from communications. But in this case, strategy was just an extension of comms. As an example, the Grid could have set out in advance a week of talking about bringing back secure, well-paid jobs to northern communities. It would have included a policy announcement which spoke to that objective, a high-profile visit by the leader, and shadow cabinet ministers carrying out similar activities. It would have a strategic aim, with all the events that week designed to lead to a specific outcome. (For instance, those accustomed to working in functional organizations were used to SWOT Analysis: identifying Strengths, Weaknesses, Opportunities and Threats. This was entirely missing in the Corbyn leadership.) Instead, Corbyn would be sent out each week to do an all-member mobilization in a different constituency. Sure, these were often target seats, but having the leader talk to the already converted, rather than the wider community, was not a good use of resources. 'Say you get three hundred people in a room in a marginal seat,' explains one member of the comms team, 'and of those three hundred, if two hundred become campaigners or regularly go out campaigning, it's worth it. But to me it felt like the boss comes into town, does a speech, does selfies, signs stuff for the raffle, leaves.' Rather than planning ahead for, say, a new announcement and agreeing on a constituency to unveil it, the operation would put the cart before the horse. When a visit to a certain town was decided upon, the team was asked to find a hook for media coverage. They were effectively trying to shoehorn a story into visits and then inviting the media, hoping for coverage. Because the communications and strategy operation was so dysfunctional, it was left to the events team to run the Grid; it was more of a diary than a Grid precisely because of the lack of strategy informing it.

Milne's operation would have been even more disastrous without his de facto number two: James Schneider, a former journalist recruited from Momentum in October 2016. Although there was some resentment at the increasingly tight-knit partnership between two public schoolboys – both had attended the elite Winchester College, and were sometimes labelled 'Jeamus' – Schneider was organized, extremely bright and became one of the most competent senior members of Corbyn's staff.

Ultimately, though, Milne was a poor delegator, insisting on accumulating executive power, rather than accepting his limitations and devolving responsibility elsewhere. After the 2017 election, Andrew Murray wrote a strategy paper splitting strategy and communications. One proposal was to bring back Kevin Slocombe, former head of media, but he agreed only if he was made executive director of communications, taking away that portion of Milne's job. But Milne fought back, fearing that it would be seen as a humiliating public demotion. There was another problem, too: after the 2017 election success, the team believed they would be inundated with applications, but that did not happen. Finally, in May 2018, former BBC executive Anjula Singh was hired as communications director. Staff members recall the day she started: she was plonked at a desk, told that someone would set her up with IT, and that was it. When she asked a senior member of staff – who was playing Solitaire – if they wanted to go for a coffee, they gruffly asked 'Why?' With no proper introduction, Singh found herself widely ignored. The set-up was so ramshackle that her responsibilities were never clearly defined, often leaving her in limbo and deprived of the power to manage staff. Exasperated, she tried to resign three times, eventually deciding to stay only out of loyalty to Corbyn.

The same went for other appointments. In a desperate effort to professionalize the team, John McDonnell had brought on board Bob Kerslake, the former head of the civil service. Kerslake told Milne that he needed to hire people to deal with strategy – looking forward, planning ahead, and linking together with the shadow cabinet team – rather than just focusing on day-to-day stuff. Accordingly, Kirsty Major was hired from the *Independent*, Mark Dearn joined from the NGO War on Want and Jack McKenna was headhunted from then backbencher David Lammy's team, where he had gained praise for his work on injustices such as the Grenfell Tower disaster, the deportation of Windrush Britons, educational inequality, immigration and racism. On his first day, he turned up at 9 a.m. at the leader's office. The first to arrive, he found the doors locked and was left waiting outside. When he finally got in, there was no desk or laptop for him. Nothing had been sorted out. McKenna had been told that his new role was vital to the success of the Corbyn project. Unfortunately, no one else had been. No meeting had been called with the political advisers of the frontbench to introduce him, and when he turned up to a shadow cabinet team meeting, no one knew who he was or why he was there. Shadow cabinet ministers with under-resourced operations formed the impression that McKenna was someone who could help write press releases and do media work. But that wasn't what he'd left his old campaigning job to do. It was a waste of talent.

The policy department excepted, new staff had no induction process, found themselves scrabbling about to find out which WhatsApp groups to join, and were given no guidance about how they should allocate their time. One senior aide tells me that the lack of inductions was symptomatic of how overstretched they were. Inductions, though, are time-saving measures. If three hours are spent telling new staff members how things work, they don't have to spend weeks trying to find out for themselves rather than committing to the job at hand. For those privately educated white men, brought up with an ingrained self-assurance, it was perhaps easier to navigate such needless challenges; for others, less so.

Milne's talents and skills are undeniable, and he would have fared well as a trusted political adviser to Corbyn and an eloquent columnist. But as a senior aide puts it, 'Seumas never wrote a coherent strategy in the time he was there, ever.' Another aide compares Milne to the Arsenal football player Mesut Ozil: 'so gifted, a level of intricacy and flair and playmaking ability that's just unparalleled. But he wouldn't do the dirty work. If you have a team with him, you need them to do the stuff that he won't, like tracking back.'

The blame should not all be loaded on Milne. Ultimately, he too arrived with good intentions but without the necessary experience. By virtue of the left's protracted spell in the political wilderness, there wasn't anyone obvious who had both the right politics and the right set of skills. Ultimately, leadership had to come from the leader – and it didn't. 'Jeremy is not the most strategic person, and the issue comes from the top,' says one of the most senior advisers. With no serious forward planning, the team were left taking each day as it came. This was no way to run a political party.

For many of Corbyn's enemies within the Labour Party, it was his foreign policy positions more than his domestic policies which rendered the Labour leader illegitimate. Throughout his political career to date, many of these positions had been vindicated. He had challenged British support for Saddam Hussein's dictatorship when the Iraqi regime was gassing the Kurds; been arrested on an anti-apartheid protest at a time when the Conservative government regarded the African National Congress as terrorists; and had vehemently opposed the 2003 invasion of Iraq. But Milne's and Corbyn's combined political idiosyncrasies regarding international affairs caused the Labour leadership a profound headache.

In early March 2018, the former Russian military official turned double agent Sergei Skripal and his daughter, now living quietly in the cathedral city of Salisbury, were poisoned. Immediately, the finger was pointed at the Russian state, which had form in poisonings on British soil: back in 2006, the former KGB spy Alexander Litvinenko had been fatally poisoned with polonium-210 in a London sushi restaurant.

Milne is not the Putin apologist that neo-Cold Warriors portray him as, and is on the record repeatedly criticizing the Russian leader, including for his 'authoritarian-conservatism'; rather, he believes the Western encirclement of Russia is a threat to world peace, and is sympathetic to the idea that the emergence of stronger powers such as Russia served as an important counterweight to US hegemony.[2]

A hostile media, though, was always going to seize upon not just Corbyn's involvement in anti-war efforts, but zone in too on Milne's perceived baggage to frame their coverage of Labour's response. Back in October 2014, the spin doctor had chaired a discussion with Putin for the annual Valdai club in Russia's Black Sea city of Sochi. The picture of the two shaking hands graced several newspaper pages. But Labour's Milne-crafted response to the Salisbury atrocity inflicted unnecessary damage on Labour. Some hills are worth dying on, this was not one of them. Indeed, privately, aides tell me Milne said: 'There's no way Russia is responsible, it's not in their interests.'

In Parliament, on Wednesday 14 March 2018, Corbyn condemned 'an appalling act of violence', described the use of nerve agents as 'abominable' and 'utterly reckless' in a civilian environment, denounced donations by Russian oligarchs to the Conservative Party, and expressed solidarity with Russia's democratic opposition. When he left open the possibility that the nerve agent could have been used by someone other than the Russian state, suggesting Putin could have 'negligently lost control', he was met with cries of 'Shame' from the Tory benches. However, Theresa May had also floated this possibility two days earlier, though now she condemned 'the culpability of the Russian state'.

But it was a briefing by Milne to journalists that proved deeply damaging. 'There is a history in relation to weapons of mass destruction and intelligence which is problematic, to put it mildly,' he declared, before going on to suggest that the nerve agent could have been produced during the Soviet period, and have since ended up 'in random hands'. All of which exemplified a recurring frustration for many Labour aides that, rather than voice a coordinated line agreed in advance, Milne would brief journalists with his own (and by extension Corbyn's) political views, in the process providing them with ample ammunition to use. As Tory MPs made hay with Milne's comments, the drama was compounded by a question scripted by a policy officer: Corbyn asked the prime minister how she had 'responded to the Russian government's request for a sample of the agent used in the Salisbury attack to run its own tests'.

Given that Labour would inevitably end up accepting that the Russian regime was behind the Skripal poisoning, it was hard to see what was to be gained by voicing such scepticism, particularly since it allowed the leadership to be demonized as Britain-hating extremists, with newspaper headlines such as 'CORBYN, THE KREMLIN STOOGE' and 'PUTIN'S PUPPET'.

Characteristically, too, nobody had briefed Corbyn's wider press team in advance. 'I kicked off over that; I was really angry,' says a Corbyn-supporting Labour press officer. 'It was one of the few times I had a head to head with Seumas. It felt like we were shooting ourselves in the foot. There was no support for that position in the PLP, the shadow cabinet, or staffers in Corbyn's office. It was just Seumas's and Jeremy's personal view being carried out because it's what they believed.'

In the wake of the Skripal case, Corbyn's personal ratings plummeted.[3] The fact that Labour, in response, supported the expulsion of Russian diplomats and proposed significantly tougher measures than the Tories – backing the so-called Magnitsky Act to clamp down on 'dirty' money from Russian oligarchs – was entirely eclipsed by the row.

As well as being a classic example of the kind of needless fights the leadership chose to pick, the Skripal case exposed what was to prove a deepening rift between the political outlook of Corbyn and Milne on the one hand, and, on the other, the influential John McDonnell. Especially through his long-standing involvement with the Stop the

War coalition, which he had chaired until the Labour leadership election of 2015, Corbyn was always far closer to 'tankies' – those aligned with a pro-Soviet perspective – and Trotskyists with absolute anti-imperialist politics than McDonnell. While some traditional Corbyn allies feared that drawing attention to human rights violations committed by repressive regimes hostile to Western interests played into the hands of warmongers, McDonnell was rather more flexible – for instance, in becoming the parliamentary voice of a group he formed to support democratic movements against the authoritarian regime in Iran.

Privately, McDonnell was severely frustrated by the leadership's response to the Skripal case. Publicly, while characteristically loyal, he intervened to shift Corbyn's stance, arguing that the leader's position had been 'misread', and announcing that Labour agreed 'Russia's to blame'[4] and called for Labour MPs not to appear on Russia Today, Russia's state-run international news channel.[5] This was a clear example of how McDonnell's tactical approach – defending the red lines that mattered, not needlessly picking damaging fights which did not – could, if properly harnessed, have saved the Corbyn project much unnecessary hurt. Unfortunately, it wasn't. In time, the rift between shadow chancellor and leader's office would only deepen.

The Corbyn leadership's relationships with the Parliamentary Labour Party and its bureaucracy were bad from the get-go, and a significant chunk of it was irreconcilable to Corbyn from the start, no matter what he did. But here, again, Corbyn and those around him didn't help themselves; in fact, they made a bad situation worse.

While there were Labour MPs who were bitterly ideologically opposed to Corbyn and would never engage with the leadership in good faith, others lacked strongly entrenched politics: what they worked for, above all else, is a Labour government. This group was open to being nurtured, and indeed, in the early days, efforts were made. One aide spent the first fortnight having coffee, drinks and dinner with practically every Labour MP. An 'open day' policy was instituted every Wednesday afternoon after PMQs, in which MPs could come and visit the leader; and each Wednesday evening, there were parties with different groups of MPs, for example the new intake, and then by region. Some Corbyn allies were assigned MPs to speak to. This strategy was to the irritation of much of the so-called 'core group' of Labour MPs, that is, the marginalized Corbynite faction within the PLP who felt taken for granted. 'We didn't concentrate on them because they're in the bag; we need to build alliances,' suggests Anneliese Midgeley, then deputy chief of staff. But this approach was abandoned before it was clear whether or not it would work. Two months into Corbyn's leadership, Katy Clark, the former left-wing Labour MP for North Ayrshire and Arran, who was defeated in the SNP landslide of May 2015, was appointed political secretary. Placing a former Labour MP there was an error. Parliamentarians are factional beasts, and don't necessarily feel like being bossed around by someone who was once one of them. In any case, Clark abandoned the parties and open-door Wednesdays in favour of focusing on the core group, and then building outwards. Of course, with some MPs, trying to construct bridges was a waste of time. But surely it would have proven possible to build relationships with a wider group of MPs without diluting politics? Combined with a more competent organization, 'good faith' critics could at least be separated from those driven by bad faith and nothing more.

It wasn't just Corbyn's internal enemies, though. Months into his leadership, disillusionment had also spread to those who had championed him. Jon Lansman had worked on Tony Benn's deputy leadership bid back in 1981. He went on to play a pivotal role in Corbyn's 2015 campaign and founded the grassroots Corbyn-supporting movement Momentum. By spring 2016, Lansman was disillusioned with the leadership. 'It was clearly dysfunctional,' he tells me. He even approached McDonnell to suggest he take over, much to the shadow chancellor's chagrin.

Lansman wasn't the only one. That summer I feared for the whole project. It would collapse, I felt, opening the way for Corbyn's vengeful opponents to crush the left. I found myself privately speculating, with other sympathetic members of the Labour leadership and left-wing commentators, that Corbyn could act as a transitional figure, before passing the baton to a younger politician upholding the same vision to fight the next general election, then scheduled for 2020. The most plausible candidate seemed to be Clive Lewis, newly elected MP for Norwich South and one of Corbyn's most vocal supporters, and someone I'd campaigned for long before the 2015 election. He had an attractive back story. He was a mixed-race working-class guy from a Northampton council estate, whose service in the army seemed to make him better placed to resist media smears about left-wing politicians hating Britain or posing a threat to national security. Even though he was inexperienced, his former job as a BBC journalist made him a better media performer than some seasoned politicians, and he was photogenic, handsome even, someone you could imagine playing a prime minister in a fictional political drama. Lewis was far from ready, but then a general election was not expected for some time to come. There was another potential advantage: a new left-wing leader might learn from the experiences of Corbyn's then-unprepared team and make a positive impression on the electorate from the outset.

The attempted internal coup against Corbyn, following the June 2016 Brexit referendum, destroyed that fantasy timetable. So, too, did the rumours that the Tories planned to call a snap general election. That July, they had their own leadership contest in the wake of David Cameron's departure, electing the former home secretary, Theresa May, who played to the media presentation of her as the new Margaret Thatcher[6] by doing an impression of the Iron Lady in her first appearance in Parliament. The similarities would end there. But at that point the Conservatives, confident in their new prime minister, slavered at the prospect of bringing about Labour's electoral annihilation.

That summer, the whole deck of cards was thrown in the air. Even some of those closest to Corbyn didn't see how he could go on with some 90 per cent of the parliamentary party ranged against him. One of them was Cat Smith, who had been Corbyn's parliamentary researcher before becoming MP for Lancaster and Fleetwood in 2015. In the midst of the slew of shadow cabinet resignations that triggered the coup, she tried to arrange a one-on-one meeting with Corbyn, but his team were extremely suspicious, demanding to know what she wanted to discuss. Finally, she persuaded them. Late that June, she sat with him alone in his parliamentary office and talked it through, suggesting he could resign, having created a new climate for the discussion of left-wing ideas – an achievement in itself. Corbyn sat quietly, saying nothing, withdrawn.

Meanwhile, chatter continued to circulate around Clive Lewis. About this time, he received a phone call from Seumas Milne, who quietly asked the Norwich MP how he was. 'So, so. What's happening with you?' replied a jittery Lewis. 'You know, it's like, not great,' came the voice on the end of the line. 'I'm hearing you're being suggested as a leader.' Anxiety hit Lewis, who feared he was being set up, or accused of stabbing Corbyn in the back. 'Yes, it's been said – but it's not me saying it, it's not what I want.' Then, to his astonishment, Milne ventured: 'Do you want to do it?' Lewis paused, nervous, then replied: 'If I had to, and there was no other alternative, then of course I would.' 'OK, that's good to know,' Milne told him. 'Stay by your phone, things are moving fast.' Milne cannot recall any such phone call and denies he would float such a suggestion. He is emphatic that he never even considered Corbyn's departure.

Whatever the case, nothing happened. The party's NEC ruled that Corbyn's name would appear on the ballot paper in the forthcoming leadership election and, with Corbyn again supported overwhelmingly by the party's grassroots, his victory was assured. Like Lewis, I voted for Corbyn for a second time. In the election's aftermath, the sense of trauma that had permeated the leadership dissipated, and was quickly replaced by triumphalism. The atmosphere had swung from one extreme to the other. In Corbyn's office, it appeared, there was no treating those twin impostors, triumph and disaster, with a healthy scepticism. I feared that no lessons would be learned from the events of the last months, and that this dysfunctional operation would continue until it was, eventually, swept away in a general election and the left driven permanently into political exile.

Pondering how best to use my position as a critical but increasingly disillusioned friend of the leadership, at the end of July I wrote a blog entitled 'Questions all Jeremy Corbyn supporters need to answer'. In it, I expressed my fear about 'the left failing, and even disappearing forever', adding that while 'the last few months have been a story of relentless Establishment hostility towards Corbyn's leadership', there had been 'an utterly ineffective strategy to deal with it and cut through with a popular message'. I then set out some broad questions: 'How can the disastrous polling be turned around?', 'Where is the clear vision?', 'How are the policies significantly different from the last general election?', 'What's the media strategy?' and 'What's the strategy to win over the over 44s?', the demographic most hostile to the Corbyn project.[7] The blog caused fury among Corbyn's most ardent supporters, and I was hauled into the office of one of the most prominent leaders of the labour movement, who demanded, bluntly: 'What the fuck do you think you're doing? You've practically resigned from the left and need to find a way back.'

I didn't agree with that, of course. My actions could be construed as naïve – and they were – but they were carried out in good faith. Through late 2016 and early 2017, left-wing commentators and junior members of Corbyn's team would come round to my flat, and we'd argue over how the Corbyn project could be salvaged. But the triumphalism in the leader's office proved short-lived. Theresa May's assurances that she wasn't about to call an early general election seemed increasingly unbelievable with the Tories' poll lead soaring, and Corbyn's personal ratings continuing to plummet. As the operation grew ever more demoralized there was a growing exodus, including Corbyn's highly competent press spokesperson, Matt Zarb-Cousin; his former chief of staff, Simon Fletcher; his trade union liaison officer, Nancy Platts; the head of events, Gavin Sibthorpe; Mike Hatchett, the head of economic policy; Jayne Fisher, his stakeholder manager; and his head of media, Kevin Slocombe. Even some who continued to back the Corbyn project in public were privately giving up. It all seemed to be falling apart. The leadership election was an opportunity for a reboot which had not been taken.

But the rumours continued. So, too, did my doubts over Corbyn, which only increased when, at the end of February 2017, Labour was routed in a by-election and nearly defeated in another. I wasn't sure about much by this point, but what did seem clear to me, as I wrote in a *Guardian* piece at the time, was that Labour under Corbyn would lose the next election, whenever it came, and the Labour Party would hurtle off to the right. If Corbyn couldn't sort out the mess the party was in, I concluded, he had to stand down in favour of a younger MP who would be committed to the policies that had inspired Corbyn's supporters in the first place.[8]

In March 2017, speculation over a successor to Corbyn continued to swirl. Starting to lose patience, Unite's leadership had begun to favour Emily Thornberry as a successor to Corbyn should things not improve in six to twelve months. This was an attractive proposition for some on Labour's right, who believed that the non-Corbynite Thornberry could eventually lead the party back to the centre ground. Believing that the Corbyn project was on the verge of collapse, I had a conversation with a couple of Labour MPs in which Clive Lewis's name came up. It was swiftly leaked to the *Telegraph* newspaper.[9] Corbyn's key allies were privately incandescent at what they saw as my manoeuvring. Meanwhile, Corbyn's new chief of staff pulled Clive Lewis aside. 'Word of advice,' she told the MP shortly in her Glaswegian tones. 'Wind Owen's neck in, wind his fucking neck in, because if he doesn't stop going on about it, I'm going to have to start believing you're sanctioning it, OK?' Lewis's protests of loyalty to Corbyn were brushed aside. 'Listen big guy,' she countered. 'You will be leader one day and I will run that campaign for you, but that isn't now.'

This was a new tone from the leader's office: direct, decisive, with undertones of menace. In an attempt to bring order to the chaos of Corbyn's operation, the leadership had appointed one of the most extraordinary characters of this time, someone who would become one of the most powerful figures in the history of the Labour Party: Karie Murphy.

'She's a force of nature.' Wherever you stand on Karie Murphy, it's impossible to argue with this character assessment by one of her closest allies. 'A thunderbolt,' a senior aide concurs. Murphy was born to an Irish Catholic family in Glasgow's East End. The Irish Troubles blazing on her television screen when she was a teenager had a profound impact on her political upbringing. She trained as a nurse and health visitor, then worked in nursing for nearly a quarter-century in the city's poorer East End, where she encountered extreme levels of deprivation which further made her question the profoundly unequal and unjust society in which she lived. Involvement in the trade union movement eventually led her from Scotland's biggest city to national Labour politics. In the 2000s, with the party still in power, she worked with two MPs. Through the second, David Anderson, a former miner representing the Northeast constituency of Blaydon, she came into contact with another Labour MP, Tom Watson.

Now politics, by and large, is not – or shouldn't be – seen as a soap opera; it's about competing social forces and conflicts between groupings in society with fundamentally different interests. But the role of individuals can be consequential, too. There is no doubt that it's impossible to comprehend fully the evolution of Labour's civil war during these years without understanding the growing psychodrama involving Karie Murphy, Tom Watson and Len McCluskey.

Let's start with Watson. He came from what you might call the 'Old Right' of the Labour Party, a faction which, predating Tony Blair's New Labour, was more well disposed towards social democratic policies and the trade union movement, but which nonetheless had a burning animosity to the left. Before entering Parliament as an MP, Watson was the political officer of the Amalgamated Engineering and Electrical Union. Its leader, Sir Ken Jackson, openly called for a strike-free Britain and for the Trade Union Congress to scrap its annual conference in favour of a joint event with the Confederation of British Industry, the bosses' organization. Unsurprisingly, he was described as Blair's favourite trade union leader. Watson, though, led an attempted coup against Tony Blair in favour of Gordon Brown in 2006, which became known as the 'curry house conspiracy', the plot having been concocted over a biryani in Wolverhampton. The then Labour prime minister branded Watson as 'disloyal, discourteous and wrong'. It was the start of what would become a pattern of plotting against Labour leaders on Watson's part. Yet, some years later, under the leadership of Ed Miliband, Watson seemed to have embarked on a political journey, departing from his moorings on the party's right in favour of anti-establishment politics.

Around this time, in the early 2010s, Watson launched a campaign on the fraught issue of phone hacking by newspaper outlets owned by the Murdoch empire, and asked Karie Murphy: 'How about working with me?' Murphy, whose politics remained well left of Watson's, was at first reluctant. But she liked Watson: 'His intellect allows him to be charming, it's quite an attraction.' So, too, was Watson's aversion to Blair: 'He told me New Labour was dead and buried.' The two developed a close relationship, and Murphy became Watson's office manager. Like him, she had campaigns she was passionate about – such as Justice for Colombia, justice for the Hillsborough families, and justice for the miners assaulted by police at the notorious 1984 'Battle of Orgreave' – and encouraged Watson to support them.

Meanwhile, Watson, who had recently split up with his wife, rented a flat on the Old Kent Road from Jim Mowatt, a boisterous Scottish Unite official and close ally of Len McCluskey. For a time, Watson and McCluskey were flatmates; the pair and Murphy were 'thick as thieves', says Jonathan Ashworth. 'It was a good laugh,' recalls GMB political officer Lisa Johnson. 'They were always quite fun to be around. They have a way that group, you want to be part of the gang.' Intense political discussion would be punctuated by drunken karaoke nights out in Soho. Meanwhile, Murphy later offered Amy Jackson, a Unite official, a job in Watson's office, and an alliance was forged between the women which endures to this day.

There was, though, something impulsive about Watson. He could treat someone like his best friend, then quickly transfer his attentions to another. The same went for his causes. He would always have an obsession, whether it'd be the phone hacking campaign, or cycling, or later – with dramatic effect – dieting. Close to Ed Miliband, he was appointed chair of the Labour Party, but became increasingly frustrated with Miliband's leadership, and particularly with those around him. When Karie Murphy stood to be Labour's parliamentary candidate in the Scottish seat of Falkirk and was embroiled in a firestorm over alleged – and disproven – vote rigging, Watson backed her against Miliband's leadership, and was genuinely disgusted by the treatment of his office manager, who he felt had been hung out to dry. He had been told that senior Labour figures had been ordered to find a reason to stop the selection and to brief against her to the media.

On a hot day in July 2013, at the Glastonbury music festival, I sat on a stage with Watson at 'Left Field', a series of talks and performances organized by iconic musician Billy Bragg, debating the future of the party. 'Almost to a man, woman and child the people wanted me to give them the route map back to supporting and believing in

Labour,' Watson later wrote about the event for Vice News, describing people's yearning for the party to offer a more radical alternative to Tory austerity. 'Yet I couldn't traverse the chasmic gap between the words coming out of my mouth and the voices in my head. The audience cheered my nemesis, the left-wing polemicist Mr Owen Jones. They were polite to me, at least, but markedly unenthusiastic about what I had to say.'[10] His long-standing disillusionment coming to the boil, a week later he resigned. 'You've become a working-class hero,' McCluskey told him. 'But if you ever betray the left, they'll never forgive you.'

But Watson and Murphy's relationship started to become strained. Murphy didn't believe Watson shared her socialist convictions. Indeed, she didn't believe he had any overarching vision of how society should work, instead simply fixating on whichever cause had attracted his attention at any given moment – a more dangerous Mr Toad, you might say. Approached in 2012 by a man called Carl Beech, who claimed to have uncovered a Westminster paedophile ring, Watson fell for the story, which became his grand new cause. Accordingly, his office became a hotline for survivors of child abuse to phone, or for people to ring from prisons asking for help. 'We were not equipped in any way to deal with it,' says a former Watson aide. 'You're asking me to speak to people who are victims of child abuse. I've got no training for this. I thought it was really mental.' Carl Beech, it would transpire, was a fraudster, a liar, and indeed a paedophile himself. He had made the whole story up, and was later jailed for eighteen years.

In October 2014, Murphy declared she was going to donate a kidney – something she had long planned to do – which would mean time off work. To her astonishment, Watson declared that didn't suit him, because he intended to do a tour around the country, paving the way for a deputy leadership bid after Ed Miliband's anticipated routing at the forthcoming general election. (Watson, a pre-diabetic whose weight peaked at 22 stone, did not want to stand for leader, he declared, because 'I'm fat and fat people don't win elections, people will recognize that.') Murphy duly donated her kidney on 10 December 2014 and returned to work her notice period, and then the pair parted ways. Murphy then went to work in the office of left-wing backbencher Grahame Morris. But McCluskey and Watson remained tight, and in 2015, Unite bankrolled Watson's deputy leadership campaign, which he duly won, becoming – in theory – Corbyn's right-hand man. Less than a year later, though, by the time of the attempted 2016 coup – during which, it was said, Watson hoped the leadership might come his way – he was drifting apart from Corbyn's operation, despite still being in office. 'I've got to be honest, having started off as someone who got on with him, I can't stand him,' says one former ally of Watson and a shadow cabinet minister. It was perhaps Watson's record of undermining successive Labour leaders that helped this former ally arrive at the conclusion that 'he's selfish, self-indulgent, all about himself.' As McCluskey saw it, Watson had, unforgivably, betrayed the left during the coup, and the once-tight trio split: Murphy and McCluskey on one side, Watson on the other. And when, in early 2017, Watson backed Gerard Coyne, a challenger to McCluskey's tenure as general secretary of Unite, the relationship turned toxic.

Meanwhile, a genuinely formidable power alliance was forged between McCluskey and Murphy in the first year of Corbyn's leadership. Like most others, McCluskey was increasingly frustrated with Corbyn's shambolic operation. Senior Labour figures, exasperated at a shadow cabinet full of Corbyn's political opponents and hostility from the whips' office, decided that Corbyn badly needed a change, not least because his then chief of staff, Simon Fletcher, was an exceptionally good analyst, but was as conflict-averse as the leader himself. That change came in the shape of Murphy, who was definitely not averse to conflict; on the contrary, she relished it. In February 2016, with the support of Unite and the approval of John McDonnell, she became executive director of the leader's office. That summer, the office announced a new 'flat structure', in which Fletcher was incorporated into a leadership team also including Murphy, Milne and political secretary Katy Clark. But, according to social media manager Jack Bond, the reshuffle meant one thing. 'That was the Karie take over,' Bond says. 'That was just a way for Karie to have a power grab.' From that point on, indeed, she gradually accumulated power and control.

Murphy is keenly aware of her reputation. 'I came in [to Corbyn's office] and designed a full staffing structure with clear roles and responsibilities for all. I then enforced that. Some people recented that discipline. Is that aggressive? I resent the term. I'm Scottish. Unless you're working against our socialist project for the right wing of the Labour Party, you have nothing to fear from me. But if I'm going to war, I'm going to fight to win. I'm like John McDonnell: I'm headstrong and determined.' When she became chief of staff, Corbyn told her he wanted three things delivered: a social movement, a more democratic party, and a left-wing party in terms of policies and the politics of it. And, Murphy says, she gave Corbyn all three.

Everyone agrees that Murphy is the person who made things happen and got things done. She arrived as office manager, appointed herself chief of staff, and began systematically removing anyone she believed was in the way – like the Agatha Christie novel *And Then There Were None*, as one aide describes it to me, where guests were murdered one by one. 'She was always able to get a decision out of people,' says Frankie Leach, who worked on the events team. 'If I needed a sign-off and I couldn't rely on Seumas to make a decision, I'd go to Karie and she'd get it out of him. She was very able to cut through the bullshit.' Here there is consensus: if she's on your side, you have no better ally – she has your back. 'She saw herself as maternal, caring, a warm but fiery and feisty Glaswegian figure,' explains Laura Murray, Corbyn's former stakeholder manager. 'And she can be that, she can be really warm and caring. When she's on your side, she's a really good person to have there. She's good at conflict. *Very* good at conflict. She's good at bollocking MPs, she's good at schmoozing with the right people.' Murphy was particularly keen on nurturing young talent – and especially younger women. But as one former press aide puts it to me: 'If you fuck her over, you are done.'

When Murphy assumed control, the leader's office was poorly respected by headquarters, understaffed and besieged. She turned that around, and staff saw her as a champion. 'She's an extremely effective organizer,' Andrew Fisher tells me. And extremely effective is what Corbyn desperately needed. Before Murphy turned up, staffers recall, the front office was often empty; people would wander in and out, and there was little sense of anyone visibly in charge.

Under Murphy's guidance the operation became more

professionalized and disciplined; jobs were defined. With Corbyn frequently unable to take decisions, Murphy filled the vacuum. 'She was great at top–down stuff,' says one former Corbyn ally in the shadow cabinet, 'she actually delivered decisions. But she wouldn't *win* arguments, she'd just drive things through.'

Even some of her ardent opponents could not help but admire her. Tom Baldwin, Milne's predecessor under Ed Miliband, was now communications director for the People's Vote campaign, whose objective Murphy passionately resisted. When the pair met in the leader's office in December 2018, with the Christmas tree baubles shimmering in the background, Murphy laid into him: witty, sarcastic, cheeky, she demanded that he explain precisely how a new referendum would offer a pathway for Labour to win an election. 'I gave him everything so he'd know he'd been in the ring with me,' she tells me. For his part, Baldwin was dazzled by Murphy – and it wasn't just the Christmas cheer. 'I thought she was magnificent in a way,' he ruefully concedes. 'Wrong, but magnificent. If she was on my side, I'd love her.'

Murphy's proudest achievements were facing down Corbyn's internal opponents, which she did with relish. One such was Rosie Winterton, who Corbyn had kept on as chief whip – even during the 2016 coup – despite her clear lack of support for the leadership. In early October that year, Murphy wrote out a script for Corbyn to read. He rang Winterton, removing her from her post and offering another position as Shadow Leader of the House of Commons. Protesting that this was a *de facto* sacking, Winterton insisted on meeting Corbyn in person. He couldn't find it in himself to refuse – even with Murphy mouthing 'no, no!' alongside him. Winterton duly marched into the boardroom of the leader's office with an aide, who was asked to leave.

Murphy sat next to Corbyn as Winterton made a vigorous defence of her job, to which the Labour leader responded with a muttered, 'I know, I understand, thank you.' With Corbyn unable to deliver the *coup de grâce*, Murphy said, simply, 'Sorry, Rosie, it's over.' The fallen Chief Whip was stunned and – as Corbyn stuttered that they could discuss other posts, such as the Council of Europe or the House of Lords – she started to cry. The meeting over, Corbyn couldn't leave the room fast enough. As a distressed Winterton was escorted to Milne's office to agree on the wording of the announcement, Murphy duly marched into John McDonnell's office where Andrew Fisher, Jon Trickett and Diane Abbott were gathered, and relayed Corbyn's stammering recalcitrance. They all cracked up at this classic example of the Labour leader's dithering. Murphy picked up a marker pen and drew a snake on McDonnell's flipchart. Then she drew a line across to cut off its head.

Murphy would later play a key role in facing down the hostile party machinery. In January 2018 Corbyn's supporters won a majority on the party's National Executive Committee, and now had the power to replace the general secretary, Iain McNicol, with one of their own. The following month, Corbyn met McNicol in his office. But although Murphy had once more written out a script for the leader, and although he was flanked by both Murphy and McDonnell, he was again unable to deliver the final blow, instead spending over ten minutes engaged in pleasantries. Much to their chagrin, they were both forced to intervene to tell McNicol it was all over. A slew of McNicol's allies promptly resigned, leaving Murphy nervous about the loss of institutional knowledge from the party – but that was a risk she had been prepared to take. In the aftermath, one resigning staffer declared at an open-invite leaving drinks: 'We've cleared out the Trots before and we'll do it again.' Despite Murphy's triumph, they were biding their time.

In the months to come, Murphy would accumulate astonishing power in the leader's office. For many, her reign had a dark side. 'What I saw happen to her over the years made me think: this is how dictatorships happen,' says one former aide. 'I'd never seen that happen before to anyone. I thought: this is how it happens, how Stalin happens. You start off with a decent vision and then it all ends up about your power. It blew my mind, the whole thing.' Many are adamant that Murphy was only ever kind and supportive to them. For James Schneider, she was 'the only person who took an interest or was understanding'. But a common complaint – including among sympathizers – is that she would make appointments on the basis of personal loyalty to her, rather than based on talent or ability; for some appointments, there were no interviews and barely a selection process at all. Some who crossed her found themselves sidelined. 'Loyalty to her was more important than any other aspect of somebody's professional input,' says a former staffer.

Some of those who came into conflict with Murphy were young, idealistic staffers whose political awakening had taken place in leaderless movements, and who struggled with the rigid, top–down discipline Murphy imposed. On one occasion, late in the evening at the 2018 Christmas party, Murphy accused a shadow cabinet member's researcher of bringing Lib Dem members along. The researcher strenuously denies having done so, but rather than take time to investigate, Murphy subjected her to a prolonged public tirade, reducing her to tears. It is an incident Murphy regrets. Another aide who fell out with her says he was accused of alcoholism (something Murphy denies) and told to see a doctor. In the end he did; not to register as an alcoholic, but to be signed off sick. 'I went to the GP and told him I worked for Jeremy Corbyn,' he recalls. 'The doctor said: "How long do you need?"'

Some of those outside the senior management team felt infantilized, robbed of any kind of agency or power. 'A complacency played itself out,' says Jennifer Larbie, Corbyn's former head of international and equalities policy, 'and a concentration of power and control among the senior management team. There was a failure to delegate, and it almost became an impenetrable force. It's important they worked closely together and shared the same vision, but over time it sometimes felt separate from Jeremy and separate from the rest of the staff team.' When staff grievances came to the boil, Murphy would call team meetings and tell them how lucky they were to work there. Some allege that she would encourage people to submit complaints against those who crossed her (Murphy is emphatic this did not happen). There was a 'general atmosphere of fear', says one aide. 'People would regularly talk about the fact that they would tense up when she walked in the room and breathe a sigh of relief on Fridays, when she was usually in Glasgow. There was a widespread fear right across the office and it demoralized and demotivated a lot of people in the operation.' As dissatisfaction with the operation as a whole mounted, twenty-four members of the leader's office signed a letter protesting about 'bullying and intimidation'. Murphy, though, is insistent that any such allegations are entirely false, that she was a strong-willed manager who had to impose discipline on a frenetic situation and make difficult decisions in a highly charged atmosphere while under almost constant political siege. In that, she definitely had a point. If the likes of Milne weren't up for doing the 'dirty work', as one aide put it, this was Murphy's stock in trade. And it was about to get dirtier.

5
How to Run a Campaign

It was nine o'clock on 18 April 2017, a bright, mild morning, and I was anxiously watching TV. A podium was being hastily assembled outside 10 Downing Street. Britain's Conservative Prime Minister Theresa May was about to make an impromptu address to the nation. Like everybody else, I was wondering what she was going to say.

It was spring in Britain, but for Jeremy Corbyn's Labour Party, riven by a devastatingly public civil war, a bleak political winter beckoned. That April, polling placed Labour twenty-four points behind the ruling Conservatives,[1] while Corbyn's own personal ratings were catastrophic.[2] The party had just lost a by-election in Copeland, a northern constituency held by Labour since the 1930s, to the Conservatives. Voters who had voted for the hard-right populist UKIP in the general election two years earlier had switched to the Tories. It was the first time a governing party had won a by-election since 1981. James Schneider, Corbyn's youthful director of strategic communications, had sat in the office overnight, waiting for the result. He recalled former Labour Prime Minister Harold Wilson's words: 'The Labour Party is like a stage-coach. If you rattle along at great speed everybody is too seasick to cause any trouble. But if you stop everybody gets out and argues about where to go next.' And in the previous months, the Corbyn project had lurched to a juddering halt.

Then came Theresa May's announcement. It was indeed to call a general election, to be held in six weeks' time on 8 June. Having categorically ruled it out, May and her advisers had suddenly decided an election was necessary, to provide the Conservative government, so May said, with a greater public mandate to negotiate Britain's departure from the European Union after the referendum of the previous year had left the country sharply divided over whether to go or stay; to provide, as she put it, 'certainty, stability and strong leadership'. Nobody really believed that – either in the Labour Party, or the country as a whole. Her plan was to eliminate her opposition, or, as the Tory-supporting *Daily Mail* screeched the next day, 'CRUSH THE SABOTEURS'; to slap down the 'remoaners' of all parties looking to remain in the EU; and to wipe out Corbyn's Labour Party once and for all. In the Labour leader's office, Corbyn's combative chief of staff, Karie Murphy, stared at the TV, mouthing 'Oh fuck.' In nearby Labour HQ, there was uproar. 'It was like a scene out of Dad's Army,' remembered Andrew Gwynne, a shadow cabinet minister and Labour's campaigns and election chair. 'Don't panic! Don't panic!' May had presented the upcoming election as a second referendum on Brexit, an issue that had split the Labour Party. It was, as Labour press officer Joe Ryle recalled, 'the worst nightmare for us'.

That afternoon, College Green, the stretch of manicured lawn opposite the Houses of Parliament, was a tangled mess of TV cameras, stressed producers, ashen-faced Labour MPs and Tory MPs grinning like Cheshire cats. A tag team of two right-wing pundits and a *Sky News* presenter barracked me, demanding to know why Jeremy Corbyn was a suitable prime minister. 'I think he'll lie awake at night, worrying about the failure to build housing for people to live in, about the lack of secure, well-paid jobs, about the fact that in this country the rich aren't paying their taxes,' I said in the sort of defiant tone you can only conjure up when feeling utterly cornered and out of options. One of the pundits, from the ardently pro-Tory *Sun* newspaper, cut in: 'But does that make him a prime minister?' I shot back: 'Yes, I think it does. If the definition of prime minister is someone who passionately cares about the needs of the majority of people in this country.' In his eighteen months or so as leader, Corbyn had rarely been seen as prime ministerial material – if, that was, you defined 'prime ministerial' in the conventional, stuffed-shirt, shiny-suited, PR-friendly sense. It was already clear that if he was going to stand any chance in the upcoming campaign, that definition had to change.

Not that some on Corbyn's own team gave him much chance at all.

In the already demoralized Labour leadership operation – in the weeks before May's announcement, there had been an exodus of staff – the immediate reaction among many was that Labour would be wiped out, and that blame for electoral defeat would be laid firmly on the left-wing policies championed by Corbyn, Corbyn himself would have to go, and the left would be back in the political wilderness.

Statisticians at Labour HQ crunched the numbers, projecting election results according to the current polling, in which Labour was some twenty-four points behind. The outcomes looked terrible for Labour. Andrew Gwynne, who had just been out on College Green defending Labour's prospects and had been openly laughed at, searched for his own seat, Denton and Reddish, which he had won with a healthy 10,511 majority less than two years earlier and which had been a Labour seat in all its previous guises since 1945. Now, it was projected to fall to the Tories. The blood drained from his face.

The day after May's announcement, a shell-shocked Parliamentary Labour Party packed out Committee Room 14 of the House of Commons, a room that for months had been the scene of angry clashes between hostile MPs and the Labour leadership. Even some of those who'd campaigned for Corbyn doubted his effectiveness as a prime ministerial candidate. Michael Walker, who had previously been involved with Spain's radical Podemos party before joining the left-wing media organization Novara Media, contrasted Corbyn's leadership with left-wing movements abroad. Podemos leader Pablo Iglesias was 'one of the best orators you've seen, had an excellent answer to every question, constantly strategizing, never slipped up, surrounded by a clique who had driven a political project for a decade, done PhDs in political communication, had built a machine. And you'd look at Bernie Sanders in the United States and see this amazing orator.' Then there was Corbyn, who 'came here by accident, surrounded by a fairly motley crew'. In short, Walker concluded, 'I wasn't sure he was up to this.'

In British politics, holding a general election was no longer – as it used to be – in the gift of the prime minister. A piece of legislation called the Fixed Term Parliament Act, passed by David Cameron's coalition government in 2011, stipulated that two-thirds of MPs had to approve the calling of an election outside a new five-year fixed term – or a majority of MPs had to vote no-confidence in the government of the day. In practice, however, Labour had no choice but to endorse May's election announcement; refusal to do so would look like it was running scared. May had already claimed – wrongly – that Labour was attempting to subvert the will of the people over Britain's efforts to leave the European Union, so anything that looked like trying to block an election would be political suicide. Corbyn promptly went in front of the TV cameras to pronounce Labour's support for the election – mixed with some bravado about the party's chances. It was easy to mock. The media duly mocked.

In Labour HQ, meanwhile, the general gloom soon dissipated. With staffers whipped into line by the sergeant-majorly figure of Karie Murphy – 'It's a six-day week, ten hours a day,' she told them – there was a sense, as press officer Joe Ryle recalls, that 'this was it. We've got to throw everything at it, we have six weeks, this project will live or die, nothing else matters.' The sense of adversity brought people closer. 'There was a unity of purpose. If this is going to be our last hurrah, let's go out with a bang.' Corbyn, meanwhile, seemed galvanized. He gave his team a pep talk. 'We're in the fight of our lives,' he told them.

Much of this fight involved the effective communication to the wider public of what Corbyn's Labour Party actually stood for, which in the two years since Corbyn had become leader had been hampered by the party's own internal chaos and division and the related barrage of hostile media attention on the issue of Corbyn and his leadership. The party, somehow, had to shake off its defensiveness and get on the front foot.

Shifting the political narrative was critical. May wanted the election to be defined by Brexit, and Labour was particularly vulnerable to divisions over the EU referendum. Its supporters included Remainers despondent at the referendum result, especially younger voters in major cities such as London and Manchester, and those rejoicing over the narrow mandate for Leave, epitomized by older working-class voters in Labour seats, particularly in the ex-industrial North and Midlands. There was a real risk that Labour's already diminished voting base could disintegrate further, with anti-Brexit Liberal Democrats scooping up Labour Remainers and Labour Leave voters drifting to May's Tories and the right-wing populist party UKIP. If the campaign had been all about 'who is better at steering us through Brexit', says Andrew Fisher, 'she'd have won her landslide. We had to close down Brexit as an issue. Moving the debate on to different, domestic terrain was our only hope.'

Here, though, lay opportunity. Although for decades people had been widely resigned to the ideals of market fundamentalism, these ideals – even in the heady days of Tony Blair – had never really enjoyed enthusiastic support. The problem for the proponents of 'There Is No Alternative' was that, well, people thought there was.

In polling, for instance, Britons often plumped in a healthy majority for the renationalization of major utilities: water, gas, electricity and railways. A majority backed hiking taxes to fund the NHS, increasing regulation, capping the salaries of business chief executives, introducing worker representation at senior executive and board level, abolishing zero-hour contracts. Britons also believed capitalism was 'greedy' and 'corrupt', and had a more favourable view of socialism than capitalism,[3] while nearly half believed socialist ideals 'were of great value for societal progress'.[4] What these statistics revealed was that Margaret Thatcher had been wrong. 'Economics are the method,' she had once said, 'the object is to change the heart and soul.'[5] But while most had come to accept it as an unavoidable fact of life, they did not like the social order she had built. If people could be genuinely convinced that there was an alternative, everything could change.

On 20 April, Corbyn made his first major election speech at Church House in Westminster. Whatever pressure he was feeling, he came out swinging. Studiously avoiding Brexit, he launched an unashamedly populist assault on elites. He pledged not to play by the rules of the establishment and – naming a notorious rail franchise and two notorious business tycoons – declared that, 'If I were Southern Rail or Philip Green, I'd be worried about a Labour government. If I were Mark Ashley or the CEO of a tax-avoiding multinational corporation, I'd want to see a Tory victory. Labour is the party that will put the interests of the majority first.'[6]

After eighteen months of internal civil war, and the lack of a coherent alternative being presented by Labour, suddenly Corbynism had found its purpose, as an insurgent, take-on-the-elite populism: the people vs the establishment. Here, on the stump, Corbyn was in his element, and this speech, putting across a focused message, was just what his team had desperately needed. 'It was a self-confident, clear, comprehensive expression of our politics,' says James Schneider. There was a sense that maybe – just maybe – the Tories would not get to fight the election on the turf they wanted. 'The Tories underestimated us, they didn't see us coming out of the blocks there,' says Joe Ryle. 'The journalists got our message and took it. Within twenty-four hours, we redefined the election.'

Nonetheless, with polling suggesting a Conservative majority of 180 and Labour reduced to under 200 seats – a gap that hadn't been seen since 1935 – Labour had a daunting amount of ground to make up. When the polling was leaked to me, I set up an online crowdfunder, 'Stop The Tory Landslide', to pour money into vulnerable seats: £30,000 was raised in days, underlining how desperate many feared the situation to be. Meanwhile, believing that, in the aftermath of Labour's anticipated electoral slaughter, there would be another coup attempt against Corbyn by those on the right of the party, members of the leader's office and the Corbynite movement Momentum began discreet preparations for a third leadership contest that, it was felt, would follow the inevitable general election defeat to come. There was the odd optimist. James Meadway, an economics adviser to John McDonnell, was particularly bullish about Labour's prospects, provoking consternation and ridicule among some of his colleagues. Meadway believed that in its membership Labour had a trump card. Corbyn's leadership had swelled the party's ranks and, with half a million members, it was one of the biggest parties in the Western world; the Tory membership, on the other hand, had shrivelled to perhaps a fifth of that number. Meadway had read and inwardly digested *Ground Wars*, a book by the Danish academic Ramus Kleis Nielsen, who argued that activists talking face-to-face with potential voters played a critical role in swinging competitive elections. The proof could be seen in recent US presidential elections: Barack Obama had been able to mobilize such a resource; Hillary

Clinton hadn't. 'You need people on the ground talking to people,' Meadway says. 'They don't trust the media or politicians. If you talk to people directly, they'll listen and trust you.'

Then there was what Meadway calls 'objective circumstances'. Since the financial crash, living standards for Britain's workers had been squeezed for the longest period since perhaps the 1750s.[7] In the same timeframe, only Greece had endured such a dramatic fall in wages. Furthermore, he continued, there was 'real anger' over austerity, particularly among those relatively younger Britons who had been hit hardest by it. 'If you walked around Britain before the election, after the last seven years of Tory government, would you have found a happy settled society full of people who wanted it to carry on as it was? No way!' Meadway declaimed.

Labour needed a pithy slogan, a theme that provided a coherent, overarching narrative. Many ideas were discussed; nothing felt quite right. At one meeting, Seumas Milne had a lightbulb moment. He recalled the Labour Party's current constitution. In 1995, in his repudiation of socialism, Tony Blair had abandoned the iconic Clause IV, the statement of the party's aims which enshrined a commitment to public ownership. But there was a phrase in the new Clause IV that struck Milne, about building a society 'in which power, wealth and opportunity are in the hands of the many, not the few'. Besides, it also echoed a line from Percy Bysshe Shelley's great radical poem 'The Mask of Anarchy', written in the aftermath of the 1819 Peterloo Massacre, which Corbyn became fond of quoting: 'Shake your chains to earth like dew, which in sleep had fallen on you: ye are many – they are few.' Milne barged into a room in the Labour leader's office and asked everyone there: 'For the many, not the few' – what did they think?

For Corbyn's Labour, the slogan underscored the party's ambition to make a direct assault on vested interests at the top of Britain's establishment. Whatever the Conservatives' apparent strengths, there were areas in which, as Andrew Fisher put it, 'we knew they had weaknesses. On public services, on pay, on redistributive taxation, the economy and on public ownership, they were out of sync with public opinion.' Three months before the election was called, the leader's office had been exploring a new mantra: that Britain had a 'rigged' society, rigged in favour of arrogant, greedy elites who needed to be confronted and challenged. This narrative was now at the core of Labour's election message. Nothing short of a dramatic redistribution of wealth and power would suffice. In the following weeks, this 'For the many, not the few' slogan would become the prism through which all of Labour's policies would be seen and understood.

For all these positive steps, Labour's fears of electoral disaster remained – and, on 4 May, were reinforced by results in local elections across the country. These were terrible for Labour, losing seven councils and haemorrhaging 382 councillors. Labour won a projected 27 per cent of the vote in the local elections, compared to 38 per cent for the Tories – for whom it was the best local election outcome in ten years. If history was any guide, the party was on course to do even more poorly in the general election in five weeks' time. Curiously, however, some in the leadership team saw hope in the results. 'I wasn't happy about losing councillors,' says James Schneider. 'But I was very happy that we were closing the gap on the Tories. The local election results put us eleven points behind the Tories, rather than the twenty-four points in the opening polls. So we had caught up a lot over the course of three weeks.' The country's leading pollster, Professor John Curtice, seemed to share Schneider's view. The results, he opined, were 'perhaps not quite as good' as the Tories would have liked.[8]

Both the Tories and the Lib Dems – batting their eyelashes at Labour Leave and Labour Remain voters respectively – desperately hoped that Brexit would define the election. But this was before the Brexit polarization had really set in, and there were already signs on the ground that that might not happen: Brexit rarely came up on the doorstep in London, and even less frequently outside the capital. Moreover, the centrist Lib Dems were proving useless. Not only had they characteristically misunderstood the mood of the country by pledging a second referendum on Brexit, but within days of the election, their leader Tim Farron was dropping clangers left, right and centre. After initially refusing to state whether or not he thought gay sex was a sin – a non-admission that would dog him throughout the campaign until he clarified that he didn't – he confessed that as a schoolboy he had had a poster of Margaret Thatcher over his bed.[9] Then, in apparent discord with his party's resolutely Remain campaign, he claimed to be 'a bit of a eurosceptic'[10] but thought Britain was better off in the EU. All this before an interview from 2007 surfaced, in which Farron had expressed anti-abortion views – a sharp contrast with his 2017 declaration that he was 'pro-choice'.[11] All of which confirmed what most thought: that the Lib Dems were hardly an appealing home for disillusioned urban liberal voters and therefore were hardly likely to attract Labour Remainers.

One of the most important strategies for any political movement radically challenging the status quo is to expand the electorate, to mobilize the previously disengaged to vote. One of the promises of Corbyn's initial campaign for the Labour leadership was that, of all the candidates, he would best appeal to both young voters and non-voters, and with only 44 per cent of 18- to 24-year-olds voting in 2015, there was a big overlap between these two demographics.[12] As soon as the 2017 general election was called, the Labour leadership earmarked hundreds of thousands of pounds for voter registration initiatives, which paid immediate dividends: in the five weeks after May's announcement, nearly 3 million Britons signed up to vote, of whom just over a million were twenty-four or younger.[13] The higher the voter registration numbers, the worse it was for the Tories. What's more, they knew it.

In the run-up to the 2015 general election, the Conservative–Lib Dem government had introduced a new form of voter registration which meant fewer younger and private tenant voters (least likely to support Conservatives) on the voting rolls. They were also toying with introducing voter ID, which Republicans had promoted in the US knowing that Democrat-leaning poorer and minority voters were least likely to own ID. 'I don't think the Tories put a single penny into registration,' says Andrew Murray. 'They're like the US Republicans: minimize the electorate, suppress turnout, *de facto* limit voting to the older and richer.' By contrast, as part of its strategy to expand the electorate, the Labour leadership operation set up a series of outreach and engagement programmes, focused on women, black and minority communities, different religious communities, LGBTQ people, the young in general and students in particular – to name a few.

Meanwhile, the challenges to Labour's campaign arrived thick and fast. Some, predictably enough, came from the direction of Labour

HQ itself as the resentful parliamentary party and Labour Party bureaucracy united in their shared nostalgia for the New Labour project and their concomitant hatred of Corbyn and everything he stood for.

Now, in a general election campaign, you might have expected Labour's staff – whatever their views on the leadership – to put their heart and soul into maximizing their party's success at the ballot box. You'd be wrong. Many in anti-Corbyn circles craved electoral disaster, and seemed to consciously undermine the party's efforts.

As they looked forward to exacting revenge on the Corbyn project in a post-election leadership contest, dark talk of retribution was common. 'Death by fire is too kind for LOTO,' declared one official three weeks into the election campaign. 'Thornberry is awful,' messaged another. 'She should pay in the reckoning.' When a YouGov poll suggested that Labour's support was surging in late May, one official wailed: 'I actually felt quite sick when I saw that YouGov poll last night.' Others tried to reassure their colleague: 'With a bit of luck this speech will show a clear polling decline and we shall be able to point out how disgusting they truly are . . . I personally think we are going to do very badly indeed, and I think it will shock a lot of them how badly we do, including JC. So everyone has to be ready when he is in shock. It has to be clean and brutal . . . These crazy people who now make up our membership never want us to win in any case. They are Communists and Green supporters.' Polls which showed bad results for Labour were celebrated. For example, two such surveys, conducted by polling companies TNS and ORB, were greeted with 'Always loved TNS' and 'Good old ORB'. Another poll on election eve which suggested a twelve-point Tory lead was met with 'Boom.' When they discussed Labour's final mass election rally in Islington, one staffer urged: 'Truncheons out lads, let's knock out some Trots', another responding with: 'Water cannons, please.'

Despite Karie Murphy's appeal to staff to work 'ten hours a day, six days a week' during the campaign, staff at Southside reportedly did the bare minimum of what was expected. Contrary to the Labour leadership's vision of an insurgent campaign, Southside officials wanted to run the most defensive campaign possible, prioritizing safe Labour seats over winnable marginals – and, as they were in charge of the party's expenditure, they controlled the campaign's purse strings. A secret project – named Ergon House, the London Labour headquarters where it was supposed to be enacted – was discussed by Labour HQ staffers to ensure campaign resources were diverted to favoured MPs on the right of the party, while one staffer reportedly ordered his colleagues not to allow Ben Soffa, the left-wing head of digital organizing, to see how digital campaign funds were being managed. When senior figures from the Labour leader's office called for the party to target non-voters, Labour HQ figures had a familiar glib retort: 'The problem with non-voters is they don't vote.'

Jon Lansman, Momentum founder and a veteran of grassroots political campaigning, saw an irony here. 'We'd been told for decades that we didn't want to win, that we were just purists,' he says. 'Actually they just defended safe seats. *We* wanted to win and *we* fought for supposedly safe Tory seats – because if we were going to win, we needed to do just that.'

In all this, the Corbyn camp looked for inspiration to Bernie Sanders's insurgent left-wing candidacy for the US Democratic presidential nomination, and how mass rallies had spurred on his campaign, creating a buzz beyond existing core supporters, and impacting both social media and mainstream media coverage. 'Obviously having indoor events became impossible very quickly, there weren't enough big spaces in Britain,' says one aide who accompanied Corbyn across the country throughout the campaign. 'We wanted big rallies in parks, town centres, wherever.'

According to the aide, however, Labour Party officials were markedly unambitious, 'just were not having it, they didn't want it. They booked tiny rooms, and said that's what the regional parties wanted.' Labour HQ would even fail to tell local groups about Corbyn events. 'All of these things sound mundane in the bigger picture. But when party regions were running defensive campaigns, when a huge membership was willing to do anything but weren't given direction – not even *told* their own party leader was coming – I mean, it was a constant bunfight, we were totally undermined.'

Karie Murphy was typically blunt about the situation. The Corbyn leadership, she said, had spent two years fighting Labour HQ 'and we knew they wouldn't disappear – quite the reverse. They wanted us to be beat. We knew they were gearing up to get rid of us – we had to keep tabs on everything they were doing. It was exhausting and challenging with one barrier after another. Labour HQ under McNicol spent every day frustrating progress. We knew they'd disproportionately fund their friends and our enemies, and areas we wouldn't necessarily need additional funding to go to. Using community organizing, we needed to engage communities: there was no place we wouldn't go.'

Throwing caution to the winds, Corbyn's campaign was indeed incredibly ambitious. Shadow Cabinet Minister Jon Trickett had drawn up a strategy paper before the election setting out how Labour could aim for 40 per cent of the vote – or the same level as Tony Blair achieved in his landslide win in 2001. Above all else, Trickett emphasized, Labour's vision should not be transactional – simply handing out electoral goodies – but be transformative in its aim to fundamentally build a new society. He proposed that the party target key groups of voters – the young, BAME people, working-class communities and the North. 'We had the strategy,' recalls Murphy, 'the idea is you don't go to young mums and say, "here's an extra tenner a month", or make it all about basic transactions. Instead, we'll provide, say, a bus service. The whole transformative strategy was Trickett's, [using] Corbyn's vision and politics . . . Seumas worked with him, we all contributed, and Andrew had to come up with the policies.' In other words, here was the leadership working as a solidly united team with a common agreed vision: Milne refining the messages, Murphy making sure things happened and fighting internal opponents of their strategy, Fisher devising the manifesto. For once, the leader's office was a well-oiled machine – and it quickly clicked into gear.

Critical to Corbyn's, and Labour's, chances were the broadcasting neutrality rules, which kick in during the period of an election campaign. Corbyn had what one aide described as 'unprecedented recognition at this stage of the electoral cycle': 94 per cent recognition with the public. His approval ratings, the aide added, 'are minus forty'.

Since becoming leader, Corbyn had been defined by an overwhelmingly negative press. The only opportunities he had to put his side of things were brief, occasional, heavily edited snippets on television, often involving questions about his leadership. No opportunity at all, in other words. On the other hand, Corbyn hadn't been around for that long. So yes, the public had a broadly bad perception of the leader, but the negativity around him hadn't yet put down roots; it was, in the parlance, 'soft'. An election campaign meant that Corbyn would be on television constantly, for long slots of time, unfiltered, able to present his case clearly and lay out the positive reasons to vote for Labour. 'Most people just don't take that much notice in politics outside of election periods,' says Matt Zarb-Cousin, Corbyn's former spokesperson, in his softly spoken Essex twang. 'They were ambivalent about Corbyn, they'd seen a few stories about him, thought he was a bit of a joke. But when it comes to an election, you think of positive reasons to vote for someone, rather than negative reasons not to like them.'

And, as the campaign went on, so it proved. Corbyn had an affable, zen-like demeanour on television. Viewers could swiftly see the contrast between his media image – dangerous terrorist-loving extremist – and a reality which seemed poles apart. In one media outing in front of a studio audience, veteran interviewer Jeremy Paxman tried to coax out of Corbyn his supposedly dangerous radicalism, at one point asking why abolishing the monarchy wasn't in the manifesto, given Corbyn's republican views. 'Look, there's nothing in there, as we're not going to do it,' Corbyn replied, unfazed, to audience laughter and whoops.

What was more, Corbyn was a different sort of politician from those the public were used to. Usually, prospective prime ministers appeared desperate to stay on message, to stick to pre-prepared lines created by PR firms, spinners and focus groups, and shrivelled the further they got from Westminster. Corbyn loved campaigning: public walkabouts, meeting voters, mass rallies. He spoke with genuine conviction, a true believer in his own policies and ideas. And a previously sceptical public, seeing him for the first time as himself, increasingly trusted him as someone who said what he meant and meant what he said. That enthusiasm proved contagious.

Theresa May's campaign had the diametrically opposite effect. 'Before the campaign began, you could see why people had a good impression of May,' says Harry Richie, at the time Momentum's social media officer. 'She seemed like a normal politician getting on with the job, competent – because everyone says she is.' So confident were the Tories of Theresa May's popularity that her name was painted in huge letters on campaign literature, posters and buses, eclipsing the party's name in size. The election was all about Theresa. The problem was that the more people saw of her, the less they liked what they saw. May's public appearances consisted of contrived, heavily controlled meetings with small, selected gatherings of Tory activists, often in workplaces where the real employees had already been sent home, while questions were vetted beforehand.

It had to be said that Labour's decision to have Corbyn speak to crowds of thousands in town squares was not without risk; a security nightmare, it was also a potential PR disaster waiting to happen. But it was worth it to expose the glaring contrast: Corbyn addressing mass rallies, talking to voters, hugging supporters, offering an unvarnished vision of hope; May cocooned in staged rallies of diehard supporters, sticking to a stale and uninspiring script. There were certainly obstacles to Corbyn's strategy of relentless campaigning across the country, some Labour MPs, for example, tried to block him from coming to their constituencies. One offered a surreal litany of excuses, claiming that a visit from the leader would mean them losing their seat, going bankrupt, and causing their father to die from grief.

Nor did it help the Conservatives that their campaign was run by Lynton Crosby, a right-wing Australian political strategist with a notorious line in campaigning techniques and – rather belying his ruthless reputation – a patchy history when it came to election campaign successes. Crosby suggested the Tories should stick to a slogan and hammer it to death. The slogan dreamed up for May was 'strong and stable', a phrase she dropped clunkily into sentences, inviting inevitable mockery. Her failure to answer questions, and her robotic responses and demeanour led the *Guardian*'s John Crace to dub her 'the Maybot' – a soubriquet which stuck. 'She had the warmth of an ice cube, and not much more personality,' was how one senior aide put it. At one point, when asked by a TV reporter what the naughtiest thing she'd ever done as a child was, she clutched desperately for an answer, responding that it was 'running through fields of wheat'. She deployed increasingly lame excuses for refusing to debate with Jeremy Corbyn, an encounter she seemed to fear. All of which turned her into a laughing stock.

The leaders' conflicting personalities, though, were only part of the battle. The gamechanger in the campaign could only be the policies Labour proposed to the nation. Andrew Fisher, the man tasked with bringing Labour's election manifesto together, had about three weeks to come up with a prospectus that would decide Labour, and the left's, survival. No pressure then. The meticulous Fisher, though, had spent the preceding months building up an impressive library of detailed policy documents. The shadow Treasury team, meanwhile, had been costing specific ideas. If corporation tax was restored to its 2011 levels, what would it raise? How much revenue could be amassed by a clampdown on tax havens? Needing somewhere quiet to concentrate, Fisher was often holed up in his Croydon home. Sometimes, he would take half days in Southside, then get the train back to south London and work through the night.

With the Corbyn project's emphasis on grassroots political participation, the membership were asked which issues and policies they thought were most important. There were tens of thousands of responses and, despite the multiplicity of voices, they mapped closely onto the policies Fisher was drawing up: vindication, seemingly, of the ambitious policies the leadership was determined to champion.

Back in 2015, Corbyn had won a decisive mandate from Labour's membership because of two commitments above all else: to end austerity and to tackle Britain's grotesque levels of inequality. Both would form the core of an ambitious, radical manifesto, one that, attempting to defy the usual narrative that the left made expensive commitments that could not be afforded, was properly and fully costed. Here, Shadow Chancellor John McDonnell was acutely aware of the potential traps that awaited Labour. He believed that one of the main reasons Labour lost the 1992 general election – which it had been widely expected to win – was the Tory onslaught focusing on the threat of 'Labour's Tax Bombshell'. In the 2015 election, the Tories had committed not to hike income tax, National Insurance or VAT – while simultaneously highlighting Labour's supposed fiscal imprudence. This time round, the Conservatives were so confident that they didn't repeat these pledges. And McDonnell stole their thunder, with a commitment that, under Labour, 95 per cent of Britons would not pay any more income tax. 'It neutered the Tories,' says James Meadway, then one of McDonnell's aides. 'We closed down tax as an issue for Labour, which is normally a bugbear for the party.' The philosophy was 'spending for the many, taxes for the few'.

Labour's tax plans showed how politically savvy the united leadership had become. Given that the average British worker was still poorer than they were before the 2008 crash, a commitment to raise taxes across the board to fund public services was seen as politically fatal. Accordingly, McDonnell decided to lower the top rate of tax – then 45 per cent – from a threshold of £150,000 to £80,000, while a new 50 per cent tax band for those earning more than £123,000 would be introduced. Why £80,000? The party's polling showed that most people thought earning £60,000, even £50,000, qualified you as rich (median household disposable income in Britain being just £27,200).[14] But there was another question: what did people think they would be earning in five years' time? 'They might think £60,000, and they'd probably be wrong, but they'd still see it as plausible,' explains James Meadway. 'So if you, say, hit them at £60,000, they might think, "that's me in 5 years"! Nobody thinks they're going to hit £80,000, though.' And £80,000 or more also happened to be the income of the top 5 per cent of earners – a nice clean number. There was another factor, too. If wages were going up, Labour could make the case that, as everyone was better off, taxes could go up to support the NHS. But after the longest squeeze in wages for generations, this was deemed an impossible sell.

The manifesto would prove to be the most radical programme put to the British people by Labour since 1983, when the party had been pummelled by Thatcher's landslide victory: investment paid for by hiked taxes on the rich, the abolition of student tuition fees, a statutory living wage, public ownership of utilities. The 1983 election defeat had been a millstone around the neck of the left ever since, and a salutary lesson, so right-wing naysayers had it, of what happened when Labour got too radical. The Corbyn leadership was determined to disprove it. Although the manifesto was quickly put together, process was nonetheless rigidly observed: policies were talked through with shadow cabinet ministers and their teams; trade union leaders were allowed to scrutinize a draft in a designated reading room (but not take it away). This process of internal consultation, carried out before the manifesto was approved by the Labour leadership, was supposed to be watertight. It wasn't.

I remember the moment well. I was live on *Sky News*, on the evening of 11 May, and the presenter turned to me and told me that the manifesto had been leaked – something unprecedented in British electoral history. The first to hear of it was Corbyn's Head of Strategic Communications James Schneider, who got a call from Jack Blanchard, then a *Mirror* journalist. 'Hi, mate, I've got the whole manifesto!' came the crowing voice in triumph down the phone. Next to ring was the *Telegraph*'s Kate McCann. It was clear the whole media had their hands on it.

Outwardly, speaking to journalists, party representatives were calm; deep down they were anything but. 'It was absolute shock and horror,' says Schneider. Andrew Fisher, the manifesto's author, was devastated. 'He looked grey,' says one aide. There was much flapping around as the comms team prepared lines.

Where the leak had come from was unclear, though there was a prevailing assumption that it was from within the anti-Corbyn brigade in Labour HQ. But there was nothing opaque about the response of the right-wing media, which went into predictable overdrive. The manifesto would 'take Britain back to the 1970s' screeched the *Telegraph*; for the *Mail*, it was a 'socialist manifesto that is red in tooth and claw and dripping with class envy'. Some anti-Corbyn Labour MPs and candidates were happy to go on the record with their views: one described the manifesto as 'childish', another as 'a ten-year-old's letter to Santa Claus'.[15]

A few hours after the leak, around 2 a.m., a bleary Schneider phoned campaign chair Andrew Gwynne. Shadow Justice Secretary Richard Burgon, scheduled to appear on ITV's *Good Morning Britain* to discuss justice policy, was unreachable – presumably blissfully asleep and unaware of the building shitstorm that was about to be unleashed in the morning media. Burgon was stood down; Gwynne would go on in his place. 'Muggins here was doing it instead,' says Gwynne ruefully. Trying to buy time, Schneider briefed Gwynne neither to confirm nor deny the manifesto's contents but to 'dance on a pinhead'. Gwynne's job was 'to avoid being drawn into talking about policies we haven't launched, but at the same time not to make them sound like terrible crazy ideas – probably the hardest brief you can give anyone. Go and defend something without talking about it.'

On his round of radio and TV programmes that morning, Gwynne, faced with this Sisyphean task, put on a positive spin. Suddenly we're not talking about personalities, he ventured to interviewers, we're talking about policies. 'I threw an aside to [BBC presenter] John Humphrys that he'd probably have had a downer on Attlee's manifesto for a government if he was a reporter in 1945. We offered something transformational: large parts of the UK, particularly young people, felt that they could believe in something and vote for something they could believe in.' This new manifesto, he said, exploded the usual stale politics. 'Gwynne,' says Schneider, 'was an absolute hero.'

What happened next underlined just how divorced from popular opinion the manifesto's critics were. Polling by the *Mirror* found that – as the paper put it – 'almost every Labour policy announcement went down well with voters'. Even a majority of Tory voters backed hiking income tax on those earning more than £80,000 a year.[16] When, finally, key party stakeholders met to approve the manifesto, aides were feeling more upbeat. Journalists assembled outside the room. 'Then Jeremy came out and did an absolutely confident, pitch perfect prime-minister-in-waiting speech to the assembled journalists,' recalls Schneider. 'He was completely in control of the situation.'

The manifesto – and its leak – proved a turning point. Rather than being the focus of just one burst of publicity, it was discussed and debated on TV and in newspapers for days. Manifestos usually have very limited public purchase, but this one was the most shared political link on Facebook in the week of its launch, and discussed more extensively than any such document for many years. 'In hindsight, it was utter strategic genius to have leaked it, even if it was clearly done maliciously,' says Fisher. Usually, manifestos had little impact on election campaigns, but then, 'Nobody had put anything like this forward for at least a generation.'

People under the age of forty had never experienced an election in which there was such a marked difference between the two parties, or where Labour had offered a radical departure from the status quo. In 2015, Labour had appeared timid, apologetic; this time round, it was bold. Corbyn travelled the country, waving the manifesto everywhere he went. The radical alternative was unapologetically and forcefully presented. On doorsteps across the country, campaigners, even those Labour MPs hostile to Corbyn, experienced the same reaction: people liked the manifesto, and it was encouraging them to consider voting Labour. The political consensus – always built on a widespread sense of resignation, not enthusiasm – was crumbling.

The Tories retained two key advantages over Labour. The first was money. In the run-up to the election, they received £25 million in donations from wealthy vested interests, more than twice the Labour total.[17] The second advantage was the support of the vast majority of the British press, among the most vitriolic, aggressively right-wing in the Western world. Their campaign against Corbyn and his key allies was unrelenting. A particular obsession was Shadow Home Secretary Diane Abbott, Britain's first black female MP, and a huge target of racist abuse. A bad interview, in which she forgot how much money was required to fund Labour's pledge to reverse Tory cuts to the police, led to the *Daily Mail* devoting no fewer than fourteen pages of its election eve issue to portraying the Labour leadership as terrorist sympathizers.

Labour, though, had two assets of its own. Its financial counterweight to the Tories' lavish corporate funding was the trade union movement. Unite, the biggest union, had £12 million in its political fund. A campaign plan targeting Unite's hundreds of thousands of members was drawn up. 'We identified key movers and shakers in key workplaces whose job it would be to get the message out face to face,' Unite's former political officer, Anneliese Midgeley, tells me. It was these in-person conversations that the Labour leadership held to be so crucial to their chances of persuading swing voters. Labour's second asset was a mass, energetic grassroots army, both online and on the streets.

Momentum, the grassroots organization founded in 2015 to harness the political energy of Corbyn's first leadership campaign, was an experiment, an attempt to combine the strategies of the Labour left of the 1980s and new, tech-savvy young radicals. Its leading lights were young Britons who had become disillusioned with – and politicized by – the betrayals of New Labour, the financial disaster and the reality of Tory rule: people like Beth Foster-Ogg – then only twenty years old but a force of nature – and Adam Klug, the son of a left-wing Jewish academic, who gave up teaching to throw himself into the Corbyn movement.

After months of tortuous internal battles, now was the movement's opportunity. Since its foundation in October 2015 following Corbyn's election as Labour leader, Momentum had swelled to over 150 local groups and thousands of members. Before the election, its role was unclear and factional battles over its internal structures had crippled it. But suddenly there was a unity of purpose, clarity of direction and a tangible goal. Within a week of the election being called, explains Momentum's Emma Rees, 'we had a clear sense of the campaign ahead. We needed to train up as many activists as possible to feel confident on the doorstep.' This was key. Despite the surge in Labour's membership, most were new to campaigning, and it was here that Foster-Ogg's community organizing came into play.

'We knew we could mobilize huge numbers of people', said Foster-Ogg. But she didn't just want activists to knock on doors, ask which party they were voting for, then move on. Instead – inspired in part by Bernie Sanders's US campaign for the 2016 Democratic presidential nomination – she was interested in persuasive conversation, in listening to people's concerns, fears, hopes and aspirations, and seeking to win them over. Some, she said, were sceptical that this could work. 'They were like – there's six weeks until an election, how will you do that?'

Clarity of message on the doorstep was key. Foster-Ogg's strategy went like this: if you couldn't explain a policy in ten seconds, it wasn't worth it. 'And the Labour manifesto was a series of ten-second policies,' she explains, from taxing the rich to investing in public services, introducing a living wage, abolishing tuition fees, bringing utilities into public ownership. Or as another Momentum activist, Rachel Godfrey-Wood, summed it up: 'When you're in a club when every song is a banger, that's like the manifesto!' Momentum understood all this. What they now needed to do was communicate it.

Foster-Ogg launched thirty-eight training sessions across the country for potential canvassers. At one, in north London, 300 volunteers turned up, cramming into the meeting room. Some were experienced activists, others were just frightened about an impending Tory landslide and wanted to do something. Many had never canvassed before. This was one of Momentum's key aims, to turn otherwise mostly passive Labour Party members into activists.

Another of Momentum's critical contributions was maximizing turnout at Corbyn's rallies across the country. Conventional wisdom – which I myself had bought into – suggested that these would bring together only the true believers, the already converted. But with mass outdoor rallies, anyone could turn up – and they did. At one, in a Reading car park, passing office workers stopped to listen. This wasn't a case of talking to long-standing Campaign for Nuclear Disarmament activists in a church hall. As the then *Channel 4 News* reporter Michael Crick put it, Corbyn 'has probably addressed bigger meetings in 2017 than any leader since Churchill'.[18] These events were often in safe seats, but they drew people from surrounding areas, and, critically, were shown on regional TV news. They had a decisive impact. According to post-election research by the London School of Economics, in Labour seats Corbyn didn't visit, the party's vote share went up by 9.8 per cent; in those he did, the surge was an astonishing 18.7 per cent. In the case of Theresa May, the Tories' share of the vote went up by 5.9 per cent in seats she didn't visit; in those she did, their vote share went down.[19]

The story of Momentum's campaign in the southwest city of Bristol, home to arguably the movement's most active group at the time, was a case in point. 'We believed we needed a strategy that put us on the offensive,' says Phil Bates, a member of Bristol Momentum. Told by Labour HQ to focus on defending existing local MPs, Momentum nevertheless believed they should be far more ambitious. Accordingly, they targeted the adjacent constituencies of Bristol North West and Stroud, both with a Tory majority of less than 5,000; and Gower, with a Tory majority of just twenty-seven. They sent hundreds of activists to constituencies which the party in London had written off. All these seats would be won by Labour in 2017.

Momentum employed a number of approaches. Focusing on their

target constituencies, they used Momentum's phone canvassing app to mobilize activists from adjacent areas, regularly getting between thirty and fifty people out at very short notice. 'We wanted to create a pulse of activity twice a week,' says Bates, 'that'd give confidence to local activists to come out, make them feel a seat is winnable, and to give candidates a boost, too. Frankly, some were lacklustre.' Moreover, many of the MPs they canvassed for deliberately omitted any mention of Corbyn in their leaflets, believing the leader was a liability rather than the asset he was becoming. When they delivered the flyers, Momentum activists wrapped them in specially designed leaflets about the manifesto and the Labour leader. These activists were encouraged to conduct listening campaigns, to look at each electoral ward, identify the key issues – whether it be hospitals being closed down or struggling local schools – and tailor their message accordingly.

Stockwood ward in Bristol East is a housing estate with an overwhelmingly white, working-class population and little Labour Party presence in the past twenty years. The Tories had triumphed there in the last council elections; a fifth of voters had opted for UKIP. This time, fifty activists, from students to pensioners, turned up. Most had never met before. First-time canvassers were buddied up with experienced members to give them confidence. The whole ward was leafleted in two hours; then, the activists retired to the pub, where they could bond and exchange experiences. As in many wards, people in Stockwood would angrily decry the fact that no Labour canvasser had knocked on their door for years, if ever. These campaigns achieved dramatic results: Stockwood would end up decisively voting for Labour.[20] Former Tory aide Tom Edmunds puts it to me, tellingly: 'If you ask Conservative candidates which stood and lost in seats we thought were winnable, they'll say Momentum were there.'

Nationally, Momentum used innovative techniques to mobilize members. One method they imported from Bernie Sanders's campaign was text relaying. Texts were used not to broadcast information, but to start a conversation. They were intended to be personalized, chatty, friendly: 'Hi Jenny! You around for a campaign event this weekend?' Suggested set responses were mapped out in advance so they could be swiftly sent and, if necessary, edited. For example, if they replied 'Sorry, no', a response could be sent back along the lines of: 'Sorry to hear that, can you come to another one?' What was more, while many people didn't answer phone calls or respond to emails, they were far more likely to reply to text messages: the response rate was 40 per cent. Throughout the campaign, Momentum reached an astonishing 90,000 activists in this way.

Momentum's social media campaign represented an extraordinary departure in British politics. In 2017 there existed for the first time a rival online anti-Tory political ecosystem which could serve as a counterweight to the overwhelmingly hostile mainstream press. Tom Edmunds should know: he was on the receiving end, having run the Tories' 2015 and 2017 digital campaigns. As he stirs a cappuccino in a theatre café on London's South Bank, he recalls how much changed in just two years. 'In 2015, the only people churning stuff out were political parties,' he says. 'But look at the registered participants in 2017 – that is, the groups that are allowed to spend up to £700,000 – using followers they'd already built up beforehand. Around seventy to eighty signed up, and of those just two were Tory. The rest were either pro-Labour or anti-Tory.'

Edwards reels off a list of groups the Tories had to contend with: 'Pro-Remain groups, like Open Britain. Anti-austerity groups, like the People's Assembly. Animal protection charities taking on fox hunting. Labour groups, like Momentum. Broadly progressive campaigning alliances like 38 Degrees and Avaaz. Single-issue groups, against cuts to education, or the NHS. There's a lot of political content online – but the content that comes through most comes through third-party groups.' One striking example he gives is a video on school cuts released by the National Union of Teachers which had over 4 million views on Facebook.[21]

All this gave Labour's digital campaign an advantage. Political parties have to be careful with the videos they release. If they're too negative, or have content or facts or spin that can be disputed, then party leaders risk being ripped apart at press conferences. But these informal rules don't apply to third-party groups. Their existence also meant that it was easier for Labour to focus on a positive message – because the negative anti-Tory messages were extensively covered elsewhere.

At the centre of the anti-Tory ecosystem, Momentum helped bridge the online and offline worlds. Harry Richie, then thirty years old, coordinated the social media campaign. He was the only full-time Momentum digital employee, but had a core team of around five helping him. They created videos – optimum length, just a minute long – which explained, in accessible terms, how to canvass. A website called 'My Nearest Marginal' allowed you to type in your postcode, and then told you which nearby constituency was a priority, with details of how to get involved. Another campaign, 'Pledge The Day', signed up 8,000 people to commit to taking election day off work to knock on doors and get Labour's vote out.

Momentum didn't have access to electoral rolls, or marketing or polling data, and they didn't have the means to micro target swing voters. Instead, they prioritized the creation of content which would spread organically, without needing finance to drive it; that is, content people would choose to share voluntarily on their Facebook walls, rather than having it promoted there by paid advertising. 'We wanted to make it super accessible, engaging, maybe funny,' says Richie. 'And we looked at the way people receive this, mostly on their phones, to try and grab their attention.'

Above all else, the focus was on reaching outside the political bubble and recognizing that most people don't follow politics in great detail. Going into policy detail wasn't going to work. Instead, each video had to carry a key message or sentiment. That could include capturing key TV moments. In one press conference, Theresa May was challenged about why she refused to debate with Corbyn. 'She completely floundered, tried to make a joke, but no one laughed, it was really awkward.' And indeed, they titled the video 'This is so awkward', subtitled all of her 'uhms' and 'ahs', including her mixing up her words. It got more than 4 million views. Even if many hadn't seen the whole video, Richie reasons, such content would help chip away at the positive impression so many had of May at the start of the campaign.

Some of Momentum's videos were unapologetically edgy. One was set in Tory Britain in 2030. In a supposedly loving scene between a father and his daughter, she asks him why she doesn't have free school meals or university education like he did. 'Because I voted for

Theresa May!' he says with a chuckle. 'Daddy, do you hate me?' she asks. 'Obviously!' he responds.

The video went viral – around 7 million views – particularly among younger people, tapping into a well of bitterness and the sense that Tory politicians were stealing people's futures. Other videos featured Corbyn speaking at mass rallies the length and breadth of Britain, including shots of passionate crowds. It was footage that made viewers want to identify with an exciting, inspiring movement, while eroding the negative portrayal of Corbyn that had been carefully crafted by the British press. Another initiative was 'Grime 4 Corbyn', promoting pro-Corbyn musicians, like Awate and Maxsta, with huge youth fanbases. Under the direction of stakeholder manager Laura Murray, Corbyn's Twitter account was used to direct-message celebrities and ask for their support. To begin with, many were cautious, responding that their management would not let them say anything or be party political, but after a tipping point halfway through the campaign, they were much more positive. When Stormzy, a British rapper with a colossal youth following – came out in support, it encouraged others to do the same. Somehow, this previously obscure backbencher in his late sixties had acquired the thing all politicians craved and practically none had: cultural cachet. Corbyn, simply put, was cool. All of which contrasted sharply with Corbyn's electoral opponent. 'Imagine taking Theresa to see Stormzy,' one Tory aide reflected to me, before trailing off into an eloquent silence.

Momentum's digital campaign was a collective endeavour. The core team sent out a request for help from those with creative skills in, say, videos, filming, editing, and such. They built a database of 450 people – 'we put a lot of focus on that,' says Richie, 'working with these people, building relationships' – whom they could quickly call on. Independent film crews working around the country would send in a rough cut of footage – say, at a rally or campaign day – and the talented central team would finish it off and make it shareable on social media. Other times, people the Momentum team had never met would edit footage off site, or come into the London headquarters near Euston to finish the videos. 'It really amplified what we could do,' says Richie, who had previously been sceptical about the power of social media. All told, Momentum spent less than £2,000 on social media advertising during the 2017 election campaign. It was quite the investment.

Momentum's digital campaign dovetailed with Corbyn's own. This was almost entirely run by Jack Bond, a workaholic former youth community worker. His social media strategy was simple: to amplify popular policies and communicate directly to Labour supporters, especially by maximizing the use of video. Both Facebook and Twitter allowed the leadership to describe their own policies in their own terms, without media filters. From the outset, Corbyn was clear that the video output from his accounts had to be relentlessly positive. When the video team mocked up a humiliating interview by Michael Fallon, the then defence secretary and main Tory attack dog, they got a call from Corbyn. 'It's not hopeful,' he said. 'It's them making a mistake, I don't want us to attack them. I want everything we write and put out to be hopeful. If we're attacking them, it should be on their record, not on their mistakes.' At the time, the team was deeply frustrated, knowing that the video had the potential to go viral. In hindsight, Jack Bond tells me, Corbyn was right. 'They voted for him because what he's saying is hopeful and transformative – one of many ways Jeremy isn't a normal leader.'

If Corbyn's integrity was an asset in Labour's social media campaign, May's qualities were anything but. One Tory aide told me that 'Theresa May's fucking terrible at online stuff. She bombs. She can't deliver it. Whatever you think about David Cameron, fuck me, he's good, he delivers the speech. You'll do three takes, including close-ups, and he'll nail each time with passion and charisma.' Asked to communicate warmth, the aide recalled, May 'came back with a manic smile'.

A clichéd argument about social media is that it is a bubble where people carve out isolated spaces made up of those with similar beliefs to their own. But the 2017 general election disproved this claim. 'People's friendships on Facebook are far more expansive than they are in real life,' says Richie. 'In real life, most people don't talk about politics with their friends. But they might see friends sharing things online – it's quite a powerful endorsement.'

The numbers speak for themselves. During the campaign, Corbyn's Facebook published twenty videos which reached over a million people, Momentum had fourteen, and the Labour Party had just two, excluding two party election broadcasts and a video about a final rally they had nothing to do with. Jeremy Corbyn's social media operation managed to get 1.25 million Facebook shares; Theresa May's far more well-financed page managed 100,000 shares. On Twitter, Corbyn's account got 1.42 million retweets, May's, 96,000. The Facebook reach was even more dramatic: over 47 million unique people saw Corbyn's page. A poorly resourced, often ramshackle – but, crucially, politically, culturally and technologically savvy – operation smashed the Tories' online offensive. 'In the final week, we got video views of 13 million, and 150 million appearances on people's screens on Facebook, all organically shared,' says Richie. 'All that stuff would have cost a fortune in paid advertising.'

Crucially, the online offensive cut through where it needed to. In Canterbury, where Labour would end up winning for the first time ever, over four in ten Facebook users watched a Momentum video in the last week of the election; in Sheffield Hallam, where ex-deputy prime minister and former Liberal Democrat leader Nick Clegg was booted out of his seat, the figure was over half.[22]

Labour's approach to the campaign, summed up, was this: using modern technology to expound creatively a politics which was unapologetically about the majority versus the elites. But the party was helped by the Tories' own campaign, which was a case study in hubris. Coming just days after their own near-fiasco, Corbyn's team were nervous about the Conservative manifesto launch. Would there be some audacious raid on Labour territory, or some traditional Tory short-term tax-cutting bribe? One policy in the Tory manifesto pre-briefing, though, stood out like a sore thumb. It suggested that the Conservatives were planning to make adults pay for their own social care through a 100 per cent tax on the value of their assets (their house included), above a £100,000 threshold. It looked like a stinker of a policy, but Corbyn's team were convinced that there would be some surprise, because the Tories would surely brief out the more contentious elements of their policy prospectus in advance. They hadn't.

This policy, which turned out to be the centrepiece of the Tory manifesto, was initially lauded by the right-wing press. But Labour and its supporters christened it the 'dementia tax' because, while those suffering from cancer would have access to free NHS care, those with a condition such as dementia – more prevalent among an older demographic more inclined to vote Conservative – would be compelled to pay. Labour and its allies successfully turned the Conservatives' flagship policy into their Achilles heel. It got worse for Theresa May: her proposals to means-test pensioners' winter fuel payments, and to abandon the existing 'triple lock' guaranteeing sustained rises in pensions proved a toxic electoral combination. It seemed that the Tories believed that pensioners would vote for them come what may and so had decided that they could start repealing their benefits and rights. Other Conservative policies included allowing a free vote on fox hunting and abandoning a ban on the ivory trade. For Momentum's Foster-Ogg and her team of canvassers, it was perfect for the doorstep. 'The only Tory policies you could sum up in ten seconds were fox hunting, legalizing hunting rhinos, and the dementia tax,' she says smiling.

The Conservative manifesto indicated another, more profound, victory for the Corbyn project. One section was entitled 'We believe in the good that government can do', and spoke of the need for a state 'that is strong and strategic, nimble and responsive to the needs of people'. That included requiring 'government to play an active role, leading a modern industrial strategy'.[23] On a rhetorical level, at least, the Tory leadership was acknowledging the polling – and abandoning the viscerally anti-state ideology to which they had been wedded since the late 1970s.

This campaign, however, was not a story of ever-escalating hope and optimism. On the evening of 22 May, in the foyer of the Manchester Arena, a 22-year-old man detonated a bag packed with improvised shrapnel at an Ariana Grande concert. The area was packed with teenagers, children and parents accompanying them or waiting to drive them home: twenty-two were murdered, dozens of others left with terrible injuries.

That evening, before the shocking events at the Manchester Arena, Corbyn's campaign had been at its most buoyant. Corbyn himself was in an excellent mood after a day of mass rallies in Yorkshire, including what was described by one local newspaper as 'a rock star reception' in Hull.[24] 'Even the weather was with us,' says an aide. The Tory campaign was at its lowest ebb. Theresa May had attempted a partial U-turn on her disastrous dementia tax, and at a cringe-inducing press conference had been openly ridiculed by journalists when she declared repeatedly 'Nothing has changed!', like a short-circuiting political robot.

Later, as Corbyn and his team sat in a Premier Inn restaurant in Doncaster, the BBC's *10 O'Clock News* contrasted May's calamitous day with footage of the Labour leader and cheering crowds. Then, to their horror, came the news from the Manchester Arena. 'Manchester was particularly horrible,' says James Meadway. 'It was really obnoxious and horrible in a way we haven't seen in this country for a while – the methodical targeting of little kids, with a degree of planning.' There was no question about the instant response. 'There had to be days of mourning and respect,' says Joe Ryle. All parties agreed to pause the election campaign. Because during this time there was technically no government – and two possible governments-in-waiting – Corbyn's team were given regular security briefings. Many of them were up all night, trying to process what was happening.

Corbyn wanted to go to Manchester to show solidarity with the victims, and he attended the vigil there. But, just sixteen days before an election, it was impossible not to think of the political consequences of the atrocity. As Andrew Murray puts it, 'Terrorist attacks are normally to the benefit of the right, or to the government of the day – and they were the same people in this case.' The Tories had long positioned themselves as the party of security and law and order. 'I knew the kids of friends caught up in that attack,' says Andrew Gwynne. 'There's the horror. You also think, God, this is awful on a political level. It allows May to be strong and stable, statesman-like, she's the PM, she'll do a great speech at Downing Street, which will be seen as the right thing to do, and garner support across the political spectrum.' The underlying dynamic, he feared, played to the Tory narrative that Corbyn was soft on terrorism, and indeed friends with terrorists. In this campaign, the Tories and their media outriders in the British press had made a strategic decision to portray the Labour leadership as terrorist sympathizers. The implication was clear. Before the attack, Labour had all the campaigning momentum, but the pause in the campaign would allow the Tories to surge back.

As the team left Manchester, the government announced that troops would be deployed on Britain's streets. The mood on the train journey south was quiet. 'We just sat thinking, it's all over,' recalls Sian Jones, Corbyn's head of media. 'I felt sick to my stomach.' She was concerned that May's team were cynically trying to weaponize the attack politically. 'We thought they were trying to fuck us over, to use this for political advantage, to portray them as strong on security, and Jeremy as weak.'

After the initial period of public mourning had ended, a fierce argument broke out among the campaign team as to how Corbyn should respond politically. Some were uneasy about doing anything other than condemning the attack, praising the emergency and security services, then pivoting back to politics as normal as quickly as possible. But Andrew Murray, Andrew Fisher and Seumas Milne firmly resisted this argument. 'I said, "You wouldn't be Jeremy Corbyn if you did that,"' states Murray. 'You had to say: "Why are these things happening? Why, when we're so deep into the war on terror, is terrorism not only not going away, but as bad as ever or getting worse? What has gone wrong with our foreign policy which is enabling it – without taking moral responsibility away from the criminals who did it?" This was the wider agenda of issues that a democracy has to be mature enough to address.' But in the Labour Party press office there was heavy resistance to the strategy; privately, some were disgusted by it. Even some of Corbyn's aides had doubts.

Yet, as the Labour leadership knew, the terrorist attacks would be cynically weaponized against them. Whatever happened, they would be painted as a threat to national security. It was crucial, they felt, to get on the front foot. Pressing ahead with Murray and Milne's plan, the team drew inspiration from the so-called 'Philadelphia moment': Barack Obama's speech in May 2008 during the Democratic presidential race against his competitor Hillary Clinton. In response to controversy over comments made by his former pastor who had vehemently condemned racism in US society, instead of going on the defensive, Obama made a powerful speech about the traumatic history of race in the US. Four days later, Corbyn made his intervention in the Cumbrian city of Carlisle. Pinning the blame for the attack squarely on the terrorist, he went on to explain that the war on terror was simply not working. 'Many experts, including professionals in our intelligence and security services, have pointed to the connections between wars our government has supported or fought in other countries and terrorism here at home.' And then came a critical line of attack. Before Theresa May had become prime minister, she had been home secretary for six years, and had overseen a reduction of 20,000 police posts. Indeed, she had, in the past, denounced the police for 'crying wolf' over the threats to national security posed by slashing police numbers.[25]

Swiftly, predictably, Corbyn came under attack from the Tories' Michael Fallon and Boris Johnson – the latter calling the speech 'absolutely monstrous'. Some Labour MPs were furious, too. I was among those privately berated by Labour politicians for arguing Corbyn's case. Yet public, as opposed to establishment, opinion was on Corbyn's side. One poll found that 53 per cent thought British foreign policy was partly responsible for terrorist attacks in Britain; just 24 per cent believed it played no role.[26]

Days later, on 3 June, terrorists ploughed a van into pedestrians on London Bridge, before indiscriminately stabbing punters drinking in pubs in nearby Borough Market. Eight were murdered. 'We are all shocked and horrified by the brutal attacks in London,' declared Corbyn. Britain could not, he unapologetically argued, have security on the cheap. This was simply not an approach a 'conventional' Labour leader would have taken – and it resonated. Suddenly the consequences of Conservative cuts to spending had been starkly exposed in a grimly tangible way: such cuts put British lives at risk. When Theresa May responded to the atrocities by questioning multiculturalism, Labour flipped the discussion to the uncomfortable conversations Britain's government should be having with its Saudi and Gulf allies who were exporting terrorism. In his solidly working-class northern constituency, Gwynne found that people were blaming the government for police cuts that left them feeling more insecure and less safe.

A clip of the head of the Police Federation berating Theresa May over cuts made when she was home secretary went viral. 'How do you sleep at night?' he had pointedly asked her.

Corbyn's response to these twin atrocities encapsulated so much of what, at this time, he was about. Anathema to much of the political and media elite, it struck a resonant chord with many people throughout Britain.

During the election Corbyn himself had been exceptionally positive. 'He's just like – "we have to do this",' says staffer Faduma Hassan. 'He's seen it all, so he was more assured, perhaps.' His impact had been astonishing. From rallies in the early days of the campaign, when Corbyn aides would come back from trips on the road talking of electrifying experiences, to Corbyn's countless inspirational interactions with people. Hassan recalls him meeting a young family in Wales. The father was crying. 'He was saying: "I have a disabled son, I can't work full time, I'm not getting anything, you're my only hope."' Hassan pauses. 'To see a grown man crying who had never voted – it's those sorts of moments, that this is real, not just about our politics or some factional fight, but about people.' On 21 May, Corbyn appeared – unannounced – onstage at the Wirral Live music festival at Tranmere Rovers football ground. The 20,000 festival-goers there 'went bananas' and began chanting his name, 'Oh, Jeremy Corbyn!', to the tune of The White Stripes' 'Seven Nation Army'. Soon, it was being sung everywhere.

The day before the election, Corbyn travelled to six constituencies across Britain, starting in Scotland, then the North of England, then Wales, and ending in Islington's Union Chapel, where the last rally of his first leadership campaign was held. Each stop required multiple teams to be sent up in advance to lay the groundwork. That final day was testament to the metamorphosis, in the space of six weeks, of a ragtag, often chaotic team into a highly sophisticated and complex operation. Beginning in anxiety and panic, the Labour campaign had become one of the most creative, transformative and inspiring of modern times. 'I knew we'd run the best campaign we could,' said Joe Ryle. 'We were proud, confident and proud.'

*

It was 8 June, election day. Despite the transformation in Labour's campaigning, an unprecedented rout was widely predicted. 'I was nervous,' recalls Andrew Fisher. 'Really nervous. The polls were so divergent.' The latest polling showed Labour behind by a range of thirteen points to five points. Just one polling agency, Survation, placed Labour a tantalizing 0.9 points behind, with a 40.4 per cent share of the vote. The party's internal polling had Labour on just 34 per cent, a modest four-point improvement on the disaster of 2015. The leadership hoped that the unfiltered data of the different pollsters suggested a very close result between Labour and the Tories; it was only when filters were applied to take into account differential turnout that these wildly differing poll results emerged. Those polls with the biggest Tory leads made the calculation that Labour voters – particularly younger Labour voters – were not going to turn out in as great numbers as the data suggested.

On polling day itself, many of Corbyn's team were out canvassing. I was with some of them in Battersea, a Tory-held seat in London being contested by left-wing Labour firebrand Marsha de Cordova. WhatsApp messages pinged on the phones of aides all day, with optimistic reports of high turnout dotted across the nation. A couple of hours before the exit poll was released, I rang the Labour leadership office as I biked back from Tooting, a marginal Labour seat whose team had sent out a frantic text warning of weak Labour turnout. How did it look? 'Mixed', came the answer. What did mixed mean? 'Good in London, difficult in the Northwest, the Northeast and the Midlands,' I was told. 'But . . . that's basically England outside of the Southeast?' I spluttered. It wasn't a happy moment. One relatively optimistic senior aide predicted that, of Parliament's 650 seats, Labour would end up on anything between 215 and 260 seats.

Andrew Murray had drafted four scenarios of what might happen: from 'disaster', Labour ending up below its 2015 vote share, to the most optimistic, a hung Parliament. But he didn't think that was particularly likely. Neither did many in Momentum HQ. On election eve, Beth Foster-Ogg and Emma Rees had met up to discuss the structure of Corbyn's third leadership campaign which would be triggered by the inevitable electoral defeat Labour was about to suffer.

It was five minutes to 10 p.m., when the exit poll would be released:

crunch time. 'I was sitting with Corbyn's media team, and no one spoke,' says Joe Ryle. 'My body was tensed up. I was struggling to breathe. I don't think I've ever been so nervous in my entire life. I'd never thrown so much energy into something before, and it all hinged on one announcement.'

I was in the ITV studios as an election night commentator. I remember the countdown to the exit poll as the longest two minutes of my life. And then came the announcement. As soon as BBC presenter David Dimbleby proclaimed that the Tories were the 'largest party', it clicked that Theresa May had lost her majority. Labour were due to gain some 30 seats in what would be a hung Parliament. Corbyn's team went crazy. 'There was a huge release of excitement,' says James Schneider. 'Just elation at first – then we didn't believe it,' says Joe Ryle. 'We're on the left – we don't normally win things!' Andrew Fisher punched the air as the exit poll was announced, yelling, 'Please be fucking right, please be fucking right.' Another recalls one half of the room being ecstatic, while the old Labour HQ guard were 'shellshocked, dazed, couldn't believe it'. Their responses – both distraught and furious alike – were what you would expect from messages exchanged between Conservative officials, not senior Labour figures responding to substantial gains by their own party. 'We will have to suck this up,' mourned one staffer. 'The people have spoken. Bastards.' Another suggested they should have bet on Labour's surge because then 'at least you'd get something good from the disappointment'.

One colleague had an unkind metaphor for the Southsiders: it must have been like accidentally finding yourself in Stasi HQ when the Berlin Wall fell. 'They were like, everything I thought about the world turned out to be horribly wrong.' The initial outburst of joy soon subsided to a nervous caution. James Mills, John McDonnell's fast-talking press aide, told the shadow chancellor to wait until 1 a.m. before he accepted the exit poll was right, pointing out it had been wrong two years earlier. Then, the results unfolded. When Canterbury, a Tory constituency since the nineteenth century, fell to Labour, Mills told McDonnell: 'Not being funny, John, but I've never seen anything like it before.' 'Stop it!' McDonnell responded, trying to suppress his own excitement. In Battersea, south London,

Foster-Ogg was in the local Labour Party headquarters when the results were announced: a near-8,000 Tory majority had been overturned into a Labour gain. 'Everyone was just screaming! It was complete and utter joy!' Amidst the euphoria, Andrew Fisher instructed staff not to drink too much as Labour could be entering coalition talks the next day.

In Conservative headquarters, the atmosphere was rather different. A Tory aide reportedly vomited into a bin, and Theresa May broke down in tears. 'It was pretty bad,' recalls campaign manager Tom Edmunds. The Tories, he concluded, had targeted the wrong seats. At certain points in the campaign, they genuinely believed they could win Bolsover (Labour won with a 5,000+ majority), Sedgefield (Labour won with a majority of more than 6,000 votes) and West Bromwich East (Labour majority of over 7,500). 'We thought, as the results came in, what was the point in targeting those seats? It made you realize the message focus on Brexit was a fuckup. We lost the likes of Canterbury, and Tory Remainers, because we banged on about Brexit so long we became the Brexit Party.' By the end of the night, Edmunds felt something like relief, because at one stage he thought Corbyn was going to be Britain's next prime minister. Only the Tories' breakthrough in Scotland stopped them being evicted from Number 10.

Theresa May had called her election to extinguish Labour as a political force. Instead it had plunged the Conservative Party into chaos. Labour had experienced its biggest vote surge since 1945, and gained the highest share of the vote since 2001; indeed, it won almost the same percentage as Blair's second landslide. Labour had started twenty-four points behind the Tories; it ended with a two-point deficit. It was clear that the party bureaucracy, though, had been planning for a Labour rout. As soon as the exit poll dropped, the leadership team found that their key fobs no longer worked in Southside. They were to be locked out, possibly in preparation for a coup.

How had Corbyn's Labour – seemingly a lost political cause when the election was announced six weeks previously – come within a few thousand votes in a few constituencies of being able to form a government?[27] The post-election narrative, that it was all about Brexit with Remainers flocking to Labour to thwart the Tories' plans to leave the

EU, was wide of the mark. Corbyn was committed to implementing the referendum result, while the profound polarization on the issue had yet to set in. Few offered Brexit as their reason for voting Labour. While May's campaign had been poor, this didn't explain how Labour secured 40 per cent of the vote. It was also what Labour offered the British people, a policy prospectus which captured the spirit of the age, and the Corbyn project's ability to tap the vast disillusionment with the social order, something with which no previous Labour politicians had yet dared to engage. The election result proved that when radical policies were spelled out without apology, but defiantly and in primary colours, people were hungry for them.

For a brief period after the election, there was an air of triumph about the Corbyn project. The leader himself seemed untouchable. Labour MPs who had attempted to depose him now enthusiastically joined in the chorus of 'Oh, Jeremy Corbyn'. By contrast, Prime Minister Theresa May was, in the unsavoury words of former Chancellor George Osborne, a 'dead woman walking'. A week after the election, dozens of working-class people burned to death in Grenfell Tower on a housing estate in west London. The bungled government response, and the questions raised about the kind of society that could lead to such a catastrophe, only fed into a sense of mounting existential crisis for Britain's Conservative rulers.

Two weeks after the election, Corbyn attended the Glastonbury Festival and was met by tens of thousands singing his signature song; his position as an icon of hopeful change seemed secure. Touring Europe, he gained rockstar receptions from members of European social democratic parties in crisis, desperate to know how Britain's Labour Party had turned its fortunes around. 'He was the most wanted politician in Western Europe,' recalls Mark Simpson, Corbyn's Brexit lead. 'We'd go to Brussels and venues would be filled out. Normally there'd be twenty people at Party of European Socialists meetings; now they were oversubscribed by hundreds. In Prague, we were mobbed by hundreds of people. It was an eye opener.'

Amid the jubilation, few noticed – or wanted to notice – some uncomfortable signs. While Tory strategists were devastated not to have taken those prized Leave-voting Labour seats, they had made substantial progress. In Bolsover, the Labour majority had more than halved; in Sedgefield, the Tories had surged by over 5,000 votes; in West Bromwich East, the Conservatives enjoyed a vote share increase of over 13 percentage points. Theresa May's lead over Labour among pensioners was 50 per cent higher than David Cameron's had been just two years earlier. What was more, with no party obtaining an overall majority, Parliament, as Seumas Milne warned his deputy James Schneider, 'will be a real site of struggle'. Fearing that such attritional Westminster politicking would sap the energies of Corbyn's insurgent movement – indeed, went against everything it stood for – Schneider could not suppress a mounting sense of unease. 'Fucking hell,' he thought, 'we are done for.'

PART II

Fall

6

The Brexit Bandersnatch

The dystopian science fiction series *Black Mirror* features a fictional TV show called 'Bandersnatch', in which the viewer could interactively make decisions for the main character, Stefan Butler, a computer programmer creating a video game in the mid-1980s. You could decide on his behalf to take a job at a video game company, to pour tea on the computer, to shout at his father, to jump off a balcony, to take LSD. But in one respect it didn't make any difference which scenario you picked: they all ended badly for the character. Some endings were grimmer than others – in one, he ended up in prison; in another, his father was brutally murdered – but whatever decisions you elected to make, the outcome was not pretty.

When looking back at Labour's involvement with Brexit, it's difficult not to recall that show in that, whatever decisions the party made, it would not have ended well. Nothing inflicted so much terminal damage on the Corbyn project as the protracted national crisis that followed Britain's narrow vote in June 2016 to leave the European Union.

To understand why, it's worth recalling that the most fundamental pillar of any left-wing movement is class politics: the idea that the majority in society have different, conflicting economic interests from those at the top, which transcend cultural divisions. Brexit revealed and exacerbated existing divisions in British society which cut *across* classes, unleashing a fierce culture war – something that struck at the foundations of the Corbyn project. As the nation polarized, new political and cultural identities were cemented: now we were no longer Labour or Tory, working class or middle class, but Remainers and Leavers. As a result, cracks in Labour's electoral coalition were disastrously widened, between voters who tended to be younger, more diverse, living in urban areas and with more socially progressive views, and those who for the most part were older, more socially conservative, living in small towns. For well-funded bad faith elements on the Remain side, Brexit offered an opportunity to create a wedge between the Labour leadership and its natural supporters, and to toxify Corbyn in the process.

After the 2017 election, Brexit sucked the oxygen out of British politics. With its popular domestic policies no longer able to win a hearing, Labour came to be defined by its increasingly indecipherable approach to this one tortured issue, in trying vainly to appeal to its different voting demographics, it ended up satisfying few and alienating many. In the process, Brexit all but destroyed Corbyn's appeal as a straight-talking man of principle, and shattered the unity of the Labour leadership.

Fatally, Labour's leading lights hubristically clung to the belief that whatever pain Brexit caused the party, it would always prove a greater existential threat to the Tories; indeed, that it could even end up ripping the Conservative Party apart for the first time since the Corn Laws in the mid-nineteenth century. They were wrong.

The European question has long gnawed at both Britain's major political parties. In the post-war period, as Britain contemplated the benefits and demerits of joining the European Community, it was by and large the Tories who were keen to embrace Europe, with Labour deeply divided on the issue. The Tories were a largely enthusiastic pro-European party, who under Ted Heath unexpectedly won the 1970 election with a manifesto pledging that, with the right deal, 'it would be in the long-term interest of the British people for Britain to join the European Community'.[1] When, the following year, Parliament voted on entry, just 10 per cent of Tory MPs voted against; the Labour Party was significantly more split, with nearly a quarter of its pro-European MPs rebelling against their leadership to vote with the Tories.[2] But when Labour won the 1974 general election on a manifesto committed to renegotiate the terms of entry, it was now the anti-European left in open rebellion.

Tony Benn had favoured European integration in the 1960s, but, as he shifted leftwards, he came to see the EC as an undemocratic, bureaucratic menace which enshrined market dogma and threatened to block the radical aspirations of a future Labour government. 'I think the reason why both Labour and the Tories have reversed their positions over the years is that in the 1970s we, the left, regarded the EU as a capitalist conspiracy, about movements of capital and so on,' says former Labour MP Chris Mullin, one of Benn's key allies. For Heath and Thatcher, on the other hand, Europe was a means to break the post-war social democratic consensus. 'In their view, the EC was about defending capitalism, the market economy, and making it harder for socialist governments to interfere in the market,' as British historian Robert Saunders puts it to me. 'If Thatcher liked anything, it was a market, and the fact it was a common market was important to her.'

As a parliamentary democracy, Britain has generally shunned referendums as instruments of autocratic demagogues. In 1945 Labour leader Clement Attlee rejected Winston Churchill's suggestion of a national vote on whether the wartime coalition should continue during the peace: 'I could not consent to the introduction into our national life of a device so alien to all our traditions as the referendum, which has only too often been the instrument of Nazis and Fascism.'[3] Trying to manage a fractured Labour Party, its wily leader Harold Wilson increasingly saw a referendum as the only possible route. 'Labour was so divided by 1974 that it just couldn't have formed a cabinet to take a "for" or "against" position,' says Saunders, 'so it had to lift it out of cabinet and put it to the public, rather like David Cameron took it out of internal Tory politics to get the electorate to deal with it instead.'

The 1975 referendum was almost a mirror image of its equivalent four decades later. Backed as always by a vociferous right-wing press, Margaret Thatcher campaigned for Yes wearing a jumper embroidered with European flags. Wilson, meanwhile, playing a high-wire act, presented himself as a moderate Eurosceptic who, on balance, felt Britain was better off in the EC,[4] a position that helped reassure those Labour voters who were themselves sceptical but open to persuasion.

The Eurosceptic campaign was led by Benn, who was, in Saunders's words, 'the blazing meteor of the campaign, the figure around which the whole No campaign revolved'. Yet Benn was loathed by Liberals and Tories, and, with Leave becoming synonymous with Bennism, the Europhiles won a landslide victory, two thirds opting for 'Yes'.

Throughout the 1980s, Thatcherite free marketeers embraced Europe as deeply as the left rejected it – until, late in the decade, a fundamental shift took place in the thinking of both. The catalyst was a speech in September 1988 by then President of the European Commission Jacques Delors to Britain's Trades Union Congress, in which he enthralled his audience with talk of a 'social Europe' that enshrined workers' and social protections.

For a labour movement traumatized by Thatcherism, a lifeline seemed to have been thrown from Brussels. For Thatcher, on the other hand, Europe was suddenly metamorphosing into a menace. 'We have not successfully rolled back the frontiers of the state in Britain,' she famously thundered in Bruges twelve days after Delors's speech, 'only to see them re-imposed at a European level with a European super-state exercising a new dominance from Brussels.'[5]

From that moment on, Euroscepticism became predominantly associated with the Tory right. The left, meanwhile, came to find the EU more appealing. Some of its leading lights even became EU enthusiasts, such as the former firebrand leader of the Greater London Council, Ken Livingstone, who even advocated adopting the euro.[6]

Like most of the British left at that point, Jeremy Corbyn had voted 'No' in the 1975 referendum and had consistently voted against legislation which granted more powers to the EU. But in truth, Corbyn had little passion or interest when it came to matters related to the EU, rolling his eyes at the Euroscepticism of his fellow left-wing MP Kelvin Hopkins. In his then backbencher's office, Corbyn's staff would sometimes hear him expressing bafflement about why his colleague was so fixated on the issue. His closest ally, John McDonnell, was even more agnostic – and pragmatic, believing that Labour's position on EU membership should be dictated by whether it made an election victory for a left-wing policy programme more or less likely.

In the 2015 general election – the Labour disaster which proved the catalyst for Jeremy Corbyn's unlikely rise – the Tories won their majority on a manifesto committed to a referendum on Britain's membership of the EU. As he campaigned for the leadership, Corbyn announced that he wouldn't rule out supporting Leave because he feared that the EU deal Conservative Prime Minister David Cameron wanted to negotiate was 'about trading away workers' rights, is about trading away environmental protection, is about trading away much of what is in the social chapter'.[7] This was not paranoia. It was reported in July 2015 that Cameron was seeking to negotiate opt-outs to laws such as the working-time directive and agency workers' directives.[8]

There were discussions – which I was part of – to withhold automatic support for Remain without guarantees that existing rights would be protected. They prompted me to suggest the left debate the case for a 'left exit' – or, as I called it, Lexit.[9] 'Lexit' remains my only contribution to the English language. It's not one I'm particularly proud of.

This refusal to provide a blank cheque for Cameron worked. 'Cameron drops demand for full immunity from EU labour rules' was the *Financial Times*'s splash on 1 September, the paper adding it was a 'bid to keep unions and Corbyn with the "in" camp'.[10] It also, apparently, worked for Corbyn. On becoming leader in September 2015, he issued a joint statement with the shadow foreign secretary – Hilary Benn, son of Tony – to commit to campaigning for Remain in the forthcoming referendum.

This was just as well, because active support for Brexit among the left and the labour movement was at that point very low: all the major unions backed Remain, as did the vast majority of the Labour membership. And, for the Lexit tendency – who objected to the neoliberal elements of the EU and believed that it was impossible to reform those defects out of existence – this was a problem that never went away. Their objections, indeed, were a decisive factor for very few who voted for Leave in Britain, the vast majority of Leave voters had entirely different reasons for wanting to get out of the EU.

But if the new Corbyn leadership had been brought onside for Remain, this didn't mean campaigning alongside the Conservatives shoulder to shoulder. A year earlier, Labour had been persuaded to do precisely this in the referendum for Scottish independence. The official campaign, Better Together, had a bitterly negative approach, described as 'Project Fear'. Although it won, and Scotland remained part of the UK, the campaign was a catastrophe for Labour; many of its natural supporters, repelled by the alliance, defected *en masse* to the Scottish National Party. In the UK general election of 2015, a once-dominant Labour presence north of the border was all but eliminated. Labour, which had previously held forty-one of Scotland's fifty-nine parliamentary seats, was left with a solitary Member of Parliament.

Labour's self-distancing from the Conservatives, however, wasn't just down to the traumatic memory of the Scottish campaign. When Corbyn assumed the leadership in 2015, both he and John McDonnell met Hilary Benn and Angela Eagle, the new shadow first secretary of state, to discuss the campaign and suggested – to their chagrin – that Corbyn emulate Harold Wilson's more detached approach in the referendum. While Benn and Eagle wanted what McDonnell calls a 'straightforward, "we back Europe" campaign, with no criticisms of EU institutions', McDonnell himself concluded that, with most Labour members and Labour voters backing Remain, in order to safeguard the left's political project, the party must do the same, but he wanted a more 'sceptical' stance towards the EU – something which reflected a more widespread contempt for uncritical Remainers among the Corbyn leadership. As one senior aide puts it dismissively of the pro-EU lobby: 'The EU was their religion, they thought it was the highest level of social development you could aspire to.'

It wasn't hard to understand this scepticism. The official Remain campaign, Britain Stronger in Europe, epitomized the corporate, pro-big business neoliberalism which Corbynism had rebelled against. Its funders included corporate titans such as Goldman Sachs, Morgan Stanley and Airbus. A well-funded organization comprising some 180 staff, it was directed by figures antithetical to the Corbyn project: New Labour stalwart Peter Mandelson; former Lib Dem cabinet minister Danny Alexander; former Tory minister Damian Green; Roland Rudd, a financial services PR executive and brother of the Tory cabinet minister Amber; and Stuart Rose, the former head of Marks & Spencer and a Tory peer. All its key strategic decisions were made by Prime Minister David Cameron and his sidekick George Osborne in Number 11.

From the perspective of the Labour leadership, if this cross-party pro-EU campaign wasn't appealing, neither was the official Labour Remain campaign. Alan Johnson, who headed up the latter, hailed from the Blairite wing of Labour and hated everything Corbyn and his team stood for. 'He resented being in the same room as them,' says Andrew Fisher, Corbyn's policy chief, with the result that 'nothing was ever coordinated'. Johnson's contempt for the left was visceral. At the parliamentary vote on approving military action in Syria in December 2015, the left-wing Labour MP Clive Lewis couldn't get a seat in the rammed parliamentary chamber, and sat on a step. Seeing Johnson sitting at the end, Lewis greeted him. 'He turned around and said, "Fuck off, and tell your fucking Momentum Trot mates who are plastering my surgery with shit to fuck off as well. You've ruined this party."' Lewis protested that Momentum members were not all nasty or indeed 'Trots'. Johnson ignored him, staring straight ahead.

There was another problem: Johnson was also widely considered to lack political energy and commitment. 'I supported him when he stood for the deputy leadership in 2007, but he just didn't organize,' former Labour Deputy Prime Minister John Prescott told me. 'I said to him, "Do you want this, because you're not putting up a fight," but he didn't.' Another long-standing official of the Communication Workers Union – the trade union Johnson once led – told me: 'He's a bit lazy. I don't think he's driven the way other politicians are driven.'[11] If true, this may have explained his involvement in the referendum campaign itself. Or rather, lack of. Johnson was largely invisible – to me, anyway.

The referendum campaign itself was an internal Tory psychodrama laid bare. Desperate to cement his reputation in history, Cameron veered from an obsessive fear that the referendum would tear the Tories apart whatever the result, and – having won the Scottish referendum and 2015 general election – a belligerent hubris. 'I'm a winner, I can win this,' the prime minister puffed to EU leaders in December 2015. Cameron settled on the same strategy that he had used to secure his narrow victory in the Scottish referendum: to focus on the terrible economic shock that would follow by voting the wrong way – or 'Project Fear', as it was successfully dubbed by the Leave campaign.

The Remain side was hobbled from the start. Britain was in the grip of the Conservatives' austerity policies, wages were being squeezed for the most protracted period since the early nineteenth century, and were lower than they had been before the 2008 financial crash. Although the Tories had benefited from a temporary increase in real wages in the run-up to the 2015 election,[12] those were again stagnating or declining during the referendum campaign.[13] A referendum on the status quo was being held when so many – understandably – were disillusioned with it. The EU became a lightning rod for their grievances.

Then there was the poisoned ground on which the referendum would actually be fought: immigration. The previous summer of 2015 saw a peak in Europe's refugee crisis: a million humans fled war, violence and persecution across the Mediterranean; nearly 4,000 drowned as they did so. British newspapers splashed with headlines such as 'SEND IN ARMY TO HALT MIGRANT INVASION' and 'THE "SWARM" ON OUR STREETS'. Ironically, David Cameron himself had spent years demonizing migrants, fuelling an issue that drove the Leave campaign. In 2011, he declared that 'for too long, immigration has been too high', berating migrants' failure to integrate, causing 'discomfort and disjointedness' in communities. It was a speech the *Daily Telegraph* headlined as: 'David Cameron: migration threatens our way of life'.[14] Cameron set an impossible target to reduce yearly net migration to tens of thousands; when it was repeatedly missed, it undermined faith in democracy and also fuelled the idea that immigration was a problem. During this period, Labour cravenly failed to combat this migrant scapegoating, making repeated interventions which only helped stoke the issue, and, during Ed Miliband's 2015 general election campaign, even selling election mugs emblazoned with the slogan 'Controls on immigration'. By the time of the referendum, immigration frequently topped polls as voters' main concern. With very few in public life willing to make a pro-migrant case – and with government policies fuelling social crises, ranging from falling living standards to a lack of affordable housing to crumbling public services, for which migrants were now being blamed – the backdrop for the referendum could hardly have been less favourable for Remain.

In the first months of Corbyn's leadership, Labour was split on how to approach the referendum: whether to follow Hilary Benn's wholehearted embracing of the EU; or Corbyn's own strategy of 'Remain and Reform' – a phrase coined by Seumas Milne – acknowledging that there were things wrong with the EU and reforms were needed, but that it was right to stay in. Both messages were being promoted: one by the Labour leadership, the other by the official Labour Remain campaign. The result was confusion – which, predictably, the anti-Corbyn brigade in the Labour Party sought to exploit. Ten days before the electorate went to the polls, a senior Labour official opined to a like-minded colleague that they thought Remain would win 'but at least if not, Corbyn will clearly be seen to be responsible'. In other words, the Labour bureaucracy would have been all too happy for Corbyn to be the fall guy.

From exchanges like these, a story has since been spun that Corbyn's leadership intentionally sabotaged the Remain campaign because of its own Leave inclinations. There was in fact no conspiracy – but there were plenty of cock-ups, of a kind that bedevilled the leader's office. And there was, too, a hint of deliberate obstructiveness.

Mark Simpson is the son of a Labour Member of the European Parliament and worked for about eight years in Brussels as the political officer for the party's MEPs. He was therefore well placed to become Corbyn's key lead on EU matters; one colleague describes him as 'unique, as a non-Corbynite in the centre of the Corbyn camp'. During the referendum campaign, Simpson's job was to look after Corbyn, help write his speeches, and liaise between the leader's office and the party's largely anti-Corbyn HQ at Southside. Ideally, in a campaign with which Labour were supposed to be engaged with the seriousness of a general election, the leader's office would have imposed its will on the uncritically pro-EU Southside. Whether that was politically possible or not, it failed to do so.

While Corbyn's strategy and communications director, Seumas Milne, had Leave sympathies, most staffers – such as chief of staff Simon Fletcher and policy chief Andrew Fisher – were sincerely committed to Remain and Reform. Corbyn himself seemed equivocal. Twelve days before the referendum, he appeared on *The Last Leg*, a late-night comedy TV talk show, where he rated his passion for staying in the EU as a 'seven, or seven and a half' out of ten.[15] Corbyn, Simpson implies to me, was more agnostic than that, describing his Remain position as 'values driven, like working together on climate change', and while Corbyn subscribed partly to the idea that the EU was a 'capitalist club, entrenching capitalism and neoliberalism, he didn't do so wholeheartedly; it didn't turn him on in any way'. In this, Corbyn mirrored the British electorate at the time: even among Remainers, fervent support for the EU was a fringe position in 2016.

For all that, Corbyn did his bit for the pro-EU cause, making big set-piece speeches at pro-Remain rallies across the country; there were frequently queues around the block to hear him. But there was, characteristically, the absence of a media strategy – sometimes, journalists were not invited to those events – and for that, Mark Simpson blames Milne. 'He was really, really difficult in it all,' says Simpson. 'Seumas is always deeply worried about being tarred with the "establishment" brush.' This, he suggests, was the worst sort of campaign for Milne: one that could so easily be construed as an 'establishment stitch-up'. Fearing that Labour's embrace of Remain would alienate working-class communities and fatally suppress the insurgent spirit of Corbynism, Milne therefore took up an equivocal position on Remain. It was, Simpson concludes, a serious mistake: 'the idea that the blame [for Brexit] would fall on the Tories, not us, was completely naïve, it was fanciful.' When the *Daily Mirror* organized a letter with a 'Remain and Reform' theme, it was signed by all but six Labour MPs; Milne removed Corbyn's name. For others in the leader's office, there were more mundane reasons for failures in the campaign. 'Corbyn did loads of events, and the reason it didn't get lots of pick-up wasn't because we didn't try,' said one staffer, 'it was that we just didn't know how to get pick-up.'

It was true that with much of the media framing the referendum as a battle for the soul of the Conservatives, Labour struggled to get into the spotlight. Laura Parker, Corbyn's private secretary, recalls how he made a persuasive, high-profile pro-EU speech in front of senior journalists at the Institute of Engineering Technology just off the Strand in central London, three weeks before the referendum.[16] 'It was a very good speech, he turned up on time, he had a decent suit, the big guns were there,' Parker recalls. When the team later returned to the office to watch the coverage, they found themselves staring instead at an extended clip of Boris Johnson auctioning off a cow in Clitheroe, southwest England, in a stunt focusing on the

Common Agricultural Policy.[17] 'I understood then that we were really in trouble,' Parker tells me. 'But I didn't sense other people thinking that.'

Nonetheless, those who staffed the Corbyn project – attracted by the ideals of socialism, not fighting a status quo referendum campaign on behalf of David Cameron's Conservative government – were bored by the whole thing. Rory Macqueen, an adviser in John McDonnell's office, looking back at his notes from the time, which showed he expected Remain to win, admits he 'found the whole thing fucking tedious' and wished it was all over. Joss MacDonald, Corbyn's speechwriter, agrees: 'Most people in LOTO did not take it seriously at all. Most thought if we left, it wouldn't really cause us any political difficulties.' That attitude went right to the top of the leadership. Corbyn's aides are insistent that he voted to Remain – despite later widely circulated conspiracy theories that he opted for Leave – but that he regarded the whole referendum campaign as a huge inconvenience, and indeed would rather talk about anything else, and that he was convinced that a vote for Leave would be far more politically damaging for the Conservatives.

The prevailing attitude in Corbyn's team was that, while the victory would be narrow, Remain was a near-certainty to triumph in the referendum. As one senior aide said, 'I thought basically the polls were running very close, but a small percentage would take flight, hear stories about the supermarkets not stocking food and ATMs not working if we voted Leave.' In Mike Hatchett's words, convinced that Remain would win regardless, the Labour leadership 'focused on landing in the right place politically'. But it was in this equivocal support for Remain that Labour's later problems were born – and even at this point, the gaps were beginning to open between Leave and Remain factions within the party. With the leadership having more or less switched off, they failed to take account of what individual Labour MPs – mostly in England's de-industrialized North – were picking up during the referendum campaign: the strength of support for Leave.

At the time, Gloria de Piero – a plain-speaking former broadcast journalist, often to be spotted puffing at an e-cigarette – was MP for Ashfield, a former mining area in the East Midlands with depressed wages and a lack of amenities. She stopped knocking on doors early on, realizing she was inadvertently doing 'Get Out The Vote' for the other side by reminding the Leave-inclined when the referendum was. 'Whenever I spoke to them, it was a bit to do with immigration, and of going back to the sense they think the best days were behind them, not ahead,' she explains. 'It was: "we can be good on our own again, like we used to be, standing on our two feet".' On the doorstep, she found that people were happy, positive, looking forward to leaving the EU. A schism was opening up in Labour's electoral coalition. De Piero's best friend, Vicky Foxcroft, Labour MP for Lewisham Deptford, an overwhelmingly Remain constituency in southeast London, came to visit Ashfield during the campaign. 'She said, "Fucking hell, all of these Leave posters,"' recalls de Piero. Both represented Labour heartlands, but while Remain stickers plastered the windows of houses in Foxcroft's constituency, Leave paraphernalia blanketed Ashfield. 'They couldn't fucking wait to vote Leave,' says de Piero. 'There was nothing I could do to persuade them, nothing at all.'

As the referendum date approached, and it was increasingly evident that things were in the balance, the anti-Corbyn Labour HQ's attitude suddenly shifted. 'When they realized things were going wrong and they weren't reaching parts of the left, they wanted Jeremy out more and more,' Andrew Fisher tells me. Indeed, polling in the run-up to the referendum showed that Corbyn was the most trusted politician in Britain on the issue – especially among the Remain-inclined.[18] Labour HQ started trying to script portions of Corbyn's speeches, demanding he weave in what Fisher described as 'combining Project Fear with unalloyed EU fandom'. The leader's office pushed back. This was simply not how Corbyn spoke and would therefore be inauthentic, they countered. The result, once again, was muddle instead of clarity. Days before the referendum, Corbyn spoke in the northern town of Rotherham (where over two thirds of voters would plump for Leave), just near Orgreave, the site of an iconic pitched battle in the Miners' Strike of 1984–5. 'Jeremy should have gone across the road and spoken in the field, got 1,000 ex-miners there, spoken about collectivism, on his own terms and language,' says one leading Corbyn ally. 'But because there was no engagement in how the campaign was designed, he ended up a hostage to the Alan Johnson campaign and its narrative.'

Ultimately, it wasn't Labour's leadership which doomed Remain. The official campaign acted as though it was taking a calculator to a knife fight. Where the Remain side concentrated simply on a cold economic argument lacking any soul, Vote Leave focused on emotion, deploying the devastatingly effective 'Take Back Control' and scaremongering about migrants, concocting the false claim that Turkey would join the EU, and distributing lists of EU rapists and murderers in Britain. The Leave campaign, too, had learned a lesson from the Scottish referendum. Then, the pro-independence movement had published a White Paper offering what the SNP's First Minister Alex Salmond described as the 'most comprehensive blueprint for an independent country ever published'. In doing this, the SNP opened itself up to scrutiny. Rather than a happy abstract idea, independence became something real, tangible – and it could be attacked. The Leave campaign, accordingly, didn't define its plan for Brexit at all: with no plan, there could be no risk. They portrayed the referendum as simply a vote to leave the EU, with no sense of how close or distant the ensuing relationship would be. Trying to scrutinize Brexit was like nailing jelly to a wall.

On 26 May 2016, four weeks before the referendum, the Office for National Statistics revealed that net migration to the UK had risen to 333,000, only 3,000 fewer than the recorded peak.[19] Just two days later, more than 8.5 million postal votes were issued for the referendum, and would end up comprising over a fifth of the total votes cast.[20] Millions were voting with these high migration figures at the forefront of their minds. According to the early returns, Remain was losing 70–30 on postal votes. Given postal voters tended to be disproportionately older voters who favoured Leave, a majority for the latter would be expected, but these margins were dangerously high. To win the referendum, Remain needed to win 54–46 on polling day itself.

Then came the darkest day. On 21 June, I was sitting in a studio in the *Guardian* building near King's Cross station, recording a video called 'Brexit: prepare yourself'. In it, I warned that a Leave victory was likely and would be followed by a right-wing Tory power grab, an escalation of anti-immigration sentiments and an early general election. A push notification flashed up on my phone: a Labour MP had been stabbed and shot in West Yorkshire. Some hours later, as I arrived at St Pancras station to catch a train to Nottingham for a rally held by the left-wing Remain and Reform movement Another Europe Is Possible, I received a text: the Labour MP Jo Cox had been murdered. We cancelled the rally. It later transpired Cox was the victim of a far-right terrorist who later gave his name in court as 'Death to traitors, freedom for Britain'.

Corbyn had spent the day delivering big speeches in Doncaster and Sheffield in South Yorkshire. Mark Simpson was with him as news of the attack on Jo Cox came through. When they arrived in London, met by a police escort, a phone call confirmed her death. Simpson was personally devastated: his girlfriend had been very good friends with Cox. 'Jeremy was absolutely phenomenal that day,' he recalls. 'The way he handled it, the way he led on it, the way he brought people into the leader's office to update them with the information. He had my utmost respect. He was quite a rock to a lot of people who were upset, very scared and worried. He was top notch.'

The next day, for the only time in the campaign, Corbyn and Cameron appeared alongside each other in public to leave floral tributes in Birstall, where the MP had been killed. Less than a week before the referendum, campaigning was suspended for two days.

Inevitably, the different campaigns considered the impact of an act of political murder so close to a referendum – including, egregiously, the Brexit-championing UKIP leader, Nigel Farage, who stated that his side did have momentum until this terrible tragedy. On the weekend before Thursday's vote, a senior BBC journalist told me that he believed Remain would be boosted; many on the Remain side, by contrast, felt that the suspension of campaigning had come just as they had been building momentum.

On referendum day, 23 June 2016, the last poll of the campaign landed, giving Remain a ten-point lead. When I arrived at the ITV studios near King's Cross that evening for the results programme, a senior figure from the *Sun* newspaper told me that No. 10 believed the poll, expecting a slam dunk victory.

The results trickled in: Sunderland was 61–39 in favour of Leave, but nearly exactly what the campaign had expected, 60–40. Newcastle, they projected, would be 52–48 for Remain; it came in 51–49. Britain had voted 52 per cent to 48 per cent to leave the EU. Postal votes had proved pivotal. Ironically, on the actual day itself the country had voted 52–48 in favour of Remain.

Whatever the failings on Labour's part, the later claim that responsibility for the result lay with Corbyn belies the actual evidence. While a large chunk of Labour voters – people let down by the deindustrialization of the 1980s and then by austerity – voted Leave, two thirds of Labour supporters did opt for Remain – a similar proportion as the voters of the avowedly pro-Remain Scottish National Party. Where it went so badly wrong is that only 40 per cent of Tory supporters voted Remain. The wavering demographic that in the end plumped for Leave was, explains the head of Britain Stronger in Europe, Will Straw, 'the 10 per cent of well-to-do shire Tories who had not very much to lose – probably retired owner-occupiers. They were essentially fed up with David Cameron, and quite liked flirting with Johnson and Gove. That's what cost us the referendum.'

But the Labour leadership wasn't prepared for the result, nor for the opprobrium that followed – from Labour HQ. 'It was depressing, people were openly hostile to us, the staff were just blaming us, just treating us like shit on their shoes,' recalls one senior Corbyn aide. 'It was a very hostile atmosphere.' Yet the leader's office had drafted nothing in advance of the result: no statement, not even a tweet. In the early hours of 24 June, as the outcome became clear, Andrew Fisher sat in Labour Party HQ thrashing out a script with Seumas Milne and Simon Jackson, Labour's director of policy and research. As far as the Labour leadership was concerned, this was a defeat for David Cameron and the Tories and a repudiation of Conservative austerity policies. In hindsight, Fisher thinks this first statement was misjudged: 'a little bit emotionally cold to people's feelings about having lost the referendum. It was more a tone of "we are leaving and must respect the vote", not, "oh my goodness, we're leaving the EU which means this and that".'

In Corbyn's first TV interview after the result, he struck much the same note. Stating his acceptance of the referendum result, he listed the social reasons that drove people to vote Leave, and said that Article 50 of the Lisbon Treaty, whose triggering would begin the process of leaving the bloc, 'must be invoked now'. It was a comment that provoked outrage among Corbyn's critics. As one of his closest allies acknowledges, 'it was a blunder, unfortunate language' and it fuelled the sense that Corbyn had been a secret Leaver all along. But Andrew Fisher is adamant that it was not a gaffe, that 'he meant now not as in immediately, but as now, as a consequence of this event'. For Corbyn's enemies in the Labour Party, the interview helped weaponize the Brexit issue among Labour's broadly pro-Remain membership, becoming the pretext for the attempted leadership coup that summer.

The referendum result was, for many, a moment of genuine trauma. Labour MPs wept down their phones to their advisers. 'It was absolute meltdown,' says Jonathan Ashworth, a non-Corbynite who served in the shadow cabinet throughout Corbyn's tenure. 'We hadn't properly understood just how visceral it was for a lot of Labour MPs, about how much the EU meant to them,' says Andrew Fisher. For all this, the leadership challenger that summer, Owen Smith, ran on a platform of a second referendum, which even many staunch Remainers thought a big mistake. Smith's crushing defeat underlined that most of the membership prioritized socialism over membership of the EU.

In summer 2016, just after the referendum, Gloria de Piero sat at a bus stop in Ashfield with her partner, on the first leg of their journey back to another world, Westminster. A woman sitting next to them, in perhaps her late sixties, recognized de Piero and asked: 'Do you think we'll actually leave?' De Piero was baffled. 'I said "Of course we will, there's been a referendum." Not for one second did I think otherwise. I thought it was an odd question. But she was wiser than I was.'

At first, Labour's commitment to upholding the referendum result didn't seem controversial. When, in February 2017, some eight months after the referendum, the government called a parliamentary vote on triggering Article 50, the then besieged Labour leadership knew it had no choice but to support the move. Otherwise the Tories would call a general election on the basis that Labour was obstructing the referendum result. Although some Labour shadow ministers resigned because they feared angering their strongly Remain constituencies, they did not do so to undermine the leadership. Indeed, the most high-profile of these resigners, Clive Lewis, was rooted firmly in the party's left and had backed Corbyn in both leadership elections. Meanwhile, the likes of Chuka Umunna and Wes Streeting – both of whom hailed from the party's right and in time would become champions of a second referendum – wrote an article explaining their support for triggering Article 50, arguing that 'We believe as democrats that we must abide by the national result which is a clear choice to leave the EU', and that 'to stand against the decision of the country would be to deepen Labour and the country's divisions'.[21] Though forty-seven Labour MPs rebelled along with Lib Dems and nationalists, over three quarters of parliamentarians voted to trigger the start of the Brexit process. Nonetheless, Labour was notably more divided than the Tories. As Labour's lead Brexit researcher Mark Simpson admitted, 'You saw the beginnings of a split in the Tory Party, but it was completely minor compared to where we were.'

The first meaningful splits in the party leadership came with the six tests Labour drew up in March 2017 as conditions for backing a Brexit deal: a 'strong and collaborative future relationship with the EU', the 'exact same benefits' of the single market and customs union, fair management of migration, defending rights and protections, protecting national security and delivering 'for all regions and nations of the UK'. The tests were internally divisive, to say the least. Shadow cabinet member Jon Trickett, is pithy in his dismissal of them. 'Look at the details of Labour's tests. They simply were piss weak.' Above all else, he objected to a 'status quo argument' of just retaining existing rights and conditions in the labour market. 'You can't sell that to people in my constituency thrown out of mines thirty-five years ago and who've got nowt even now,' he thunders. 'Why would we support exactly the same so-called rights which they already have, but which have held back the Yorkshire coalfield? They voted Brexit to reject the status quo. If Labour was insisting that our response to Brexit was to say: let's keep what we already have, they will think "hang on we voted to leave and now we are being told by Labour stick with what we have got. Get stuffed." The same applies to all the de-industrialized regions in our country.' At one strategy meeting, Trickett made his objections so forcefully that Corbyn was described as 'visibly pale'. Whatever the individual merits of the pledges, they were effectively a holding position, and summed up what would become a growing problem for Labour: having a stance on Brexit that was indecipherable and impenetrable to most. When asked, shadow ministers, even Corbyn himself, would struggle to remember the tests.

Not that these internal fractures were immediately visible. Theresa May's intention to frame the 2017 general election as a Brexit-focused, 'people versus Parliament' contest, did not work. After all, unlike the 2019 election contest, there had not been two and a half years of wrangling and deadlock, and there wasn't an imminent departure deadline hovering over the nation. Labour's manifesto declared uncomplicatedly that it 'accepts the referendum result', although it declared a 'strong emphasis on retaining the benefits of the Single Market and the Customs Union'. Suitably vague wording, which allowed it more or less to brush the issue aside. 'In the 2017 election, everyone was of the same mind,' recalls John McDonnell: 'that we had to accept the result, but get a best result, with a nod and a wink, as near as damn it to EU membership. I can't remember many interviews in the campaign where Brexit was thrust in my face as a challenge. We managed it through the whole campaign.'

The myth later spread by some Remainers that Labour's gains in the 2017 election were essentially won with Remain votes was demonstrably wrong. Chuka Umunna, the bitterly anti-Corbyn, then Labour MP, swanned smugly around Parliament claiming that his increased majority in his Streatham constituency was down to his personal commitment to the single market and customs union – a claim comprehensively disproven by the case of neighbouring Vauxhall, an equally Remain constituency which had nonetheless handed an increased majority to Labour MP Kate Hoey, a zealous Brexiteer who had campaigned alongside Nigel Farage in the EU referendum. That did not stop Umunna tabling an amendment soon after the election trying to bounce Labour into backing the single market. 'The relationship between the whips' office and Umunna was very very

very difficult,' says Chief Whip Nick Brown. 'He wouldn't speak to us, though he was obliged to because of his membership of the Labour Party, and told me that I shouldn't indicate to his face what the voting was going to be. It got to the point where I was required to get him to abide by it. He was a very unpleasant individual in my opinion.'

Yet the election result contained warning signs for Labour. Despite gaining thirty-six seats across the country, it lost six seats in the North and Midlands: all had heavily voted for Leave. Gloria de Piero had been convinced she would lose her Ashfield seat. In the end, while her vote actually went up, the Tories nearly doubled their support in her constituency, reducing her majority from approaching 9,000 to a wafer-thin 500, forcing a recount. There were, too, swings against Labour in 130 constituencies, notably in strong Leave seats such as Bolsover, while the Tories won their highest vote share in the Leave-voting Northeast since 1983.[22] De Piero was scathing about the post-election hubris in the Labour leader's office: 'While everyone was getting intoxicated with depriving the Tories of a majority, no one wanted to look at what had happened in coalfields, in white working-class areas,' she says. 'There were warning signs – but nobody wanted to look at them.'

That wasn't entirely true. Some Corbyn advisers, like Seumas Milne, Jon Trickett and Andrew Murray, had undoubted Eurosceptic leanings, but their ideological bent was trumped by sincere electoral considerations which they held in good faith: the swing against Labour in Leave-supporting constituencies had left the Tories within striking distance of taking them, while many strong pro-Remain seats had huge Labour majorities where the party could afford to haemorrhage support. Meanwhile, in forty-one out of the fifty-four Tory-held target seats Labour needed to win if it wished to form a government, a majority had voted to Leave[23] – and the nature of Britain's non-proportional electoral system meant that the party had to prioritize voters in marginal seats over safe seats. 'It was fucking mad to go in a Remain direction given where the votes are,' says Andrew Murray. 'You have to win under a first-past-the-post system, and we could see from 2017 where we were vulnerable.'

It's at this moment, however, that Labour made a fatal mistake. In the aftermath of the 2017 election, Corbyn had immense political capital. Labour MPs who had very recently been plotting to overthrow their leader were now serenading him with 'Oh, Jeremy Corbyn!'; he even received an extremely irregular standing ovation from his MPs in the House of Commons. His approval ratings with the electorate had soared. The Tories, by contrast, were in utter turmoil, and Theresa May was 'a dead woman walking'. It was the ideal moment for Corbyn to make categorically clear that Labour would never support a new referendum, and would seek to implement the 2016 decision. And, while acknowledging the hurt of a majority Remain membership, Corbyn should make the case that it would be impossible for Labour to win a general election by overturning the referendum result. That way, Labour could present a clearly defined Brexit plan that would include close relationship with the EU (assuaging uneasy Remainers by focusing on workers' rights, environmental rights and protecting jobs, as well as presenting the potential economic upsides of Brexit), and demand a meeting with May's government to hammer out the details, allowing Labour – and the country as a whole – to pivot back to the domestic issues which mattered.

In order to sell such a message, though, Labour would have first needed to define its Brexit position clearly – and it didn't. The unfocused detachment that the Labour leadership had shown in the referendum aftermath simply continued – especially when campaigning in those precarious Leave-voting Labour seats in the Midlands and the North. The top team – not least Seumas Milne – persisted in its belief that Labour's Brexit position should be kept intentionally vague, and the party should avoid talking about it at all in favour of domestic policies: this was, after all, the approach that secured 40 per cent of the vote and deprived the Tories of their majority. The vagueness was only exacerbated by profound differences among the leadership over what a Labour Brexit should actually look like.

But hindsight is a marvellous thing. After the 2017 election, it really did seem as though the Tory government was enveloped in an existential crisis, and that Brexit would finish it off. For the first time, Corbyn's Labour had a moment of unity. Why would you choose that moment to kick up a fight, to alienate currently jubilant members, aggravate liberal Remainers who were now willing to give Labour a chance, to distract attention away from the Conservatives' travails – or worse, to look like you are trying to bail them out over Brexit? And indeed, would such clearer positioning have worked? Or would it merely have provided more of a focus for Corbyn's hostile pro-Remain opponents to congregate around? Moreover, no one who knows Corbyn truly believes he would ever have wanted to take on the Labour membership – on this or indeed anything. 'We were on a conveyor belt to this fucking disaster show back then,' a senior adviser told me. 'The Brexit problem, we've always been getting there. Could we have done it better? Obviously, had we tried to nail the argument back then, maybe. But it doesn't seem credible or realistic.'

Instead, there was a tentativeness surrounding Brexit in the leadership team, with Corbynites tiptoeing around the issue as if it were some kind of unexploded bomb. 'Internally there was never any policy coherence in response to what Brexit should be,' says James Schneider, Corbyn's former spokesperson and head of strategic communications. 'There were two coherent Labour policy positions: one, the EU is not that great anyway, democracy is important, let's chart a progressive course to leaving. The other one is, leaving the EU is very bad, so we should try and cushion the blow as much as possible, and if possible, stop it.' But there was never a means to have that debate within the party – according to Schneider, Labour 'hummed and hawed between the two positions'. Schneider recalls McDonnell declaring as early as November 2016 that Labour 'must embrace the enormous opportunities to reshape our country that Brexit has opened for us'. 'The internal backlash we got on that was dramatic,' Schneider recalls. Such exercises were rarely repeated. 'The balance of forces within the labour movement were hugely on the side of "Brexit is bad, let's try and cushion the blow and stop it." Which is totally understandable because the older generation had been broadly convinced by the Delors speech to the TUC in 1988, and the younger people had never heard a Eurosceptic argument which hadn't been made by some arch-reactionary.' This was precisely why there existed a cross-generational anti-Brexit position among Labour's membership: older members had come to see the EU as a lifeboat in a sea of icy Thatcherism, whereas younger people understandably associated Euroscepticism with migrant-bashing Farageists.

The leadership, accordingly, found itself shying away from talking about Brexit in any positive way at all. 'It was very difficult to talk about any potential benefits of Brexit,' says Alex Nunns, one of Corbyn's speechwriters. 'Identify any opportunities for a socialist government outside the EU – even while acknowledging the drawbacks – and you'd have ultra-Remainers frothing at the mouth and creating a fake controversy that would probably drown out rather than amplify the message. So the most we felt we could do was acknowledge the sentiments of Leave voters in wanting to kick the establishment.'

In February 2018, Labour formally committed to staying in the European customs union, a position backed by the likes of John McDonnell, the increasingly influential Corbynite Shadow Secretary of State for Business Rebecca Long-Bailey, and the Remain-leaning Shadow Brexit Secretary Keir Starmer. 'Keir thought it was the way to go,' recalls Andrew Fisher, 'and Jeremy wasn't hostile, he was OK with it, he thought it was a logical extension of what we said in 2017.' Predictably, Seumas Milne was opposed to the shift, believing that Labour did not need to be that explicit about its Brexit plans. The problem, however, was that by this point the narrative around Brexit had begun to polarize: on one side, a growing Remain movement; on the other, a Conservative government with a full-throated endorsement of Brexit. As the two sides pulled further apart, Labour was left trying to sit on two stools and its position started to look like a weak compromise. It was the usual problem. Convinced that, as Mark Simpson pointed out, 'Brexit is worse for the Tories than us,' the divided Labour leadership sat tight and waited, refusing to reveal its non-existent hand.

In 2018 the pro-Remain movement gathered pace. As far as Unite chief of staff and Corbyn adviser Andrew Murray is concerned, Labour's failure to stick to a firm position on Brexit opened up a space for such a movement to develop. There are convincing parallels, he believes, with the movement against the war in Iraq. 'About a year lapsed between Bush and Blair signalling their intention to go to war: that's space to mobilize and win arguments,' he suggests. 'I think Labour similarly created the space for a mass Remain movement.' That April, Britain Stronger In Europe, relaunching as Open Britain, spearheaded the People's Vote campaign, whose founding premise was that any Brexit deal should be put to the British people in another referendum (aka a 'People's Vote') alongside another option: to remain in the EU. People's Vote's professed neutrality on the issue was completely unconvincing. Whether or not they supported it, the British people saw the campaign as a route to stop Brexit; frankly, it would have been better to be open about it. Once again chaired by Tory Home Secretary Amber Rudd's brother Roland, People's Vote largely comprised an amalgamation of Labour MPs who were becoming increasingly hostile to Jeremy Corbyn, the Liberal Democrats and pro-EU Tory MPs like Anna Soubry. People's Vote quickly amassed hundreds of thousands of emails, launched a parliamentary lobbying operation and organized increasingly large and passionate demonstrations. As far as most of the Corbyn leadership were concerned, though, People's Vote was – like its previous incarnation – a hostile entity.

The Remain movement was not homogeneous: it had good faith and bad faith actors. The good faith brigade believed straightforwardly that Brexit was an act of terrible self-harm which would damage the country's economy and its international standing; those of a leftish bent abhorred the nativism and xenophobia that underpinned the Tory interpretation of Brexit, and feared the slashing of workers' rights, social protections and environmental measures that it betokened. But there was also an extremely influential bad faith element who, while they may well have agreed with much of this analysis, saw Brexit as a convenient wedge issue, something to provoke a split between the Labour leadership and the largely pro-Remain Labour membership and voter base. 'Some MPs thought it was a way to destabilize Jeremy Corbyn with the membership,' says Gloria de Piero (who was herself no Corbynite, having voted against him in both leadership elections and resigned from the frontbench in 2016). De Piero herself wasn't sure where the line lay between good and bad faith actors – but she had no doubt of the latter's influence. One such was former New Labour spin doctor Peter Mandelson, who became a key figure in the People's Vote campaign, and who publicly declared: 'Why do you want to just walk away and pass the title deeds of this great party over to someone like Jeremy Corbyn? I don't want to, I resent it, and I work every day in some small way to bring forward the end of his tenure in office. Something, however small it may be – an email, a phone call or a meeting I convene – every day I try to do something to save the Labour Party from his leadership.'[24]

Remain, then, became a means for a political faction that had become consigned to near irrelevance to revive itself. Spanning Labour's Blairites and those elements of the Conservative Party who clustered round David Cameron and George Osborne, this faction combined support for market economics and a generally hawkish foreign policy stance with inconsistent support for social liberalism: champions of equal marriage, they have a patchy history on immigration rhetoric and policy. (Thumbs up for markets and gays, in summary.) It was also united by the fact that its various elements had been cast into the political wilderness by the Corbynite and Brexit groups which had triumphed within their respective parties. The most common term applied to this faction is 'centrist' – though this is itself profoundly misleading. The centre ground in public opinion favours more state intervention and more social conservatism, the direct inverse of their own worldview, in other words. But in the absence of a consensus over any other descriptor, that's what we'll use.

At the elite level, these 'centrists' included former senior politicians, political special advisers, party bureaucrats and think tank wonks, alongside newspaper columnists, senior political reporters, editors and producers in the mainstream press and broadcast media. Many of these figures now found their access to networks of power and influence – always something they had previously taken for granted – barred. They were brought together by a sense of nostalgia for a golden age of rational, stable, 'centrist' politics – apparently represented by the Blair or Cameron years, which they had bestrode. They understood the subsequent political polarization on left and right since as mass irrationality, a hysterical departure from sacred liberal values. For them, Remain was a golden opportunity, a cause to crystallize around. It also provided the ghosts of New Labour past – like former spin doctor Alastair Campbell – a chance to claw back relevance, to loom large once more in a new present.

Tom Baldwin, the fast-talking, gruffly cheerful former director of communications and strategy to Ed Miliband, arrived at my flat two months after the fateful 2019 election and weeks before the coronavirus lockdown. Back in June 2018, he became the director of communications to the People's Vote campaign. Baldwin joined People's Vote in good faith: he genuinely wanted a new referendum in order to stop Britain's divorce from the EU, a divorce that he believed would damage his country, which he loves. But it was soon clear to him that many of those he was working with had other priorities. As he recalls the experience across my dinner table, he sounds strained, as though reliving some sort of trauma. 'When I joined, I was slightly taken aback by the extent to which People's Vote was dominated by the political personalities of Chuka Umunna and Anna Soubry, with Chris Leslie and others in the background.' The three names Baldwin mentions – the then Labour MPs Umunna and Leslie, and the Conservative Soubry – were classic 'centrists', deeply at odds with their party leaderships.

There's no disguising Baldwin's frustration with People's Vote. It was, he says, 'seen as quite exclusive': those running it didn't appear to want to expand the campaign's political range, to collaborate with a broader spectrum of Labour or Tory politicians beyond the already out-and-out convinced and passionate supporters of another referendum. When Baldwin proposed getting Labour on board, they batted it away: 'we've tried, forget it, it's over.' Here, Baldwin believes, is where ulterior political motives came in. The major players in People's Vote, he says, had a strategy 'to say that Labour was going to betray a Remain vote which had propelled it to a decent [general election] result in 2017. And that was their language and what they were doing in Parliament.' When, in June 2018, the first mass People's Vote demonstration – attended by 100,000 people – took place, 'they were looking for an opportunity to define themselves against the Labour leadership. That was not the view of the campaign staff or James McGrory [the director of People's Vote] or myself – but Chuka and Anna were quite dominant characters at that time.'

In response, Baldwin tried to preserve the neutrality of People's Vote. He sought to broaden the range of Labour voices in the campaign, to emphasize that it had no views on the Labour leadership, and to focus on securing a new referendum – and, he says, he came down hard on anyone who 'tried to cloud that'. Initially, he had some success: both Umunna and Soubry began angrily complaining that their roles in People's Vote had diminished. They repeatedly, though unsuccessfully, pushed for an early parliamentary vote on a new referendum, knowing that by doing so, they would put Labour on the spot. Corbyn's MPs would vote against such a move, allowing Umunna and Soubry's allies to turn ardent Remainers against his party. Within Labour, this faction of the People's Vote MPs caused huge frustration among Keir Starmer's operation, who believed that they were trying to cause difficulties for the leadership, rather than advance the Remain cause.

'It was really clear to a lot of us,' Baldwin continues, that a few – by no means most – of the MPs backing People's Vote were using the campaign to do something else. 'They were mobilizing to create a breakaway party,' a new political party driven by unabashedly pro-EU, 'centrist' values. Baldwin himself vociferously argued for not conflating the two projects – the questions of a new referendum and a new party must not be confused, he told his employers. Increasingly, however, his voice was drowned out. On the eve of the general election, the People's Vote chairman, Roland Rudd, staged a boardroom coup sacking Baldwin, as part of his drive to get the campaign to use its resources to back the Liberal Democrats. But there was one meaningful consequence: the People's Vote campaign imploded.

Throughout 2018, as Conservative Prime Minister Theresa May's Brexit ran into the sand, another distinct Remain insurgency gathered speed within the Labour Party. The left-aligned Remainer movement Another Europe Is Possible had very different motives from those of the People's Vote campaign. It believed that the anti-Brexit movement should be embraced by the left because it was bound up with progressive causes such as immigration, environmentalism and internationalism – issues at the heart of the Corbyn project. Calling openly for the 2016 referendum result to be reversed, the movement began a mass campaign within the party membership, with one central aim: to get the Corbyn leadership, and the party, to commit to the principle of a 'people's vote' at the Labour Party's upcoming 2018 conference. Combined with other initiatives – such as Remain Labour – they carried out a forensic, highly effective operation to mobilize the membership behind Remain. As national organizer Michael Chessum tells me, 'the fact that it was the left running this campaign helped reclaim the idea that it was not just the right who cared about a public vote or about a firmer stance on Brexit. We detoxified the anti-Brexit cause.'

But there was a problem. Corbyn loyalists, who viewed the People's Vote with understandable suspicion, believed that while Another Europe Is Possible might be acting in good faith, it was providing left cover for a Remain insurgency which could only inflict political damage on the Corbyn project. They gave the movement short shrift, despite their otherwise overlapping political beliefs. 'There was this narrative from the ultra-loyalist crowd of "this is a plot, you're working with the right to undermine Jeremy Corbyn",' says Chessum, 'and that was from every level of the Corbyn project.' After the 2016 referendum, indeed, Labour depressingly abandoned a principled pro-migrant argument, believing that this was unavoidable given a referendum result which was largely driven by opposition to freedom of movement. It was all the greater a betrayal given that the likes of Corbyn, McDonnell and Diane Abbott had, in their wilderness years, steadfastly defended the rights of migrants and refugees at a time when it was unpopular to do so.

Nonetheless, as the Labour conference approached in September 2018, the Remainers within the party felt optimistic. 'At the time,' as one Starmer ally puts it, 'there was a growing feeling for some Remainers that all of Brexit was looking shit, maybe actually there is a way out of it.' It was at this point, he tells me, that then Shadow Brexit Secretary Keir Starmer started to shift. 'He had very much been in the "second referendum is stupid, it's not going to happen, let's just move to a soft Brexit" camp, but just before the 2018 conference he started to come around to that's where it should be.' The Corbyn leadership, however, thought otherwise. Convinced that supporting a second referendum would destroy its chances of winning the Leave-voting constituencies it needed to gain to form a government, it was determined to block the idea.

As far as the Labour leadership's increasingly embattled 'respect the referendum' faction was concerned, the membership's overwhelmingly pro-Remain leanings were entirely unrepresentative of the country as a whole. 'This is what caused all the problems. I was ecstatic at the huge growth in the Labour membership, but this brought new divisions between Southern and Northern members,' says Ian Lavery, then chairman of the party and MP for the Northumberland constituency of Wansbeck. Lavery's view was backed up by recent research showing 'an interesting – but, given the importance of London, by no means total – mismatch between the party's electoral heartlands, which are in the North, and where nearly half of its grassroots supporters are located, in London and the South.'[25] This, Lavery tells me, is a deeply problematic imbalance. 'At conference, you've got thirteen fucking thousand people there – brilliant, absolutely fantastic.' But while 'I don't want to have a battle with anyone about who the heartlands are, and there's lots of people in poverty in London and the Southwest as in the rest of the country,' he qualifies, 'look at how many are from the North and [how many from the] South.' It costs a significant amount of money to attend conference, he notes, and as a result conference is self-selecting, excluding many working-class supporters.

Gloria de Piero passionately agrees with Lavery. Having grown up in poverty in a working-class Bradford community, she recalls there being no central heating or double glazing – 'it was fucking freezing'. De Piero expresses anger that a workers' party has ended up with an overwhelmingly middle-class membership. 'It's not on. The working class get fucked over every day of their lives, decisions don't go their way, but obviously when the middle class suffer something they didn't want happening, they get uppity, "we don't want this!"'

De Piero makes a powerful point. It's true that while a significant majority of Labour supporters were Remain-inclined, those who voted Leave were indeed under-represented in the party membership. Yet it's not as simple as this. For instance, even if you accept the simplistic definition of working class and middle class used by pollsters, looking at the 2016 vote through the lens of voting age gives a very different picture: a majority of working-class people under thirty-five voted Remain – including in the working-class heartlands of Liverpool, Manchester and London – while a majority of middle-class pensioners voted to Leave. Looked at by age, in other words, De Piero's view of the 2016 referendum is turned on its head.

Whatever the case, it was quite clear that, given the groundswell of support for a second referendum among the party grassroots, blocking its official endorsement at the Labour conference wasn't going to be easy. Delegates massing at the conference centre in Liverpool with their 'Love Corbyn Hate Brexit' badges and T-shirts showed the size of the task.

Accordingly, the Labour leadership tried to defuse the issue. Rather than one motion on the party's adoption of a second referendum, to be voted on by the membership present, Corbyn's political secretary, Amy Jackson, argued that there should be two motions: one setting out Labour's opposition to the Tories' approach to Brexit, and a separate, watered-down and non-binding resolution endorsing the referendum as one of many options. Keir Starmer, however, pushed back. There must be, he insisted, one unified motion which included the possibility of a second referendum.

This, it was clear, was where the membership were at: second referendum supporters, so the thinking went, had the backing of about 90 per cent of the room. The unions were less clear-cut. Unite remained opposed to a new 'people's vote', while others – including GMB, the third biggest trade union, and the left-wing transport union TSSA (which had hosted Corbyn's leadership campaigns and housed Momentum's headquarters for a long time) – were pushing for it. Nonetheless, these unions were agreed that a compromise had to be struck to stave off an insurgency which looked as if it would end up committing Labour not just to back a second referendum, but to back Remain as well.

All of which presented Corbynism with a fateful paradox. One of the key planks of Corbyn's leadership campaigns had been the democratization of the Labour Party. He tapped into long-standing resentments among party members, who felt they had long been treated as mere fodder to deliver leaflets and knock on doors at election times, but were otherwise regarded as embarrassments who had no business sticking their noses into important political questions that were better left to advisers in the leader's office. Corbyn, however, was the self-styled tribune of the membership, particularly in his second leadership bid in which he mobilized the support of the grassroots against a recalcitrant, hostile Parliamentary Labour Party.

Since these successes, and the positive result of the 2017 election, many within the party felt that the leadership, having got what it wanted, was once again closing its ears. In mid-2017, for instance, Karie Murphy organized an awayday for all leader's office staff. In one session, she stood at the front with Andrew Fisher and Seumas Milne, giving a talk on election strategy and Labour's election surge. Milne's explanation of the communications strategy, however, caused widespread amusement because it was the first anyone present had heard about it. Murphy then handed out manifestos, autographed by Fisher and Milne, as if they were some kind of superstars. The mood in the room was simmering. 'We sat there thinking "We were there, we did a lot of the work",' says one researcher present. 'It was treating us like we should be fans and learning from them.' Another time, Murphy put a giant 'For The Many Not The Few' correx poster on the wall, signed by the top team. Irritated by a sign championing the many but signed by the few, staffers added their signatures *en masse*, underlining the word 'many'.

Blocking the referendum vote at conference, however, wasn't just a question of irritating a room full of staffers. Rather, it would be a sure signal that the leadership was prepared to chuck its deeply held, loudly trumpeted democratic principles overboard in order to get the outcome it wanted. How could the leadership stand decisively against the aspirations of the membership on the biggest domestic political issue since the Second World War? The membership might have been unrepresentative of the country as a whole, but it was the only membership that the party had.

The motion finally agreed upon, and on which conference delegates would vote, was a fudge, a Rorschach inkblot which could be interpreted differently depending on how you looked at it. The wording accepted 'that the public voted to leave the EU', but not that they were 'voting for fewer rights, economic chaos or to risk jobs'. It championed 'full participation in the Single Market', opposed Theresa May's approach as 'a threat to jobs, freedom of movement, peace in Northern Ireland and the NHS', and enshrined Labour's unmemorable and unwieldy six tests, committing the party to vote against any deal which did not meet them, as well as 'vigorously' opposing a No Deal exit. The motion's priority – if a Tory Brexit deal was voted down in Parliament, or No Deal was on the cards – was an 'immediate general election that can sweep the Tories from power'. If that proved not possible, 'Labour must support all options remaining on the table, including campaigning for a public vote'.

Then, on Monday 24 September, the day before conference was due to vote on the motion, John McDonnell declared on BBC Radio 4's *Today* programme that the public vote the Labour leadership was backing would be only on the nature of the Brexit deal itself, without the inclusion of Remain on the ballot paper.

It was, explains Andrew Fisher, a genuine slip on McDonnell's part: 'John just got a bit caught and hadn't answered in the way he wanted to.' Privately, McDonnell was insistent that he had misspoken and apologized to Starmer. The next day, from the conference podium, Starmer endorsed the motion, then doubled down. 'Nobody is ruling out Remain as an option,' he asserted, an apparent contradiction of McDonnell that met with a spontaneous, rapturous standing ovation in the packed convention centre. Some believe this was opportunism on Starmer's part – a man with future leadership ambitions who knew where the sweet spot of the membership lay. Fisher, though, feels Starmer saw it as a necessary corrective to McDonnell's interview. Having spent hours hammering out the wording of the motion, the shadow Brexit secretary felt duty bound to uphold its spirit.

The problems stemmed from the motion itself, an indecisive stew of perspectives and qualifications; even those who had devised it didn't seem to know what it stood for. The leadership interpreted it as Labour's commitment to focus on delivering a soft Brexit, with a second referendum one of several distant alternative options, while Remainers would increasingly claim that the leadership was in violation of its own democratically agreed policy. It was, said a senior aide, 'at that point people started to have no clue what our position was. It was a disaster.'

Shadow cabinet member Jon Trickett agrees. The lack of a firm position on Brexit left the party at sea on the issue – 'adrift' was how he repeatedly put it. 'In the absence of the leadership saying "we have to go with the referendum, the popular vote and the wishes of the British people", the party gradually drifted – as it would naturally – to oppose the Tories. The Tories were for Brexit, they'd led the Brexit campaign, we'd been equivocal. As the party membership drifted – some didn't drift, they were already there – into an oppositional movement against the Tories, that meant being against Brexit.'

It was natural for Labour as the opposition to – well – oppose the government. Brexit made up almost the entire policy programme of Theresa May's administration. Coupled with the fact that Corbyn's Labour was viscerally opposed to Toryism, shifting to a position which seemed opposed to any form of Brexit, and therefore the result of the 2016 referendum, became almost an inevitability.

Hours after Starmer's speech, delegates at the conference centre on Liverpool's waterfront voted overwhelmingly for the motion; only a smattering voted against. The Remain movement had secured a seismic victory. A growing proportion of the membership and the party's voter base was becoming convinced that, rather than having to tolerate Brexit, there was a way out; it could be reversed. And the party's leadership had no choice but to cater for their political interests.

Two months later, Theresa May secured a deal with the EU for a withdrawal agreement: freedom of movement would end, but a compromise to deal with the vexing issue of Northern Ireland had been struck. A cornerstone of the 1998 Good Friday Agreement, which ended the bloody thirty-year-long Troubles, was that there would exist a porous, open border between the North and the Republic of Ireland. For Unionists, the six Ulster provinces would remain part of the territory of the United Kingdom; but for Nationalists and Republicans, they could live as though a united Ireland was a reality. This proved a formidable obstacle to any Brexit deal. If the UK left the single market and customs union and created its own tariff and regulatory framework, it would necessitate a hard border between Northern Ireland and the Republic to allow for customs checks – which would in turn destabilize the peace process. The alternative was to create a new border in the Irish Sea; but that was unacceptable to the hardline Northern Irish Democratic Unionist Party, upon whose ten MPs May relied for her government's parliamentary majority. In any case, the full name of May's party was the Conservative and

Unionist Party. 'No UK prime minister could ever agree to this,' she declared in the House of Commons in February 2018, Boris Johnson nodding vigorously one seat away from her. The solution, in May's deal, was to kick the can down the road with a temporary 'backstop'. The UK would *de facto* remain in a customs union until alternative arrangements could be agreed.

May's deal was butchered within hours. Hostile fire came from all directions: the Tory Brexiteer right, the so-called 'European Research Group' (ERG); the right-wing press; the Democratic Unionist Party; the Labour leadership, the majority Remain contingent of the PLP and Momentum; the Greens and the Liberal Democrats; the Scottish nationalists; the Remain movement; Nigel Farage's Brexit Party; and the liberal press. This cacophony of voices dominated the airwaves and the newspaper splashes. May's deal was portrayed as Brexit in name only by the right-wing Brexiteers, as too hard a Brexit by Labour and its sympathizers, or simply as a bad incarnation of an always inherently bad Brexit by ever angrier Remainers. There were few voices to defend it, because the government had announced the deal before it had been discussed by cabinet – and in any case, many cabinet ministers had eyes on their political futures and were keenly aware of where the Tory membership was at. In a parliamentary vote in January 2019, May's deal was obliterated by the biggest margin in the history of British democracy: an astonishing majority of 230 against. In the second defeat two months later, this opposition began to crumble – but a majority against of 149 was still absurdly high.

Yet there were those in the Labour leadership who not only believed that May's deal would in fact pass, but felt it was desirable for it to do so. A deal would end the Labour Party's own increasingly torturous Brexit dilemma, they thought, and provide a reset button for British politics, allowing the national debate to shift back onto Corbynism's favoured territory: popular domestic politics articulated through an antagonistic relationship between the majority and the elites. Besides, May's deal was not the end point: the withdrawal agreement was a divorce arrangement, with a future relationship with the EU still to be negotiated. Once in power, Labour could simply adjust the deal according to its own values and priorities, including preventing a race to the bottom in workers' rights, consumer protection and social legislation.

It was simply politically impossible, however, for Labour to come out and vote for May's deal. The idea that Corbyn could now be seen to bail out a Tory government and the cornerstone of its legislative programme was unthinkable. The membership would be traumatized, along with much of Labour's voter base, and Corbyn's opponents in the PLP would have an exceptionally strong pretext to dislodge him, probably successfully this time. 'Labour would have been to millions the party that enabled Brexit and did a deal with the Tories,' explains one senior aide, 'and which failed to take the opportunity to do them in and get a general election when they had a tiny majority.'

During this time, the old narrative – that Brexit was primarily a Tory problem, inflicting more damage on the Conservatives than Labour and therefore more likely to rip the former apart – emerged with redoubled force. May's Conservative government was seen as so unstable that it could collapse at any moment, paving the way for a general election in which Labour could triumph. 'The hung Parliament probably sowed some of the seeds of our destruction,' says Carl Shoben, Labour's director of strategy, 'because from that moment, rather than thinking about a long-term strategy of winning an election, we were in an election mode, thinking that the Tories could collapse at any time and it was our job to make them collapse. Possibly the energy going into making a Tory collapse pushed us into a Brexit position it would have been better not to be in.'

There was another option. Through the early months of 2019, opposition among Tory MPs to May's deal was beginning to crumble, as they feared their precious Brexit was imperilled. In a third vote, at the end of March, the majority against fell steeply from 149 to 58. What if Labour MPs representing Leave seats – who were being angrily berated by constituents unable to understand why something they had voted for going on for three years earlier had not yet happened – allowed it to pass? Between forty and sixty such Labour MPs – including Gloria de Piero and Lisa Nandy – had formed an internal 'Respect the Result' caucus. Seumas Milne, Corbyn's chief of staff, Karie Murphy, and Amy Jackson, who like many

Labour MPs viewed the whips' office as the beating heart of the Remain cause in the party (Murphy, indeed, was keen that Chief Whip Nick Brown be removed), duly bypassed it. Meeting privately with the 'Respect the Result' MPs, the trio suggested they could abstain on key votes without any disciplinary consequences: the MPs should 'do what you have to do'. They were also offered comfort by Unite General Secretary Len McCluskey, whose powerful union remained resolutely opposed to a second referendum, and who assured them that he would provide them with political cover if they did so. 'At the time, they were looking to me to be their shield so they could break the Labour whip and support the Theresa May deal,' McCluskey tells me. 'They needed a shield. They were afraid they would get deselected for going against Corbyn's three-line whip.'

Though Gloria de Piero was an instinctive Blairite, she found herself increasingly isolated by this faction, as it embraced the Remain cause with ever greater zeal. 'These were my colleagues who I thought were friends,' she tells me. 'I've never believed in "no compromise with the electorate" – but the "centrists" took an extreme position and I'm not an extremist. They thought an extreme position was a normal position.' Ironically, de Piero now sought political sanctuary with elements of a left-wing Labour leadership she had strongly opposed. 'We were in there all the time with Amy and Karie and James Schneider and Seumas – it was so weird that they were my fucking safe space. They knew we were right. Jeremy knew we were right, but he just wouldn't stand up to the membership.'

There were a number of reasons why the likes of de Piero could never, in the end, stomach voting for May's deal. For a start, the deal had been so successfully rendered toxic, it was hard to break ranks to back it. And, as Labour MPs stampeded towards a more organized, better funded and louder Remain movement, those in the Respect the Result grouping grew ever more isolated. At the same time, the Corbynite grassroots movement Momentum was pushing for further democratization of the party and, at the 2018 conference, had succeeded in making it easier to deselect sitting Labour MPs. The Respect the Result Labour MPs feared that, if they crossed the line, they would find themselves kicked out of the party.

With the Labour leadership already being squeezed from all sides, the vice tightened further in mid-February 2019: eight Labour MPs – most notably, Chuka Umunna – broke from the party and, joining with three Tory MPs, including Anna Soubry, formed The Independent Group. This new centrist party rebranded itself as Change UK, but in any case it soon tanked.

The Labour leadership was initially worried by Change UK. John McDonnell in particular had long feared a breakaway party, not because it had any realistic chance of picking up a significant number of seats, but because, by dividing the anti-Tory vote, it would weaken Labour's electoral chances. McDonnell recalled the trauma of the breakaway Social Democratic Party in the early 1980s: in splitting the Labour vote, they allowed the Tories to take, among others, the West London seat of Hayes and Harlington, which he finally regained for Labour in 1997. Although McDonnell's internal critics – such as Murphy –believed he had become irrationally obsessed by this issue, McDonnell firmly believed that if seventy or eighty MPs defected to another party, they were sunk. The main concern, he tells me, was to stem the trickle of defections. If Labour had resisted a referendum, 'we'd have had more defections. It'd have split the Parliamentary Labour Party on a bigger scale – one that maybe we'd never recover from. There was no point in risking giving them a tool or weapon to use against us.'

All of which led McDonnell to lean more towards Remain for purely tactical reasons. He met up with the leading lights of People's Vote, including Alastair Campbell, Tom Baldwin and Roland Rudd – which, inevitably, aggravated Karie Murphy and Seumas Milne. For McDonnell, however, Change UK had to be stopped from using the People's Vote campaign to further their party's interests. If, he told People's Vote, a new referendum with Remain on the ballot paper was truly their objective, then Labour represented their only route map.

The Labour leadership's long-standing fear, that People's Vote had become a means for their bitterest opponents to destroy the left, only deepened when People's Vote embraced somebody who had become one of the most disliked figures within Corbynism, the Labour Party deputy leader, Tom Watson. On Brexit, as in much else, Watson was a political butterfly. After the 2016 referendum result, he had been vocal in his insistence that Brexit must happen.[26] Since then, he had experienced a Damascene conversion to the Remain cause, and in March 2019, he addressed a mass People's Vote protest in central London. Tom Baldwin is emphatic that Watson, now a true believer, had done something 'brave and courageous' despite his 'reputation for being tricky and Machiavellian'. But much of Labour's top brass, including Starmer's Remain-leaning team, thought otherwise, that in involving himself with People's Vote, Watson was simply trying to foster divisions between Corbyn and the membership. His interventions, they believed, were profoundly unhelpful.

The problems presented by Change UK were most evident in the deadlocked Parliament, where, on 14 March, the new party's MPs tabled a 'second referendum' vote. While Labour ordered their MPs to abstain, seventeen Labour MPs in Leave seats rebelled to vote against, including five resigning from frontbench roles to do so, underscoring growing discontent from pro-Brexit figures within the party. The vote failed by a massive margin, setting back the second referendum cause. For Change UK, however, its main aim was to foster disillusionment among Remainers with the Corbyn Labour Party. Fearing that this was indeed Change UK's ultimate agenda, Tom Baldwin had been briefing that People's Vote had nothing to do with the new party. 'It was a big blow for People's Vote,' he says. 'A lot of MPs who'd been thinking of going with Change UK thought, "hold on, they're not working in our best interests". The scales fell from their eyes, and they didn't.' Indeed, Change UK didn't simply despise Corbynism: they hated Keir Starmer, too, believing that he gave the Labour leadership a Remainer lick of paint, and – given widespread agreement that the ex-director of public prosecutions was highly able – made it harder for them to denounce the party for incompetence.

Now, however, Labour was becoming dangerously enmeshed in parliamentary battles whose intricacy made them largely incomprehensible to the wider public, and fed a sense of exhaustion and boredom in the electorate.

Meanwhile, Parliament had become entangled in a knot of increasingly convoluted procedures. On 25 March, MPs voted to seize control of the parliamentary agenda from May's ailing government.

Two weeks later, they held a series of indicative votes to establish whether there was a parliamentary majority for any option, including a customs union; a new referendum; the so-called 'Norway option', in which Britain would leave the EU but remain a member of the single market; or revoking Article 50 to prevent No Deal. There was no majority for any option.

Perhaps the most telling of these parliamentary votes, as far as Labour was concerned, was that for the new referendum. Labour's leadership instructed its MPs to vote for the amendment (which had itself been tabled by two Labour MPs, Peter Kyle and Phil Wilson) – but forty Labour MPs voted against or abstained in defiance of the leadership's orders, including shadow cabinet members Jon Trickett and Ian Lavery, who abstained. The Kyle-Wilson amendment failed to pass by twelve votes. Corbyn's response – or lack of it – to the mutiny was telling. 'I tendered my resignation fucking twice,' Ian Lavery tells me, regarding the amendment as an unacceptable fudge. 'I thought – bloody man, Jeremy should bloody sack us!' The conflict-averse Corbyn simply ducked the issue.

In a polarized nation, Corbyn's own disinterest in Brexit didn't help. 'Jeremy always spoke on the issue with the enthusiasm of someone reading a photocopying manual,' is how Andrew Fisher describes it. 'He wasn't passionate about it. He was passionate about international affairs, housing and austerity. You could see the difference, the marked contrast, when he was talking about child poverty versus how he spoke about Brexit.' The result, Fisher concluded, was that he was incapable of providing leadership on the issue. 'One of the things I'd reflect on – and any future Labour leader should reflect on – is you don't just get to lead on issues you want to lead on. If you're the leader you have to lead on everything, not just the things you care about.'

With Brexit swamping everything, Labour's domestic policies could not get a hearing, and in an ever more deafening culture war, neither could Labour's 'For the many, not the few' narrative. The leadership tried to build class solidarity across the Brexit divide. In a powerful speech on Brexit in the Leave-voting Yorkshire town of Wakefield, Corbyn pointed out the parallels between Remain and Leave voters, who were struggling whatever they thought of Brexit. 'You're up against it. But you're not against each other.'[27] But it was just too late, and – classic Corbyn – it wasn't part of a broader communications strategy. A set-piece speech, in itself, was a drop in the ocean; it needed to be part of a relentless campaign of messaging. It wasn't, and it was duly drowned out by the Brexit din.

The original deadline for Britain to leave the EU, 29 March 2019, came and went without resolution. But one deadlock did break. Since the 2017 general election, Labour and the Tories had polled roughly neck and neck, around 40 per cent apiece. That now changed. With Labour generally perceived as adrift on Brexit, its polling tanked. Increasingly, Leave voters regarded No Deal as the only truly authentic Brexit, while Remainers, for their part, increasingly wanted Brexit to be reversed. That April, one poll found that 38 per cent backed a No Deal exit, while 40 per cent opted for revoking Article 50 and stopping Brexit, underscoring that the middle ground had collapsed.[28] With this polarization came vocal fury. Corbyn was despised by the radical wing of Remain: 'Where's Jeremy Corbyn?' was chanted with abandon at People's Vote rallies. Because Brexit day had been cancelled, Britain now had to participate in the upcoming European elections, a contest that gave other resurgent parties – the Brexit Party, the Lib Dems, the Greens – a national platform. (Change UK, on the other hand, had lurched from crisis to farce and was increasingly reduced to irrelevance.) Two weeks before polling day, the Brexit Party had soared to an 18 per cent share of the vote; the combined Lib Dem–Green share was 23 per cent.[29] With Labour and the Tories both on a sagging 24 per cent, panic enveloped both main parties.

At the beginning of April, realizing that she could not get any Brexit package through Parliament without support from the opposition, Theresa May called for negotiations with Corbyn. She announced she was 'taking action to break the logjam. I am offering to sit down with the leader of the opposition and to try to agree to a plan that we would both stick to, to ensure that we leave the European Union.' But it all felt too late. Such an approach should have been made after May's parliamentary majority had evaporated in the general election twenty-two months previously, not when her administration was on life support.

The talks went ahead. Corbyn's team were well disposed to a deal if it could be done. 'A lot of effort was put in, particularly by Jeremy's policy staff, who worked very hard and sincerely on the issues, not just on the headlines, but going into the weeds,' says Chief Whip Nick Brown. The Labour team, including Milne, McDonnell and Starmer, trooped into the grand Cabinet Office building at 70 Whitehall. Awaiting them around the table were the government representatives, including Chancellor of the Exchequer Philip Hammond, Michael Gove and May's chief EU negotiator Olly Robbins, a tall, serious figure who was the architect of her deal, and who came to be respected on the Labour side. 'He was extremely competent, to give him his due,' says McDonnell, 'and relatively straightforward.' Much of the first two weeks was taken up by Robbins making a passionate case for his deal. Stressing that while it ended freedom of movement between Britain and the rest of the EU, it provided everything Labour really wanted, that the 'backstop' was the customs union that Labour were seeking. Not that they could describe it as such because to do so would have antagonized Tory Brexiteers.

'I've come to the conclusion that Robbins negotiated a really clever deal which prevented a border in Ireland, and which both he and May thought would lock the UK into the single market and customs union over time but deal with the issue of Brexit,' one non-Corbynite senior aide tells me. The trouble was, he continues, that the Labour leadership were thinking, as they had done for so much of Corbyn's tenure, 'in two- to three-month periods, skirmish to skirmish'. Robbins, by contrast, was 'thinking what it would look like in twenty years' time'. The Labour representatives, though, felt confident that they were running rings through a clearly divided Conservative team. The Tory chief of staff, Gavin Barwell, seemed particularly desperate for a deal, while Robbie Gibb, May's director of communications, was clearly opposed. The Tories would openly disagree in front of their opponents, and their strategies never seemed particularly clear, even to themselves. Michael Gove, in particular, would weigh in with baffling contributions. When McDonnell raised this phenomenon with Philip Hammond in a private meeting, the chancellor muttered, 'You haven't seen him in cabinet.'

The negotiating teams were their respective parties in microcosm: both contained elements which wanted a deal, and elements which didn't. While McDonnell felt that 'at one point Keir and I thought we might be able to get a deal', Starmer grew increasingly concerned about the idea. His own seat, Holborn and St Pancras, was a Remain stronghold, and he was being berated by his constituents. McDonnell used the weakness of May's government to extract concessions on workers' rights, while expressing scepticism to his colleagues about a deal that would save May's government and deliver Brexit. What would Labour get out of that? Clouding the picture further, Unite boss Len McCluskey, who was convinced that Starmer 'frankly just didn't want a deal', was himself negotiating separately with the government's team. In early May 2019, sitting in 10 Downing Street, he proclaimed: 'We are negotiators, professional negotiators, and I can tell you that if you sent us away over a weekend with what I know is on the table, we'll be able to cut a deal.' Later, in Parliament, he told Corbyn, McDonnell, Starmer and key Labour aides that a deal was on the cards, 'if you want one. But in my opinion, you don't.' While Corbyn sat there in his now customary silence, McDonnell summed up the dilemma. 'Lenny,' he said gently, 'you have to understand that it's like negotiating with a company that's going into administration.'

McDonnell's point was inarguable. By this time, May's authority within her own party had evaporated. As a *de facto* Tory leadership campaign raged, May's would-be successors played to the Brexiter gallery, making it clear they would rip up any deal done with Labour. Whatever way you looked at it – whether Remain or Brexit – a deal with May's ailing administration appeared highly unattractive.

Yet with Labour now being devoured alive in the polls – the Lib Dems, recovered from the mauling they had suffered in the 2017 general election, and pitching themselves as the Remain party, were eating steadily into the Labour Remain vote and were now at around 20 per cent – the political space for any deal had disappeared. Labour's two dearly held principles – freedom of movement and permanent membership of the EU customs union – were shut down by the Conservatives ('What's the point of doing Brexit if you don't end freedom of movement?' Philip Hammond asked Keir Starmer. 'That's what Brexit means.'). In mid-May, after six wasted weeks, negotiations collapsed.

Corbyn's social media manager, Jack Bond, remembers the day well. On the evening of Thursday 16 May, a week before the approaching European elections, Bond was informed that Labour was to pull out of the negotiations the next day 'so we don't get completely hammered next week for possibly facilitating a Tory Brexit'. Corbyn was due to do a broadcast interview explaining Labour's reasons for ending the talks, and Bond arranged for a social media clip to be filmed directly afterwards. The next morning, Bond received a phone call from Corbyn's diary secretary telling him no driver had been booked, and he was asked if his father, a taxi driver, could pick the Labour leader up at his favourite café in Finsbury Park. With the TV interview set for 10 a.m., Corbyn failed to turn up at the prearranged time of 8.30; and as Bond waited with his father and media officer Jack McKenna and Anjula Singh, one of Milne's deputies, a new rendezvous time was set for 9.15. Corbyn finally appeared at 9.30. They sat in the café, Singh trying to brief Corbyn, who was eating breakfast and struggling to concentrate. At 10 a.m., Milne turned up to offer his own briefing. Eventually, Corbyn arrived forty-five minutes late, and was met by a group of exasperated journalists in no mood to play nice. 'It just summed up how we did things, kicking and screaming, with nothing proactive, without any plan or professionalism,' as Bond puts it. 'The story ended up running for hours without any Labour voice, so the Tories ended up shaping the narrative.' The social media clip never happened.

The ever-growing tensions throughout Britain were mirrored in Labour's increasingly stressful shadow cabinet meetings, and around the table of the party's Brexit strategy subcommittee, chaired by Corbyn. Anticipating this national hardening of views, Ian Lavery told the strategy meeting after the 2017 election that, whatever happened, 'there would be blood on the walls, that's how serious this is'. He was right. Lavery and Jon Trickett in particular became a unified bloc. Calling themselves 'blood brothers', they set the tone after the 2018 Labour conference, presenting a list of dozens of Leave seats Labour would lose if it aligned itself with Remain. While party members were increasingly demanding the reversal of Brexit, the pair argued, the ordinary rank-and-file members of the trade unions were not, and they represented the party's backbone. It wasn't just 'middle-class members in the metropolitan cities' that voted for you, Trickett would tell Corbyn, but 'tens of thousands of trade unionists' and their views should therefore count equally. By 2019, Lavery exploded at frequent intervals. Corbyn would often sit in silence while he shouted, swore and thumped the table in frustrated rage, his ire directed particularly at Starmer and Thornberry, but also sometimes at McDonnell and Abbott. On one occasion, Lavery interpreted comments by Abbott as suggesting voters in the North supported Brexit because of racist inclinations; Starmer, he believed, had nodded in agreement. 'If you ever fucking call me racist you'll know about it,' he stormed at the disconcerted Starmer; when Corbyn attempted to restore calm, Lavery spat out 'shut the fuck up'. After Thornberry made a pro-Remain intervention on television, Trickett snapped: 'What you did is send electronic shocks all the way through the fucking north of England.' Discussions descended into such aggressive bitterness that at one point one figure suggested to his detractor that they take their disagreement outside so he could 'fill you in'. All of which reflected the fury bubbling away in local communities. In just one instance, Andrew Gwynne, Labour's co-national campaign coordinator, was spat at in the streets of his pro-Leave constituency while out walking with his grandson.

Each faction rested the democratic legitimacy for their position in two different component wings of the labour movement: for the pro-Remain wing, the Labour membership; for the Respect the Result grouping, the party's trade union affiliates. Diane Abbott was genuinely affronted by anti-migrant and racist impulses involved in the Brexit movement, but focused her argument on its existential threat to Corbynism, reminding Corbyn that he could not be seen to betray the members who had delivered him an overwhelming mandate in two leadership elections. Besides not wanting to alienate the membership, Corbyn, like many other London MPs, felt growing pressure from his own Remain seat. He told allies that 8,000 constituents had emailed him to demand a revocation of Article 50 – to cancel Brexit without even a referendum – which, given that he saw himself as a constituency MP first and foremost, inevitably had an impact.

McDonnell also subscribed to this view. Though ambivalent

towards the EU, he believed that if the Corbyn project lost the membership, it was sunk. It was this, above all else, that drove his own shift towards Remain, despite the fact that he represented a Leave-voting seat. In spring 2019, he met up with Len McCluskey, who had arrived at the opposite conclusion: that embracing Remain would doom Labour's prospects. 'What the fuck is going on?' McCluskey demanded. 'Please convince me and I promise to go away and I'll bang the biggest drum!' McDonnell was blunt: 'I know better than you. I go up and down the country, and I'm telling you the army is crumbling.' It was, he argued, many of the most committed Corbyn supporters, particularly the young, who would be disillusioned by Labour becoming a midwife to Brexit. 'I hope you're right,' McCluskey retorted, 'because I'm telling you what I'm picking up in our heartlands is the exact opposite of what you're telling me.'

Yet, in just a matter of months, between the beginning of 2019 and the aftermath of the European elections five months later, more or less the entire shadow cabinet – convinced by polling that believed backing Brexit would lead to devastating political consequences for Labour – had swung round to supporting a new referendum, leaving only Lavery, Trickett and John Healey vocally accepting the result of the 2016 vote. It was, said the dwindling pro-Brexit faction, all McDonnell's fault. They had expected the likes of Thornberry and Starmer to agitate against Brexit, but not Corbyn's closest lieutenant and shadow chancellor, a figure of unimpeachable left credentials. What McDonnell had done seemed to them an act of betrayal.

Yet McDonnell was acting entirely in good faith. In part, he believed he was shielding Corbyn, by saying things the Labour leader felt unable to articulate, redirecting pressure away from him in the process. The truth was it was an impossible situation, and whatever the fury against McDonnell, he was right: Labour had no real choice. With the middle ground, which sustained the party's increasingly flaky Brexit compromise position, scorched into oblivion and Labour haemorrhaging votes to both Remain and Leave, the membership was no longer in any mood to accept the referendum result.

Corbyn himself had been catastrophically damaged by Brexit. Having never adopted a clear and enduring position, he had spent the two and a half years since the election in a constant but erratic retreat from accepting the referendum result, never making a principled, coherent case to the public about why he was doing so. In the 2017 general election, Corbyn came across to the British public as a politician who said what he meant and meant what he said, whether they agreed with him or not. No longer. By January 2019, voters had gone off him: he was seen as weak, indecisive and a flipflopper.[30] 'It all became about party management,' says Andrew Murray, somewhat bleakly. 'It's like writing a play to keep the cast happy, while forgetting about the audience who are going out the door.'

Labour was trapped in a burning building, but there were no exits. One incident among many summed up its predicament. In May 2019, just before the European elections, a meeting was convened between Jeremy Corbyn, senior Labour HQ officials and the party whips. 'We've taken the membership too far,' declared Corbyn. 'We're not going to get away with it, we are going to have to support a second referendum.' Both Karie Murphy and Amy Jackson were furious. 'This is a betrayal of the working class!' bellowed Murphy. These were comrades with shared battle scars whose unity and solidarity had sustained the Corbyn project. All that was now on the brink of total disintegration.

7
The Antisemitism Crisis

Six greedy capitalists with large noses sit around a Monopoly board counting money. The board rests not on a table, but on the backs of subjugated, slave-like human beings. Behind them is suspended a pyramid and all-seeing eye, a symbol often signifying Freemasonry; to the left, a protesting youth, fist raised, clutches a banner emblazoned with 'THE NEW WORLD ORDER IS THE ENEMY OF HUMANITY'. In 2012 this scene was graffitied in dazzling technicolour on the wall of a property off Brick Lane in London's East End by US artist Mear One. It was denounced by the borough mayor, Lutfur Rahman. 'The images of the bankers,' he said, 'perpetuate antisemitic propaganda about conspiratorial Jewish domination of financial institutions,' declaring that it would be removed. When Mear One posted an image of the graffiti on Facebook, decrying the mayor's decision (it was, the artist protested, not antisemitic), then backbencher Jeremy Corbyn was tagged in. Corbyn got involved, on the artist's side: 'Why? You are in good company. Rockerfeller [*sic*] destroyed Diego Viera's [*sic*] mural because it includes a picture of Lenin.'

When Corbyn became Labour leader three years later, he refused to deactivate his Facebook account despite the pleadings of his social media manager, Jack Bond, who predicted that his entire back catalogue of comments would be scoured through by hungry journalists. Sure enough, in November 2015, the *Jewish Chronicle* published a piece headlined 'Did Jeremy Corbyn back artist whose mural was condemned as antisemitic?' Corbyn's then head of media, Kevin Slocombe, did not respond to requests from the newspapers for comment, and the matter seemed to end there.

But the Mear One controversy resurfaced over two years later, in March 2018, at a time when Corbyn's post-2017 election honeymoon had already dissipated. On the 23rd of that month, the prominent Jewish Labour MP Luciana Berger sent a volley of incensed text messages to members of the leader's office demanding an explanation for Corbyn's response, and highlighted the episode on Twitter. Berger herself had been systematically harassed by antisemites, predominantly on the far right – some of whom had gone to prison for making death threats – but was also targeted by some claiming to be on the left.

That morning, when Corbyn's stakeholder manager, Laura Murray, logged on to Twitter, she was shocked. 'I just couldn't believe it,' she tells me. 'It was the first time I felt really embarrassed of Jeremy and of working for him.' The timing could not have been worse. That afternoon, Murray was due to attend a bi-monthly meeting with the Jewish Labour Movement, Labour's only affiliated Jewish organization, a long-standing relationship which had begun – in its earlier incarnation of Poale Zion (Workers of Zion) – in 1920. Not untypically, Executive Director of Comms Seumas Milne could not be found; his number two, James Schneider, was off sick. Eventually, Murray managed to get both on a call, but struggling to get a clear line on the issue from them, she turned up to the meeting, expressing her desperate apologies that she had been unable to speak to Corbyn or anyone who could provide an answer. It didn't look good. But it got worse.

Shortly after, Murray received a WhatsApp message from Schneider in his sick bed with the official line that she was to use. 'In 2012,' it went, 'Corbyn was responding to concerns about the removal of public art on the grounds of freedom of speech. However, the mural was offensive, used antisemitic imagery which has no place in our society, and it is right it was removed.' The combination of a 'free speech' defence – long used by the right to defend racism – and the lack of any apology shocked Murray and Corbyn-supporting press officers, and they duly demanded its amendment. When told it had already been sent out to journalists, Murray exploded with rage: 'Are you fucking kidding me?'

A new, lengthier statement was put out, emphasizing that the contents of the offending mural 'are deeply disturbing and antisemitic' and that 'the defence of free speech cannot be used as a justification for the promotion of antisemitism in any form'. This time, an apology was included. Murray then left the office for a dinner appointment, but kept an eye on her messages. When she got off the tube, she discovered the apologies had been removed. 'I thought, how fucking stupid and tone deaf can this be?' Finally, a day later, Corbyn's team coughed up an apology to Jewish leaders for his comments about the mural. Why it took so long is unclear. But it was a classic failing of the Corbyn era: resisting taking an unavoidable step, then suffering self-inflicted damage, and gaining no credit whatsoever for finally bowing to the inevitable. It was also symptomatic of the leadership's inadequate and recalcitrant response to a persistent problem within the Labour Party, and would, distressingly, become one of the defining issues of Corbyn's tenure as leader: the antisemitism crisis.

Antisemitism is ingrained in all European societies. Two thousand years of blood libel, scapegoating, pogroms, expulsions and murder, culminating in an attempt to exterminate every single Jew on the European continent by industrialized, bureaucratic means: all this ensured that this very specific form of racism set down deep roots in many different cultures. The unique trauma of the Holocaust did at least provoke some reckoning with antisemitism in Europe and the US – but it hardly eradicated it. Months before Corbyn assumed the Labour leadership in summer 2015, a poll found that a quarter of the British people believed that Jews 'chase money more than other British people'; a fifth believed that their 'loyalty to Israel makes them less loyal to Britain than other British people'; 17 per cent believed that 'Jews think they are better than other people'; and another 17 per cent believed 'Jews have too much power in the media'. Strikingly, in almost all cases, the most sympathetic to antisemitic ideas were UKIP voters, followed by Conservatives, followed by Labour supporters, with Lib Dem backers the least inclined to antisemitism.[1] Overall, the poll revealed a disturbingly large reservoir of antisemitic sympathies within the British populace. 'If you apply that to the Labour Party, you're talking about a huge number of people,' says Jon Lansman, perhaps the most prominent Jewish figure within the

Corbynite movement. 'Even if it's just a third of that number, it's a hell of a lot of people.' What's more, antisemitism is on the rise, and hate crimes have surged: in 2019, they rose for the fourth year in a row, reaching 1,805 incidents, including a 25 per cent increase in violent assaults. Most involved online hatred, but they also included the desecration of synagogues and Jewish graves.[2]

Antisemitism is a shapeshifter: it appears in many different guises. Its underlying themes, however, have remained the same. Perhaps the best definition of this awful mindset is that by Jewish academic Brian Klug:

> The Jew belongs to a sinister people set apart from all others, not merely by its customs but by a collective character: arrogant yet obsequious; legalistic yet corrupt; flamboyant yet secretive. Always looking to turn a profit, Jews are as ruthless as they are tricky. Loyal only to their own, wherever they go they form a state within a state, preying upon the societies in whose midst they dwell. Their hidden hand controls the banks, the markets and the media. And when revolutions occur or nations go to war, it is the Jews – cohesive, powerful, clever and stubborn – who invariably pull the strings and reap the rewards.[3]

Antisemitism has always existed on the left. Despite his own Jewish heritage, Karl Marx himself was not immune from expressing then pervasive antisemitic attitudes. 'What, in itself, was the basis of the Jewish religion?' he wrote in *On the Jewish Question* in 1844. 'Practical need, egoism . . . Money is the jealous god of Israel, in face of which no other god may exist.'[4] Mikhail Bakunin, the nineteenth-century Russian founder of modern anarchism, resorted to antisemitic tirades against Marx and his Jewish allies in their heated arguments.[5] The French anarchist Pierre-Joseph Proudhon, meanwhile, declared in his diaries that 'The Jew is the enemy of the human race' who should 'be sent back to Asia or exterminated.'[6] From the nineteenth century onwards, antisemitism co-opted left-wing rhetoric about greedy elites exploiting a hard-pressed working class, targeting Jewish financiers and bankers, suggesting that wherever injustice lurked then the Jews must be behind it; and was bound up in more sweeping expressions of racism. Labour's legendary first leader, Keir Hardie, claimed that 'modern imperialism is really run by half a dozen financial houses, many of them Jewish.'[7] Sidney Webb – one of the founders of the Fabian Society, the flagship reformist Labour Party affiliate – wrote in 1907 that higher birth rates meant that Britain was 'gradually falling to the Irish and the Jews'.[8]

And so it went on, throughout the twentieth century. The iconoclastic socialist writer George Orwell repeatedly aired antisemitic prejudices. A year into the Second World War, he wrote: 'What is bad about Jews is that they are not only conspicuous, but go out of their way to make themselves so . . . They make use of England as a sanctuary, but they cannot help feeling the profoundest contempt for it. You can see this in their eyes, even when they don't say it outright.'[9] After the war, Labour Foreign Secretary Ernest Bevin displayed clear and profound antisemitic leanings, making disparaging and well-worn links between Jews on the one hand, and finance and Communism on the other, leading his Under-Secretary of State Christopher Mayhew to write in May 1948: 'There is no doubt in my mind that Ernest detests Jews.'[10]

The no-holds-barred antisemitism of this era would find itself at the centre of contemporary British political debate. In the spring of 2019, Corbyn was denounced for having written the foreword for a 2011 edition of *Imperialism: A Study*, a 1901 book written by liberal historian J. A. Hobson and a common university set text, which included a strikingly antisemitic passage claiming European finance was controlled 'by men of a single and peculiar race'.

This was presented as just the latest episode in a litany of Corbyn's failures on antisemitism. Yet what it really underlined is that there has never been a real reckoning with the antisemitism of Britain's past. Indeed, there was no scandal when Theresa May unveiled a statue of the first female Tory MP, Nancy Astor, a notorious antisemite,[11] later that year. From Conservative Prime Minister Neville Chamberlain – who declared 'No doubt the Jews aren't a lovable people; I don't care about them myself'[12] – to, more recently, the Thatcherite children's author Roald Dahl – who stated 'there's a trait in the Jewish character that does provoke animosity . . . even a stinker like Hitler didn't pick on them for no reason',[13] antisemitism is entrenched in our culture.

There are distinctive elements to left-wing antisemitism. What could be described as 'leftism' in its broadest sense understands and analyses capitalism as a series of competing social forces, a system in which classes driven by rational economic self-interest have conflicting needs and aspirations. Then there is 'conspiracism', which is quite different: a belief in shadowy individuals wielding sinister unaccountable power and pulling strings behind the scenes. This can – and does – all too easily blend into antisemitism. Rather than talking about the financial sector as a whole, for example, conspiracists often rant about the Rothschilds, a long-vilified family of Jewish financiers, who don't even make the cut of the richest 1,000 people on earth. What's more, the rise of social media, most notably Facebook, and YouTube, has made it far easier for people to come into contact with such conspiracist propaganda.

Opposition to all forms of racism and bigotry should be core to the left's identity: a signature commitment. That is sadly not always true in practice, and there is a specific reason why antisemitism can become a blind spot for some on the left. Jews were the favoured targets of racists in interwar Britain. Postwar, with the striking exception of anti-Jewish riots in 1947,[14] memories of the Holocaust seemed to result in a broad consensus about the evils of antisemitism, and a new influx of immigrants arriving from countries across the British Commonwealth, black people – not least the Windrush generation – and Asian people became the main targets. 'When I first became active in the Communist Party in Hackney in the East End in the 1970s, the fight against racism was almost exclusively against what Afro-Caribbean people went through,' recalls Andrew Murray, Unite's chief of staff and a former senior Corbyn adviser. 'The fight against anti-Jewish racism was a very honoured part of our heritage: you'd meet people who'd been at the Battle of Cable Street, and there were older Jewish people in the Communist Party – but the Jewish people leading demonstrations in Hackney were leading demonstrations against racism directed at black people from the police and the National Front, which hardly targeted Jewish people at all. That was the culture you were forged in.' Meanwhile, the oppressed Jewish working class of the East End were gradually replaced by new generations of immigrants from Pakistan, India and the Caribbean.

In the 1970s, a new, largely London-based Labour left emerged, its ranks including the likes of Corbyn, Ken Livingstone (who would go on to become the first Labour mayor of London, and would be caught up in his own antisemitism furore), Diane Abbott and John McDonnell. They wanted to combine anti-racism, feminism and the gay rights movement with the left's focus on class. They understood racism as a systemic problem: that is, that it existed in the form of discrimination in the provision of housing and jobs, in harassment by the police and justice system, in degradation in popular culture, and discrimination in education. Racism was 'prejudice plus power'. This 'systemic' racism was endured by British Jews before the war; after the war, it was predominantly the turn of other minorities. Bound up in this was the question of 'whiteness', which is not a static category: race, after all, is a social construct, not a biological reality. In the postwar decades, the 'whiteness' of Irish people was perceived as ambiguous; the systemic racism they faced in Britain was summed up by the infamous guesthouse slogan 'NO DOGS, NO BLACKS, NO IRISH'. Jews were long excluded from 'whiteness', but in the post-war period, Jews have often been treated as white.

And here is how a blind spot can emerge. If Jews are judged no longer to suffer systemic racism and to have become defined as 'white', then antisemitism can come to seem less problematic than, for instance, anti-black racism and Islamophobia. It goes without saying that there are several problems with this attitude. For a start, collective trauma is absolutely central to the Jewish experience: two thousand years of persecution will do that to a minority. Throughout the history of the Jewish people, there are times of apparent benevolence, acceptance even, by the dominant Christian populations of Europe, followed by a sudden revival of persecution: a striking example being the Dreyfus Affair in late nineteenth- and early twentieth-century France. French republicanism encouraged Jews to believe that they were, above all, French citizens like anyone else. That was until Captain Alfred Dreyfus, a French Jewish military officer, was sentenced to life imprisonment for treason after allegedly leaking French military secrets to Germany. Dreyfus's innocence was eventually established – but after a vicious campaign of antisemitism, including antisemitic protests and riots and anti-Jewish campaigns by racist French publications. The episode was critical to the rise of Zionism; it seemed to prove that Jews would never be truly welcome in Europe, and needed the safety of their own homeland.

Of course, we don't have to travel back to the now distant French Third Republic. A few years ago, I stood alongside a close friend on platform 17 of Berlin-Grunewald railway station. It was deserted; weeds sprouted in between the tracks. But the signifiers of past horrors were there: a steel grate marked the spot from where, on 18 October 1941, 1,251 Jews were transported to Lodz; on 17 March 1943, 1,160 Jews were deported to Theresienstadt. My friend's grandfather met his first wife in the German capital and they had a child. Both would perish, along with dozens of his relatives, shot in the forests of Latvia before the mass gassing began. Germany had the most integrated Jewish population in Europe; but this fact did not spare its population from the most extreme act of antisemitic violence in human history.

Sue Lukes is a Labour councillor in Islington, north London. Active in her local Jewish community, she is very proud of her heritage. Her father, aged ten, fled Prague and Nazi persecution on the *Kindertransport*. 'I get the collective trauma,' she tells me, 'I'm absolutely part of it.' When she moved to London in the 1980s with her partner – who had fled Chile after General Augusto Pinochet's bloody right-wing putsch against Salvador Allende's elected socialist government – the threat of the far right and chatter of a military coup if the left ever assumed power led her to memorize the address of the Office of the UN High Commissioner for Refugees in London, just in case. She learned how to get there, with or without public transport. 'I was a mother and I organized my life,' she explains. 'I was a full-time worker and parent, and one thing I had on my list was: make sure you know where the UNHCR are, you never know when you might need it.'

Absorbing Jews into whiteness is problematic in other ways. 'I think it's a very unsophisticated understanding of how racism works,' says the left–wing writer Rachel Shabi, whose family were Jews who fled Iraq in the mass exodus of 1951. 'It relies on creating a racialized minority, and that racialized minority is maybe given temporary whiteness rights. But those rights can be withdrawn again at any point in history.' European Jews, she explains, were long called the

'Orientals of Europe': a large proportion of Israel's Jews are from the Middle East. 'We can show up as white, but we're Middle Eastern, we're not white, we "pass" sometimes, depending on the context. That entire population is also erased: Yemeni Jewish people, Iraqi Jews, Moroccan, Tunisian.' This type of dynamic leads to a constant kind of mental looking over your shoulder: you never feel secure about how you're being perceived – or when that perception is going to change, for the worse.

The relationship with Israel also complicates the picture: the relationship that many Jews have with Israel; that Britain has; that the left has. The approach of much of the left towards Israel in its early days was rather different from what it is now. The Soviet Union – and with it, the international official Communist movement – supported Israel's foundation in 1948, and initially provided it with military support. After the calamity of the Holocaust and the extermination of two thirds of European Jewry, Zionism – long controversial among the Jewish diaspora – became a dominant idea among Jews. There appeared to be an incontestable need for a Jewish homeland, and the state's founders blended their Zionism with socialist rhetoric; the collective communities of the kibbutzim seemed like incubators of a new socialist society. Those who were regarded as the torchbearers of the Labour left – such as Tony Benn, Nye Bevan, Jennie Lee, Eric Heffer, Ian Mikardo and Michael Foot – were strong champions of the early Israeli state.

What changed? In the ensuing decades, national liberation struggles against Western colonial oppression – notably the French in Algeria and the US in Vietnam – ignited the imagination of much of the radical left. When the 1967 Six-Day War led to the Israeli annexation of Palestinian lands in the West Bank and Gaza, Israel came to resemble a colonial occupier. To some, the Palestinians came to resemble the Algerians: a subjugated Arab people struggling against a European settler state. With the right-wing Likud party in power, Israel jettisoned its original socialist principles. In line with Reaganism and Thatcherism, mass privatization swept the country, kibbutzim included. Then came Israel's war with the Palestine Liberation Organization and its 1982 invasion of Lebanon, which culminated in the massacre of thousands of civilians by Israeli allies in the

Palestinian refugee camps of Sabra and Shatila – all of which further drastically eroded left-wing sympathy with the Israeli national project. By the 1990s, Israel, founded in part by Holocaust survivors, was increasingly regarded as a brutally oppressive superpower, striking in the militarization of its society and its chauvinistic nationalism; as Israel fought Palestinian *intifadas* (uprisings) with thousands of consequent deaths, and expanded illegal settlements in the West Bank, the left widely saw Israel as the last remaining European colonial-type enterprise. Because Israel received generous military and diplomatic support from Western governments, the liberation of Palestine from its subjugation became one of the great foreign policy causes of the left.

Yet while the brutality of Israel's occupation of Palestinian lands is undeniable, the situation was – and is – fundamentally different from those projects of European settler-colonialism. In those horrors, Europeans arrived to plant their flags to claim land on behalf of their own states, while Israel's founders were fleeing the flags of their old nations. Rhodesia, for example, was not founded by survivors of a genocide who had already suffered two millennia of persecution. Israel was both a state founded by victims of unimaginable horrors seeking a refuge, and a state in which many saw the characteristics of old-style settler colonialism. Anybody who doesn't desire security for the Jewish people of Israel is as dangerous as they are wrongheaded. Many Jews who are politically hostile both to the occupation of Palestinian territories and to Israel's depressing right-wing trajectory, nonetheless retain a profoundly emotional connection with Israel; a state which is seen as a refuge – however imperfect – if, once again, the winds shift and the antisemites come back for more.

For many Palestinians, the concept of Zionism cannot be separated from their lived experience of occupation and the deprivation of their own right to national self-determination. Different sensitivities apply to discussion in the West. For some elements on the Western left, 'Zionist' became the ultimate cuss word. Zionism was a political ideology, they argued, and one inherently rooted in oppression. But the imprecise usage of 'Zionism' and 'Zionist' in the West is deeply problematic, leaving it eviscerated of meaning. After all, those self-describing as Zionists include everybody from Israeli hard-right extremists, who desire the annexation of all Palestinian lands to create a Greater Israel encompassing Judea and Samaria (otherwise known as the West Bank); to Israeli peaceniks who support the end of the Palestinian occupation. A 2015 survey found that while 59 per cent of British Jews self-identified as Zionists, 90 per cent supported Israel's right to exist as a Jewish state, the traditional Zionist aspiration.[15] For many Jews, angry denunciations of 'Zionists' mean one thing whatever the intention of the speaker: purely and simply, a contemporary manifestation of age-old angry tirades against the Jews.

Things get even messier. Some cynically deploy the charge of antisemitism to shut down legitimate criticisms of oppressive policies pursued by Israeli governments. The Israeli prime minister, Binyamin Netanyahu, is among those who have falsely denounced the international Boycott, Divestment and Sanctions movement as 'antisemitism in a new garb'. Jewish critics of Israel are smeared as 'self-hating Jews'.[16] The establishment of a unified secular state of Jews and Palestinians may be a far-fetched proposition, but it is still a legitimate belief; nonetheless, it is again often treated as an idea beyond the political pale. Palestinian voices are sidelined. Then there are those whose denunciations of Israel are expressed in antisemitic terms, or are simply motivated by antisemitism. Whether or not their sympathies with the plight of the Palestinian people are genuine, those who talk of an all-powerful 'Jewish lobby', or of the Israeli state acting as a sinister global puppet master, have embraced one of the most obvious antisemitic tropes.

Some make direct comparisons between the Israeli state and the Nazis, comparing the predicament of the Palestinians to that of the Jews during the Holocaust. The realities of the Israeli occupation are grim enough on their own terms – military subjugation, the theft of land, all justified by state-sanctioned racism – without a comparison which is as offensive as it is manifestly untrue. There has been no attempt to physically exterminate the Palestinian people; the comparison is meant only to bait Jews with the memory of their most murderous persecutors. Some Jews have found that even the very mention of antisemitism leads to an immediate jump to a conversation about Israel. As Rachel Shabi puts it, 'accusations of antisemitism tend to be in some way mired or tinged with criticisms of Israel: it's the job of the person presenting the claim of antisemitism to prove otherwise'. And, Shabi reasons, 'ultimately there's no way to prove otherwise because of that abiding and enduring suspicion'.

Labour's relationship with Britain's Jews did not begin to disintegrate under Jeremy Corbyn, but under his predecessor, Ed Miliband. In the dying days of the Gordon Brown era, in 2009–10, Jewish voters were almost evenly split between Labour and the Conservatives, with secular Jews more likely to support the former and religious Jews to opt for the latter.[17] But in the 2015 election, well over two thirds of British Jews supported the Conservatives, with only just over a fifth supporting Labour.[18] This despite Miliband having chalked up the milestone of being the first ever Jewish Labour leader; if he had triumphed at the ballot box, he would have become the first self-described Jewish prime minister in British history. So what happened? According to Labour right-winger Michael Dugher, the collapse in Jewish support for Labour was down to the leadership forcing its MPs to back a motion on Palestinian statehood a year earlier, a decision he described as 'catastrophic'.[19] Anger came from other quarters, too. Maureen Lipman, a prominent Jewish actor and previously lifelong Labour supporter, publicly declared that she would vote for 'almost any other party' in response to the leadership's supposed capitulation to a 'ludicrous piece of propaganda'.[20] That an international question has a bearing on the voting habits of a British minority is by no means specific to Jews. In the 2019 election, polling suggested that many British Indian voters abandoned Labour over its support of national self-determination for Kashmir.[21]

Labour's deteriorating relationship with Britain's Jews clearly had something to do with the party's pre-existing position on Israel. When Corbyn became leader, relations were already generally bad; however, there is no point pretending that a Labour leader from his political tradition would not present further complications given the unquestionable emotional significance of Israel to many Jews. Corbyn was a passionate supporter of self-determination for oppressed peoples – including the Kurds, Sri Lanka's Tamils and the Chagos Island residents, who were driven from their homes by the British government in the late 1960s to make way for a US military base. He was also deeply committed to Palestinian justice, more so than any previous Labour leader. Equally, he could point to an extensive record opposing antisemitism and showing pro-Jewish solidarity. For example, signing Early Day Motions condemning antisemitism,[22] helping organize a counter-mobilization to a demonstration by the fascist National Front in the so-called Battle of Wood Green in 1977; taking part in a campaign to save a Jewish cemetery from being sold off to property developers in 1987; and, in 2010, calling on the British government to settle Yemeni Jewish refugees.[23]

His commitment to challenge the British foreign policy establishment and side with victims of oppression was instrumental to his appeal among many of his supporters. But for many Labour MPs committed to supporting numerous human-rights-abusing regimes as long as they were amenable to Western interests – spanning Turkey, Saudi Arabia and Israel – this was their worst nightmare. Unquestionably, Corbyn's unstinting support for the Palestinians is one reason why some of his enemies regarded him as an unacceptable Labour leader from the outset.

The first rumblings of what would become known as Labour's antisemitism crisis began in summer 2015, as Corbyn moved from rank outsider to frontrunner in the party's leadership election. Around this time, headlines were triggered by Corbyn's historic connection with a group named Deir Yassin Remembered – after a notorious massacre of hundreds of Palestinian Arabs by Israeli soldiers in 1948. Corbyn had attended the group's events, in the process meeting its founder, Paul Eisen – who had gone on to publish vile writings on Holocaust denial, and had since been ostracized by the mainstream Palestinian solidarity movement. Corbyn is emphatic that he knew nothing about this – and, indeed, no one close to him believes for a moment that he would ever willingly associate with a Holocaust denier. But the encounter spoke to a wider problem: that while most of the Palestinian justice movement abhorred antisemitism, it nonetheless attracted antisemitic elements. Further headlines drew attention to Corbyn promoting a parliamentary meeting on the Middle East conflict in which he had declared that 'our friends from Hezbollah' – the militant Lebanese organization – would be speaking, and that he had 'also invited our friends from [the Palestinian resistance movement] Hamas to come and speak as well'. In a testy *Channel 4 News* interview, he argued that the word 'friends' was used 'in a collective way, saying our friends are prepared to talk. Does it mean I agree with Hamas and what it does? No. Does it mean I agree with Hezbollah and what they do? No. What it means is that I think to bring about a peace process, you have to talk to people with whom you may profoundly disagree.' He would later express 'regret' for 'using those words'.[24] But despite a week or so of coverage, the issue of antisemitism did not truly cut through at this point.

In the first phase of Corbyn's leadership, attention focused on incidents which had occurred under his predecessor. In April 2016, it emerged that Naz Shah, the new Labour MP for Bradford West, had, during the Israeli military's August 2014 Operation Protective Edge that had resulted in the deaths of hundreds of Gazan Palestinians, shared a map superimposing Israel on the US, accompanied by the headline 'Solution for Israel–Palestine conflict – relocate Israel into United States', adding that might save 'them [the US] some pocket money'. This was dealt with swiftly: Shah resigned as John McDonnell's parliamentary private secretary, met Jewish community groups, and came to be seen as a model in rehabilitation. In other instances, councillors who had shared often gratuitous antisemitic social media posts long before Corbyn had even stood for leader were suspended.[25]

The major flare-up in this period centred on the former mayor of London, Ken Livingstone. Discussing the Naz Shah affair on BBC Radio London, he declared: 'When Hitler won his election in 1932 his policy then was that Jews should be moved to Israel. He was supporting Zionism before he went mad and ended up killing six million Jews.' A firestorm erupted, exacerbated by Livingstone's insistence on continuing on an entirely self-destructive media tour. When Corbyn was told, he was genuinely appalled. 'What the fuck has he said?' he burst out. Andrew Fisher recalls Corbyn's response. 'There was never any sense of "Livingstone's entitled to his view" or "it's a legitimate perspective",' he says. Corbyn demanded Livingstone's suspension from the party within hours of his comments. 'The pair weren't close friends,' Fisher continues, 'but Livingstone was a lifelong ally who had fucked up. Livingstone strongly denied antisemitism but Corbyn said, "He's left us with no choice."'

The issue of antisemitism within Labour, however, was not going away.

On 29 April 2016, in the aftermath of the Livingstone affair, Seumas Milne phoned Shami Chakrabarti. Former head of civil liberties organization Liberty and something of an icon in progressive Britain, Chakrabarti was close to senior Labour figures such as Diane Abbott and Emily Thornberry and had begun to engage in political campaigning on her own account. Milne pointed to the problems Labour had had with antisemitism, and affirmed the party's need to look at the problem, assess its scale, and decide what to do about it. Would Chakrabarti, Milne asked, head an inquiry into antisemitism and other forms of racism within the Labour Party? Chakrabarti, who had herself been appalled by Livingstone's comments, instantly agreed. Her two vice-chairs would be Professor David Feldman, the director of the Pears Institute for the Study of Antisemitism at Birkbeck College, and Baroness Jan Royall. That the Chakrabarti Inquiry was not entirely focused on the issue of antisemitism was later offered as evidence that the report had been diluted, but Chakrabarti had thought it necessary to place antisemitism within a broader context of racism – not least because some on the left did not recognize antisemitism as racism in the first place.

The report was described by the Jewish sociologist Keith Kahn-Harris as 'a sophisticated and empathetic piece of work' exploring several important themes: why terms such as 'Zio' should never be used; why collective responsibility for Israel's actions must not be placed on the Jewish people; and why the Holocaust should, as a general rule, not be deployed in political arguments, particularly as regards the Israel–Palestine conflict.[26] The report tried to distinguish between behaviour that was ignorant – for example, conflating terms in sloppy, lazy, but offensive ways when discussing the Middle East – and outright malice and racism. Constructively, the report suggested reforms of the party's disciplinary and complaints procedures, the appointment of a general counsel to offer legal advice on disciplinary issues, and measures to improve the party staff's ethnic diversity. The

Board of Deputies of British Jews – the largest Jewish communal organization in the country – themselves declared that they 'appreciate the careful way in which Shami Chakrabarti has engaged with our community and that she took on board and addressed some of our concerns with commendable speed'.[27] Such a key report required a thorough discussion; what happened – at the report's launch, no less – was a disaster.

The report was publicly launched at Savoy Place on London's Strand, in front of an invited audience including a number of journalists for national media, on 30 June 2016, a week after the EU referendum and during the most febrile period of the internal Labour Party coup against the Corbyn leadership. But the event was derailed when Marc Wadsworth – a veteran black anti-racist activist – distributed leaflets calling for the deselection of anti-Corbyn MPs. One of the recipients, a *Telegraph* journalist, handed their leaflet to Ruth Smeeth, an anti-Corbyn, and Jewish, Labour MP. Wadsworth then heckled Chakrabarti for not taking questions from the BAME journalists present, and stood up to denounce Smeeth for 'working hand in hand' with a right-wing newspaper, sparking fury from other MPs present. Smeeth herself left the room in tears.

Wadsworth was expelled from Labour two years later for bringing the party into disrepute, but the damage had already been done. Not only did the episode entirely overshadow the Chakrabarti report, it fuelled another phenomenon: the rise of a vocal faction on the Labour left who believed that the antisemitism crisis was entirely manufactured as a means to destroy the Corbyn project – and that the leadership, giving in to this conspiracy, was prepared to throw its members under a bus. This faction tapped into the prevailing sense of defensiveness in Corbynite circles, and various blindspots on antisemitism among some elements on the left.

Prominent in this emerging faction were older activists, many of whom had ripped up their membership cards in the Blair era, and rejoined since Corbyn's rise; in meetings, they would often alienate younger members with angry, obsessive tirades. They were exemplified by Jackie Walker, an activist eventually expelled after describing Jews as 'chief financiers of the sugar and slave trade'; arguing that 'the Jewish Holocaust does not allow Zionists to do what they want';

questioning at a Labour antisemitism training session why Jewish organizations, such as schools, needed high security; and claiming (falsely) that Holocaust Memorial Day commemorated only Jewish victims.[28] (Walker's defenders would claim this was a witch hunt against pro-Palestinian activists. It is striking, though, that her offending comments – as was the case with most of Labour's high-profile antisemitism scandals – had nothing to do with Palestine.)

These episodic flare-ups proved politically difficult and damaging, as well as distressing to Jews of varied political opinions. But, it turned out, they were only the preamble. Almost two years later, in spring 2018, the reigniting of the Mear One mural controversy, and the Corbyn leadership's desultory response to it, triggered a sequence of events from which there would be no recovering.

After the fresh complaints over Corbyn's comments about the Mear One mural – and the leadership's clumsy, self-exculpatory response – things snowballed. Amid mounting condemnation from inside and outside Labour – not just of the mural, but of antisemitism on the left in general – the Board of Deputies of British Jews and the Jewish Leadership Council organized a hundreds-strong protest, including dozens of Labour MPs, outside Parliament, under the banner 'Enough Is Enough'. Among them were angry Jewish protesters demanding Corbyn's resignation. Days later, Christine Shawcroft, a Corbyn-supporting member of Labour's ruling executive council and chair of its internal disputes panel, resigned under pressure from the Labour leader's office after it was uncovered that she had defended a council candidate who had shared antisemitic online posts. (The candidate told journalists at the time that he had posted one offending article on Facebook 'for the purpose of debate' but that he did not agree with its content.) Shawcroft declared that 'political reasons' were partly behind his suspension (though she later admitted that she had not looked sufficiently closely at the posts, which included outright denial of the Holocaust). In fact, the candidate should have been suspended long before, but party staff working under Labour's then general secretary, Iain McNicol, in the summer of 2017 had simply issued Notices of Investigation. Nonetheless, Shawcroft's suggestion that he be allowed to stand as a council candidate while under investigation itself suggested factional loyalty over properly addressing antisemitism.

At the beginning of April 2018, a week or so after Luciana Berger had drawn fresh attention to the Mear One mural controversy, the *Sunday Times* published an article headlined 'Exposed: Jeremy Corbyn's hate factory'. The piece presented various racist comments, including antisemitism, that had been posted on several Corbyn-supporting Facebook groups – groups, moreover, that counted some Corbyn staffers among their members.[29]

Here is a classic example of why being able to walk and chew gum is so important – and what happens when you can't, or don't. It is unsurprising that Corbyn staffers were members of groups named 'We Support Jeremy Corbyn', which had many thousands of followers; moreover, they were unlikely to encounter many if any of the thousands of comments being posted, let alone the extremely small proportion that were racist. Nonetheless, the fact that antisemitic comments were being posted by any self-described Corbyn supporters was – and is – a genuine problem. One group was founded and run by a Labour member, Musabbir Ali, who had shared a blog entitled 'Timeline of the Jewish Genocide of the British People', accusing Jews of being behind wars from Oliver Cromwell's time onwards.[30] 'There was stuff posted in that group like "Jews are shit, if you want to touch them you have to wash your hands" and sharing Holocaust denial, claims Jews run the world, and claims Jews are behind every war,' says an appalled Harry Hayball, Momentum's social media officer.

As examples mounted, so did pressure on the leader to do something about it. Corbyn wrote a letter to Jewish leaders on 26 March, professing that he was 'committed to eliminating antisemitism wherever it exists', and that he recognized 'that antisemitism has surfaced within the Labour Party, and has too often been dismissed as simply a matter of a few bad apples', which was a direct rebuke to those in denial. 'There needs to be a deeper understanding of what constitutes anti-Semitism in the labour movement,' Corbyn continued, acknowledging that 'newer forms of anti-Semitism have been woven into criticism of Israeli governments'. An article published under his name in the *Evening Standard* went even further, accepting that we 'must also face the uncomfortable fact that a small number of our members and supporters hold anti-Semitic views and attitudes, which need to be confronted and dealt with more rapidly and effectively'. He listed examples, including sympathy for Adolf Hitler, and added that some are drawn to the pro-Palestinian movement because 'it affords an opportunity to express hostility to Jewish people in a "respectable" setting' and that others see 'capitalism and imperialism as the product of conspiracy by a small shadowy elite'.[31]

But here was the problem – a now familiar one. These interventions were hasty, *ad hoc* responses to this specific crisis as it erupted. While they were all well and good, there was no coherent strategy within the leader's office on how to tackle claims of antisemitism. What was more, the open, apologetic tone of these pieces jarred with Corbyn's own public interventions on the issue, which were often angry and defensive, centring on his lifelong opposition to racism. Because Corbyn was capable of showing genuine heartfelt passion and emotion about other forms of injustice, the contrast with his response on antisemitism was all the more glaring.

Anti-racism is core to Corbyn's sense of identity. He believes, proudly, that he has fought oppression all his life, so being labelled a racist was a cause of profound personal trauma to him. 'On a personal level, he found it utterly bewildering,' says long-standing Islington colleague Sue Lukes, who had helped his team script videos on Jewish issues, such as Hanukkah messages. 'He never imagined anyone could find him antisemitic; it floored him.' But this, even those close to Corbyn admitted, disastrously clouded his judgement. 'I don't think Jeremy thinks there isn't a problem, or that it's all smears,' says Jon Lansman. 'But he still underestimated the effect it has on Jews.'

Rather than write an article in the *Evening Standard*, Andrew Fisher believes Corbyn should have made 'a speech, a public "I understand, we will be quicker on this" . . . But I think Jeremy didn't emotionally engage with it enough.' Corbyn, indeed, had one such speech written for him, by a leading left-wing Jewish intellectual who preferred to remain anonymous. 'It was brilliant, absolutely brilliant,' says one of Corbyn's leading allies. 'Jeremy just wouldn't do it, because he was so angry about it all. He'd say: "Why do I have to defend myself on this, it's unbelievable!" [We had] absolutely the best advisers you could have; they then get frustrated and it was almost "What do we do?" Despair, absolute despair.' Indeed, the *Jewish Chronicle* had offered to publish a piece in the early days of Corbyn's leadership, written in Corbyn's name by the same Jewish thinker. It never happened. When, in wide-ranging speeches written for him, a writer had inserted an apology on antisemitism, Corbyn would get visibly irritated. 'His line was that the media is obsessed with this,' says one aide, 'and that's making us all obsessed with it.' In particular, he would angrily query what he saw as an excessive focus on antisemitism at the expense of Islamophobia. Corbyn's intensely protective wife, Laura Alvarez, likewise felt that he was being unjustly pilloried, and that his aides were not doing enough to rebut the criticism. Sometimes, a tug of war ensued: when the likes of Milne would arrive at Corbyn's house to record a video on antisemitism, Alvarez sat trying to rewrite the script.

For Corbyn, as for many in the party, it was beyond aggravating to be savaged by accusers who were themselves drenched in racism. During the 2010s, the Conservative government had indulged in persistent anti-migrant rhetoric; it had stripped away the healthcare and housing of Windrush Britons, and carried out what seemed like a systematic programme of deportation from the UK. The most prominent Conservative Tory Muslim peer, Baroness Sayeeda Warsi, had accused the party of institutional Islamophobia, which she said 'exists right from the grassroots, all the way up to the top'.[32] In September 2018 Conservative MEPs voted to defend Hungary's far-right regime, itself the most flagrantly antisemitic government in Europe. The right-wing press, with its symbiotic relationship to the Conservative government, baited minorities such as migrants, Muslims and refugees on a near-daily basis. For them to point the finger over racism enraged Corbyn and his grassroots supporters alike.

Yet none of this was an excuse – or it shouldn't have been. Antisemitism was a genuine problem, and one causing many Jews genuine hurt. 'Once you get on to that emotional plane on an issue, you're stuffed,' one of Corbyn's senior allies tells me off the record. 'It happens to all of us, but most of us in politics have someone who shakes us and says: "This is why they're coming for you, let me deal with it." But once you've been got at on an emotional level, it's very, very difficult.'

'We delivered as much on antisemitism as we could operationally despite the failings of those in Labour HQ charged to manage the processes,' former Chief of Staff Karie Murphy tells me. 'What we failed on was politically, because Jeremy found it difficult to engage.' In August 2018, Milne and Murphy arranged for Corbyn to make a speech in front of an invited audience at the Jewish Museum London in Camden, focusing on both opposing antisemitism and defending Jewish cultural and religious practices. That was not without problems at the museum's end. Behind the scenes prominent Jewish figures pressured the celebrated institution not to host the speech, calling it a stunt[33] – and as the day approached the museum grew increasingly hesitant about holding the event. So, too, was Corbyn. Fearing that this attempt to defuse the antisemitism crisis would blow up in his face – that he might be abused, perhaps publicly denounced as an antisemite – in trademark style, he made his own discomfort clear: he went AWOL, as he tended to when trying to avoid conflict or when he did not wish to do something, and he didn't come into the office or answer his phone. The problem, one Corbyn ally told me, was that 'Milne went and did it without clearing it with Jeremy first.' Corbyn 'wasn't comfortable with the speech. Sometimes they do panic: Seumas is a last-minute jockey – there'd be nothing, then suddenly an op-ed or a speech.' Corbyn, it turned out, sought the advice of his trusted Jewish comrades, who argued that if he wasn't ready and the speech was not properly thought through, it would only make things worse. Corbyn feared being attacked and pilloried. The plan fell through and the speech was never delivered.

Meanwhile, Karie Murphy approached Lord Michael Levy, a businessman and one of Britain's most prominent Jewish figures, once described by the *Jerusalem Post* as 'undoubtedly the notional leader of British Jewry'. The son of impoverished Jewish immigrants, he made his fortune in the music industry. Lord Levy struck an alliance with Tony Blair during his tenure as Labour leader; he could never be accused of sharing Corbyn's politics. But anyone who wanted a dialogue with Britain's Jewish community would surely need to engage Lord Levy; he was president of the Jewish Free

School, a comprehensive school that was once among the biggest of its kind in the world; of Jewish Care, the largest provider of social care services for British Jews; and of the Jewish Lads' and Girls' Brigade, a national Jewish youth organization. In the first year of Corbyn's leadership, before the antisemitism crisis had reached a deafening level, Lord Levy had a one-on-one meeting with Corbyn and then arranged a dinner between the Labour leader and twelve prominent Labour-supporting Jews. In a private room at the House of Lords, Corbyn listened as several speakers briefed him on a range of subjects – from the Holocaust Educational Trust's chief executive discussing the Shoah, to the president of the Union of Jewish Students briefing about the situation on campus. But there was no follow-up from Corbyn's office. As the antisemitism crisis began to consume Labour in the spring of 2018, Karie Murphy reached out to Lord Levy – a move made in good faith on her part – and met him once a month and occasionally for dinner, sometimes with the party's general secretary, Jennie Formby. Now, Murphy asked him what he wanted from the leadership, what needed to be done. 'Some [things] I could act on, some I couldn't,' she tells me. Trying to be constructive, Lord Levy recommended that the leader's office work with Simon Morris, the jovial former chief executive of Jewish Care. Although Morris did not share Corbyn's left-wing radicalism, he was a passionate Labour supporter who wished the party well whoever was at the helm. In late June 2018, Morris – who had already met up with an enthusiastic Karie Murphy several times – attended a meeting in the leader's office, involving Corbyn, Seumas Milne and Andrew Fisher. The meeting began well: Jewish Care had a care home in Corbyn's constituency, and he spoke animatedly about social care, showing genuine understanding. But when the conversation shifted to antisemitism, the mood changed.

Morris had been asked before the meeting not to insist on any preconditions for his cooperation, in case of disappointment, but he did make one initial suggestion: that Corbyn visit Israel. Fresh in his mind was an official trip by Prince William to the Jewish state, occupied Palestine and Jordan – including a visit to a Palestinian refugee camp in Ramallah, making him the first British Royal to visit the occupied West Bank. Morris explained why the issue of antisemitism had become so sensitive for British Jews and suggested that visiting Israel would be a tangible sign: not of abandoning the Palestinians or their struggles, but recognizing the state of Israel's right to exist. Given that Corbyn is a public supporter of a two-state solution, this was his own formal position anyway. He could visit Yad Vashem, the official memorial to Jews murdered in the Holocaust, an action that, Morris argued, would demonstrate a powerful understanding of the trauma of the Jewish people. Corbyn, however, did what he did so often in conversations he found difficult or which contained the seeds of conflict: he zoned out and veered off at tangents or went down rabbit holes. Nonetheless, the meeting ended on friendly enough terms, and a place was created for Morris in the leader's office; funding for the post and a job description were both signed off. But Corbyn subsequently avoided discussions about Morris, doing his disappearing act routine to avoid awkward conversations, and Morris never took up his post. 'If he set a condition to go to Israel,' says one Corbyn ally, 'that's unreasonable, when we're spending our whole time saying that being Jewish is not necessarily the same as the government or state of Israel,' noting that Corbyn had visited both Israel and Palestine before. This might be an entirely legitimate argument – but it's one the Labour leader failed to make. Instead, he missed another opportunity to reach out to the Jewish community.

Another name in the frame was Lord Levy's son Daniel, a distinguished political scientist who had worked with think tanks such as J Street, a progressive US Jewish organization, and was a staunch critic of the Israeli government and the Israeli occupation of the Palestinian territories. Unlike his father, his politics were close to those of the Corbyn leadership. He had written nuanced, thoughtful pieces on Labour and antisemitism, arguing that the leadership had 'been slow and cumbersome' and had 'lacked in empathy or in conveying a sense of passion in fighting antisemitism', but also that prominent Jewish leaders determined to push for Corbyn's removal were making 'a terrible mistake'. Levy denounced observations by leading Jewish newspapers that Corbyn posed an 'existential threat to Jewish life in this country', and former Chief Rabbi Jonathan Sacks's comparison of Corbyn with Enoch Powell.[34] Daniel Levy, in other words, was exactly the sort of constructive, thoughtful voice Corbyn needed to be listening to, even if there were points of disagreement between the two. But the Labour leader showed no interest in meeting him. 'Because Levy was seen as "Blair's banker", knows people on the Board of Deputies, [was] a very successful businessman, Jeremy wouldn't even meet Daniel,' says one of Corbyn's most senior allies. 'I asked him to meet Daniel. It was mistake after mistake. The perception then is he doesn't give a fuck.'

In defence of Karie Murphy, those close to Lord Levy believed she genuinely wanted to help, but somehow did not seem able to do so. Later in the summer of 2018, John McDonnell phoned Lord Levy and told him, 'You're one of the only people who can help.' Levy's response was curt: 'I wish I could, but while Jeremy is leader, you can't resolve it.' For his part, McDonnell privately expressed his own repeated exasperation at the leadership's failure to grasp the nettle on the crisis.

In part, Corbyn's sometimes blinkered approach can be ascribed to his belief that he already had an extremely close relationship with the Jewish community, in the form of Jewish activists alongside whom he had marched and organized for decades through anti-war and pro-Palestinian activities. In 2017, some of them had founded Jewish Voice for Labour, an unabashedly pro-Corbyn organization whose membership grew to around 1,200 members, albeit two thirds of whom were not actually Jewish.

Yet there was a fundamental problem: JVL's own position was that while antisemitism on the left and in Labour existed, 'all the evidence shows this problem to be small, no worse than in the rest of society', and that the antisemitism crisis was 'deliberately produced' both to shut down critics of Israel and to undermine Corbyn's leadership. They were passionately critical, too, of the Board of Deputies and what they saw as the Jewish establishment. But their approach was at odds with where most Jewish people were, including many who had actively supported Corbyn. In a speech at the Limmud Festival – an annual event organized by a leading Jewish charity – Jon Lansman declared of JVL: 'It is an organization which is not just tiny but has no real connection with the Jewish community at all.'[35] His speech provoked fury from JVL: it was 'deeply disturbing', they tell me, and wrote them off as 'the wrong kind of Jew'. Nonetheless, this view of

JVL remains widespread among Jewish communities. 'I spoke to a lot of Jewish people,' explains journalist and author Rachel Shabi, who supported Corbyn in both leadership elections and had gone on record as backing him, 'and their frustration with JVL is: "How has this crank group become privileged inside the Labour Party?" They became everyone's mascot, anyone's antisemitism alibi: "They don't think antisemitism is so, and so it isn't." '

JVL senior figures believe there has been a witch hunt against Jews with dissenting views on Israel, and are indignant about the number of Jews suspended from the Labour Party following allegations of antisemitism. 'You don't get black people accused of anti-black racism; it's quite extraordinary,' their co-chair Jenny Manson tells me. But there is no question JVL became more entrenched in their views. In February 2019, their secretary, Glyn Secker, declared: 'What has happened is that there has been a major campaign of misusing antisemitism. And I say that as someone whose family has perished in the Holocaust, and my partner's family . . . These allegations have been made up in order to discredit the leadership.'[36]

While JVL's views represented a legitimate strand of Jewish opinion to be engaged with, the problem lay in the fact that Corbyn was less interested in other Jewish perspectives. There needed to be a better strategy to engage with the Jewish Labour Movement, which was undoubtedly overwhelmingly hostile to the Labour leadership, but which was the most representative organization of the diminished number of Labour-supporting Jews. Corbyn had attended the JLM's Hanukah party in December 2017 and privately met its chair in the New Year, while Laura Murray met them regularly. But after the antisemitism crisis escalated in the spring of 2018, they refused to engage further with either the party leadership or headquarters.

JVL, indeed, could prove an active barrier to dialogue with the wider Jewish community. On one occasion, Laura Murray was told to invite a range of Jewish organizations and individuals for a roundtable discussion. There was broad interest, but when the invited parties discovered JVL would be present, they began to drop out, one by one, until only JVL was left. The roundtable had been publicized in advance in the *Jewish Chronicle*; if it went ahead with just JVL, the fallout would be dramatic. Murray attempted to cancel it, but Murphy and Corbyn insisted on pushing through with it. (Another Corbyn ally strongly disputes this, saying that Corbyn understood that an event boycotted by mainstream Jewish organizations and individuals would be ridiculous. 'This isn't going to be a table, it's going to be a stool,' Corbyn joked, instructing the office to scrap the roundtable.)

Other Jewish voices – unequivocally pro-Corbyn and pro-Palestinian, but nonetheless believing that Labour needed to do more on antisemitism – were ignored. Michael Segalov is a young left-wing journalist and activist. When I first met him in 2012, he was, like many leftists of his generation, implacably opposed to Labour as an irretrievably right-wing, neoliberal party; he only joined in 2015 to support Corbyn. But when Corbyn's political secretary, Amy Jackson, suggested Segalov be brought in for advice, a senior figure informed her he had the 'wrong politics'. It was left to Andrew Fisher to reach out, occasionally seeking advice from him. Momentum founder Jon Lansman became the leadership's go-to voice, who would be sent out to defend Corbyn publicly on the issue and to show that the party was taking antisemitism seriously. Often, Lansman himself would be bombarded with virulent messages on social media, some of them clearly antisemitic in nature. 'I now feel I have been used as a Jew to defend the party, but I'm not supported afterwards,' he tells me. 'They're quite happy for me to go on fucking radio or TV to defend Jeremy, but I'm not supported afterwards.'

Part of the problem, as many of those close to Corbyn point out, is that for nearly all his political life, he was used to speaking to people he broadly agreed with; he was not equipped or prepared to deal not only with those who strongly disagreed, but those who were overtly hostile to his politics, as was undeniably the case with most leading figures in the Board of Deputies.

As so often, he needed a strategy and Laura Murray pushed for one, setting up a meeting between Corbyn and his aides and the Board for 25 April. Even if the leadership did not feel it was possible to acquiesce to all of their demands, they could at least find compromise positions. Accordingly, Murray drew up a document setting out a number of such compromises: one, in response to the Board's call for an independent ombudsman to oversee antisemitism cases within the Labour Party and report back to the Board, proposed instead that Labour provide the Deputies with monthly or quarterly updates on cases of antisemitism. The suggestions were all ignored. Corbyn and his aides marched into the meeting with little to offer. It did not help that some members of the Board brought the subject of Israel into the proceedings. One asked Corbyn why he could never say anything positive about Israel – perhaps, praising its hospitals for treating Arabs and Jews alike. When another declared that some Labour members could not get past the creation of Israel, Milne commented: 'It's not the state exactly, it's the ethnic cleansing which took place at the end.' It was hardly a productive comment at an event dedicated to confronting contemporary antisemitism. Corbyn was asked, too, if he would visit Israel. He was noncommittal, but many of his allies believed it would have cost nothing to agree, and he could have combined such a trip with travelling to Occupied Palestine. In the aftermath, the Deputies released a public letter expressing disappointment; no subsequent meeting took place.[37]

That summer of 2018, things got worse, with two key flashpoints which caused huge political trauma for Labour. Back on 12 December 2016, both Labour and the government had adopted the working definition of antisemitism devised by the International Holocaust Remembrance Alliance, or IHRA, in Budapest seven months earlier. The definition itself was uncontroversial, stating: 'Antisemitism is a certain perception of Jews, which may be expressed as hatred toward Jews. Rhetorical and physical manifestations of antisemitism are directed toward Jewish or non-Jewish individuals and/or their property, toward Jewish community institutions and religious facilities.' Accompanying the definition were a series of eleven examples, almost all of which were equally uncontroversial. For example: 'Calling for, aiding, or justifying the killing or harming of Jews in the name of a radical ideology or an extremist view of religion' or 'accusing Jews as a people of being responsible for real or imagined wrongdoing committed by a single Jewish person or group, or even for acts committed by non-Jews.'[38]

There were, however, two examples over which several pro-Palestinian voices raised concerns. The first of these read: 'Denying the Jewish people their right to self-determination, e.g. by claiming that the existence of a State of Israel is a racist endeavour'; the second stated:

'Applying double standards by requiring of it [Israel] a behaviour not expected or demanded of any other democratic nation.' In autumn 2018, I met British-Palestinian lawyer Salma Karmi-Ayyoub, to try to understand why Palestinians were so worried about them. As far as the first of these examples was concerned, Karmi-Ayyoub told me, pro-Palestinian activists feared that it would extend to 'prohibiting people from being able to talk about the state of Israel and how or if it is a racist endeavour from the Palestinian perspective'. This seems an entirely reasonable concern. It is surely right that Palestinians themselves should feel unencumbered in describing their own lived experience since 1948: the deprivation of their right to national determination; the expulsions which accompanied Israel's foundation; their land in the West Bank stolen; and a so-called 'nation-state law' passed in 2018 which was denounced by opposition parties as racist and akin to apartheid because of its downgrading of the rights of the Arab minority.[39] The second example, Karmi-Ayyoub feared, would be used to argue against the Boycott Divestment and Sanctions campaign that urges action to pressure Israel into complying with international law. In Karmi-Ayyoub's words, 'unless you're calling for a boycott of every country that abuses human rights you're then accused of applying a double standard and therefore being an antisemite'.

In August 2018, Professor Manuel Hassassian – the Palestinian ambassador to the UK – made an even more passionate plea. 'Anybody who is serious about understanding the historical context in which Israel was created will know that 750,000 Palestinians were ethnically cleansed by Zionist terror militias and 500 Palestinian villages destroyed,' he declared. 'It is difficult not to define this as a racist endeavour.' Agree or not, this was a debate in part about the Palestinians, but almost largely without their involvement.

It wasn't just pro-Palestinian activists who expressed these concerns. David Feldman, the director of the Pears Institute for the Study of Antisemitism, declared that the definition's key passage was 'bewilderingly imprecise' and there was 'a danger that the overall effect will place the onus on Israel's critics to demonstrate they are not antisemitic'.[40] This was an issue that also preoccupied parliamentarians across the political spectrum. Indeed, ardent anti-Corbynite, then Labour MP, Chuka Umunna declared on behalf of Parliament's cross-party Home Affairs Select Committee that 'although we broadly accept this definition, we propose additional clarification to ensure that freedom of speech is maintained in the context of discourse about Israel and Palestine, without allowing antisemitism to permeate in any debate'. That included emphasizing it was 'not antisemitic to criticise the Government of Israel without additional evidence to suggest antisemitic intent' and that 'It is not antisemitic to hold the Israeli Government to higher standards than autocratic nations and dictatorships around the world, or to take a particular interest in the Israeli Government's policies or actions, without additional evidence to suggest antisemitic intent.'[41] The IHRA Plenary had themselves emphasized it was a 'non-legally binding definition', and did not describe the examples as set in stone, instead clarifying: 'To guide IHRA in its work, the following examples may serve as illustrations.'

There were valid criticisms of the IHRA examples, not least from the perspective of the Palestinians themselves. Corbyn, with his passionate commitment to the Palestinian cause, agreed with them. But Corbyn's Labour did not have the political capital or space to engage in this debate, and pro-Palestinian voices were largely excluded by the media. 'When you're a party accused of antisemitism, saying "we're going to define antisemitism, we know better than an international panel of Jewish academics agreeing with it" – it's just a fucking idiotic thing to do,' says Andrew Fisher wearily. Fisher himself had argued for the party to adopt the examples in full from the start.

Initially, however, the Labour leadership's reservations went under the media radar. When, in December 2016, Seumas Milne briefed the press that Labour was only accepting the definition, his qualification went unnoticed. In July 2018, Labour drew up its own Code of Conduct, adopting the IHRA definition, but replacing the examples with its own guidelines described as 'in part derived from the IHRA working examples', and specifically omitting the two at the centre of controversy.[42]

Several figures close to Corbyn, who had tried to persuade him to adopt the IHRA examples in full, despaired of his stubbornness over the issue. Among them was Unite's Len McCluskey. 'Because that's what Jeremy is like,' McCluskey tells me with a sigh. 'Here you have a principled decent man, and all his life he's been able to say what he wanted, and if someone thinks it's outrageous, he'd take the criticism and defend himself. Suddenly he's the leader of a political party and your views have to be tailored accordingly, you can't just say something and say it's your view, happy to be criticized, happy to defend yourself. You can't, you're the leader of a party.'

For all this, it was Milne who was the most vociferous opponent. He was undoubtedly passionate on a point of principle as a lifelong supporter of the Palestinian cause. Privately, his reasoning was this. If the IHRA was passed in full, Corbyn's enemies would trawl through the back catalogue of comments made by the Labour leader and Milne himself, then submit official complaints to the party on the basis that they stood in violation of the definition. That would trigger a disciplinary procedure, leading to their possible suspension, necessitating Corbyn's removal as leader; he would then be replaced by his deputy, Tom Watson, who would proceed to purge the party's left. As Andrew Fisher pointed out, however, this was nonsensical: there was a pro-Corbyn majority on the party's National Executive Committee, and the general secretary, Jennie Formby, was a committed Labour leftist who would never countenance such a move.

At a meeting of senior Labour figures called to discuss IHRA, convened in Parliament at the beginning of the summer of 2018, Milne and Shami Chakrabarti – now the shadow attorney general – locked horns over the wording of the second half of the seventh example: that 'claiming the existence of a State of Israel is a racist endeavour' constituted antisemitism. As far as Milne was concerned, the statement was inherently flawed. His argument internally went like this. The wording was so convoluted and subtle that anyone with anti-Zionist sympathies – or any Palestinian who regarded their treatment as racist – would be targeted. In the half-example that was objected to, the indefinite article could easily be lost, denying the right of Palestinians to talk about their own discrimination, including the ethnic cleansing of 1948, or the discrimination in Israel where they were forbidden from returning to their homes. Accordingly, one form of discrimination, abuse and bigotry – and the right to talk about it – would be set against another. These were certainly arguments many Palestinians identified with, and they were largely left unheard in the debate on the IHRA examples.

Chakrabarti demurred. She thought that the distinction between 'a' State of Israel – which is what the example said, and which could refer to any hypothetical Israel – rather than 'the' State of Israel, was crucial to any sensible interpretation. When Milne again disagreed, the exchange blew up. 'We'll disagree,' Chakrabarti angrily replied, 'and you can take the whole project down with you.' It was far from the only clash at the top. At another meeting, when Andrew Fisher proposed adopting the IHRA examples in full, Karie Murphy – who largely took a backseat in this particular saga – warned the party risked selling out the Palestinians.

Amy Jackson, Corbyn's parliamentary secretary, told him that there was a majority on the NEC to pass the IHRA definition and its examples in full and without exception, regardless of whatever Corbyn did or said. But Corbyn – encouraged by Milne – refused to countenance it. Accepting the IHRA definition would, he maintained, have an awful impact within the Labour Party for anyone criticizing Israel; it might, indeed, lead to their expulsion from the party. Yet circumstances in which any Labour Party member would ever be expelled were extreme indeed. 'Is the party ever going to end up in a position where people can't criticize the actions of the Israeli government?' asks one senior aide, contemptuous of the idea Labour would use IHRA to silence Israel's critics. 'That was the summer of awful, awful, awful attacks, and that was his own stupid fault.'

Apart from anything else, what should surely have given Corbyn pause for thought was that two key pro-Corbyn members of the NEC, Jon Lansman and Rhea Wolfson, were Jewish – and were determined to vote for the IHRA examples in full. Effectively, then, Corbyn was antagonizing otherwise politically sympathetic Jews.

It was yet another example of Corbyn choosing to die on the wrong hill. Labour was inevitably going to adopt the IHRA definition. It was surely better for the leadership to do so proactively, than to zig-zag there incoherently, provoke lots of avoidable outrage and lose plenty of arguments along the way, and in the end gain no credit for accepting the IHRA position. But at least it would – well, what?

*

If all this weren't bad enough, that summer things escalated further. In mid-July, after a series of votes on Brexit, Margaret Hodge, another prominent Jewish Labour MP, launched into a furious tirade at Corbyn over the IHRA saga behind the Speaker's Chair in the House of Commons, reportedly yelling: 'You're a fucking antisemite and a racist. You have proved you don't want people like me in the party.' (Hodge denied swearing.) Corbyn's outward response was calm: 'I'm sorry you feel like that.'[43] Privately, he was enraged. Hodge and Corbyn went back a long way, and not in a good way. Hodge had been a long-standing councillor in Islington, Corbyn's own borough, and led the council for a time, where they had clashed. Hodge herself had moreover co-sponsored the vote of no confidence against Corbyn back in 2016.

Shortly afterwards, on his way to an event marking the memory of the late socialist writer Mike Marqusee, his friends noticed that Corbyn was shaken up. As far as his allies were concerned, Hodge's attack declared open season for newspapers to denounce Corbyn as a racist and an antisemite – because, their lawyers concluded, the Labour leader would not sue. 'It was a real sea change in how he was talked about,' says a senior aide.

The leader's office, however, doubled down. While Corbyn continued to insist on an apology, Karie Murphy was determined that disciplinary action should be initiated against Hodge by the party itself, with a view to suspending her. Chief Whip Nick Brown argued against doing so, as did John Mc Donnell, while Seumas Milne was privately anxious about the optics of taking action against a high-profile Jewish MP. Their fears were overridden, and the party general secretary, Jennie Formby, issued Hodge with a Notice of Investigation. So began an entirely self-defeating enterprise.

Meanwhile, Nick Brown sought to broker a conversation between Corbyn and Hodge. One mediator was John McDonnell, who, en route to the Norfolk Broads for his annual holiday, phoned Hodge, attempting a conciliation. The pair had known each other since the 1980s when she was chair of the Association of London Authorities and he was chief executive. Hodge told McDonnell that the matter was already with her lawyers. However, she did not rule out a conversation with Corbyn, and suggested the leadership set up a panel involving both British Jews and Palestinians to offer advice on resolving the IHRA controversy. But for the next few days, Corbyn refused to take calls or respond to texts from his allies. Throughout the summer, senior Labour figures, including McDonnell, begged Corbyn to seek a rapprochement with Hodge, shake hands, and offer to set up a panel involving both British Jews and Palestinians to give advice on resolving the IHRA controversy. 'I won't do it without an apology,' Corbyn said emphatically, 'it's never going to happen.' While Corbyn was genuinely very upset, some of his allies believed Murphy was goading him. Privately, Lansman warned senior figures that the debacle could destroy the leadership. He wasn't far off.

Things continued to escalate. At a shadow cabinet 'Preparing for Government' awayday on 23 July 2018, attendees learned that Murphy planned to send Hodge another letter informing her that disciplinary action would be dropped only if she apologized in full. Calling Corbyn to an urgent meeting – at which Milne, Murphy, Fisher and Corbyn's son Seb were also present – McDonnell made a forceful argument against the letter; Corbyn apparently agreed. Later that day, the letter was sent anyway. Furious, McDonnell went ballistic at Karie Murphy, who he believed had turned Corbyn's head. Murphy responded by saying that Corbyn, hurt and angry by Hodge's allegations, was driving the disciplinary action and that there was nothing she could do. McDonnell went public, calling for the party to drop the action and – genuinely fearing that any attempt to remove Hodge from the parliamentary party would provoke a number of MPs to resign *en masse* – again attempted to defuse the growing tension, declaring that Hodge had a 'good heart'.[44] Corbyn, meanwhile, was now refusing to speak to his longest-standing ally, angry at what he perceived as McDonnell talking to Hodge behind his back. For his part, McDonnell went silent, refusing to engage with the leader's office for weeks. 'Everyone,' says Karie Murphy, 'was emotionally in a very dark place.'

Parliament had emptied out for the summer recess, and most Labour researchers were working five-hour days in shorts and T-shirts. But the leader's office was bombarded relentlessly with media queries about past trips, meetings and speeches Corbyn had done over the years: most strikingly, his visit to Tunisia in 2014. There, Corbyn had taken part in a ceremony commemorating the innocent victims of a 1985 Israeli air strike, during which wreaths had been laid for the Palestinians accused of taking part in the terror atrocity at the 1972 Summer Olympics in Munich. 'It was just constant,' recalls one aide. 'People must have been looking at this stuff for I don't know how long, digging it all up.' Staffers spent days rummaging through files, letters, emails and receipts from trips dating back twenty, twenty-five years. Corbyn, meanwhile, 'was pretty much detached from staff for much of the summer', according to Karie Murphy. 'This was a man who was beyond broken-hearted, that, as a proud antiracist campaigner, he was being accused of racism. So he was paralysed. He was being asked to do things that in some way would confirm in people's minds that the reason he had to do these things was because he was antisemitic. It wasn't true – no one will convince me that he has an antisemitic bone in his body – but he could have found strength if he'd embraced people.'

At the best of times, Corbyn's schedule lacked announcements or stories for the media to report on. But that summer, as the communications strategy seemed to break down completely, there was a clear story to fill the vacuum: antisemitism. In one supposedly short interview for a news clip, eleven minutes were dedicated to antisemitism. 'It was just awful, it was *awful*,' recounts one aide who had been on the road with him. 'He looked defensive, he sounded defensive, because our position was just getting hammered from all sides. It was a hot summer, and it was just incessant.'

Both the Margaret Hodge and the IHRA affairs ended in predictable and humiliating climbdowns. In August, the disciplinary action was quietly dropped – without Hodge having offered Corbyn's demanded apology. At the beginning of September, the NEC met to discuss the IHRA examples. Corbyn brought along a statement, written by Milne, which had been briefed to journalists as an additional document to be passed by the NEC as a clarification of the definition. Together with commitments to stand in solidarity with the Jewish people and fight antisemitism, it emphasized that the IHRA definition and examples would 'not undermine freedom of expression on the Israel–Palestine conflict', that 'it cannot be considered racist to treat Israel like any other state or assess its conduct against the standards of international law', and 'nor should it be regarded as antisemitic to describe Israel, its policies or the circumstances around its foundation as racist because of their discriminatory impact, or to support another settlement of the Israel–Palestine conflict'. The day before, Milne had been told that there were not the numbers to pass the document – but, with journalists already having been prematurely briefed on it, Corbyn brought it along anyway and read it out to the committee. When it became clear that there was a majority opposed to passing it, the meeting was abruptly adjourned. After it recommenced, Corbyn simply said that his statement was not intended to be taken to a vote. 'It was so humiliating, so ridiculous,' says one aide. 'It just cemented in people's minds that Jeremy is the problem.'

In normal times, the parliamentary recess gives the opposition an opportunity to try to set its stall out to the British public. The events of the summer, however, had damaged and divided the leadership, and bred more distrust and anger with Labour among Britain's Jews. More generally, people were left with a vague impression of crankiness and infighting, and – although the antisemitism issue with Labour was not widely understood – a general sense spread of something untoward, not right about the party.

Then there was the other story. In marked contrast with the eagerness to discipline Margaret Hodge, the party machine was accused of being notably slow to move against cases of antisemitism within Labour. These accusations were spot on – though it has to be said that, from where I was standing, much responsibility lay not with Corbyn's allies, but with the largely anti-Corbynite party structures, which until March 2018 were presided over by General Secretary Iain McNicol. During this time, the recommendations of the Chakrabarti review (which reported in mid-2016) were not implemented, and – despite repeated prodding by John McDonnell – the vast majority of complaints had, according to newspaper mentions of the leaked report, not been acted upon by Labour's Governance and Legal Unit (GLU). Indeed, a later investigation by the Labour Party found that, between 1 November 2016 and 19 February 2018, just thirty-four investigations had been initiated out of more than 300 complaints. The report speculated that this lack of action could have been due to 'incompetence, mismanagement, prioritising other work and/or lack of motivation to take disciplinary action when there were not factional gains to be made'. (A former GLU staffer thought rather differently, batting aside the contents of the report as 'A highly selective, retrospective review of the party's poor record . . . conducted in the dying days of Corbyn's leadership in order to justify their inaction.)[45] During this time, just ten individuals were suspended, with another twenty-four Notices of Investigation issued in relation to antisemitism. At least 170 cases identified as antisemitism meriting investigation were not acted upon.

Some of the cases are genuinely disturbing. One member was found to have posted comments supporting Holocaust denial, called Jews 'cockroaches', declared 'never trust anything a Jew says' and shared a post which said 'Jews admit organising White Genocide'. Suspension from the Labour Party should surely have been automatic – yet there was no evidence this was discussed. Instead, the GLU issued a Notice of Investigation, which merely amounts to informing the member in question that they're being investigated. The case of another member who had been reported for Holocaust denial was not even logged, let alone investigated. Elsewhere, twenty-six cases were submitted to the GLU by Labour Against Antisemitism (LAAS); according to the Labour report, at least twenty-two of these should have led to suspensions for an assortment of gratuitous and deeply offensive antisemitic statements and the sharing of antisemitic material, including explicit Holocaust denial and conspiracy theories. One stated, 'speaking for myself I despise Jews I think they are vermin and the scum of the earth'; another explicitly wrote 'I am a Holocaust denier' as well as 'Israel is a shameful little prostitute of The Big American Bank Robbery', combined with talk of the 'Zionist owned Western media'; another shared a video entitled 'Gentiles will be the slaves of Jews'; yet another shared material from the infamous Holocaust denier David Irving, and promoted an article entitled 'The HolocaustTM and the Phony Six Million'. These cases should have been met with immediate suspension as the first step to expulsion – yet they weren't.

It wasn't that the GLU couldn't move fast – when it wanted to. During the two leadership elections of 2015 and 2016, the GLU had worked in overdrive to purge Corbyn-supporting members, often on the flimsiest excuses, such as evidence that members had voted for the Green Party. For some reason, the most abhorrent and deranged antisemitism did not appear to require the same urgency. It's hard not to conclude, in the words of the Labour report, that the 'hyper-factional atmosphere prevailing in party HQ' had something to do with it.

Former anti-Corbyn staffers in Labour HQ later publicly claimed that Corbyn's office had intervened in antisemitism cases, suggesting that they did so to prevent action being taken by the party machine against those accused of antisemitism. But the evidence here suggests that staff in the leader's office *did* intervene, broadly speaking, for two reasons.

First, they asked for updates on high-profile cases, on the basis that these needed to be brought to a swift conclusion. In the cases of Ken Livingstone and Jackie Walker, the vice-chair of Momentum, staff repeatedly chased GLU to take action against the pair. In one such email, dated 17 October 2017, Stakeholder Manager Laura Murray wrote to the head of GLU asking for an update on these and other cases, a timetable for their hearings by the NEC, and a date for a final decision to be delivered. Murray added that the Jewish Labour Movement 'expressed frustration that these cases have taken such a long time to be heard, as they feel that it is difficult to begin the process of rebuilding trust between the Labour Party and the Jewish community whilst we have still not dealt with these cases'.

An intervention from Corbyn himself made precisely the same point. In February 2018, he wrote to party general secretary Iain McNicol, stating that 'it is clear that the current processes are far too slow to meet the volume of disciplinary cases the party has to deal with', yet 'no procedural changes to the Party's disciplinary processes have been brought forward by Party staff for consideration by the NEC'. Venting his frustration at the GLU's failure to implement the Chakrabarti recommendations in full, Corbyn added: 'it is a cause for real concern that Jewish voices from across the political spectrum of the Labour Party still feel that we do not take antisemitism seriously enough'. When two NEC members wrote to McNicol requesting updates on complaints by Labour Against Antisemitism, they suspected they were misinformed by the party bureaucracy about how much progress had been made.

Second, when in early 2018 Iain McNicol stood down as general secretary and his replacement had yet to be appointed, Corbyn's office intervened in response to requests for assistance by GLU staff. On 26 March 2018, a GLU staffer emailed Laura Murray and Amy Jackson, writing 'thank you for your help' and 'it's been really helpful to have your input' and suggesting that in future he 'raise each case with [them] before we take further action on it'. Another staffer chipped in approvingly: 'very good'. Murray responded that she thought 'that sounds like a really good way forward for the time being. Given the unfolding urgency of getting this problem under control, it is helpful to have more people speeding the process along, which I can help with.' Rather than intervening to block action on antisemitism, the leader's office intervened to *un*block it; there were twice as many suspensions in the week and a half of involvement from the leader's office as GLU had ordered for the whole of 2017.

Three days later, the head of Corbyn's office, Karie Murphy, queried why GLU staff were emailing the leader's office at all on this subject. 'Complaints do not usually come to LOTO like this,' she wrote, 'why are they being sent across in this format now?' Who, she asked, 'has given authorization for the changes', adding, 'something is amiss here'. These email exchanges were later presented by much of the British media as evidence of the leader's office unduly interfering in the processing of antisemitism cases – which, as it happened, was a reversal of the reality. 'The [GLU] staff started copying us in: "should we suspend this person or that person",' Laura Murray tells me. 'And we in good faith said, "yes, obviously suspend them". This was leaked to the press as improper involvement.'

In March 2018, Iain McNicol's replacement as general secretary, Jennie Formby – an avowed Corbynite – came into the job with a genuine determination to deal with antisemitism. Yet her efforts quickly ran into the sand, bogged down in part by the IHRA saga that summer. Reform was slow, partly because it took time to change staff, and partly because by this point Jewish community groups no longer trusted the Corbyn leadership; moreover, Formby was struggling with breast cancer. She soon came under fire after placing Dan

Simpson, Labour's most senior Jewish official – who, along with other party staff belonging to the old order, had already resigned with a substantial payoff and was working his notice – on gardening leave, which she only did at the recommendation of a McNicol ally. Media headlines denounced the removal of Labour's most senior Jewish official, and Formby was barracked by angry MPs over the move at her first encounter with the Parliamentary Labour Party.

Genuinely important changes were made on Formby's watch. A comprehensive system for logging complaints – inexplicably lacking before – was put in operation. The handling of antisemitism cases was speeded up: specially constituted panels would now hear cases each month, rather than four times a year, and were granted the power to expel members in clear-cut cases of egregious prejudice. An independent barrister was brought in to advise the panels, while rules were changed to ensure that all antisemitism complaints were investigated nationally. Investigations by staff were transformed, with new tools to help search through social media and allowing them to launch their own investigations, rather than simply passively responding to new complaints received. Dossiers on antisemitism in Labour-supporting Facebook groups and the key individuals involved were reported to the social media giant. Instead of those accused having to be investigated in person, thus delaying the process, reform allowed remote investigations.[46] As a result, the improvement was marked: forty-five members were expelled for antisemitism in 2019 (with another 104 quitting during the proceedings), compared to ten in 2018 and one in 2017, and after further reforms in September 2019, twice as many people were expelled in two months as in the whole of 2018. Disciplinary panels heard 274 cases related to antisemitism in 2019, ten times more than in 2017, and 296 members were suspended because of antisemitism in 2019, nearly 200 as many as the year before.[47] Important initiatives came from the leader's office too. James Schneider – a high-ranking Jewish member of staff – authored an eight-page pamphlet designed as a political education tool for members. Entitled *No Place for Antisemitism*, it acknowledged the 'unsettling truth' that 'a small number of Labour members hold antisemitic views and a much larger number don't recognise antisemitic stereotypes and conspiracy theories'. Nonetheless, in a devastating blow, at the end of May 2019 Labour was referred to the Equality and Human Rights Commission to investigate whether the party was guilty of institutional antisemitism.

But serious errors continued to be made. One Labour councillor appointed to the Governance and Legal Unit, Thomas Gardiner, was believed by some colleagues to lack good judgement when it came to antisemitism. When, in one notorious example, a Labour member shared a picture of the Statue of Liberty's face smothered by an alien tattooed with the Star of David and the comment 'The most accurate photo I've seen all year!', Gardiner opined that the image was 'anti-Israel, not anti-Jewish': a patently ludicrous decision, in my view. Some staff expressed their frustration to me, and voiced a feeling that, after Formby took over, though Gardiner did support the drive to improve the handling of antisemitism complaints he was prone to lacking urgency and dragging his feet if they, as lower-ranking staff, proposed reforms. They felt that the drive to bring reforms into being really emanated from the leader's office. Gardiner strongly disputes this interpretation of events – and of his actions – telling me it is 'directly contradictory to the facts' and 'doesn't even make sense'. He says that he guided 'very major reforms' through Annual Conference in 2019, this being, he says, the first opportunity for any reforms proposed in spring 2019 to be passed by the Party.

Across the board, the party – including the leader's office – failed to support members of the operation in their efforts to confront antisemitism. Both Laura Murray in the leader's office, and Georgie Robertson, a member of Labour's press team, poured commitment and energy into trying to fix what had become an ever-growing crisis within the party. In the spring of 2019, they co-authored a new proposal to tackle antisemitism, which they submitted to Jennie Formby and Karie Murphy. Warning that the lack of progress made on the issue risked a 'new wave of stories and splits' that could be 'extremely damaging to the Party', Murray and Robertson suggested a detailed series of reforms, including a comprehensive political education programme, a plan to tackle antisemitism in Labour-backing social media forums, and 'ensuring greater consistency and speed in decisions on, and conclusions to, cases'. The proposal was thoughtful, constructive and empathetic, and Murray and Robertson even offered to help implement it outside their working hours. Given the hole that Labour was now in over the issue, you might think that senior staff would have warmly embraced the initiative.

They didn't. Karie Murphy's response was to fire off an angry email. 'I have struggled for 12 months to manage Laura Murray's workload,' Murphy typed. 'She has become fixated on Antisemitism and is now, as a consequence, not at all balanced. Her judgement and views on managing this subject are concerning.' The email added that, as a consequence, 'we have no relationship with any other BAME [black and minority ethnic] community groups or individuals, little input into any Disabilities group or Woman's groups'. Murphy is adamant that she was concerned about Murray and Robertson burning out, but it was, to say the least, a poorly worded message. (While Murphy does believe there were concerns about the failure to do outreach work with British Muslims, she is insistent that what Murray 'does is phenomenal – she's a fantastic worker'.)

Furthermore, Murphy's email added, Robertson 'will not undertake any task bar what she decides is of interest. Her option of course is to focus solely on the media management of Antisemitism. While the paper may look like a positive initiative from two enthusiastic members of staff it absolutely is not. It's symptomatic of a broader issue. Some staff think they can work to suit themselves.' As Murray herself points out, before March 2018 dealing with Jewish stakeholders such as the Jewish Labour Movement and Board of Deputies had constituted about 10 per cent of her role; it ballooned to 95 per cent. But that was hardly her fault. The failures of others had led to the 'broader issue exploding'; Murray was dealing with the fallout.

The lack of leadership on antisemitism left a vacuum; it was filled in part by elements of the membership who believed that Corbyn had had his hands tied on the issue, and that Labour had simply surrendered to bad-faith actors. More broadly, they had a conspiracist mentality. Privately, exasperated senior Labour officials referred to them as 'cranks'. In this, as in so much else, the lack of leadership was a real problem. As one Labour press officer put it, Corbyn needed 'to show members who think it's all a smear that no it isn't, [antisemitism] is real, and while it's a small minority and not most of the party, denying and downplaying it makes it worse'. While *ad hoc* interventions by Corbyn – often in written form – did make that clear, 'it wasn't enough; there should have been a sustained campaign from the leadership to persuade the members, and we never rolled out political education'.

With no such campaign forthcoming, the grassroots movement Momentum resolved to take the initiative on antisemitism. They called out antisemites on social media, organizing joint protests with the Jewish Labour movement against alleged antisemites such as David Icke, and produced five political education videos about antisemitism, one of which – on Rothschild conspiracy theories – attracted two million views on social media. But not only did Momentum feel unsupported in their efforts by the leader's office, they resented that several prominent pro-Corbyn social media outrider accounts that dismissed antisemitism as a smear campaign were cultivated at the very top, among them those belonging to a WhatsApp group which included some senior figures in the leader's office. 'Privately, they cited these high-level contacts as authority for opposing and shutting down attempts to oppose antisemitism on the left,' says one pro-Corbyn Labour official. 'Instead of backing Momentum's efforts to oppose antisemitism on the left, the leader's office let the idea that there was no real issue and Jon Lansman was a Zionist stooge spread instead.' As a result, social media content posted by Momentum that challenged antisemitism was often piled on by those deemed 'cranks'.

If those described as 'cranks' had a king, it was Chris Williamson. Williamson was elected Labour MP for Derby North in 2010; his political history didn't place him on the left. As leader of Derby City Council, he implemented pro-privatization Private Finance Initiative schemes and formed an alliance with the Conservatives in order to govern.[48] In 2010, rather than back either of the two left-wing candidates for leader – Diane Abbott or John McDonnell – he opted for the eventual winner, Ed Miliband. I met him at the time. He was a middle-of-the-road 'soft left' MP who would tweet countdowns about how many days remained until a Miliband government would usher in 'responsible capitalism'. Williamson supported the war in Libya, Western airstrikes in Iraq in 2014, and refused to vote against

Conservative workfare programmes in 2013 – hardly the stuff of Corbynism. But when he lost his seat in 2015, Williamson apparently re-invented himself as a revolutionary, his new political outlook proclaimed by a Twitter profile picture of Fidel Castro accompanied by Nelson Mandela. Re-elected in the 2017 general election, he returned to the House of Commons, positioning himself as the tribune of the membership. To the fury of fellow Labour MPs, he launched a 'Democracy Roadshow' to promote the party's democratization, travelling to constituency Labour parties. This was interpreted by his colleagues as a 'Deselection Roadshow' to encourage the removal of anti-Corbyn Labour MPs, but for some grassroots members infuriated by attempts to undermine the leadership, it made him a champion.

But it was Williamson's role in the antisemitism crisis that proved toxic. To quote Labour's report into the party's dealings with antisemitism, he 'engaged in a pattern of behaviour . . . which was widely regarded as offensive and as baiting the Jewish community'. Williamson constantly championed members expelled for reasons linked to antisemitism. He retweeted a Holocaust denier writing about Venezuela; tweeted his pleasure at meeting Miko Peled, an Israeli-American author who had said 'Jews have a reputation for being sleazy thieves', and that free speech meant Labour members should be able to ask 'the Holocaust: yes or no?'.[49] On being presented with the evidence by Labour press officers, Williamson refused to remove the tweets. He tweeted in support of Gilad Atzmon, a jazz musician banned by Islington Council because of his alleged (albeit denied) history of relentless antisemitism, before belatedly deleting it. Shortly after the Pittsburgh Synagogue massacre on 27 October 2018, he tweeted: 'Wow, well blow me down' as he shared an attack on the president of the Board of Deputies of British Jews, again refusing to delete the tweet when asked. Williamson joined a protest outside Labour HQ when Corbyn was attending a National Executive Committee meeting, which incensed the leader's office. In early 2019, he booked a House of Commons room to host an event with the suspended activist Jackie Walker to coincide with Corbyn addressing the Parliamentary Labour Party on antisemitism down the corridor. When Amy Jackson approached Williamson, demanding to know if it was true, he retorted with provocative flippancy, 'That's for me to know, and you to find out.'

Senior officials within the leader's office – including Karie Murphy – pleaded with Williamson to desist from making inflammatory comments and, over and over again, to stop sharing panels with expelled members, emphasizing how much political damage he was inflicting. He refused to listen, lecturing them that 'if we keep running, they'll keep chasing'. When, in a fiery speech in February 2019, Williamson declared that the party had been 'too apologetic' on antisemitism, Jennie Formby, who had run out of patience with him, suspended him. Four months later, he was readmitted to the party by an NEC panel, sparking further fury.

Williamson became a topic that caused mounting anger and frustration within the leadership, including Corbyn, who, according to senior aides, privately called him an 'idiot' and wished that 'he'd shut his fucking mouth' – unusually personal language from the largely mild-mannered leader. According to one Labour adviser, 'the Chris Williamson defence league was a one-woman operation': that is, Karie Murphy. (However, while Murphy initially saw him as a counterweight to right-wing Labour MPs, she increasingly shared the view of other Corbyn allies that he was arrogant, driven by ego and a liability.) The Labour leader was on a visit to the Northeast which was now entirely overshadowed by the news that Williamson's suspension had been lifted; Corbyn angrily asked his aides why the decision had been made; with his support, Williamson was re-suspended two days later. But that wasn't the end of it. To the frustration of senior Labour figures, Corbyn never told Williamson that his behaviour was causing the leadership serious problems, thereby allowing him to push back at Formby's reprimands by arguing he had not been told he was acting against the leader's wishes. The Williamson saga would run and run – right into the 2019 general election campaign, with immensely damaging results.

What complicated attempts by some on the left, who sincerely wanted to deal with the seriousness of antisemitism, were undoubted bad-faith attacks launched by some of Corbyn's most embittered opponents, who now spotted an opportunity. In spring 2019, the Blairite MP Siobhain McDonagh suggested in a BBC Radio 4 interview that antisemitism is 'very much part of their [Corbyn's] politics, of hard left politics, to be against capitalists and to see Jewish people as the financiers of capital. Ergo you are anti-Jewish people.' When the presenter asked, 'In other words, to be anti-capitalist, you have to be antisemitic?' she was affirmative: 'Yes. Not everybody, but there is a certain . . . there's a certain strand of it.'[50] On another occasion, Corbyn's team produced a video marking ten years since the financial crash. 'The people who caused it now call me a threat. They're right,' Corbyn added. Stephen Pollard, the passionately anti-Corbyn editor of the *Jewish Chronicle*, responded on Twitter: 'Been hesitating to tweet this because I keep thinking it can't be, surely it can't be. But the more I think about it, the more it seems it really is. This is "nudge, nudge, you know who I'm talking about, don't you?" And yes I do. It's appalling.'[51] Both attempted to conflate antisemitism with any left critique of capitalism – any attempt, in other words, to suggest that challenging the increasing concentration of wealth and power in the hands of a tiny elite, or holding the financial system to account for the crash, was somehow a display of anti-Jewish prejudices. This, in turn, only encouraged those on the Corbyn left who were determined to claim that accusations of antisemitism were nothing more than smears against the leadership. It was a vicious circle, and it turned to nobody's benefit – least of all Corbyn's, while causing more hurt and distress to Jewish people.

Part of the problem, once again, was a lack of education or understanding among some leading Labour figures about what really constitutes antisemitism. This was all too evident in the case of Derek Hatton, the former left-wing firebrand deputy leader of Liverpool City Council in the mid-1980s, who was suspended from the party for antisemitic statements just two days after being readmitted. During the 2012 Israeli offensive against the Gaza Strip, Hatton had tweeted: 'Jewish people with any sense of humanity need to start speaking out against the ruthless murdering being carried out by Israel!' Seumas Milne was unambiguous that Hatton needed to be suspended. This was classic antisemitism, he declared, which bestowed collective responsibility on the Jewish people for the actions of the Israeli state. But Karie Murphy's initial response was bafflement. She didn't see what the problem was, asking – as someone with a Catholic heritage – whether it would constitute bigotry if her religious group were asked to speak against abuse in the Catholic Church. 'She was totally schooled,' says one aide. 'She just hadn't understood it.'

Labour's antisemitism crisis was a profoundly depressing episode. The party's relationship with a minority which, historically, had been central to the development of left-wing ideas and struggles was fraught before Corbyn arrived on the scene – but, on his watch, it deteriorated cataclysmically. Worse, it need never have happened. But while there were bad-faith actors opposed to Corbyn's politics, ultimately there were severe and repeated errors by the leadership, which resulted from those two characteristic failings: a lack of both strategy and emotional intelligence. From the start, the leadership should have done two things: displayed an uncompromising opposition to antisemitism, and offered more vocal support for the Palestinian cause (something which was largely missing in any case). Although most of the seven Labour MPs who in February 2019 quit the party to form the short-lived Independent Group, would have done so come what may, this is unlikely to have been true for Luciana Berger, a Jewish Labour MP who, while she didn't share Corbyn's politics, was genuinely anguished by antisemitism and the personal abuse to which she had been subjected.

It has to be reiterated that the former leadership and the vast majority of Labour's membership abhor antisemitism. The small minority – ranging from those displaying grotesque antisemitism to others who dabbled thoughtlessly with antisemitic tropes – caused genuine upset to a Jewish community whose history left them with every reason to fear bigotry directed against them. Others still were in denial, claiming that the antisemitism crisis had been entirely manufactured by a media 'out to get' Corbyn; or that antisemitism wasn't about Jews at all, but all about Israel – claims which served to compound that hurt and fear. However unwittingly, attitudes like this served only to set back the cause of Palestinian justice and freedom.

The damage to Corbyn's Labour was grievous. The crisis led to months of media coverage, a prolonged dripfeed that helped fundamentally change the British public's sense of Corbynism from something positive and hopeful to something poisonous and sinister.

One poll found that, on average, the British public thought 34 per cent of Labour members faced complaints of antisemitism, over 300 times the actual total. The emotional damage to Corbyn himself was lasting: he was less sunny, less zen, angrier, more defensive. At meetings on the subject with senior officials, he would become distracted, offer garbled responses, play around on his phone. His allies increasingly feared that his personal sense of anger and hurt at his deeply held anti-racist credentials being defiled led him to disengage and shut down when antisemitism was discussed.

'I fear Jeremy has had a lot of the stuffing knocked out of him,' a senior Corbyn ally told me. Corbyn's slow-motion collapse encapsulated that of the movement. The relationships within the leader's office had started to crumble: over Brexit, antisemitism, communications and strategy. It was all beginning to fall apart.

8

'A Blizzard of Lies and Excuses'

Theresa May's Conservative government had long been described as a zombie premiership, but as any connoisseur of the genre knows, zombies can do a lot of damage and are famously hard to kill off. It finally came to an end in the wake of the European elections, held on 23 May 2019, in which the Tories polled a miserable 8.8 per cent: the following day, Theresa May tendered her tearful resignation outside 10 Downing Street. The contest to succeed her, bubbling away in Conservative ranks for months, finally burst into the open. Until a few months earlier, Boris Johnson's long-standing dreams of becoming prime minister seemed to be over. Most Tory MPs thought he was, variously, a charlatan, incompetent, lazy, unsuitable for high office and a walking gaffe machine. Now they saw him as the only plausible candidate, in the age of populism, who could simultaneously roll back the tides of Farageism and Corbynism. It was soon clear that Johnson's triumph was a near inevitability. The Labour leadership had sixty days to prepare for the announcement of the new Conservative leader and prime minister. Their response was shambolic.

Labour's own European election campaign had been a farce. The party had both touted Labour's alternative Brexit plan and – without securing changes to the government's deal or a general election – proclaimed that it would 'back the option of a public vote'. It was a mess of a compromise. 'We were so miserable, so fucking miserable,' recalls Jack McKenna, one of Corbyn's press team. 'The Brexit compromise literally fell apart: you could just feel the quicksand disappearing beneath our feet every week.' If the elections were a disaster for Theresa May's Conservatives, they were almost equally terrible for Labour, who polled just 13.6 per cent of the vote. The chief victor was Nigel Farage's Brexit Party with 30.5 per cent – a stunning success, given that it had been founded only seven months earlier – followed by the Lib Dems who, defying their political obituaries, came second with 19.6 per cent.

Profoundly shaken by the results, Corbyn was especially worried about the Lib Dem result. In the run-up to the EU elections, fearing an impending Labour rout, he had already – much to Seumas Milne's chagrin – made an impulsive commitment to a second referendum. On Monday 27 May, in a conference call with members of his inner circle, he stated that all attempts to break the Brexit deadlock had failed and that, respecting the will of the membership, he intended to declare that Labour backed a new referendum in all circumstances. According to one shadow cabinet minister on the call, Milne chipped in, declared that this wasn't the right place to have the discussion and 'told Corbyn off like a schoolboy'. As Corbyn backtracked under pressure from the pro-Brexit faction around him, Labour's public position on Brexit grew incoherent. Over the following week, the leader went from a bullish 'we are ready to support a public vote on any deal', to a call for a general election with the idea of a public vote a distant second.

One thing was clear: the European elections had scorched what was left of Labour's Brexit compromise out of existence; according to a YouGov poll, only 45 per cent of Labour's own members had voted for their own party.[1] When former New Labour spin doctor Alastair Campbell declared on national television that he had voted for the Lib Dems and – on the instruction of the party's general secretary, Jennie Formby, without Corbyn being informed – was duly kicked out of the party, he became a martyr to a Remain cause embraced by most of Labour's membership. (Campbell knew perfectly well what would happen when he made his announcement: the party's rules had after all been partly crafted in the New Labour era.) As #expelmetoo trended on Twitter, I was personally bombarded by messages from Labour members who declared that, while they had voted for Corbyn twice in previous leadership elections, they had opted for the Lib Dems or Greens as a Brexit protest vote. When Corbyn eventually found out about Campbell's expulsion, he was furious, believing it to be a heavy-handed authoritarian move at odds with his commitment to party democracy. So was Shadow Chancellor John McDonnell. The episode was, he believed, a completely unnecessary fight to pick, and one which would play into the hands of their political enemies.

It was clear to me where this was heading. Labour, as usual, was going to be forced kicking and screaming – this time by a membership revolt – to an inevitable conclusion: backing a new referendum in all circumstances. In the process there would be an almighty ruckus, from which it would gain no political credit. Having spent the last three years urging Labour to accept the referendum result, I now surrendered to what seemed to be the inevitable. In a despairing column, I outlined how a second referendum was a bad option for Labour, but possibly its only option.[2] As a result of my piece, Len McCluskey asked to see me. I accepted, with some trepidation. McCluskey's Unite union saw itself as the last significant bulwark against this shift in Labour policy to backing a People's Vote. But when we met, in a quiet corner of an Italian restaurant across the road from the union's headquarters, McCluskey was in a conciliatory mood.

McCluskey and Unite saw things rather differently from the Labour leadership. As far as they were concerned, the EU election results were a red herring. The turnout was a measly 37.2 per cent, and those who had voted were protesting against Labour and the Tories; such a result would never be replicated in a general election. Moreover, for all the focus on how the Lib Dems and Greens had scooped away Remain support from Labour, Unite drew attention to how well the Brexit Party had done in Labour-held constituencies in Wakefield, Barnsley and Doncaster. In McCluskey's view, Labour's reaction to the EU election results had been sheer panic. 'I am amazed, utterly amazed that anyone – including yourself – took any notice of these useless unimportant elections,' he said. 'I pleaded with people to stop panicking, to calm down.'

But the red lights were flashing on Labour's dashboard. The party's national polling was ruinous: one survey placed the party on 20 per cent, tied with the Lib Dems and only just over double the Greens. Labour's only comfort was that the government had come fifth, on 8.8 per cent – but it was cold comfort. With May's impending departure, the Tories had a clear route back, in the shape of front-runner Boris Johnson, whose Brexit populism would make large inroads into the 26 per cent of the vote gained by the Brexit Party.[3] The Tories, in other words, were altering course dramatically in the wake of the EU election drubbing; Labour was not. As James Schneider put it to me: 'We didn't have an agreed position to deal with Brexit, and if you can't deal with Brexit, how do you deal with Johnson?'

On 23 July, in London's Queen Elizabeth Centre, the Conservative leadership contest reached its inevitable conclusion: Boris Johnson was proclaimed leader and Britain's new prime minister. In the Labour leader's parliamentary office, Seumas Milne stared at rolling coverage of Johnson's assumption of power, muttering 'not good, not good' repeatedly to himself. Glued to Johnson's inaugural speech, in which he declared his commitment to 'answering at last the plea of the forgotten people and the left behind towns' by unveiling a new agenda of investment, Milne was worried: 'He's stealing all of our lines.' When the appointment of Dominic Cummings – widely perceived as the architect of Vote Leave's triumph in the referendum – as Johnson's chief special adviser was announced, the mood in the room darkened further. Usually calm, Milne was spooked.

That July, as he took power, Johnson – untrustworthy, with a record of dishonesty and lies, and a history of racism, homophobia and bigotry – was polling as the most unpopular new prime minister since records began. Yet the Labour leadership was frozen in the headlights of Johnson's victory. It was hopelessly divided on how to respond – and it showed.

'It was a massive abdication of responsibility at the end of July when Johnson came in,' recalls Mike Hatchett, Labour's director of policy and research. Over the past weeks and months Labour's policy and research team, acknowledging that Johnson would be much harder to pin down than May, had worked hard in preparation for this moment. 'We did a lot of analysis and concluded Labour should settle on "you can't trust Boris", hammer it home. Early on we needed Jeremy to do a big pitch, shape the narrative.' According to Milne's deputy, Anjula Singh, 'We had an attack package ready outlining Johnson's personal and political failings and plans for a Jeremy response, but we didn't punch through with a coordinated plan.' Milne himself, bogged down in philosophical discussions over different media approaches, seemed paralysed and the moment was missed.

The initial plan, for Corbyn to film a response to Johnson's victory, was abruptly cancelled. In its place, party chair Ian Lavery would put out a press release detailing Labour's response. There was a logic to this: Lavery was an authentically working-class MP in a Leave seat, committed to upholding the referendum result: an antidote to Johnson's nascent populism. But, as the leadership team knew – or should have known – this isn't how news works. A press release from a politician few had heard of was hardly likely to cut through. Some desperate arm-twisting by Corbyn's two speechwriters, Alex Nunns and Joss MacDonald, succeeded in getting Milne's sign-off for a high-profile op-ed to be placed in the *Guardian* newspaper – but it couldn't go out in Corbyn's name because the Labour leader couldn't be contacted. The piece finally went up on the *Guardian* website the next evening – but it didn't even make the print edition. Astonishingly, Corbyn's senior management team did not meet until 2 p.m. on 24 July – the day Boris Johnson became prime minister – to discuss their response to Britain's new Tory management.

Meanwhile, Labour politicians put up to broadcast were given seven bullet points – characteristic overcomplication, here – which failed to include examples of Johnson's dishonesty and cosy ties to big business, or any attack lines on Johnson's new cabinet appointments. As a result, different spokespeople said different things; the messaging was all over the place. Labour's one vague central theme, that Johnson had no plan, was contradicted by the raft of announcements now emanating from No. 10.

Labour's online response was equally weak and poorly shared. When Corbyn himself finally got around to recording a video, it was nicely made but too late and, again, lacked a clear message. Johnson addressed Parliament for the first time as prime minister on 25 July to set out the mission statement of his new government. It was a prime opportunity for Corbyn to deliver attack lines which would help define the new occupant of No. 10 in the public imagination. He did so – but not in the way many aides hoped. The excerpt used in BBC headlines was: 'Corbyn: "He [Johnson] says he has pluck, nerve and ambition. Our country does not need arm-waving bluster."' Repeating 'pluck' and 'ambition' merely helped Johnson – and who uses language like 'arm-waving bluster'?

Johnson, meanwhile, revelled in the Tories' new strategy against the Labour leader, portraying Corbyn as an evasive, indecisive triangulator at the mercy of his advisers. Corbyn had been 'captured, jugulated, reprogrammed by his friends', Johnson spluttered, and had 'turned now into a Remainer . . . Of all the flip-flops Corbyn has performed in his tergiversating career, this is the one for which he will pay the highest price.' Which was rich, coming from the arch-tergiversator himself – but nonetheless, Johnson had punched Labour's bruise. Corbyn seemingly had no effective comeback. When he finally got round to giving an interview on *Sky News*, a full five days after the Johnson era began, the Labour leader provided no big takeaway other than calling for a general election. It was a demand that seemed perfectly rational at this point: while Labour's polling was poor, so was that of the Tories thanks to Nigel Farage's upstart Brexit Party. It was, moreover, better to trumpet a call for an election than talk about Brexit which had Labour hopelessly divided. The problem was that a politics-weary public had no appetite for yet another electoral contest.

In the vacuum, Johnson was allowed to define himself. Purging his cabinet of those associated with May's failed government, he presented himself as a fresh start, wooing Brexit voters by abandoning May's deal and prioritizing investment in schools, hospitals and the police. 'What effort was being made to define him?' asks one Labour aide, still angry. 'As he started a general election campaign outlining his policy platform and key pledges over the summer, what was our alternative response? We were silent. We let him have the airwaves for that whole summer: on police, hospitals, almost no response. It was very concerning.'

How could such an opportunity have been so disastrously missed? If you want to be generous, Johnson was no easy politician to define. A former journalist, in the loosest sense of the word, he had been sacked twice for dishonesty, once by a newspaper editor, another by a Tory leader. His lack of principles was on show before the 2016 Brexit referendum, when he wrote two newspaper columns, one supporting Remain and the other Leave, before casually opting for the latter. His record of overt homophobic, Islamophobic and generally racist behaviour was unparalleled for a modern British politician of his prominence. Yet none of the mud seemed to stick. None of this had damaged his political career.

Then there was the fatigue. While Johnson's team were fresh, match fit, Corbyn's team were, as one aide puts it, 'fucking exhausted', ground down by four years of interminable internal and external conflict. The Corbyn team's Achilles heel (or one of them), its ingrained lack of strategic planning, had been on full display in the local elections of May 2019. The leadership told Labour's press team to target older people: an aspiration, not a strategy. Characteristically, they were offered little guidance from polling research, and there was no discussion of who they were specifically trying to reach, or why; what they were trying to say; or how messaging should be tailored for specific groups.

By this point the operation was, in short, a factionalized, fragmented mess. One aide who joined the leader's office in the summer of 2019 had adopted the brace position in advance based on negative rumours swirling around – but, nevertheless, was shocked. He told me he found a half-empty office, dotted with workaholic aides staying late into the night, desultory staffers who drifted in and clocked off at 5 p.m. and a miasma of bad morale. All this, when Boris Johnson had just become prime minister. 'It did not feel like a place fighting for its survival and future,' the aide tells me. One senior member of staff, he recalls, would get drunk every night at conference and struggled through a terrible hangover each day. Meanwhile, with Parliament deadlocked and Boris Johnson desperate to consolidate his position with a parliamentary majority, the spectre of another general election began to loom.

If, as seemed increasingly likely, an election was going to happen later in the autumn, then Labour's conference that September was realistically the party's last chance to showcase itself to an increasingly sceptical public. Yet barely a week before conference, Milne's team hadn't even settled on the crucial unifying slogan, despite weeks of focus groups and polling (of which the rest of the operation wasn't even aware). Petitioned by the fretting conference organizers, John McDonnell rang Milne, who was still dithering. McDonnell was exasperated: just choose something, he told the comms supremo. In the end, ditching the memorable 'For the many, not the few' line used in 2017 – too stale, Milne thought – his team settled on the anaemic 'People before privilege'. Truly weak, the slogan was quickly ditched. It didn't bode well.

There was another catalyst for this descent into total confusion. Through their many battles against enemies inside and outside, Corbyn's top team had remained more or less united as comrades who knew that, whatever disagreements existed, they belonged on the same team. But by summer 2019 this was no longer the case. So long as the three pillars of the Corbyn operation – Fisher, Murphy and Milne – still stood, not all was lost. 'They were the triumvirate. They were hegemonic when they stuck together, like Octavian, Mark Antony and Lepidus,' as Clive Lewis put it. 'Then one of the pillars collapsed.'

In truth, the relationship of policy chief Andrew Fisher with Milne had always been strained. That summer, it cracked. In part, inevitably, this was over Brexit. Fisher's belief that Labour had no choice but to back a new referendum put him at odds with Milne and Murphy. But there were other reasons. Fisher, fed up with years of struggling in a dysfunctional operation, had had enough.

When, as an over-enthusiastic 21-year-old university graduate, I first worked alongside Fisher in the mid-2000s, I was struck – intimidated even – by his competence. Well over a decade later, that remained the judgement of his colleagues. 'Andrew Fisher has this astonishing ability to write a zillion words an hour,' recalls speechwriter Alex Nunns. 'Andrew stands out,' agrees another senior official. 'He's like a machine. His work output is incredible and he listens to people.' In mid-September, a week before conference, Fisher wrote one of his typically fluent communications to the elections' strategy WhatsApp group. It was a letter announcing his resignation.

The message was an outpouring of total despair. It began with a litany of recent examples of gratuitous incompetence: a speech he was working on abruptly cancelled; a pamphlet pulled without warning; the lack of a conference strapline; and nothing to show for the tens of thousands of pounds splashed on focus groups and polling ('there is no end-product', he fulminated, 'just a blizzard of lies and excuses'); a confidential document prepared for the leader, widely circulated; and two policy stories leaked to the media without his knowledge. 'None of these things individually would be enough to make me leave,' he wrote. 'All of them happening three or four years ago wouldn't have been enough to make me leave. All of them happening yesterday are not why I am leaving. But they are a snapshot of the lack of professionalism, competence and human decency which I am no longer willing to put up with daily. I've tried to resolve some of these issues for a long time, but have been unable to – and yesterday just proved that I never will.' Just over a week later, the letter was leaked and splashed on the front page of the *Sunday Times*.

Karie Murphy and her allies were enraged by Fisher's letter. In their eyes, its real target was the endlessly indecisive Corbyn, with the intention of forcing the leader to choose between Milne and Fisher and, as Murphy tells me: 'That WhatsApp message from Andrew put a stake in the heart of the Corbyn project. It was an extraordinary act, criticizing Jeremy and others in such a manner that appeared ripe for public consumption.' But the target wasn't Corbyn at all. The letter was overwhelmingly aimed at Milne. Fisher had had enough. He wasn't trying to force Corbyn into a choice – but he did think it needed spelling out, in primary colours, that the project was in existential crisis.

Coming at the end of another disastrous summer for Labour, Fisher's resignation seemed the last straw. With Corbyn distressed by the schism between Milne and Fisher, his two most trusted advisers, with the operation crumbling, and with the Brexit culture war reaching fever pitch, any semblance of shadow cabinet collective discipline – never strong – began to collapse. There were rifts wherever you looked. Furious Brexit disagreements often left Jon Trickett and John McDonnell at loggerheads; the relationship between party chair Ian Lavery and Niall Sookoo, the party's executive director for elections and campaigns, had collapsed; Andrew Fisher and Amy Jackson, Corbyn's political secretary, bristled at each other. Meanwhile, deputy leader Tom Watson and Keir Starmer both tried to force the leadership into an unambiguously Remain direction; Karie Murphy and Amy Jackson, meanwhile, urged Corbyn to sack Starmer from his post as shadow Brexit secretary.[4] Senior party figures went on national media to declare their support for Remain in the event of a new European referendum, in violation of the leadership's own official position. Attending a Remain march at conference in a blue dress with a necklace of yellow stars, Shadow Foreign Secretary Emily Thornberry – once Len McCluskey's chosen successor as Labour leader – had essentially decked herself out as the EU flag, to the glee of right-wing media. 'Emily Thornberry, the shadow foreign secretary, dared Jeremy Corbyn to sack her last night as she appeared to trash the party's proposed position on Brexit,' was how *The Times* wrote it up.[5]

These frontbenchers were undoubtedly causing Corbyn's senior aides a headache. Media-savvy, with the sympathetic ear of the liberal media, they were drowning out anything the leadership was trying to say. The confused messaging – pro-Remain shadow cabinet ministers pushing the dial further and further beyond what was agreed, followed by public slapdowns and clarifications from the leader's office – merely left voters all the more bewildered.

As Labour conference convened in Brighton late that September, the infighting broke into open warfare. On the eve of conference, Friday 20th, I got a text message telling me that Jon Lansman would be leading a push at a meeting of the party's National Executive Committee that weekend to abolish the position of deputy leader – or 'abolishing Tom Watson', as some later joked. It seemed far-fetched. I dropped a line to a senior Corbyn ally, who had heard nothing, But, crazily, it turned out to be for real. Suddenly it looked like conference would be overshadowed by an epic piece of score-settling – apparently, on the part of Karie Murphy against her one-time boss.

Over a week earlier, Watson, who by now had almost no relationship with the leader's office and rarely attended shadow cabinet meetings, had blotted his copybook once too often. At the Trades Union Congress in Brighton, Corbyn had unveiled Labour's latest incarnation of its Brexit policy – another contortion, which involved endorsing a future referendum with a 'credible Leave option' on the ballot paper, but refusing to commit the party to Leave or

Remain – while Watson made his own speech in London, advocating that Labour commit to Remain. The speech had been widely briefed in advance – but there had been no prior consultation with Corbyn's team, who, when they finally got wind of it, asked him to desist. It was 'too late' to stop the speech, Watson's assistant answered airily. When news reached Corbyn, he was enraged. Though he couldn't sack Watson from the shadow cabinet – the deputy leader was there by right – Corbyn immediately declared his intention to dismiss him from his post as shadow cabinet minister for digital, culture, media and sport. Murphy, Watson's former office manager, now his arch-foe, strongly endorsed the move, ordering aides to put the plan into action.

Desperate to prevent the party splitting, McDonnell tried to calm the situation. He pleaded with Corbyn to argue that Watson's sacking would make him a martyr to the Remain cause. Proposals to dilute Watson's power were discussed – the appointment of an additional female deputy leader, perhaps – but Corbyn was wary of any move that seemed undemocratic. 'It'd be a bit Pol Pot-ish,' he conceded.

By late afternoon, some of the heat had gone out of Corbyn's anger. McDonnell tried to persuade his friend not to move against Watson – the shadow chancellor's priority, above all else, being to keep the party together. Especially with a general election on the horizon, the last thing they needed to do was open up a new round of civil war. Corbyn, equally keen to avoid intra-party conflict, began to change his mind.

As far as Karie Murphy was concerned, Corbyn had had his head turned by McDonnell, and, as she told the leader bluntly, 'we don't work for John, we work for you'. As she saw it, Corbyn wanted Watson gone, but McDonnell was standing in the way – and, as usual, Corbyn, when faced with an impasse, had gone AWOL. As conference approached, she tried to contact Corbyn to discuss what he wanted to do about the Watson problem, but Corbyn wouldn't return her calls. Finally, on the morning of Friday 20 September, the pair met and Murphy presented to Corbyn a way of carrying out the scrapping of Watson's position without having to be personally present at the NEC ruling. This, Murphy implied, sealed the deal.

At midday, Murphy messaged Jon Lansman, asking to meet him

and Jim Kennedy, Unite's rep on the NEC, at the red-brick beachside Metropole hotel at 3 p.m., where she formally asked them to proceed with the scrapping of Watson's position. It was at this point that I first heard about it. Later, Murphy contacted Lansman to tell him Corbyn had changed his mind, but that she would work on him. Lansman was not told to halt the manoeuvre.

Murphy is emphatic that, personally, she was beyond caring about removing Watson; besides, he was on his way out anyway, convinced that he was going to lose his seat in the coming electoral inferno. Whatever the case, despite prolonged faffing around by Corbyn at the NEC meeting, the attempted sacking went ahead. It failed, the NEC chair ruling it out of order for discussion on the Friday – a decision which would have taken a two-thirds majority to overturn – and that it must be tabled the next day instead. Amid the ensuing uproar, and chatter of more Labour MPs resigning, Corbyn tabled a motion the following morning suggesting the position could be reviewed. Murphy told allies that it hadn't happened because Corbyn had been pressured by John McDonnell into changing his mind.

The non-sacking completely overshadowed conference. That weekend, when Watson spotted Lansman, he yelled across the road: 'The hitman that missed!' As the dust settled, Corbyn fulminated about the episode: 'It makes us look like a fucking student union.' He told Jack Bond, his social media manager, that he'd said to the senior management team: 'You don't abolish a position because you don't like the person, that's not how democracy works.'

At the conference itself, with Labour's two Brexit tribes ranged against each other, delegates were presented with two options to vote for. While both committed to a new referendum with Remain on the ballot paper, one option advocated that the party adopt a position of neutrality; the other mandated it to campaign for Britain to stay within the EU. (Like the rest of the leadership, both Fisher and Murphy backed the former, but there were heated clashes between the two about the overall wording before a consensus was reached.) When UNISON – Labour's second most powerful union – announced it was backing the Remain motion, Unite's Len McCluskey was furious, privately denouncing them for 'doing the dirty' on the other unions. 'Looking back,' says one senior GMB union official, it was all about manoeuvring for position as to who would succeed Corbyn as leader: 'It was all about Keir Starmer, they were backing him. Keir wanted us to be Remain, UNISON decided to back it too, it was all tied to that.' For Corbyn, in the minds of many present, the writing was already on the wall.

It wasn't just UNISON, however. With most of the conference delegates instinctive Remainers, Karie Murphy and Unite led a counter-offensive. While McCluskey worked the fringe meeting circuit, urging delegates in a series of barnstorming speeches to vote down the Remain motion, Murphy swung into action in the main hall.

On the day, the delegates voted for a referendum, but rejected an outright embrace of Remain. Murphy watched with satisfaction as the chant of 'Oh, Jeremy Corbyn!' swept across the main hall. Yet during the whole process Corbyn himself had been withdrawn, almost invisible.

Corbyn was unhappy; on that everyone agreed. The internal divisions clearly affected him. His zen had gone. A year previously, he had developed an eye condition that some thought was triggered by stress. Even more than usual he avoided coming into the office. When he did turn up, 'you always knew he was in a bad mood because he'd always wear a green suit that he was told he wasn't allowed to wear', says one Murphy ally. 'If he has that on, he has the hump at people telling him what to do, he was wearing it passively aggressively.' According to another in Murphy's camp, 'he became even more rebellious, he thought "people like the fact I'm a shambolic old granddad so I can do what the fuck I like"'.

Others were genuinely worried for Corbyn, and feared that, having suffered over four years of relentless battering, he was in a bad place. 'He'd had enough, a man who's an incredible, remarkable individual,' says one shadow cabinet ally. 'I think he might have had a breakdown, to be honest. He was pulled at from all sides, the criticism his family was getting was unparalleled in political history. The only parallel I can think of is Arthur Scargill and the National Union of Mineworkers. It was just desperate times, really desperate.'

By that time, some close to him believed, Corbyn had lost patience with both Murphy and Milne, and was now deferring to McDonnell and Abbott – who were, after all, his original political allies. 'By the time it got to 2019 party conference, Jeremy was literally fed up with both Seumas and Karie,' a Corbynite shadow cabinet member tells me. 'It was over the ridiculous failed hit job against Tom Watson and the leaked Andrew Fisher memo to the *Sunday Times*.' Yet, by this point, the defensive shield that Murphy and Milne had constructed to protect Corbyn seemed to have assumed total control of him: those calling Corbyn's phone sometimes found Murphy's key ally Amy Jackson answering or texting them back. 'The honest truth with what happened around the leader's office was that it was a ring of steel,' says one of his most senior allies. 'Jeremy lost control of it completely.'

Both Murphy and Milne, on the other hand, were privately emphatic that all they did was to follow Corbyn's orders, enforce his will. They maintain that while they're often seen like advisers in pre-revolutionary Russia – where there was an abiding myth that the tsar, pure as the driven snow, could do no wrong, and that if his administration *were* ever responsible for injustice, that responsibility lay with wicked and malign advisers – the reality was rather different. Murphy and Milne argue that, even if they'd wanted to, they couldn't have taken a genuinely independent line; they couldn't have done their jobs without being closely attuned to Corbyn himself. Key Murphy ally Marsha-Jane Thompson argues: 'Karie was of course one of the people involved in making decisions – but ultimately Jeremy made the decisions . . . She would then convey those decisions on his behalf, but it was Jeremy saying "I want this done or that done", he'd rely on Karie to get it sorted.' For many of those in the leader's office, this was simply not the case: rather, Murphy often went beyond Corbyn's expressed wishes, and took no response as permission to proceed.

Others go further, contending that, on Murphy's watch, decisions were made without consulting Corbyn, an extreme example being the abortive coup against Watson. One Corbyn loyalist in the shadow cabinet recalls that when a staffer told Murphy that they were acting under Corbyn's instructions, she responded: 'This is a left-wing collective. There's no one leader.' Another aide on the events team claims that Corbyn's trust in Murphy, already diminishing, all but evaporated after the Watson debacle. 'Trust is the only thing that matters to him,' she says. 'You can be the most right-wing politician, but as long as Jeremy trusts you, he can have a relationship with you.' None of this, she continues, absolved Corbyn of responsibility, opining that the reason the relationship broke down was 'partly his fault, because he never confronted her'. One senior figure tells me that Murphy would often complain that Corbyn did not give a strong enough steer, that he wasn't decisive enough – which is undoubtedly true. 'That doesn't mean you insert your own views in that vacuum and space,' he adds, 'and she did.'

Often chaotic, under Murphy's aegis the atmosphere in the leader's office had become poisonous – if, that was, a welter of allegations made by staff in the leader's office was to be believed. Their simmering resentment burst open on a team awayday in Loughborough in November 2018, when staff noticed that Corbyn's private secretary, Iram Awan, had disappeared: suspended at Karie Murphy's behest. Senior management were coy about what had happened, claiming simply that it was 'very, very serious' and that Awan had 'put the whole project in danger'. What happened here is strongly contested. Anyone who works in Parliament has to have their passes vetted by the security services. Awan's pass had long been delayed, and Murphy, Milne and Corbyn were all sympathetic to the idea that official anti-Muslim prejudice could be involved. When the fact that she had not been issued with a pass for nine months – normally clearance took weeks – was leaked to the media,[6] office managers suspected foul play either by the parliamentary authorities, the government or the security services. The same month, an article appeared in the *Sunday Times* stating that Corbyn 'has been summoned for a personal briefing by the head of MI5 on the terrorist threat to Britain amid his approach to national security'.[7] While there were indeed negotiations under way about a meeting between the Labour leader and Andrew Parker, director general of MI5, the way this was presented – as though Corbyn was a naughty or naïve schoolchild who needed to be educated about the facts of life – was regarded as an undemocratic intervention by the supposedly impartial security services. Accordingly, a letter was drafted to MI5 expressing concern about Awan not receiving her pass, as well as the briefing about it to the media, and the *Sunday Times* article.

One story goes like this: Karie Murphy accompanied Awan to a meeting with the security services on the parliamentary estate to discuss why a pass was not forthcoming. When security personnel asked whether Awan had been sensitive about matters relating to her family, Murphy requested them to leave to allow her to speak to Awan alone. According to Murphy's allies, Awan admitted to Murphy that her brothers had extremist connections, and that one had gone to Syria. Although Awan was angry that the actions of her relatives should be used against her, when the official personnel came back into the room they accepted her explanation, emphasizing they only wanted a full and honest account and did not wish to implicate her. Awan had previously joked to Corbyn's political secretary that she knew 'bad people', and that might account for the delay in issuing her pass. When her bosses in good faith genuinely believed Islamophobia might be involved in the delay, her failure to offer up this crucial detail about her brothers caused anger.

Subsequently, in meetings with MI5 and MI6, Awan – as Corbyn's private secretary – decided who should attend. To the consternation of senior management, she invited herself and excluded Amy Jackson, even though the political secretary was part of the senior team. In the meeting with MI5 Director General Andrew Parker, it is alleged she intervened two thirds of the way through the discussion and berated him over the security services' failure to treat far right extremism with the same seriousness as Islamist terrorist activity. This was a legitimate argument, but it was for politicians, not private secretaries, to intervene in such discussions, so the argument goes. Awan was also alleged to have subsequently angrily confronted Murphy, telling her that she took orders from the leader, not the chief of staff.

Those close to Awan have a very different perspective. They are adamant that her brothers had nothing do with extremist groups. They were simply conservative Muslims, who were constantly stigmatized in society: Islamophobia, they believe, was the real reason for the delay in her pass being issued. This was something Awan had raised with senior figures in the leader's office, only to regret it, believing it was subsequently used against her. Awan herself, however, is a self-described liberal Muslim married to a white, non-Muslim man. One of her brothers had gone to Syria – but as a journalist. Sources close to Awan claim Murphy told staff members that her brothers were ISIS supporters – something denied by Murphy – but in any case, they are adamant it is categorically untrue. They are emphatic that their conservative interpretation of Islam means they see ISIS as heretical deviations. Awan had believed she attended a meeting with the security services with Corbyn's sanction, that she had directly told him she was attending and he had not objected, and that nobody at the time mentioned her speaking out of turn – and even if she had, that did not qualify for a suspension. She had, however, discussed lodging a formal complaint against Murphy two days before the disciplinary action alleging bullying and unprofessional comments related to a miscarriage Awan had suffered. (Murphy for her part denies this, and claims she told colleagues that Awan was unwell, to encourage them to offer sympathy.) Awan's allies believe that Murphy didn't like her protesting, and was simply looking for an excuse to get rid of her.

Whatever the truth, Awan's case was a catalyst for a string of complaints by staff members about the way the leader's office was run. They gathered on the parliamentary estate – well away from the prying eyes of the leader's office – to discuss their grievances. Fearing retribution if they submitted a complaint through Human Resources – now, they believed, in thrall to Murphy – or through the Joint Trade Union Committee (given the number of anti-Corbyn figures on it and the tendency of union meetings to leak) on 3 December, several staff members wrote an anonymous letter supported by twenty-five of their colleagues in the office. Contrary to the values of 'a socialist movement with workers' rights at our core', the letter asserted, 'bullying and intimidation of staff' by senior management was rife. That same management fostered a 'divisive and toxic' office culture, which included 'pitting staff against each other', and 'weaponizing of complaints made by staff, including "fishing" for potential complaints and encouraging staff to make complaints against colleagues'. Management was accused of lying about colleagues; of 'sexist behaviour, including comments made in front of colleagues about female members of staff's appearances or clothing'; and of 'disciplinary and grievance cases by SMT' [Senior Management Team] being discussed in defiance of confidentiality and 'any assumption of innocence'. Meanwhile, the letter alleged, the same management often perceived 'constructive criticism and feedback . . . as personal attack'. Though the letter mentioned 'management' throughout, it was Murphy the staff mostly had in mind.

The letter was sat on for a while. With key parliamentary wrangles over Brexit under way, staff members who were, after all, dedicated to the Corbyn project did not wish to cause trouble at a sensitive moment. But just before Christmas, the office union representative handed copies of the letter in person to three managers: Murphy, Milne and Fisher. Murphy immediately took the representative into a small meeting room and yelled at him for ten minutes: the letter was complete rubbish and nonsense, all lies, the majority of staff didn't back the allegations, and so on.

In January 2019, Corbyn called a meeting of senior figures – Murphy, Milne, Fisher, Anjula Singh and Niall Sookoo – to discuss the letter. Murphy came out fighting. As far as she was concerned, this was a minority of disgruntled staff who simply would not tolerate being managed. It was a view echoed by another senior official speaking on condition of anonymity. 'A lot of Labour staff just wouldn't accept any kind of management,' they tell me. 'It was "we know best, we're activists ourselves, we know better than anyone",' that was the approach from some in the leader's office. It was subtle, no one actively refused to do things that were asked, it just felt like a constant war of attrition and difficulty in getting things done. They had a lot of arrogance, they didn't like having some kind of management.' But good workplace relations are the responsibility of management, not the workforce – and surely this should go without saying in the party of the workers. Yet this was an office in which some of those in charge did not even do proper staff appraisals, let alone one-to-ones. 'It was an office of committed socialists who couldn't even put in a formal complaint because we were so scared,' as one aide puts it. 'So we had to resort to an easily dismissed anonymous letter, which is so fucked up.'

As the operation became more divided and polarized, staff discontent could not be wished away. In June 2019, staff members across the

Labour Party threatened strike action over a below-inflation pay rise. An attempt by Murphy's allies to encourage staffers to sign a letter expressing no confidence in their union – itself an eyebrow-raising suggestion given the leadership's and Murphy's own exceptionally close affiliation to the union movement – only caused further antagonism. At the beginning of July, the staff's union branch passed a near unanimous motion condemning the leadership for denying staff the chance to raise concerns about management processes and undermining 'the ability of branch officials to represent members by implying that bringing concerns to the union would result in leaks to the media'. The motion demanded that the allegations be treated 'with the utmost seriousness . . . any attack on our union branches or our workplace representatives, is an attack on every single one of us and our rights as workers'. Murphy and her allies, however, continued to refute the allegations. 'People treated her really, really badly,' recalls former director of campaigns and events Marsha-Jane Thompson. 'They tried to portray her as a bully, but she wasn't. It was because she was a vocal woman.' For Thompson, the allegations were down to one thing, and one thing only: 'It was sexism.'

That same summer John McDonnell and Diane Abbott, never previously the closest of allies, had already tried to persuade Corbyn to sack Murphy as chief of staff, shifting her instead to Labour HQ; and to move Seumas Milne to one side, stripping him of operational responsibilities and making him a political adviser instead. At a meeting with Corbyn at his Finsbury Park office, the leader appeared to agree, pledging to call Andrew Fisher the next day to go through the details. As they left, Abbott turned to McDonnell: 'That sounds really good, very positive, it's a great new dawn'; McDonnell, more sceptical, suggested they 'give it twenty-four hours'. Corbyn duly did his usual disappearing act, refusing to answer his phone for days. Murphy remained in office.

After the Watson debacle at Labour conference that September, however, Murphy had become too big a problem for even Corbyn to ignore. He was deeply troubled by reports of the atmosphere in the leader's office, communicated to him by the veterans of his old backbench operations Jack Bond and Nicolette Petersen, his former long-standing personal secretary. Murphy's strength, an unwavering commitment to force action through, had begun to grate on the leader. 'Jeremy found Karie's manner too hectoring when under pressure,' says a senior aide. 'There's no point talking to him like that, he'll just close down. He found her too full on.' Of all Corbyn's senior team, moreover, it was Murphy who found reasons to be constantly at his side. 'She briefed him ten times a day, sometimes a bureaucratic list of things to sign off, and Jeremy didn't work like that. He didn't like it.'

Finally, at the beginning of October, Corbyn took the plunge. What followed was a palace coup. On holiday in Spain, Murphy was asked to return. Entering Corbyn's office, she was greeted by the leader and, at his side, McDonnell. It was McDonnell who spoke, informing Murphy that she would be moved from the leader's office to party headquarters, to help prepare for an election. 'That's very interesting, John, but I work for Jeremy, not you,' Murphy shot back. McDonnell turned to Corbyn: 'Tell her, Jeremy.' Conflict-averse as always, Corbyn barely spoke. McDonnell asked Murphy to leave the room briefly. When she was readmitted, a mumbling Corbyn told her to talk to Sir Bob Kerslake, the former head of the civil service and a McDonnell ally who had been brought in to review the operation of the leader's office. Murphy took his hand, and told him: 'If you want me to leave and work at Southside I'll do it: look in my eyes and tell me.' Avoiding her gaze, Corbyn again insisted she speak to Kerslake. At an office meeting shortly afterwards, Corbyn told his team that Murphy was being shifted over to headquarters to prepare for the general election that was now surely coming. He seemed transformed. 'Jeremy was assertive for the first time,' says one of the team at the meeting. 'I'd never seen him like that before or since.'

Now it was McDonnell in the driving seat. Since the 2017 general election, McDonnell had lost much of the power he once had, and came to feel that his advice was being systematically ignored. Relations with the leader's office had virtually collapsed, leading Milne acidly to tell allies that he was 'sulking in his tent'. But Andrew Fisher had convinced him to reassert himself; and now, Corbyn turned once again to his long-standing ally in his hour of political need. McDonnell saw his role as that of troubleshooter: stabilizing the operation, covering Corbyn's back, keeping the rickety show on the road, and trying somehow to develop a policy agenda for government. Kerslake, meanwhile, found a replacement for Murphy in Helene Reardon Bond, a former high-ranking civil servant with impeccable working-class credentials: the daughter of a builder and a cleaner, she had grown up on a council estate in Kentish Town. Non-factional and highly competent, Reardon Bond was what Corbyn's office had been crying out for for years. A lifelong Labour supporter, she was also going into the situation with eyes wide open.

Murphy, however, was not going quietly. She was devastated by her sacking. As far as she was concerned, she had been given the boot not by Corbyn, but by McDonnell, who was now effectively running the show. Her passionate and sincere view was that she had contributed decisively to the continuance of the Corbyn project by stabilizing the operation during the precarious summer of 2016 and taking difficult but necessary decisions to protect Corbyn's leadership from its internal enemies. She fought back angrily, successfully demanding to retain her title of chief of staff, and to be supported in her new role by eight members of the leader's office, close allies whose loyalty to her was absolute. Murphy had been pushed out – but not entirely. Reardon Bond, meanwhile, had her hands full. Reorganizing the leader's office into a functioning entity would, she told Corbyn, take six months. As it turned out, it was six months they wouldn't have.

For Murphy, Milne and those around them, what they saw as 'McDonnell's coup' – despite the fact that it was the Labour leader who had ordered the personnel change – was bound up with Brexit, and turning Labour into a categorically Remain-supporting party. As all the staff jobs in the leader's office were reviewed, and each team member was interviewed by Kerslake, 'it felt like the People's Vote campaign had come into the leader's office and taken over', one member of staff tells me, noting that Kerslake's fellow interviewer sported a bracelet emblazoned with the EU flag. (When I put this to him, Andrew Fisher waves the speculation away. 'It's just complete conspiratorial and dishonest bollocks,' he says. 'Literally no one in the office at that time had any links to the PV campaign. Who? It's just rubbish.')

The timing of the coup against Murphy was far from ideal, though. At the beginning of September, when opposition parties joined with

Labour rebels to take control of Parliament's agenda to block a No Deal Brexit, Johnson called for an election. With all opposition parties resistant to an election defined by Brexit and believing they had the government exactly where they wanted it, they voted it down. But it was clear that they could hold out only so long. 'It is quite difficult for an opposition to say: "This is an evil Tory government that should go as soon as possible – but we demand it stays!"' as the chief whip, Nick Brown, tells me. What was more, Labour was up against a new formidable opponent.

The old rules simply did not apply with Boris Johnson and his wily senior adviser Dominic Cummings. The rulebook didn't suit them, so they just tore it up. That August, Corbyn's former spokesperson Matt Zarb-Cousin received an email from Cummings, newly installed in Downing Street. Would Zarb-Cousin like to pop over to his house for a few beers? Whatever Cummings's motive – trying to get an insight into the thinking of Corbyn's team – this encounter was profoundly revealing as far as Zarb-Cousin was concerned. Cummings was expansive about plans to deal with internal dissent within the now hungrily pro-Brexit Conservative Party. Any Tory MPs who voted to back a parliamentary motion to take No Deal off the table would, he told Zarb-Cousin, be barred from standing as candidates for the party in the next election. And if the government was obstructed in Parliament, it would do one of two things. Either they would call a general election and set the date for 1 November, the day after the Brexit deadline, when the country's membership of the EU would expire and Britain would automatically leave without a deal. Or they would call the election for 30 October and tell the electorate that a vote for the Conservatives was a vote for Brexit to happen within twenty-four hours.

Corbynism was supposed to be the insurgent, anti-establishment force in British politics. But now Johnson and Cummings had seized their populist clothes. The Conservatives' new mantra was 'the People versus Parliament': the popular will expressed by the referendum of 2016 was being deliberately obstructed by a shamelessly undemocratic and out of touch political elite. It was a framing which Milne and other aides had feared, but failed to counter.

In real terms, this was nonsense. Britain is a parliamentary democracy, and the referendum result was supposed to be about clawing back sovereignty to the House of Commons. What's more, a year after the referendum, Britain's electorate voted for a Parliament which delivered a majority against a No Deal Brexit. But politics is more about sentiment than facts, something Cummings at that point probably grasped better than anyone in frontline British politics. While the Labour leadership had spent the last few months of Theresa May's premiership winning parliamentary battles with the Conservatives, these were Pyrrhic victories. Nobody really seemed to care – except the Labour Party. The public was sick and tired of political machinations, of being trapped in an eternity of Brexit limbo, while in Leave areas many voters simply interpreted each government defeat as another attempt to sabotage their now three-and-a-half-year-old democratic vote. Johnson and Cummings understood what Labour didn't. And they were ruthless. What Cummings told Zarb-Cousin came true. When twenty-one rebel, Remain-leaning Tory MPs voted with the opposition parties at the beginning of September to back a motion blocking No Deal, they were summarily kicked out of the Parliamentary Conservative Party. Among the casualties was former Chancellor of the Exchequer Philip Hammond and Winston Churchill's grandson Nicholas Soames. Meanwhile, the prime minister's own brother resigned from government and announced he was standing down as a Tory MP. Nothing seemed to touch Johnson – and Labour's leadership looked on with envy. Corbynism was constantly portrayed in the media as an authoritarian, Stalinist cult – yet in four and a half years of Corbyn's leadership, not a single Labour MP had been deselected, while within weeks of becoming Conservative leader, Johnson had purged a huge chunk of the so-called 'liberal' wing of his party. It was a massive gamble – and it showed the British public that he meant business over Brexit.

Nonetheless, in dismissing the rogue twenty-one MPs, Boris Johnson had also shorn himself of his slim parliamentary majority. Opposition parties discussed a new plan: why not simply remove him as prime minister through a vote of no confidence and create a new transitional government to block No Deal before calling a general election in 2020, or even a new referendum? Should Johnson be forced to resign, Corbyn, as leader of the opposition, would – constitutionally in any case – be offered the prime ministership. It was a prospect that clearly energized Corbyn, who drove the discussions. 'He held together that rough alliance, that was absolutely him,' says Anjula Singh. 'He was brilliant in those meetings.' For all Corbyn's energy, however, the move would need the backing of all the other opposition parties and a smattering of newly expelled Tory MPs. The problem was the Lib Dems (fuelled by recent Labour defectors such as Chuka Umunna) and Change UK would not touch Corbyn with a bargepole. Privately, John McDonnell was unconvinced the Labour leadership could have got even its own party behind such a proposition. With the deadlock unbroken, the parliamentary machinations continued – and not to Labour's advantage.

In the 2017 general election, Corbyn had been the firebrand insurgent, the man of principle. Now, he came across as an intriguer and schemer, part of the parliamentary establishment – which was hardly his skillset, but the image stuck. His irascibility bubbled over, whether in angry speeches in Parliament, or having a go at journalists parked outside his home.

All of which weakened Corbyn further as he plummeted to catastrophic levels in the polls. Oddly, his team had become resigned to his terrible ratings, as though they were simply a fact of life. There were never genuine, strategic discussions about how to turn around those public perceptions – which itself seemed an admission of the impossibility of the task.

As if all this weren't enough, the Labour leadership, together with the Remain movement, made another disastrous assumption: that Boris Johnson could not possibly get a more favourable Brexit deal than the botched offering his predecessor Theresa May had managed. They were making what was in hindsight a basic error. May's wafer-thin parliamentary majority depended on the Northern Irish Democratic Unionist Party, which refused to accept a customs border down the Irish Sea that would split Northern Ireland from the rest of the UK. But Johnson had no intention of running a minority government in which the Conservatives in a hung Parliament had to rely on the grace and favour of the DUP; in any case, having kicked out a number of Tory MPs, he could hardly govern for long anyway. He could afford to toss the Conservative alliance with the DUP into the Irish Sea – and did exactly that. When in mid-October Seumas Milne was told that Johnson had struck a deal with the EU on a withdrawal agreement, his answer was dismissive: 'Not possible, he's never going to get a deal.' But he had.

In an extraordinary attempt to drive the deal through in advance of the 31 October Brexit deadline, the government forced Parliament to vote on the new EU withdrawal agreement that same weekend. For months, the atmosphere in Parliament had been like a pressure-cooker; now it was going to explode. MPs knocked back the government's attempt, forcing Johnson to seek an extension until the end of January 2020. One Labour aide recalled hearing his colleagues cheering and whooping outside the office in celebration. He himself felt despair, knowing perfectly well how these parliamentary games would play with the country. 'I just thought: we're fucked,' he says. 'We've just voted and destroyed the chances of a socialist government, we've played into their hands, we've created the narrative the Conservatives want: we're the establishment.' Despite having spent the last two years furiously demanding an election, Labour had been resisting going to the country since Johnson assumed the premiership, claiming that the government could use any dissolution of Parliament to throw Britain into the chaos of No Deal. With the Brexit cliff edge pushed back, that imminent threat seemed to be removed – and with it went Labour's justification for holding out against Johnson's demand for a general election.

9
Things Fall Apart

If there was any consensus among the fractured Labour leadership and the parliamentary party in that autumn of 2019, it was that an election fought on Brexit and on Boris Johnson's terms was a very bad idea indeed. That you should avoid fighting an election on issues where you are weak is surely a cardinal rule of politics. Brexit consolidated the Tory vote. It was associated with country, sovereignty and being tough, all themes relished by right-wing populists. Labour's ostensible reason for opposing an election had been to remove the threat of a No Deal Brexit first, but the party had its own reasons. When, in mid-September, members of the campaign and data teams crunched Labour's terrible polling data, the results were grim, suggesting a majority approaching 150 for the Tories. However, now Labour had run out of excuses for blocking a general election – especially when its key opposition ally, the Scottish National Party, indicated that it would back one. And on 22 October, Boris Johnson's Brexit deal passed its second reading. This was surely the moment for the Labour leadership to start urgently mobilizing for an election campaign which, after all, might determine the future of the country for a generation, and risked ending in the left's political destruction. Or so you might think.

Throughout October, union general secretaries aggravated by a lack of frontbench discipline on Brexit called meetings with the leader's office. Many lacked organization. On one such occasion, Len McCluskey took up a place at the head of the table in the leadership office meeting room; others present included Corbyn, a selection of union representatives and McDonnell. The discussion lacked both structure and urgency. Abruptly, Corbyn decided to make everyone a cup of tea, so got up and started doing it. McCluskey cut short the speaker, UNISON General Secretary Dave Prentis. 'I'm going to stop you there, Dave,' he said heavily, 'because Jeremy has got up to make tea, so I'll wait until Jeremy sits back down.' Corbyn, seemingly oblivious, pottered about. After tripping over the phone line, accidentally disconnecting an attendee on speakerphone, he turned to one of the union officials present, asking tangentially after his former aide Gavin Sibthorpe. All of which was classic Corbyn: generous to a fault, treating everybody as equals, not above making the tea like everybody else. It would have been endearing, in normal circumstances. In the current, seismic context, it was infuriating.

When union leaders turned up to the next meeting, they found no politicians present. Corbyn's chief of staff, Helene Reardon Bond, looked mortified, while Andrew Fisher had to keep restarting the meeting, as other union officials who had phoned in kept cutting out. 'This is how we were deciding whether to have a general election,' says one of the officials in the room at the time. 'The entire thing felt like a Carry On film. If you imagined the level of disorganization and the way it would be that was it.'

Yet these were also classic Corbyn evasion tactics: he was torn on what to do. Within the shadow cabinet and the leader's office there was a spectrum of belief ranging from optimism to outright fear. Remainers like Emily Thornberry passionately argued that the party should resist an election which could only be on Johnson's terms, and should hold out instead for a second referendum. Others, especially Karie Murphy and her team, passionately made the case for going to the country. Party chair Ian Lavery was sent to attend the weekly Parliamentary Labour Party meeting to address MPs, who overwhelmingly opposed an election, 'We are the most prepared we've ever been for a general election,' he declared bullishly, to general disbelief. (Lavery since told colleagues that those words are a 'noose around my neck'.) At the regular shadow cabinet meeting, the mood was solemn and emotional. Many fretted that the dark, cold nights of a winter election would suppress Labour's big advantage – a ground army and mass campaigning – and that an election on the Tories' preferred date of 12 December would disrupt voting for a key constituent part of Labour's electoral coalition: students, who would at that point be travelling home for the Christmas holiday. Corbyn himself, in classic style, swung back and forth between embracing an election and continuing to hold out.

Meanwhile, other opposition parties forged ahead. John McDonnell would speak daily with Ian Blackford, the Westminster leader of the Scottish National Party; their relations were warm. But Blackford made it clear that the SNP were minded to push for an election – and, with Labour dithering, they turned instead to the arch-Remain Liberal Democrats. On Saturday 26 October, Reardon Bond was on a conference call when Liberal Democrat leader Jo Swinson's number lit up on her phone. Swinson had phoned to say that, at 11 a.m., the Liberal Democrats would announce a joint call, together with the SNP, for a general election, demanding that it be held not on 12 December but the 9th, thereby pulling the election into university term time. Reardon Bond was shocked at what she saw as Swinson's naivety. 'Why would you do that?' she retorted. 'You're just playing into the Tories' hands.'

At this point, the Lib Dems were deluded enough to be pitching Swinson as the next prime minister – something she herself seemed to believe, claiming that her party was 'within a small swing of winning hundreds of seats'.[1] Embracing a policy of Revoke (reversing Brexit without even a new referendum) – which most Remainers, let alone Leavers, considered an anti-democratic affront – Swinson reserved her strongest invective not for Johnson but, astonishingly, for Corbyn. She did so in the belief that the fortunes of the Lib Dems – who, after all, had formed an austerity coalition with the Conservatives back in 2010 – depended on picking up Tory votes. Such wavering Tory voters, though, needed to be convinced that in no circumstances would her party prop up a Labour government. Whatever the case, with the SNP and the Lib Dems backing a general election, it was practically impossible for Labour not to acquiesce.

Some in the leader's office were still convinced that the magic of the 2017 election could be recaptured. Back then, at the start of the campaign the Conservatives had been even further ahead – one poll put them on 48 per cent, twice Labour's predicted support – and Theresa May had been supremely popular: despite all this, Labour had achieved a hung Parliament. This time, Corbyn was catastrophically unpopular, but other factors weighed on the scales: Johnson did not have the enthusiastic support May had originally attracted, and his party had a significantly lower lead over Labour. With electoral broadcasting rules in place, Corbyn's campaigning zeal, and the mobilization of Labour's mass membership, opposed to a gaffe-prone politician in Johnson, could history not repeat itself? The DUP would be unlikely to prop up a Conservative government again, so even a new hung Parliament would mean Johnson's departure. But it was seriously unlikely that the Tories would run such a dire campaign again. Negative perceptions of Corbyn had had less time to settle back in 2017; now they had hardened. Brexit polarization was infinitely more profound. And, of course, there was no longer a unified team in the leader's office.

On the evening of 29 October, a group of left-wing commentators, myself included, sat around a table in the leader's office for a briefing by John McDonnell about the coming election, committing to an unashamedly radical programme. That day, opposition parties had sought to amend the existing government's one-line bill which provided only for an election, in order to to allow sixteen- and seventeen-year-olds and EU nationals the right to vote. All proposals had been defeated. As debate raged about Labour's Green Industrial Revolution – a sweeping set of policy commitments to tackle the climate emergency and improve living standards – the parliamentary division bell sounded, calling MPs to vote on whether or not to call a general election. As he left the room, McDonnell looked haunted. Shortly after, it was clear that the Tories had got their way: the vote to call an election for 12 December was passed by 438 to 20 votes. Labour had five weeks to pull itself together and win an election. In a cringeworthy attempt to rouse enthusiasm, I banged the table. But the mood of most Labour MPs was despairing; many thought they were marching off a cliff.

From the outset, a hopelessly divided Labour leadership had no clear election strategy – and it never developed one. Strategy meetings involving Corbyn and senior figures such as Milne and Andrew Murray had supposedly been taking place throughout 2019. But, from a tight-knit core group, the meetings had expanded to become an unwieldy talking shop, at which Corbyn often did not seem fully present, fiddling with his phone – a frequent source of irritation for his allies – and barely engaging with the conversation. A recurring problem was that Corbyn's team did not always know what the leader wanted – perhaps unsurprisingly, as Corbyn didn't appear to know himself. His contributions would often be monosyllabic and contradictory, and aides would disagree on what had been concluded. On one occasion, when a strategy paper on international affairs was discussed, his demeanour was transformed, his eyes lighting up as he spoke on issues ranging from social justice in Latin America to peace in the Middle East and unilateral nuclear disarmament. But this was not the terrain on which the general election would be fought. By the time the election was declared, however, the Labour leader had long since tired of the meetings, cancelling them altogether some two months previously.

When asked by Reardon Bond where she could find the election strategy, witnesses recall Milne telling her airily that 'we don't write it all down, it's all too fluid, we have to deal with politics as it is each day'. Yet for months, Milne's colleagues had been asking him for a campaign script and a clear communications and election strategy. Back in April, John McDonnell made precisely this request of Milne, at a group presided over by election co-chairs Andrew Gwynne and Ian Lavery. The executive director of strategy and communications had promised to deliver it by July. It never materialized.

When it failed to appear, Andrew Murray – at the encouragement of Karie Murphy – was chiefly responsible for drawing up a ten-page document headed 'GENERAL ELECTION STRATEGY' and ambitiously subtitled 'Destination Labour Government', which was circulated weeks before Johnson became Conservative prime minister. Labour, Murray wrote, would need to define the coming contest as 'a change election' with the party as the 'agent of change', while reinvigorating the spirit of 2017 in a mass mobilization of members and an 'atmosphere of optimism, determination and enthusiasm'. It also set out the project's main obstacles. The new Tory leader would avoid a repetition of Theresa May's disastrous manifesto and offer tax cuts. And Labour no longer had the 'novelty of surprise', because its leader and policies were not new. Presciently, Murray warned that

May's successor could declare the end of austerity and turn on the spending taps, nullifying a key advantage for Corbyn. Rather than dealing with specific injustices, the paper advised, Labour had to focus on how it would transform society for the better. More than ever, then, it had to sidestep the 'debilitating, divisive and ultimately phoney "culture war" ' – which meant not getting trapped on Brexit, where Labour's messaging had been 'confused or conflicting'. Whichever way Labour turned on Brexit, the paper warned, it was in trouble: its position of accepting the referendum result meant leaking votes to pro Remain parties; properly embracing Remain meant haemorrhaging them to the Tories and the Brexit Party. It had, somehow, to shift the terms of the debate: to emphasize the party's progressive social values to Remainers; and, to Leavers, to address disenchantment in de-industrialized areas of the country. But the paper left more questions hanging than it answered, reflecting the basic fact that Labour was now in an unsolvable mess.

Later that summer, Milne updated the paper, arguing that Corbyn's Labour must reposition itself as 'the real challenge to the establishment and the elites'. Fretting about the election becoming a proxy second referendum, he wrote that Labour had to make the coming election about 'not in or out, but the many not the few'. Labour's enemies would portray Corbyn's Labour as 'tired, stale, hopelessly divided, indecisive, toxic and extreme' compared to Johnson's Tories as 'fresh, optimistic, decisive, action-orientated', offering a right-wing populist brew of enacting Brexit, ending austerity and slashing taxes. Labour had to paint Johnson's Tories as untrustworthy and looking after their own, the rich, while Labour could be trusted to deliver and take on the elites. 'Our objective must be to win a majority,' was its defiant cry, 'and that must underlie everything we do in the campaign,' including where the party's resources and spending were allocated. All of which was fine, so far as it went. But while the document contained apt observations, it was a position paper, not a detailed strategy paper: full of generalities, it offered vague, platitudinous answers to existential questions.

To be fair to Milne, he had consistently pointed to an unavoidable reality. Labour-supporting Leave voters might be in a minority, but they were concentrated in the marginal constituencies that the party needed to retain and to win in order to have any chance in a general election. Passionate Remain voters tended to be concentrated in safe urban seats. But while he was right about this, there was no attempt to solve the central strategic problem that dogged Labour: how does a proudly democratic party, led by a self-professed tribune of the grassroots, deal with the fact that its membership demanded a new referendum?

By the end of September, Milne had come up with another iteration of the paper. Again, it circled round the same rhetoric, while offering very little in terms of concrete strategy. As one senior aide put it to me at the time: 'If you can decipher the clear headline messages or any strategy, do let me know.' When Reardon Bond saw the document, she chuckled wearily in front of Milne's staff, saying: 'If you went to a board with that you'd get laughed out.'

On 11 November, five days after Parliament was dissolved, Milne wrote a 599 word 'narrative arc'. It outlined three 'phases'. Phase one, 'The Country at a crossroads – the challenge we face', spoke of a billionaire wealth grab under the Tories, powerful interests fuelling global warming, and both Tories and Lib Dems dividing the country over Brexit. Phase two was 'Winning the battle for change', which claimed Tory promises to end austerity could not be trusted, Tory Brexit would mean a race to the bottom in rights and protections, while Labour's final say over a sensible deal would settle Brexit in six months. Phase three, 'The future we will make', outlined core policies, such as a Green Industrial Revolution, public ownership and a housebuilding programme. It all sounded great – on the conceptual level. But it was airy rather than solid.

The centrepiece of any political campaign is a slogan. It provides an overarching narrative, ensuring that policies and speeches are brought together with an overall theme, rather than becoming a random jumble. Labour's 2017 election slogan, 'For the many, not the few', was astonishingly effective. Its policies slotted into the slogan's narrative: taxing the rich and big business to invest in public services; scrapping VAT exemptions on private school fees to fund universal free school meals. In 2019, Milne and his team strongly felt that a new slogan was needed, which made sense – but only if it was really powerful . . . After testing in polling and focus groups – one message,

'Sod Brexit – Rebuild Britain Instead', apparently went down well with Leave-leaning women in the North and Midlands. But eventually a new slogan was settled upon: 'It's time for real change'. Its target was Boris Johnson, whose presentation of himself as the change candidate was mere sleight of hand, given that he was in fact the face of a Conservative Party that had been in government for the last nine years. The only meaningful *real* change – or so voters were supposed to understand – was for the opposition to form a government and decisively break with the policies Johnson had supported and voted for. But it was too complex, too abstract, and could not compete with the Conservatives' foursquare, concrete 'Get Brexit done'.

'If that's your strategy with the slogan, you have to show *how* you're real change,' explains Andrew Fisher. In other words, all your policies and announcements and attacks on your opponents have to link to that central theme. This, he tells me, was never worked out – and, indeed, it didn't cut through. When the party belatedly realized this, it rotated through different slogans: the abbreviated 'Real change', 'On your side', 'Putting money in your pocket' and the old favourite, 'For the many not the few'. Three weeks into the five-week campaign, John McDonnell held an election strategy meeting in party headquarters to try to clarify Labour's key messages. While he scribbled them down on a whiteboard, Murphy declared she would lock the door and no one could leave until everyone was agreed on what the messages were. But nothing decisive was concluded.

At the start of the campaign, and in the absence of any detailed strategy or communications plan, Andrew Fisher – who, remember, had already tendered his resignation and was due to leave at the end of the year – took it upon himself to sit down with Niall Sookoo, the executive director for elections and campaigns, to thrash out a campaign, with policies and a basic 'Grid' – the schedule and key themes of the campaign.

A big part of the problem was the lack of any clear single figure in control – whether it be Murphy, Reardon Bond, Milne or McDonnell – and the divisions that had opened up in the senior management team. 'What is true is that people did not agree, there were too many cooks in the kitchen, and because of tensions in our team, people were working in silos,' says a senior aide. 'In a political operation, you can't run policies, comms and strategy separately; they all have to be integrated together to work to feed into each other. That was the product of the internal schism.'

Astonishingly, in an election campaign that would mean life or death as far as the Corbyn project, was concerned, 'the election team was full of tensions', says Anjula Singh, 'and coordination was tricky. Everyone was doing their own bits and that spanned both strategic and operational decision-making.'

Nowhere was this operational collapse more evident than in the lack of a plan for the Labour leader himself. It was abundantly clear that Corbyn was seen as Labour's Achilles heel and that there would be a renewed media onslaught against him – yet there was, extraordinarily enough, no strategy to combat it. 'It's hard, because we all love Jeremy and think he's great,' says one Labour press officer. 'We knew it was grossly unfair how the media treated him, but people around him never got round to how we could counter that. The scale of the challenge was huge.'

Neither was there much effort made to identify different voter groups. What planning there was centred on what was called a '99 per cent strategy': rather than being defensive and trying to hold on to what the party had, it should behave as though it could win almost anywhere, or at least as though 600 or 650 seats were in play. This exceptionally ambitious plan was trumpeted by Karie Murphy, who declared at a party staff meeting that there was 'nowhere we won't go'. Others, like Niall Sookoo, proposed beginning with a more defensive strategy: to pour resources into seats the party already held to stop them falling to the Tories – and then, when the foundations were rebuilt, gradually becoming more ambitious. But with the 2017 election in mind, when a cautious approach on the part of hostile party staff had been blamed for Labour's failure to win enough seats to form a government, Milne dismissed it, along with Murphy, who retorted: 'We're not losing any of these seats.' This time, they had control of the party headquarters, and they were determined to use it.

Whether or not, as Murphy contends, the '99 per cent strategy' came from Corbyn, messaging and strategy came under the purview of Milne and Murphy, whose dismissal from the leader's office had made little difference to her ability to influence matters. Still retaining her technical title of chief of staff, she played a key role in coordinating election efforts. Such an ambitious campaign was, it transpired, blue-sky to the point of delusion: taking the 2017 election as a template in completely different political circumstances; assuming that Corbyn would play as well with the electorate as he had two years previously, as though the Brexit culture war and the antisemitism crisis had never happened; and, in the case of one shadow cabinet minister, dismissing unfavourable YouGov polling on the grounds that the pollsters were 'Tory-owned'.

Strategy aside, the general election campaign exposed every fault-line in the Corbyn project, from the simmering personal animosities at the top to the endemic chaos in the leader's office. Before the election was even called, Labour's Grid was leaked, evidence that entrenched institutional hostility from Labour HQ had not dissipated and forcing a revision from scratch. Almost no one other than Murphy had access to this new Grid, something justified on security grounds. This provoked conspiracy theories – unfounded – among many staffers that it did not actually exist. Grid meetings, chaired by Murphy herself, would take place in the party headquarters, where Murphy and her team were now ensconced.

As it turned out, the Grid was completely ill-suited for an election campaign. Focused on where Corbyn was going each day, it pegged the announcement of new policies to Corbyn's appearances, a scatter-gun approach that would give the electorate sensory overload and allow no policy the time to sink in. 'We should have picked three or four core themes,' says speechwriter Alex Nunns, 'and just kept hammering them and developing them over the course of the campaign in speeches and policy announcements: like a Green New Deal as a massive job creation scheme in the areas destroyed by Thatcher.' Corbyn's visits, in other words, should have been secondary to the themes, with his appearances helping to sell announcements, not driving the Grid. 'I couldn't believe it,' says a senior official. 'Where's the strategy? What's this week's big message, who are we getting out there?' Press officers were left flying blind. 'We never knew where he was going from day to day,' says one. Indeed, each day of the Grid would often be revealed only between twenty-four and seventy-two hours in advance, leaving even the leader himself in the lurch. His speechwriters were sometimes given a few days' notice of a major address; sometimes, though, it was twenty-four hours at best, and often they were unable to find out his movements in advance. In the run-up to a speech in Southampton at the end of November, they weren't even told what the topic was until the evening before (environmental policy, as it happened), forcing them to stay up all night to write the leader's speech. As a result of these quick turnarounds, the sign-offs for speeches were – unsurprisingly – incredibly lax, far removed from the rigorous fact and messaging checks needed during a general election. Some speeches were not signed off at all, and the speechwriters, who should have been fed key lines by strategists, found themselves improvising messaging, which was not their job.

At Labour's election launch in Battersea at the end of October, Corbyn unleashed a powerful attack on 'the privileged few' and asked which side were we all on: dodgy landlords like the Duke of Westminster, or struggling tenants; bad bosses like billionaire Mike Ashley, or a worker who gave birth in a toilet at work because she was scared of losing her shift; billionaire media barons like Rupert Murdoch, or the overwhelming majority in society; and so on. It was an effective piece of rhetoric inspired by the US Democrat Bernie Sanders – but, cooked up only the night before, it was completely *ad hoc*.

It was symptomatic of Murphy's sometimes suffocating control that Corbyn himself was not allowed to have his own diary; sometimes he had no idea where he was going. There was no completed 'Ops note', a diary setting out the next day, until late the evening before. This was a marked difference from 2017, when things were set out to the leader days in advance. On one occasion, on his campaign bus, Corbyn gently put his glasses down and told an aide: 'You know, I don't even know what's in my diary tomorrow.' What was more, the days scheduled for him were long: he would get back at 1 or 2 a.m., then have to be back on the road at 6 a.m.

In 2017, massed crowds chanting 'Oh, Jeremy Corbyn!' had been a powerful visual expression of the campaign's growing momentum. Repeating this style of campaign was always going to be a tough ask in the cold and wet of the British winter. Corbyn began the campaign in Scotland, to small crowds. Events in English and Welsh marginals often consisted of speaking to a hundred activists and taking selfies, but often involved a round trip of four hours or more. Many of his team questioned whether this was a good use of time. It was also aggravating for Corbyn. His daily timetables were often crammed, which complicated transport and logistics. 'Why are we doing this?' was his regular demand. 'We'll never make this in time, why are we doing it?' Often, he would be hours late for an event. Once he actually arrived, it would be hard to extricate him, because there was nothing he enjoyed more than talking and listening to supporters. Which would have been fine if the rallies were getting bigger. But they weren't. 'It's cold, it's dark, it's winter,' was the usual explanation. It was the weather's fault.

Understandably, the scheduling caused Corbyn growing irritation. Towards the end of the campaign, he grew exasperated with Marsha-Jane Thompson, the general secretary's assistant and key Murphy ally, who had been charged with planning events. Frustrated that the final leg of the campaign seemed entirely unplanned, Corbyn made it clear he did not want her accompanying him on the tour bus, stating that she should instead be focusing on arranging events back at party HQ. When she turned up anyway, he took her to one side and firmly told her to leave. Upset and hurt, Thompson duly left, and blipped off the radar. Corbyn's wife, Laura Alvarez, who had proved critical to sustaining the leader's morale in difficult times, herself felt the strain, sometimes showing her anger at aides in front of watching journalists.

Then, there was the failure to portray Corbyn as, well, himself. In 2017, his events team had no difficulty doing this. Genuine, human, empathetic, he was seen enthusiastically reading Michael Rosen's *We're Going on a Bear Hunt* to primary school pupils and meeting apprentice builders to talk about Labour's housebuilding policies. The defining image of Corbyn in 2019, by contrast, was perched on a podium behind a lectern, reading speeches off an autocue. 'That's not Jeremy,' says one press officer. 'We completely failed to play to his strengths.' Which was especially problematic given his tanking personal ratings and the inevitable flak that came his way.

This time around, the media onslaught was even more vicious.[2] As the weeks ticked by, Labour aides would darkly joke: 'When do the broadcasting rules kick in?' It was compounded by a dripfeed of errors by the BBC – all of which just happened to favour the Conservatives. During the ceremonial wreath-laying on Remembrance Sunday, in the words of former Tory journalist Peter Oborne, 'a dishevelled Johnson made a mess of placing a red wreath at the Cenotaph', a gaffe which, had it been committed by Corbyn, would have seen him flayed alive in the media. (Something of this kind had of course happened to him over national anthem-gate four years previously in St Paul's Cathedral.) But nobody saw the images of Johnson – on the BBC at any rate – as the corporation substituted footage from the 2016 ceremony of, in Oborne's words, 'a much smarter Johnson placing a green wreath'. It was a mistake, said the BBC. Other slips followed: a clip of Johnson being laughed at by the audience on BBC *Question Time* was edited to show only applause; senior BBC broadcast journalists regurgitated lines fed to them by Dominic Cummings without scrutiny or interrogation.[3] To make one mistake, to coin a phrase, may be regarded as a misfortune, to make a string of them looks like carelessness – especially at a time when, in an election campaign, care badly needed to be taken. Inexcusably, however, Labour's comms team often couldn't get it together to rebut these mistakes. It regularly fell to John McDonnell, who would pester the comms team, or even ring up media studios himself to challenge inaccuracies.

In one bleak episode, several broadcast journalists – acting purely on information fed to them by Tory spin doctors – claimed that a Labour activist had punched a Conservative adviser in the face. It was proven completely untrue. Yet there were in fact two actual attacks during the campaign, both on Labour activists in their seventies: one was taken to hospital with a suspected broken jaw;[4] the other, denounced as a Marxist by her assailant, suffered suspected cracked ribs.[5] Neither incident received much attention in the media.

When Ian Austin, an obscure former Gordon Brown adviser turned Labour MP before he resigned from the party in February 2019, called for the electorate to vote Tory, it received saturation news coverage. Even though Austin was, in the opinion of a former aide to Brown, a 'thuggish right-winger', he was portrayed by senior journalists as a disillusioned Labour loyalist and successfully weaponized against the party. Letters bearing his signature were sent at vast expense to voters in key seats urging them to vote Tory. Among the MPs Austin endorsed was the hard-right Conservative MP Philip Davies, whose track record included reportedly filibustering legislation to tackle male violence against women and girls.[6] Yet when former Conservative Prime Minister John Major urged voters to support ex-Tory candidates running against his own party, the coverage was, again, minimal.[7]

The same went for media coverage of the two leaders. There was a full-on assault on Corbyn's personal integrity, particularly over Brexit and antisemitism, which might have been fair enough if the media had not all but turned a blind eye to Johnson's history of racism, Islamophobia and homophobia. Likewise, Johnson's evasiveness in the face of the media – regularly changing the conditions under which he would consent to appear, and at times failing to turn up at all – was never properly challenged. What criticism there was, as ever, failed to stick. Nothing stuck on Teflon Johnson.

Corbyn himself, worn down by a relentless battery of attacks for nearly half a decade, was far more resistant to facing the media this time round. 'He'd lost confidence,' suggests one of his closest allies. Before big set-piece interviews, he would often be stressed and grumpy, and as the campaign progressed, this got worse. When he was interrogated about antisemitism, in particular, his mood would noticeably darken.

Corbyn had always been difficult to prep for major interviews and debates. He often saw such preparation as a distraction from campaigning, and didn't regard being locked in a room with three or four people – some of whom he neither liked nor trusted – as an effective use of his time. 'We slimmed down the prep team so that Jeremy wouldn't feel like he was surrounded by lots of people trying to shove facts into him and showcasing their own cleverness,' says Anjula Singh. 'We wanted to focus on him being fully briefed and relaxed – not wound up. It was challenging to make the best use of what was often a tight schedule.' The fact, too, that Corbyn's team were unable to give him comms briefings well in advance – Milne failing to sign off these briefings in time – now became exceptionally problematic, given the compressed schedules of Labour's election campaign. For every allocated half-hour, aides found about ten minutes as they sought to brief him in trains, cars, community centres and schools. They tried to manage his rhythms, to understand when he was in the right mood and frame of mind and when he wasn't. He was easily distracted. He hated hearing anything negative about the polls. 'I wish they'd shut up about polling,' he would say. On trains, he'd flick through notes abstractedly, not seeming to take anything in. He would be bombarded with text messages, WhatsApps and phone calls, including from people he'd met on anti-war demos years previously. As ever, he found solace in everyday encounters, and would always want to have chats, with the train guard, passengers sitting next to his team, random young folk who approached him to ask for a selfie. Attempting to find moments of peace, he'd insulate himself against the outside world. Sticking his earphones in, he listened to classical music and read international novels, making it clear he did not want to be briefed.

The big interview with the BBC's rottweiler interviewer Andrew Neil, towards the end of November, would always prove the most challenging for all leaders. Corbyn's team didn't have to agree to do this – Boris Johnson successfully avoided the trap altogether – but Milne pointed to 2017, when Corbyn had done well against the big beast. For Neil, interviewing politicians on live TV was a bloodsport – and Corbyn was a prize kill. Knowing just how important the encounter would be, Andrew Fisher set aside most of the day for briefing. Things got off to a bad start when Corbyn turned up two hours late, having been campaigning in his home constituency of Islington North. Then, to the frustration of Fisher and his team, Corbyn struggled with facts and figures. The interview was predictably disastrous. Unaccountably, Corbyn refused to apologize for antisemitism within the Labour Party, even though he had already apologized repeatedly in the past, instead responding tetchily to Neil's invitation to do so.

Labour had staked much on the televised debates of the election, which had played a critical role in 2017 in transforming perceptions about Corbyn. Moreover, Johnson, despite his bluster, was not a solid debater. Before each showdown, the prime minister was twitchy, speaking in half sentences and nervously putting his arm around the Labour leader. But again, Corbyn's team struggled to prep him. It was a recurring problem, the leader's talents did not include landing agreed lines.[8] Polling after each debate suggested a score draw – not good enough when Labour were badly behind in the polls – but Corbyn felt buoyed in their aftermath: a fleeting sense of what could have been, had circumstances been different.

Corbyn and his allies eulogized Labour's mass membership of half a million activists who offered an on-the-ground counterweight to a hostile mass media. But they were often badly let down. Faiza Shaheen is a charismatic economist who stood for Labour's banner in the northeast London constituency of Chingford and Woodford Green, a seat held by Iain Duncan Smith, the architect of the Tories' assault on the welfare state. Her campaign was full of buzz and energy; there was a sense of community as activists poured in from across London and beyond. 'But there was just a complete breakdown in the party machinery,' she tells me. Her team weren't given the updated contacts of newly registered voters – between five and six thousand – until election day itself. Direct mails didn't go out on time, so that many received them *after* postal votes had already been submitted. The local region had failed to set up a Facebook campaign to locate and target their swing voters. What was more, recalls Shaheen, the leaflets themselves 'were really shit. They had no sense of direction at all. *At all.*' Here was a story repeated across the country.

Social media had played a decisive role in the glorious defeat of 2017; the videos made under the instructions of Corbyn's widely lauded social media manager, Jack Bond, had reached millions. Now, changes to Facebook's algorithms made it harder for Labour's content to go viral. The Tories, meanwhile, had drastically improved, even raiding Labour's techniques. Even though the party's official content had fewer shares and video views than in 2017, both Corbyn's operation and the social media campaign of the grassroots organization Momentum reached even more people this time round. But there was a critical difference compared to two and a half years previously. With Labour lacking a coherent message, the Tories could simply hammer away at their core lines of 'Get Brexit Done', more hospitals, more police officers, and so on. Without a clear, inspiring message to cut through, even the best social media operation in the world wouldn't have a chance.

Then there were the policies – the many, many policies. Before the 2017 election, Labour's domestic policy blitz had suddenly started generating positive media coverage; during the campaign itself, the leaking of the party's manifesto had simply resulted in extended coverage of what proved incredibly popular policies. The 2017 experience 'created a mentality, an understanding of how we get positive press: we do policy announcements', explains Mary Robertson, former head of economic policy. This addiction to dropping policies to get coverage had continued through 2018 – every time Corbyn did a speech, the comms team would ask 'What's new? We need a new policy' – but with diminishing returns. In 2019, with the party desperate to shift the conversation away from Brexit, the reliance on policy was greater than ever, but this time, unanchored by any clear narrative or vision.

Labour's election promise to roll out universal, free full-fibre broadband became a totemic example of its policy incontinence. This was grossly unfair. According to the OECD – an international organization representing thirty-seven industrialized nations – Britain ranked thirty-fifth for broadband connectivity: while 98 per cent of South Korea's premises had full-fibre coverage, in Britain the figure was less than 10 per cent.[9] Rather than market competition supposedly unleashing efficiency and reducing costs, the duplication of resources involved amounted to £6.2 billion.[10] In a society dependent as much on the internet as on road and rail networks, this was crippling. John McDonnell in particular had grasped this problem, because during various community meetings around the country, people complained to him that poor broadband was a key obstacle to attracting inward investment. Accordingly, he made broadband a key plank of Labour's economic policy and – with broadband allowing more work from home and lessening the pressure on commuting – environmental policy too. Broadband, Labour saw, was a basic twenty-first-century utility.

When Labour first announced it would roll out free universal full-fibre broadband in mid-November, it worked. Millions of people received a BBC push notification on their mobile phones unveiling the policy, and the national agenda shifted momentarily away from Brexit while the policy was debated by pundits and commentators across all forms of media. Activists were thrilled. 'It felt like the spirit of 2017, pushing what was politically accessible,' recalls speechwriter Joss MacDonald. But the policy itself – floated privately not long before – had come out of nowhere. Labour's press team first heard of it the day before its announcement. And here was the problem. Dropping a major new policy for which there was no pre-existing public appetite or demand, without laying the foundations to explain why it was necessary 'just leaves people cold', as Andrew Fisher puts it. 'And it did.'

In the absence of a coherent narrative into which to plug it, the policy appeared leftfield, random even. What Labour should have done was to spend the previous eighteen months on a nationwide campaign highlighting Britain's manifestly inadequate broadband infrastructure and making the economic, environmental and human case for transforming it. The timing of its announcement, too, was bad, coming as it did on the eve of the NHS declaring the worst accident and emergency figures on record. Due to appear on BBC's *Newsnight* to unveil a new £26 billion rescue plan for the NHS, Shadow Health Secretary Jonathan Ashworth instead found himself talking about broadband. It was the right policy announced at the wrong time with no preparation. In Len McCluskey's opinion, far from being embraced in working-class communities, billions for free broadband was seen as an absurd joke. 'There spoke the desperation, the hope that if you come up with all kinds of policies and push Brexit aside in people's minds, they'll be interested in policies,' he tells me. 'It was the exact opposite; people thought it was ridiculous.'

A week later, on 21 November, in Birmingham, Corbyn launched Labour's manifesto. In it, the broadband policy sat among a smorgasbord of transformative policies: public ownership of utilities, scrapping tuition fees, free bus travel for under-25s, a mass housebuilding programme and a huge public investment programme. Polling suggested these were all ideas popular with the British public. After the manifesto announcement, private Tory polling and focus groups found an uptick towards Labour, with the Tory lead hitting a low of four points in some seats.[11]

The party had committed to £400 billion in investment spending. Mindful that the Conservatives would inevitably attack Labour's plans as fiscally irresponsible – as they always did – an accompanying so-called 'grey book' was released to demonstrate that the programme was fully costed. The problem was, however, that those who had helped draw it up felt uneasy about it. 'I feel slightly disloyal, but when I saw the grey book for the first time in its entirety – I helped on chunks of it – I didn't think the manifesto was deliverable in that time frame,' says one senior official. 'I am so, so committed and I didn't think we can do this. It felt somewhat incredible, I just didn't think we could raise capital spending over the course of a five-year parliament.'

The other problem was the optics: to most people, the £400 billion figure felt both impossibly large and abstract. Leadership officials had briefed media commentators and community leaders that the investment would be made tangible, broken down, that there would be explanations about what the money would mean in practical terms. There were regional manifestos breaking down spending and job creation by region, for example, but their launch was bungled and never cut through. One senior staffer was a governor at her local school; at one governors' meeting, she was berated by a passionate Labour-supporting teaching assistant. 'This is a disaster,' they said. 'Every morning you're waking up and just talking billions and trillions. I'm Labour through and through but no one understands what's going on.'

One of the casualties of this haphazard, disconnected approach was the Green Industrial Revolution, a policy which had taken a huge amount of work to develop. It was, potentially, a jewel in Labour's crown, putting forward a programme intended to respond to the climate emergency while simultaneously transforming Britain, creating new skilled jobs and improving living standards. Homes would be retrofitted to a high energy-efficiency standard, reducing fuel bills and emissions; public transport, particularly buses, would be expanded, modernized and made affordable; there would be a revolution in renewable energy. But the green policy agenda barely appeared on the radar. 'The press never wrote up our green policies,' said one of its key champions, Kirsty Major, 'but then I also think it was the fault of the party for not foregrounding or briefing them, or making it more central to the sell.'

The campaign descended into policy incontinence. 'That's probably a fair way to describe it, but it's because there was literally *nothing* else,' says Fisher. 'No strategy, no planning, no themes, no narrative.' Press release after press release landed in journalists' inboxes announcing more shiny new ideas, leaving no time for any announcement to be digested. On 25 November, Labour abruptly declared that it would compensate some of the women who had lost out when the pension age had been changed back in 2011, affecting 2.6 million. Women born in the first half of the 1950s – so-called Waspi women, named after the group Women Against State Pension Inequality – would be given £100 for each week of entitlement lost: the average payment would be £15,380, and the maximum £31,300. The total price tag added up to yet another £58 billion. There was, to be fair, a rationale: Labour was struggling in the polls among older demographics, and here was a means to win them over. But it was clearly desperation. 'By that time in the campaign, we had to do something,' admits McDonnell, but 'even though I'd campaigned for Waspi women for years and there was lots of support, it was too easily attacked on the scale of expenditure'. And then came the rub: 'if there'd been a clear narrative linking policy up step by step, it'd have protected us from that criticism'. Len McCluskey was damning about the campaign: 'It was a mish mash of policies which, in my opinion, was determined by people who don't live in the working-class world.'

For all this, it was Labour's inability to deal with Brexit that harmed it most – though in truth the election was probably all over by 11 November. On that day, the Brexit Party announced it was standing down its candidates in Tory-held seats and concentrating its firepower on Labour seats. So, while the Tory vote would remain intact, Labour's would be split. Yet at that point, with a month of campaigning to go, Labour still had its opportunities. The Lib Dems, which under Jo Swinson had converted into an unequivocally Remain party, endured a catastrophic election campaign, with their leader collapsing under the modest scrutiny of their plans to cancel Brexit. The way was clear for Labour to win back swathes of Remain supporters. But again, Corbyn's team felt there was no option but to fudge it. Though there was, in theory, a strong logic to Corbyn's declaration that he would remain neutral in a new referendum, as an 'honest broker' seeking to mend rather than exacerbate divisions, it simply fed the existing narrative that he was weak and indecisive.

Corbyn did have the odd moment. Towards the end of November, in an audacious attempt to pivot towards an issue on which Labour was traditionally strong, a press conference was called at short notice. Dramatically, Corbyn waved unredacted official documents claiming that the NHS was 'up for sale' to the Trump administration. While the truth was a bit more complicated than that, it was done with panache and Corbyn pulled it off. Corbyn 'nailed it', said one aide. Like everything else Labour tried, however, it just did not cut through. It sounded too reminiscent of the notorious 'Project Fear' of the Remain campaign, and in the absence of an optimistic Labour campaign theme, seemed to project only more pessimism and gloom.

Corbyn's ratings did improve over the five weeks, as did Labour's polling. That's important to note, because conventional political wisdom suggests that there is not much poll movement during the course of a campaign. But both were starting from dire levels, because years of attacks had truly made an impression. Frankie Leach, an events officer, recalls sitting in the Royal Scot pub in the Cumbrian city of Carlisle, two days before the election. Corbyn was in the room next door giving a televised speech, and Leach sat among the pub's patrons, watching it on TV. As Corbyn spoke, punters reacted, pints in hand, repeating back Tory attack lines. 'For the first time I thought: we could be in trouble here. These were working-class people in the North who voted Leave and we had lost them,' she recalls, acknowledging a bubble that had formed around the leader, insulating him from the hostility of the outside world. 'I just wasn't hearing positive noises about Labour in that pub.'

And Corbyn knew it. Shortly before polling day, he sat with social media manager Jack Bond in a café in Archway, north London, after recording an election film. Corbyn was clearly keen to talk about something, but he skirted around it, as he often did even with close aides when difficult subjects had to be broached. At last, he ventured a comment about his terrible personal poll ratings and looked at Bond, mystified: 'Why do you think that is?'

*

By the last two weeks of the campaign, it was abundantly clear to Labour's strategists that a disaster was unfolding in the 'Red Wall', the swathe of Northern and Midlands seats which had always voted Labour, time out of mind, and on which the party had always been able to rely. It shouldn't have been a surprise: Niall Sookoo's polling had indicated this from the very beginning. Everything pointed to Labour getting a hammering.

On one canvassing expedition in Ashfield, a *New York Times* reporter accompanied the former MP Gloria de Piero and her successor as Labour candidate. Knocking on one door, they talked to a primary school teacher who had voted Remain – her husband Leave – but was 'pissed off' Britain had not yet left the EU, and was utterly sick of talking about Brexit. When the conversation moved on to the injustice of school cuts, the teacher could not agree more; but though she had voted Labour last time round, she was no longer sure how she'd vote. De Piero and her colleague said their goodbyes and walked on, but the *New York Times* journalist returned to check. The teacher admitted she was actually going to vote Conservative. 'Then I realized,' says de Piero, 'those Don't Knows were not voting for us.'

And there were lots of those Don't Knows. 'People in their sixties and seventies, former miners, were voting Tory for the first time,' de Piero goes on. 'They didn't enjoy it, not one said, "I really like Boris Johnson or I think I'm a Tory now."' But they voted Conservative anyway.

It was a story replicated across Labour's Leave-voting heartlands. In the former mining constituency of Wansbeck, Ian Lavery sought out constituents he considered weathervanes. He spoke to a miner who had been sacked in the Miners' Strike of 1984–5, a close personal friend of his, and asked him to put up a Labour Party placard in his garden. The friend refused. 'I'm not falling out with you,' he told Lavery, 'I love you to bits, but the Labour Party has betrayed me.' Lavery knocked on door after door. Many declined to say who they were voting for, some out of embarrassment or, given their family's voting history, shame. 'I saw it coming,' Lavery tells me, 'but not to that magnitude. I thought it'd be a Brexit tornado. It was a Brexit tsunami.' In the Midlands seat of Bassetlaw, where Jonathan Ashworth was out knocking on doors, it was even worse. Often when former Labour voters were abandoning their party, they'd looked embarrassed and avoided eye contact. Not this time. They told Ashworth proudly that they'd voted Labour all their life – and now they were voting Tory. There was no embarrassment at all.

On the campaign trail with Corbyn, the last two days were not good: he was tired, the schedule was overwhelming and the weather was terrible. On the day before the election, he was late for everything. When he turned up to the last rally in Hoxton, east London, the venue had been poorly chosen, with low ceilings and a stage most of the audience couldn't see. It was a fitting climax to a doomed campaign.

Throughout this ill-fated election, thousands of activists in villages, towns and cities had sacrificed bitterly cold, dark and wet evenings and weekends. They did so because of a passionate commitment to a cause they believed would free society of injustice, poverty and exploitation. On 12 December, they mobilized in vast numbers, undoubtedly saving the party from an even greater calamity. But the political headwinds they fought against were just too strong.

On election day, politicians are barred from the airwaves, and much of the team – with little work to be doing – left their posts and knocked on doors along with other grassroots activists. 'I felt nothing like I did in 2017,' admits Andrew Fisher. They looked for positive signs, such as extended queues outside polling stations, and activists out and about. Corbyn himself knocked on doors in his home patch of Islington North. In one touching moment, a group of primary school pupils caught sight of the Labour leader, came to the window and chanted: 'LABOUR! LABOUR!'

An hour before polls closed, as he drove to meet Corbyn, Seumas Milne received a phone call from Ian Blackford, the SNP leader in Westminster. Blackford had heard that the voting returns were suggesting a hung Parliament. 'I really don't know where you've got that from,' responded Milne curtly. Then Blackford began to talk about negotiations to form a government. 'If it helps, we'd want to negotiate,' said Milne, 'but I don't think that's on the cards.' It had been clear to Milne for a long time that Labour were not going to win.

Moments before the exit poll was announced at 10 p.m., Corbyn and a small group – his wife, Milne, Andrew Fisher and Helene Reardon Bond – assembled in the meeting room of Freedom From Torture, a charity located in the heart of his constituency. Across the city, in Labour Party HQ in Victoria, staffers gathered around a television as Jack Bond sent Corbyn's last tweet, thanking supporters who 'campaigned tirelessly to win so we can build a fairer country'. Then the exit poll came, predicting 368 seats for the Tories and just 191 for Labour. It was catastrophic: the party had not fallen below 200 seats since 1935. The only crumb of comfort was that the final result was not quite so bleak: 365 for the Conservatives, 202 for Labour. Nonetheless, it represented a Tory parliamentary majority of 80, the greatest since Margaret Thatcher's 1987 landslide. Even the most pessimistic in the leader's office had not predicted such a wipe-out.

Around the leader there was silence; then, from Corbyn, 'Oh dear.' His little grandson hugged him, asking: 'Are you alright?' He whispered back, 'Some days aren't good, but we'll get through it,' then walked out of the room to where other staffers were waiting. Devastated, he tried to crack a joke: 'I'm going to ask for a full recount.' Aides wept, and Corbyn hugged them, telling them to try to be positive, before leaving to attend his own count. There, in front of the nation's press pack, Corbyn announced his intention to resign as leader.

In Labour HQ the silence was punctuated by sobs and expletives; staffers walked around in tears. Corbyn arrived later, moving from desk to desk, thanking them and hugging them. 'It was very human, it wasn't at all staged,' says press officer Jack McKenna. 'It wasn't him doing what he thought he had to do. He was putting his arm around people. He didn't get into the whys and the whats.' But to many consumed with grief, only personal bereavements seemed comparable with what they were now enduring.

There was no obvious successor to Corbyn, no torchbearer for his ideas. As the election had progressed, Karie Murphy and Amy Jackson had started to prepare for a devastating rout, laying the foundations for the 32-year-old Durham firebrand Laura Pidcock to run in Corbyn's place. In the early hours, however, it was announced that Pidcock, too, had lost her seat, her 8,792 majority evaporating. For the first time in parliamentary history, Durham North West was now represented by the Conservatives.

As a new, triumphant army of Tory MPs thronged into Parliament, the weeks following the election passed like a nightmare for Corbyn's devastated staff. 'I don't think I'll ever get over it, the sight of all the Tories who won seats in the Labour heartlands queueing up for their inductions in their new suits,' says Jack McKenna.

Two and a half years previously, Corbynism seemed on the cusp of power. Left ideas and policies, long buried, were being talked about as the new common sense; the Tories were traumatized and in turmoil. That now seemed an age away. The Labour Party was shattered. There had been half a decade of tumult, of the Brexit culture wars which had divided families and communities, and which had plunged both parties into existential crisis for a while. The political system itself had teetered on the brink of collapse. This had now, apparently, given way to a new era of stability – but stability on the terms of a newly triumphalist right.

Five days after the election, on 17 December, Corbyn stood in front of the Parliamentary Labour Party, apologizing and taking responsibility for the defeat. MPs unleashed their fury at him. In the corridors outside, others began to plot what would come next. The following day, Tony Blair urged the party to ditch Corbyn's 'misguided ideology'. As Christmas came round, Johnson's Conservatives seemed masters of all they surveyed. Amid swaggering news headlines – 'Britain sees in new year on a wave of optimism', puffed *The Times* – a story that few noticed was buried in the frenzied talk of impending Brexit, Tory conquest and Labour trauma: in the Chinese city of Wuhan, some thirty people had been struck down by an outbreak of a mystery illness.[12]

Conclusion – The Centre Cannot Hold

'Fifteen minutes late.' Peter Mandelson doesn't even look up at me, glasses perched on his nose as he peers over them at his pre-prepared scribbled notes. This pillar of the governments of Tony Blair and Gordon Brown, with whom he co-founded New Labour, is sitting in a plush meeting room in the Marylebone headquarters of Global Counsel, a corporate consultancy firm he co-founded a decade ago with Benjamin Wegg-Prosser, Tony Blair's former director of strategic communications. It's true, I'm late – and I apologize, taking a seat with some trepidation.

It's 4 March 2020, and Britain is in the midst of an increasingly unsettling interlude: less than three months since Jeremy Corbyn's Labour party suffered electoral obliteration at the hands of Boris Johnson's Brexit populists, and less than three weeks before Johnson's government, belatedly recognizing the threat of the coronavirus pandemic, would impose a national lockdown. As I cycled to Mandelson's offices, England's chief medical officer, Professor Chris Whitty, was warning journalists that 'some deaths' were likely. A storm was coming, but as yet it remained rumblings of thunder in the distance. The old world was still intact, and it was ruled by a Conservative government drunk on triumphalism, rolling around in its newly acquired power, seemingly oblivious to everything else.

Mandelson – a.k.a. the King of Spin and the Prince of Darkness, among other epithets – has a unique demeanour, flashes of playfulness and mischief intermingling with menace. He does not want to do this off the cuff. Carefully, he begins to read from the notes before him, like a judge pronouncing a verdict. 'First thing I'd say is you have to see this, in my view, as ten years rather than five years,' he says with controlled anger. 'It's been a lost decade in my view for Labour, thrown away on a political experiment by two leaders, not one. I think the result of this experiment was foreseeable. I think both leaders were trying to pull off a project that was not going to work.'

In the judgement handed down by Mandelson, both Ed Miliband and Jeremy Corbyn had turned Labour's 'election-winning machine into a sort of clapped out Ford Cortina'. Mandelson continues. From time to time, he lifts his gaze, looking at me over his glasses. Corbyn, he pronounces, was doomed from the start, not because people weren't willing to give him a chance – he had total power within the party, Mandelson claims – but because he was ill-suited to the job and incapable of creating wide appeal or building a broad electoral coalition. And now, Brexit was being used by delusional Corbynites as an alibi to displace blame for their electoral failure from the real culprits: Corbyn and his team. Corbyn alienated traditional Labour supporters by never talking about his country as something he loved or had pride in, and simultaneously alienated 'as many aspiring have-something-and-want-more working-class voters in the South as he did the sort of disgruntled left-behind working-class voters in the North'.

There was truth, Mandelson concedes, in Corbyn's argument that 'the economic system is tilted in favour of the interests of shareholders and senior executives rather than employees and stakeholders and needs rebalancing'. But in Mandelson's view Corbyn lacked workable reforms or solutions: Corbyn's analysis was not matched by a realizable programme. In the eyes of many, Corbyn wasn't a viable prime minister: he was seen as weak in a crisis and uninterested in national security. Even those attracted by his radicalism didn't believe in its 'practicality, affordability; it had an incredibility around it'. When the 2019 election came, therefore, Corbyn left millions of voters unable to support him – or even the Liberal Democrats, in case they propped him up in power. Corbyn, Mandelson concludes, was more interested in taking control of the party than winning power and did not have the skills needed to win an election, while those surrounding him completely lacked the experience required. Above all else, 'he had an idealized and an ideological view of the working class and his own appeal to it, demonstrated by the fact that more of them ended up voting for Johnson than for Labour'.

For many of Corbyn's enemies, both internally and externally, Mandelson's savage critique is the only credible or legitimate interpretation of Labour in this period: an era, in their view, of self-indulgence, of childish utopianism blended with shambolic incompetence and intolerant factionalism, and morally disgraced by antisemitism. The inevitable – albeit delayed – consequence was electoral devastation and a thumping majority for the demagogic Johnson and a Conservative government infused with right-wing populism. Those who would suffer in consequence were those Labour was founded to represent – and those who the left claimed to champion most. Corbynism, in this view, was an aberration, a pointless tragedy, deserving only to be purged from political life.

This narrative deserves to be robustly countered. Jeremy Corbyn won a landslide victory in two Labour Party leadership elections – elections that were, effectively, open primaries, because his opponents had nothing left to say. All the other flanks of Labour were politically and intellectually exhausted, with no coherent vision or compelling ideas in an age of social convulsion. From 2015 to 2017, Corbyn tapped into a huge well of political disappointment in Britain, because no other credible mainstream politician was willing or able to do so.

If Corbyn was so manifestly unfit to be a leader – and, given his long exile on the backbenches, his lack of conventional leadership skills was undeniable – then what on earth does that say about his political opponents in the Labour Party who he defeated not once, but twice? Before the rise of Corbyn, there was little evidence among Labour's leadership contenders of any commitment to genuinely progressive principles; there was, however, evidence of abject moral bankruptcy. Labour had already joined in the Tory baiting of unemployed and disabled benefit claimants as lazy or feckless. After the 2015 election, a party founded to represent the working class refused to block the passage of a Conservative Welfare Bill which imposed real-terms cuts to in-work benefits for low-paid workers. What, at that point, was Labour even for? If it condoned sacrificing the living standards of supermarket workers, cleaners, bus drivers and lollipop ladies and their children in exchange for a delusional shot at power, why even bother existing? What was it seeking high office to do?

The leanings of many of Corbyn's opponents can be summed up by the jobs they took up after their political careers crashed and burned. Michael Dugher, appointed to Corbyn's first shadow cabinet as a peace offering to the Labour right, announced at the end of 2019 that he was becoming chief executive of the Betting and Gaming Council, becoming, in other words, the most influential gambling lobbyist in Britain.[1] In July 2020 Chris Leslie, briefly shadow chancellor in the months before Corbyn assumed the leadership, was appointed chief executive of the Credit Services Association, the trade association of debt collectors. The same month, Angela Smith, another co-founder of Change UK – who had once savaged Labour's commitment to public ownership of water in the Murdoch press[2] – joined the board of a private water company.[3] July turned out to be a bonanza month for Change UK alumni: Chuka Umunna joined public relations firm Edelman,[4] which in North America had run PR campaigns countering criticism from trade union-funded critics of Walmart[5] and in support of the controversial Keystone XL pipeline,[6] and which had been retained by the Murdoch empire when it was accused of phone hacking.[7] Why, you might ask, were these people *ever* in the Labour Party? What possible injustices once burned in the hearts of these eventual corporate apologists and champions of gamblers, debt collectors and water companies?

In 2015 Corbyn assumed the Labour leadership with such an overwhelming mandate because he was offering a vision that was hopeful, optimistic and brave. He presented a twenty-first-century iteration of social democracy, including ideas few would once have blinked at: corporation tax and a top rate of income tax lower than during most of the period Margaret Thatcher was in power, and a public ownership programme that was less extensive than that which existed in 1970s Britain. Indeed, most of his flagship policies – from publicly owned utilities to free university education – were to be found successfully in operation in countries in Europe and beyond. The polls consistently showed that such policies are popular; only a small minority cited them as reasons to not vote for the party in 2019. But

Labour's elite had junked even a modest form of social democracy in favour of a political no-man's land – and those who end up in such ground are gunned down by the opposition.

Today, many of Corbyn's opponents remain conceptually frozen in the late 1990s, when Tony Blair triumphed in Britain alongside like-minded political torchbearers in Western Europe and the United States. Simply through the process of laying claim to the mantle of Blairism, they believe both that they inherit a magical election-winning political formula, and that Blairism is an answer to today's challenges. Even before the Covid-19 pandemic detonated like a bomb at the heart of the global economic system, the late 1990s felt like a different, far-away political universe – and a fantasy one at that. One in which the bubble of financialized capitalism seemed to guarantee an eternity of economic growth and living standards; or, so the mantra went, a rising tide that would lift all boats. The financial crash of 2008, and, crucially, the savagely punitive austerity policies that followed, changed all that. Austerity transformed politics, fuelling the rise of right-wing populism, the new left and civic nationalism. It entrenched an unprecedented divide between the generations. If you believe that the real conflict in society is between those who have wealth and power and those who do not, then this poses a genuine challenge.

Although in today's Britain 1.9 million pensioners continue to languish in poverty – a shamefully higher rate than in most wealthy nations – successive governments have tended to legislate in their favour. Pensioners' living standards have rightly been protected, and even improved, through a 'triple lock' which ensures annual rises in the state pension; through increasing levels of home-ownership among older people, rising house prices (until Covid-19 hit), and quantitative easing inflating asset prices and equity. Governments' focus on this demographic is unsurprising: not only do they constitute a quarter of the electorate, they are the most motivated to vote. Given that this older demographic is also the most socially conservative on issues ranging from immigration to LGBTQ rights to Muslims, it's equally unsurprising that Labour has not won a majority of pensioners since 1997. At every election since, the Conservative lead in this demographic has increased.

Yet it is younger people who suffered an unprecedented squeeze in living standards, a growing housing crisis, student debt, decimated public services, slash-and-burn cuts to social security, as well as an assault on deeply held progressive social values – and who were most attracted to the Corbynite flame. Corbynism won the support of younger people in unprecedented numbers; but it also repelled older people to an unparalleled degree. That is its success and failure in a single sentence. The left's central dilemma is this: how to win the support of older citizens without betraying the hopes and aspirations of their children and grandchildren.

Those opposed to the Corbyn project claim that the left used Brexit as an excuse for its self-evident failures. Corbyn's Labour struggled to answer Britain's most serious post-war political crisis, but hubristically believed that its Conservative opponents would come off worse in the aftermath. As time went on, though – and especially after the 2017 election – Brexit sucked the oxygen out of politics, and there was little room for discussion of any other political issue in the national conversation. Corbyn's sole major advantage, as a figure of principle and conviction, was destroyed in this period. It is possible to critique the Corbyn leadership's approach to Brexit while also accepting that even a far better organized, more strategically minded operation would have badly struggled. If Labour had been led by an ardent Blairite who narrowed the differences on political issues with the Tories and was simultaneously evangelical on Remain, the party would surely have suffered an even more disastrous defeat. Although Labour's strategist in this period, Seumas Milne, has much to answer for, he was right to fear what would happen if the older working-class voters who voted for the Leave cause left Labour's fold. According to a poll taken on election day, of those who abandoned Labour in 2019, 34 per cent did so 'to get Brexit done' and 18 per cent 'to stop Brexit'; just 10 per cent mentioned policies and 5 per cent Corbyn. Among those who defected to the Tories, 71 per cent cited getting Brexit done, with just 6 per cent opting for policies.[8] Brexit underscores that culture wars are poison to political causes focused on redistributing wealth and power, rather than on cultural identity. It's an issue the left must get to grips with.

The Corbyn project, too, was the victim of long-term trends which preceded it by many years. As the election post-mortem by Labour

Together – a coalition of MPs and activists – underlined, Labour's support was being displaced over time by the Tories in ageing, largely white post-industrial areas in the North and Midlands. Brexit underlined and accelerated that process, and Corbynism did not have an adequate response to it.

Corbyn himself was subjected to a remorseless and highly personal onslaught from across the media, aided and abetted by several Labour MPs and a significant chunk of the party machinery that actively wanted their own party to fail under Corbyn: an unprecedented bombardment from inside and outside. None of this absolves Corbynism of its many failures in management, communications and, especially, strategy. After the 2017 election, Labour had a genuine shot at power. It had increased its number of seats for the first time in two decades, and enjoyed its biggest surge in vote share since 1945. The transformative policies it had offered in the election had widespread appeal. Despite subsequent attempts to revise history, there was then a broad consensus that Corbyn had every chance of becoming prime minister in the febrile months that followed; indeed, Labour's polling hovered around 40 per cent until early 2019.

The aftermath of that election could have been capitalized on, with a clear strategy to win over the voters Labour needed to secure a majority. While this was undoubtedly complicated by Brexit – such voters were most likely to have plumped for Leave – no clear coherent long-term strategy for the party was put together. As it had been from the outset, planning was done off the cuff and was invariably defensive and reactive, responding to events as they happened. In part, this approach was fuelled by complacency in the leader's office. They had, after all, proved naysayers wrong in the 2017 election, and felt it vindicated their general approach, which therefore needed little adjustment or correction. There was a sense, too, that the Tories would simply implode because of their internal contradictions.

By 2019, Labour's top brass had become crippled by divisions over Brexit. That this reflected the polarization of British society at large does not absolve the leadership of responsibility for two disastrous errors. First was its paralysed response to Boris Johnson becoming prime minister. Because Labour had no meaningful plan in place to deal with an outcome which could have been predicted for months,

Johnson, along with his chief adviser, Dominic Cummings, was able to define himself on his own terms. The second mistake, which arose from the collapse of the top team into acrimony, was a disastrous lack of strategy and narrative.

The same goes for the failures on antisemitism, the response to which was obtuse in almost every conceivable way. A clear strategy adopted earlier would have both focused on dealing with the party's processes on complaints about antisemitism, combined with speeches and initiatives reaching out to Jewish communities, and the roll-out of political education among the membership to deal with conspiracist mentalities, ignorance and bigotry which lead to antisemitism. Once again, the response was defensive, piecemeal and completely inadequate. Corbyn's political opponents would always have sought to exploit the issue, to toxify Corbynism – and did so mercilessly – but they would have been far more isolated, and far less effective, if the leadership had moved faster, further and more proactively to show genuine resolve and empathy in combating the menace of antisemitism.

What of Corbyn himself? History will undoubtedly be far kinder to the reluctant Labour leader than the judgement that currently prevails. Nobody who knows Corbyn well would ever dispute that he was driven by a genuine deep-rooted revulsion of injustice, and a desperate burning commitment to building a world free of exploitation, oppression, bigotry, racism and violence. Before he stood for leader, supporters and critics alike agreed on his compassion, his generosity of spirit, and an equal, open-handed warmth towards those who agreed and those who strongly disagreed with his beliefs, personal qualities that led some Labour MPs who opposed his politics to nominate him for a place on the leadership ballot in the summer of 2015. His aversion in all circumstances to making personal attacks, even when faced with extreme provocation, was testament to his humane values. He withstood a campaign of vilification that would have broken most. He had an unbending sense of loyalty.

But a balanced portrayal of Corbyn has to acknowledge his failures. His backbench exile for most of his political life left him lacking the experience or skillset of conventional leaders. His aversion to conflict, while appealing – few saw him as a scary demagogue – rendered him chronically indecisive, and his leadership sometimes directionless and rudderless. Long accustomed to mixing in left-wing circles where there was near unanimity on key political questions, he struggled with difficult conversations with those who passionately dissented. His otherwise commendable sense of loyalty partly explains the prolonging of Labour's agony on antisemitism, because decisive action meant facing down long-standing allies. As a backbencher, his quirkily run operation was legendary; as leader of the opposition, organization was left to the aides around him. Whatever their failures, though, the buck has to stop with him. His stubbornness ensured his survival in the face of an unprecedented assault from every direction, but it also left him all too defensive and contributed to a bunker mentality some of his allies perpetuated. It is worth remembering, too, that this was not a politician who sought power. He first stood for the leadership out of a sense of duty, not because he believed he would win – he did not – but to advance and promote causes he had championed throughout his life.

Would it not have been wise, sometime between the 2017 and 2019 elections, for another torchbearer of left politics to take his place? This is a question which benefits from hindsight. Why would a leader resign after Labour's first gains in an election since 1997? The fact that Corbyn's Labour started from such a calamitous place when Theresa May called the 2017 election and managed to turn it around had a lasting consequence: if he could do it once, why not again? Would not Brexit have wreaked the same political mayhem whoever was leader? These counterfactuals can never be tested. Nonetheless, it is a tragedy for the left that John McDonnell, long the Labour left's natural figurehead, never assumed the leadership. Whether the membership would have voted for him – whether there was something about Corbyn's personality, as many of his defenders believed, that was key to his triumph – is again untestable. McDonnell is one of the most impressive postwar Labour figures, a working-class autodidact, one of the few genuine intellects in politics, and someone who understood that the left needed to be serious and focused on winning the prize: securing power in order to transform society and overcome injustice. He will remain Labour's lost leader.

*

In the aftermath of the 2019 defeat, the Labour membership voted for a new leader. The membership, broadly speaking, can be divided into thirds: one third who will vote for whoever the left candidate is, another third who will vote for anyone but; and a middle third who are floating voters, but who passionately abhor injustice and desperately want the Tories removed from power. It was Keir Starmer who most successfully appealed to this middle third to secure his inevitable landslide victory because he convinced them he was the most electable and effective and did not represent a significant departure from their values and beliefs.

What, then, is the legacy of Corbynism? Is it, as the likes of Peter Mandelson hope, an aberration in Labour's history, to be extinguished as a period of monumental self-indulgence and moral disgrace? Maybe not. During the leadership campaign, Starmer declared: 'We should treat the 2017 manifesto as our foundational document; the radicalism and the hope that that inspired across the country was real.' He committed to ten pledges, including raising taxes on the affluent and big business, public investment, the scrapping of tuition fees, public ownership, no illegal wars, replacing the Tories' cruel social security system, and defending migrants' rights. Before Corbyn, such ideas would have been condemned as hopelessly naïve and unrealistic. Now, the most basic tenets of social democracy are embraced once again – and that is a political legacy in itself. 'We are not going to trash the last Labour government,' Starmer declared, 'nor are we going to trash the last four years.' That forms his democratic mandate. Perhaps, then, the legacy of Corbynism is to ensure that the new mainstream of the Labour Party is one that never again commits to austerity, or the baiting of benefit claimants, or the demonizing of migrants.

Whether Starmer's leadership sticks to those commitments remains an open question. Those who decide to stay members of the Labour Party should certainly fight to ensure that they do. But the struggle for change does not simply take place within the confines of political parties. Following the police killing of George Floyd in the United States at the end of May 2020, global Black Lives Matter protests against systemic racism exploded. Extra-parliamentary struggles – mass movements in the streets that are impossible for the powerful to ignore – must surely take centre stage, whether the cause be workers' rights, the climate emergency, public investment, the welfare state or peace.

Today, in the age of Covid-19 and beyond, the debates and ideas this book explores are more important than ever for the future that we hope to build, and for the future of the generations to come. Indeed, one of the legacies of the Corbyn period is that the left is no longer simply defined by what it is against, rather than what it is for. It nurtured a new ecosystem of think tanks, economists and intellectuals who are seriously engaged in debating what a new world could look like, brimming with ideas such as the four-day working week, a Green Industrial Revolution, and the democratization of the workplace and the economy.

Just over three months after the 2019 election, British society was shut down in response to the coronavirus pandemic. 'Boris must embrace socialism immediately to save the liberal free market,' boomed the *Telegraph*, as the age of coronavirus dawned. Undoubtedly, the Conservative government had no choice but to enact the most dramatic expansion of the state in peacetime, which included paying the wages of half the country's workforce. Yet this move was designed to preserve the existing failed model of capitalism, not to lay the foundations of a better alternative. A Corbyn premiership would have transformed the lives of the struggling and the insecure: from a war on poverty, to the provision of affordable housing, to the scrapping of tuition fees, to the Green Industrial Revolution which would have combatted the climate emergency, created skilled jobs and raised people's standard of living. More to the point, it would have done all this without being compelled by an unprecedented national trauma, but out of conviction. Instead, Britain was lumbered with Boris Johnson, a right-wing charlatan with a record of deceit, whose sole guiding principle is the pursuit of power, with a history of whipping up bigotry against minorities ranging from Muslims to gay people. His administration has gone on to preside – if its response can be described as such – over one of the most catastrophic national responses to coronavirus, both because of its fears that swift and decisive action would cause excessive damage to the economy (which in many decisions it seems to have prioritized over human life), and because the

British state, long before hollowed out by austerity and free-market dogma, was hopelessly underprepared for such an unprecedented national crisis. The price has been paid in the avoidable deaths of tens of thousands of predominantly older Britons.

As the most serious economic crisis since the Great Depression beckons, there are no guarantees that a more socially just world will emerge. The economic turmoil of the 1930s led to fascism; in the 1970s, it led to the Thatcherite and Reaganite counter-revolution. Today, we are haunted by the spectre of right-wing authoritarian populism. Without an inspiring and convincing alternative from those who champion a radical redistribution of wealth and power, and a society which prioritizes the needs and aspirations of the majority over those of a thriving elite, those forces will prosper. Comparisons are made between the current pandemic and the Second World War. While they are often flawed, it's striking that in 1945, at the end of the war, the incumbent government led by a Conservative prime minister was swept aside in a landslide victory for a reforming Labour government, a Labour government which shredded the old status quo in favour of a new settlement, of a welfare state, National Health Service, public ownership and state intervention. Now the war had been won, Labour argued, it was time to win the peace.

If Corbynism showed anything, then it is that ours is an age in which people are demanding radical solutions to a fall in living standards unprecedented for generations. The Covid-19 pandemic may well prove only the warm-up act for a far greater emergency that threatens human existence itself: a climate crisis, which demands a fundamental transformation of our social and economic system.

Far from being answered, the injustices that led to the rise of Corbynism have only intensified. As long as wealthy nations fail to provide security and comfort to their citizens, as long as millions are deprived of the promise that growing prosperity will deliver a more comfortable and fulfilling existence for them and their families, as long as rising global temperatures menace human civilization, there will be a demand for unambiguously radical answers. Coronavirus has further exposed the harsh realities of societies – both in Britain and around the globe – in which millions are always one pay cheque away from hardship, in which the self-employed and gig economy workforce are deprived of basic security, in which the welfare state is chronically inadequate, in which private tenants are at the mercy of landlords, in which health and social care services are under-resourced and fragmented.

Can we, together, build a new society free from such ills? This was the hope of Corbynism and the many who embraced it. Those of us who continue to believe so must learn from the successes and defeats, gains and mistakes of that time. Learning such lessons does not mean abandoning a commitment to building a new society which focuses on human needs and aspirations, or surrendering to the political pessimism of tinkering around the edges and attempting to put an acceptable face on continued injustice. On the contrary. Learning such lessons shows that we are serious about building a new world. With so much injustice coexisting with limitless human potential, building a new world isn't a utopian dream, a self-indulgent fantasy. It is the only hope for humanity.

Notes

INTRODUCTION

1. https://www.nursingtimes.net/news/policies-and-guidance/nurses-deliver-scrap-the-cap-pay-petition-to-downing-street-20-10-2017/
2. https://www.theguardian.com/politics/2018/sep/23/welfare-spending-uk-poorest-austerity-frank-field
3. https://www.ifs.org.uk/publications/14370; https://www.theguardian.com/books/2019/dec/06/britain-has-closed-almost-800-libraries-since-2010-figures-show; https://www.theguardian.com/uk-news/2019/may/07/cuts-england-museums-london-cliff-edge; https://www.thetimes.co.uk/article/leisure-centres-close-as-spending-on-council-run-sports-facilities-plunges-6tqg7gxmb; https://www.cnp.org.uk/stop-cuts; https://www.theguardian.com/society/2019/jan/28/councils-say-more-arts-cuts-inevitable-amid-rising-social-care-need
4. https://www.theguardian.com/business/2020/apr/20/british-households-face-disposable-income-fall-of-515-per-month
5. https://www.mirror.co.uk/news/uk-news/uk-food-banks-see-demand-22088998
6. https://www.ons.gov.uk/peoplepopulationandcommunity/birthsdeathsandmarriages/deaths/bulletins/deathsinvolvingcovid19bylocalareasanddeprivation/deathsoccurringbetween1marchand31may2020?hootPostID=99da561a8f846d840579c3aa49ad15fa
7. https://www.imperial.ac.uk/news/198155/neil-ferguson-talks-modelling-lockdown-scientific/
8. https://www.itv.com/goodmorningbritain/articles/locking-down-a-week-earlier-could-resulted-in-less-than-10-000-deaths-former

CHAPTER 1

1. James Curran and Jean Seaton, *Power Without Responsibility: Press, Broadcasting and the Internet in Britain* (Routledge, 2009), p. 143
2. Tony Benn, *The Benn Diaries* (Hutchinson, 1995), p. 388
3. https://www.standard.co.uk/comment/comment/joe-murphy-jeremy-corbyn-will-hang-on-as-leader-but-the-battle-is-far-from-over-a3350531.html
4. http://www.politicsresources.net/area/uk/man/lab74feb.htm
5. https://www.theguardian.com/politics/2014/mar/16/tony-benn-1980-interview-loss-thatcher-surrender-defeat-labour
6. Mark Fisher, *Capitalist Realism: Is There No Alternative?* (O Books, 2009), p. 2
7. https://assets.publishing.service.gov.uk/government/uploads/system/uploads/attachment_data/file/805268/trade-union-membership-2018-statistical-bulletin.pdf
8. http://corporate.centralus.co.uk/articles/call-centre-turnover/
9. http://www.bbc.co.uk/news/av/uk-politics-22073434/tony-blair-my-job-was-to-build-on-some-thatcher-policies
10. https://wwws.theguardian.com/politics/2001/oct/02/labourconference.labour6
11. https://www.telegraph.co.uk/news/politics/2475301/Labour-membership-falls-to-historic-low.html
12. http://news.bbc.co.uk/1/hi/uk_politics/4422086.stm
13. http://www.johnmcdonnell.org.uk/2007/02/new-labour-privatises-probation-and.html
14. https://www.trustforlondon.org.uk/data/boroughs/islington-poverty-and-inequality-indicators/
15. https://www.ft.com/content/363af3be-1236-11e8-940e-08320fc2a277
16. https://www.theguardian.com/money/2018/feb/16/homeownership-among-young-adults-collapsed-institute-fiscal-studies
17. https://www.theguardian.com/society/2020/jan/20/youth-services-suffer-70-funding-cut-in-less-than-a-decade
18. http://news.bbc.co.uk/1/hi/uk_politics/2289017.stm
19. https://www.indymedia.org.uk/en/2003/09/277888.html
20. https://www.telegraph.co.uk/news/uknews/1562023/Tories-vow-to-match-Labour-spending.html
21. https://www.theguardian.com/politics/2009/sep/15/george-osborne-speech-full-text
22. https://www.theguardian.com/politics/2010/mar/25/alistair-darling-cut-deeper-margaret-thatcher

23. https://www.theguardian.com/politics/2009/sep/18/nick-clegg-liberal-democrats-spending
24. http://www.telegraph.co.uk/news/politics/labour/4248254/MP-suspended-for-picking-up-mace-during-Heathrow-debate.html
25. https://www.theguardian.com/politics/2009/apr/21/g20-protest-video-police
26. https://www.indymedia.org.uk/en/2011/03/474954.html
27. https://www.theguardian.com/politics/2010/may/07/polling-queues-hundreds-unable-vote
28. https://www.politics.co.uk/news/2011/12/20/uk-uncut-vindicated-commons-report-backs-protest-group
29. https://www.ft.com/content/b189980a-19a5-11e9-9e64-d150b3105d21
30. https://www.ucu.org.uk/article/10342/Value-of-university-staff-pay-has-plummeted-in-last-decade-employers-own-research-reveals
31. https://www.theguardian.com/education/2019/mar/21/england-universities-in-deficit-figures-financial-pressure
32. https://www.bbc.co.uk/news/business-46459694
33. https://www.newstatesman.com/newspapers/2010/12/police-malik-caught-students; https://www.theguardian.com/uk/2010/dec/15/jody-mcintyre-protester-dragged-from-wheelchair; https://www.bbc.co.uk/news/uk-england-london-11967098
34. https://publications.parliament.uk/pa/cm201012/cmhansrd/cm101213/debtext/101213-0001.htm
35. https://www.pressgazette.co.uk/journalist-shiv-malik-injured-by-police-baton/
36. https://www.telegraph.co.uk/education/educationnews/8213287/Len-McCluskey-head-of-Britains-biggest-union-praises-magnificent-student-protest-movement.html

CHAPTER 2

1. https://www.theguardian.com/commentisfree/2010/aug/29/ed-miliband-labour-leadership-change
2. https://labourlist.org/2010/08/the-growth-deniers-ed-balls-full-speech/
3. https://www.theguardian.com/politics/2011/sep/27/ed-miliband-speech-labour-conference
4. https://www.bbc.co.uk/news/business-11153166
5. https://yougov.co.uk/news/2015/11/25/conservative-blame-spending-cuts/
6. https://www.theguardian.com/politics/2015/may/30/chris-leslie-interview-labour-shadow-chancellor-election

7. https://blogs.lse.ac.uk/brexit/2020/04/03/three-years-in-hell-fintan-otoole-on-the-disastrous-corbyn-effect/
8. https://www.youtube.com/watch?v=JaxApp3kkVI
9. https://twitter.com/lukeakehurst/status/606154157318356993
10. http://islingtonrefugeeforum.org/wp-content/uploads/2015/09/IRF-Refugee-Week-June-15-Report-Final-docx.pdf
11. https://www.theguardian.com/politics/2015/jun/15/labour-leftwinger-jeremy-corbyn-wins-place-on-ballot-for-leadership
12. https://www.thetimes.co.uk/article/social-media-could-blow-apart-labours-race-qhhz8360fx3
13. https://www.telegraph.co.uk/news/politics/11745648/Labour-behaving-like-a-petulant-child-warns-Chuka-Umunna.html
14. https://www.theguardian.com/politics/video/2015/jul/22/tony-blair-jeremy-corbyn-labour-leadership-video
15. https://www.telegraph.co.uk/news/politics/labour/11741861/How-you-can-help-Jeremy-Corbyn-win-and-destroy-the-Labour-Party.html
16. https://www.telegraph.co.uk/news/general-election-2015/politics-blog/11680016/Why-Tories-should-join-Labour-and-back-Jeremy-Corbyn.html
17. https://www.telegraph.co.uk/finance/economics/11776925/A-Corbyn-victory-in-the-Labour-leadership-battle-would-be-a-disaster.html
18. https://www.telegraph.co.uk/news/politics/labour/11767152/Tories-dont-vote-for-Jeremy-Corbyn.-It-wont-end-well.html

CHAPTER 3

1. https://www.mirror.co.uk/news/uk-news/heres-what-jeremy-corbyn-really-6438877
2. https://pressgazette.co.uk/sun-and-mail-online-both-take-down-stories-claiming-jeremy-corbyn-was-dancing-a-jig-on-way-to-cenotaph/
3. https://www.businessinsider.com/the-ridiculous-ways-the-media-misre presents-jeremy-corbyn-2015-12
4. http://www.lse.ac.uk/media-and-communications/assets/documents/research/projects/corbyn/Cobyn-Report.pdf
5. https://www.theguardian.com/media/2016/may/12/bbc-bias-labour-sir-michael-lyons
6. https://www.opendemocracy.net/en/opendemocracyuk/were-labours-antisemitism-failures-really-corbyns-fault/

7. https://www.independent.co.uk/news/uk/politics/diane-abbott-abuse-female-mps-trolling-racism-sexism-almost-half-total-amnesty-poll-a7931126.html
8. https://www.telegraph.co.uk/news/politics/labour/11764159/Jeremy-Corbyn-faces-coup-plot-if-he-wins-Labour-leadership.html
9. https://www.thetimes.co.uk/article/plot-to-oust-corbyn-on-day-one-2jk7cw8rrkn
10. https://www.theguardian.com/politics/2015/aug/20/jeremy-corbyns-honeymoon-period-will-last-until-local-elections
11. https://www.newstatesman.com/politics/2015/08/owen-jones-right-are-mocking-jeremy-corbyn-because-secretly-they-fear-him
12. https://twitter.com/shamindernahal/status/644214378296905728
13. https://www.independent.co.uk/news/uk/politics/temporary-nationali sation-of-threatened-tata-steel-plants-is-an-option-minister-confirms-a6959201.html
14. https://www.theguardian.com/society/2016/jan/23/poll-junior-doctors-support
15. https://www.telegraph.co.uk/news/politics/Jeremy_Corbyn/12021973/ Jeremy-Corbyn-faces-humiliation-as-more-than-100-Labour-MPs-plan-to-defy-leader-over-Syria-air-strikes.html
16. https://www.independent.co.uk/news/uk/politics/saudi-arabia-yemen-labour-mps-debate-bombing-intervention-woodcock-a7382706.html
17. https://www.telegraph.co.uk/news/2016/11/30/pmqs-jeremy-corbyn-takes-theresa-may-as-conservatives-edge-towards/
18. https://yougov.co.uk/topics/politics/articles-reports/2016/06/30/labour-members-corbyn-post-brexit
19. https://www.huffingtonpost.co.uk/entry/jeremy-corbyn-parliamentary-labour-party-plp-meeting-told-to-quit-margaret-hodge-alan-johnson uk_5771819ee4b08d2c5639bfc0
20. https://www.theguardian.com/commentisfree/2016/jun/29/labour-mps-vs-corbyn-war-party-members-tories-brexit
21. https://www.independent.co.uk/news/uk/politics/thousands-of-jeremy-corbyn-supporters-march-on-parliament-against-labour-party-leader ship-challenge-a7106511.html
22. https://twitter.com/aliceperryuk/status/753663563546451969
23. https://www.theguardian.com/politics/2016/jul/20/owen-smith-i-have-never-advocated-privatisation-of-the-nhs
24. https://www.mirror.co.uk/news/uk-news/listen-moment-owen-smith-made-8759470

25. https://d25d2506sfb94s.cloudfront.net/cumulus_uploads/document/0cpa7iw5l7/TimesResults_160830_LabourSelectorate.pdf

CHAPTER 4

1. https://news.sky.com/story/corbyns-cabinet-chaos-the-inside-story-10346377
2. https://www.theguardian.com/commentisfree/2014/oct/29/counter weight-us-power-global-necessity-conflicts-spread
3. https://www.theguardian.com/politics/2018/apr/14/labour-and-tories-level-corbyn-popularity-wanes-poll
4. https://www.independent.co.uk/news/uk/politics/john-mcdonnell-defends-jeremy-corbyn-russia-response-nerve-agent-a8261946.html
5. https://www.theguardian.com/politics/2018/mar/11/labour-mps-should-not-appear-on-russia-today-says-john-mcdonnell
6. https://www.theguardian.com/media/greenslade/2017/jan/18/theresa-mays-brexit-speech-what-the-national-newspapers-say
7. https://medium.com/@OwenJones84/questions-all-jeremy-corbyn-supporters-need-to-answer-b3e82ace7ed3
8. https://www.theguardian.com/commentisfree/2017/mar/01/corbyn-staying-not-good-enough
9. https://www.telegraph.co.uk/news/2017/02/09/clive-lewis-sounds-support-challenge-jeremy-corbyn-labour-leader/
10. https://www.vice.com/en_uk/article/69w7np/glastonbury-dispatches-tom-watson-mp

CHAPTER 5

1. http://www.mirror.co.uk/news/politics/tories-open-up-24-point-10259681
2. http://www.politico.eu/article/jeremy-corbyn-less-popular-than-donald-trump-poll/?utm_content=bufferd8e5c&utm_medium=social&utm_source=twitter.com&utm_campaign=buffer
3. https://www.li.com/activities/publications/public-opinion-in-the-post-brexit-era-economic-attitudes-in-modern-britain
4. https://www.ipsos.com/sites/default/files/ct/news/documents/2018-05/global_advisor_socialism_survey.pdf
5. https://www.margaretthatcher.org/document/104475
6. https://www.theguardian.com/politics/2017/apr/20/election-result-not-a-foregone-conclusion-insists-jeremy-corbyn

7. https://www.theguardian.com/commentisfree/2017/sep/25/jeremy-corbyn-power-labour-brexit
8. https://www.independent.co.uk/voices/local-election-2017-latest-analysis-john-curtice-tory-landslide-general-election-a7720801.html
9. https://www.theguardian.com/politics/2017/may/08/tim-farron-margaret-thatcher-poster-childhood-bedroom-itv-interview
10. https://www.bbc.co.uk/news/uk-politics-39761746
11. https://www.theguardian.com/politics/2017/may/16/tim-farron-says-hes-pro-choice-after-2007-interview-emerges
12. https://www.ipsos.com/ipsos-mori/en-uk/how-britain-voted-2015
13. https://www.independent.co.uk/news/uk/politics/election-uk-turnout-voters-registration-labour-tories-record-numbers-a7777931.html
14. https://www.ons.gov.uk/peoplepopulationandcommunity/personalandhouseholdfinances/incomeandwealth/bulletins/nowcastinghouseholdincomeintheuk/financialyearending2017
15. https://www.telegraph.co.uk/news/2017/05/11/labour-mps-reject-jeremy-corbyns-manifesto-theresa-may-warns/
16. https://www.mirror.co.uk/news/politics/poll-shows-people-love-labours-10404216
17. https://www.telegraph.co.uk/news/2017/08/24/conservative-donors-handed-theresa-may-record-25-million-fight/
18. https://twitter.com/MichaelLCrick/status/872158950896144385
19. https://blogs.lse.ac.uk/politicsandpolicy/constituency-visits-impact-on-ge2017/
20. http://www.electoralcalculus.co.uk/cgi-bin/seatdetails.py?seat=Bristol%20East
21. https://www.facebook.com/nut.campaigns/videos/856455754511897/
22. http://blogs.lse.ac.uk/politicsandpolicy/explaining-labours-facebook-success/
23. https://issuu.com/conservativeparty/docs/ge2017_manifesto_a5_digital/10
24. http://www.hulldailymail.co.uk/news/hull-east-yorkshire-news/jeremy-corbyn-gets-rock-star-91728
25. https://www.bbc.co.uk/news/uk-32806520
26. http://www.independent.co.uk/news/uk/politics/jeremy-corbyn-foreign-terror-links-uk-public-agree-latest-poll-labour-policies-a7764476.html
27. https://www.independent.co.uk/news/uk/politics/corbyn-election-results-votes-away-prime-minister-theresa-may-hung-parliament-a7782581.html

CHAPTER 6

1. http://www.conservativemanifesto.com/1970/1970-conservative-manifesto.shtml
2. Mark Baimbridge, Philip Whyman and Andrew Mullen, *The 1975 Referendum on Europe* – Volume 2: *Current Analysis and Lessons* (Imprint Academic, 2006), p. 88
3. Vernon Bogdanor, *The People and the Party System: The Referendum and Electoral Reform in British Politics* (Cambridge University Press, 2009), p. 35
4. Robert Saunders, *Yes to Europe!* (Cambridge University Press, 2018), p. 260
5. https://www.margaretthatcher.org/document/107332
6. http://news.bbc.co.uk/1/hi/uk_politics/1032999.stm
7. https://www.theguardian.com/politics/2015/jul/25/jeremy-corbyn-draws-fire-position-future-britain-eu-membership
8. https://www.theguardian.com/politics/2015/jul/11/david-cameron-employment-law-opt-out-eu-membership-renegotiation
9. https://www.theguardian.com/commentisfree/2015/jul/14/left-reject-eu-greece-eurosceptic
10. https://twitter.com/hendopolis/status/638453468383084544/photo/1
11. https://www.theguardian.com/politics/2014/oct/16/alan-johnson-labour-antidote-ukip
12. https://www.theguardian.com/business/2015/feb/23/uk-wages-to-rise-above-inflation-for-2015-study-shows
13. https://www.businessinsider.com/uk-wages-gdp-and-inequality-2016-3?r=US&IR=T
14. https://www.telegraph.co.uk/news/uknews/immigration/8449324/David-Cameron-migration-threatens-our-way-of-life.html
15. https://www.bbc.co.uk/news/av/uk-politics-eu-referendum-36506163/corbyn-i-m-seven-out-of-10-on-eu
16. http://www.ukpol.co.uk/jeremy-corbyn-2016-speech-on-the-eu-2/
17. https://www.bbc.co.uk/news/av/uk-politics-eu-referendum-36437136/boris-johnson-auctions-off-a-beautiful-milker-cow
18. https://www.thetimes.co.uk/edition/news/voters-turn-away-from-eu-as-trust-in-cameron-slides-jlct2rdck; https://www.telegraph.co.uk/news/2016/06/16/eu-referendum-leave-supporters-trust-ordinary-common-sense-than/
19. https://www.theguardian.com/uk-news/2016/may/26/net-migration-to-uk-nears-peak-fewer-britons-emigrate
20. https://www.electoralcommission.org.uk/who-we-are-and-what-we-do/elections-and-referendums/past-elections-and-referendums/eu-referendum/report-23-june-2016-referendum-uks-membership-european-union

21. https://inews.co.uk/opinion/chuka-umunna-wes-streeting-labour-re mainers-will-vote-trigger-article-50-529708
22. https://labourlist.org/2017/07/seema-malhotra-it-is-more-complicated-than-class-and-brexit-labour-needs-a-one-nation-consensus-to-win-again/
23. http://statsforlefties.blogspot.com/2018/11/do-i-stay-or-do-i-go-labours-brexit.html
24. https://www.theguardian.com/politics/2017/feb/21/peter-mandelson-i-try-to-undermine-jeremy-corbyn-every-day
25. https://labourlist.org/2017/10/tim-bale-inside-labours-massive-member ship-base/
26. https://labourlist.org/2016/11/watson-mocks-lib-dem-brexit-deniers-and-vows-labour-will-not-disrespect-public-by-trying-to-overturn-eu-vote/
27. https://labour.org.uk/press/jeremy-corbyn-brexit-speech-wakefield/
28. https://www.telegraph.co.uk/politics/2019/04/08/exclusive-britons-split-middle-no-deal-no-brexit-telegraph-poll/
29. https://yougov.co.uk/topics/politics/articles-reports/2019/05/13/voting-intention-conservatives-24-labour-24-8-9-ma
30. https://yougov.co.uk/topics/politics/articles-reports/2019/01/30/brexit-indecisiveness-seriously-damaging-corbyn

CHAPTER 7

1. https://d25d2506sfb94s.cloudfront.net/cumulus_uploads/document/921pn4p2fh/CampaignAgainstAntisemitismResults_MergedFile_W.pdf
2. https://www.theguardian.com/news/2020/feb/06/antisemitic-incidents-hit-new-high-in-2019-according-to-study
3. https://www.oxfordchabad.org/templates/articlecco_cdo/aid/922682/jewish/Anti-SemitismSymposium.htm
4. https://www.marxists.org/archive/marx/works/1844/jewish-question/
5. 'Introduction' in Michael Bakunin, *Statism and Anarchy* (ed. Marshall Shatz, Cambridge University Press, 1990), p. xxx
6. David Patterson, *Anti-Semitism and its Metaphysical Origins* (Cambridge University Press, 2015), p. 127
7. Robert S. Wistrich, *From Ambivalence to Betrayal: The Left, the Jews and Israel* (University of Nebraska Press, 2012), p. 205
8. George Bornstein, *The Colors of Zion: Blacks, Jews, and Irish from 1845 to 1945* (Harvard University Press, 2011), p. 25
9. George Orwell, *Diaries* (ed. Peter Davison, London, 2009), p. 286

10. Youssef Chaitani, *Dissension Among Allies: Ernest Bevin's Palestine Policy* (Sadiq Books, 2002), p. 123
11. https://www.independent.co.uk/news/uk/politics/nancy-astor-statue-theresa-may-boris-johnson-antisemitism-plymouth-a9226106.html
12. Louise London, *Whitehall and the Jews, 1933–1948: British Immigration Policy* (Cambridge University Press, 2000), p. 106
13. https://forward.com/schmooze/349771/the-5-most-anti-semitic-things-roald-dahl-ever-said/
14. https://www.newstatesman.com/2012/05/britains-last-anti-jewish-riots
15. https://fullfact.org/news/are-majority-british-jews-zionists/
16. https://www.theguardian.com/world/2014/feb/18/israel-boycott-movement-antisemitic-netanyahu
17. https://www.jpr.org.uk/documents/The%20political%20leanings%20of%20British%20Jews.pdf
18. https://www.thejc.com/news/uk-news/huge-majority-of-british-jews-will-vote-tory-jc-poll-reveals-1.66001
19. https://www.thejc.com/news/uk-news/labour-was-catastrophic-on-israel-says-shadow-cabinet-member-michael-dugher-1.66832
20. https://www.independent.co.uk/news/uk/politics/maureen-lipman-says-she-cant-vote-labour-while-ed-miliband-is-leader-9827294.html
21. https://www.ozy.com/news-and-politics/why-british-labour-is-losing-indian-voters/247320/
22. For example: https://edm.parliament.uk/early-day-motion/26545/combatting-antisemitism
23. https://www.spectator.co.uk/article/is-jeremy-corbyn-really-anti-semitic-
24. https://www.theguardian.com/politics/2016/jul/04/jeremy-corbyn-says-he-regrets-calling-hamas-and-hezbollah-friends
25. https://www.bbc.co.uk/news/uk-england-beds-bucks-herts-36009544; https://www.telegraph.co.uk/news/2016/05/02/labour-councillor-suspended-after-calling-for-jews-in-israel-to/
26. https://www.theguardian.com/commentisfree/2016/jun/30/labour-antisemitism-report-shami-chakrabarti-jeremy-corbyn
27. https://www.bod.org.uk/jonathan-arkush-reacts-to-report-by-shami-chakrabarti-inquiry-on-antisemitism/
28. https://www.theguardian.com/politics/2019/mar/27/labour-expels-jackie-walker-for-leaked-antisemitism-comments
29. https://www.thetimes.co.uk/article/exposed-jeremy-corbyns-hate-factory-kkh55kpgx
30. https://jewishnews.timesofisrael.com/musabbir-ali/

31. https://www.standard.co.uk/comment/comment/jeremy-corbyn-what-i-m-doing-to-banish-antisemitism-from-the-labour-party-a3821961.html
32. https://www.businessinsider.com/islamophobia-scandal-conservative-party-goes-right-up-to-the-top-baroness-warsi-interview-2018-6?r=US&IR=T
33. https://www.telegraph.co.uk/politics/2018/08/03/jewish-museum-bars-corbyn-speech-stunt-labour-mps-threaten-quit/
34. https://www.prospectmagazine.co.uk/magazine/the-jewish-community-must-not-become-a-sacrificial-pawn-in-labours-war
35. https://www.thejc.com/news/uk-news/jon-lansman-faces-sceptical-audience-at-limmud-1.474283
36. https://www.thejc.com/news/uk/jewish-voice-for-labour-secretary-says-antisemitism-allegations-are-made-up-1.480714
37. https://www.bod.org.uk/statement-following-board-of-deputies-and-jewish-leadership-council-meeting-with-jeremy-corbyn/
38. https://www.holocaustremembrance.com/working-definition-antisemitism
39. https://www.independent.co.uk/news/world/middle-east/israel-jewish-nation-state-law-passed-arabs-segregation-protests-benjamin-netanyahu-a8454196.html
40. https://www.theguardian.com/politics/2018/apr/28/labour-antisemitism-talks-six-key-sticking-points
41. https://labourlist.org/2016/10/chuka-umunna-clause-iv-tells-us-to-live-in-solidarity-tolerance-and-respect-but-labour-has-failed-to-deliver/
42. https://cst.org.uk/public/data/file/5/0/NEC%20code%20of%20conduct%20Antisemitism.pdf
43. https://www.huffingtonpost.co.uk/entry/jeremy-corbyn-told-by-veteran-jewish-mp-youre-a-fucking-racist-and-anti-semite-margaret-hodge_uk_5b4e34cbe4b0fd5c73bfe020?dh
44. https://www.theguardian.com/politics/2018/jul/22/labour-should-drop-action-against-margaret-hodge-mcdonnell
45. https://labourlist.org/2020/04/internal-report-lays-bare-poor-handling-of-complaints-by-labour/; https://news.sky.com/story/labour-antisemitism-investigation-will-not-be-sent-to-equality-commission-11972071
46. https://jewishnews.timesofisrael.com/opinion-jennie-formby-chief-rabbi-can-criticise-but-heres-why-hes-wrong/
47. https://labour.org.uk/wp-content/uploads/2020/01/13434_20-Statistics-Report-No-Place-For-Antisemitism.pdf
48. https://www.politicshome.com/thehouse/article/chris-williamson-its-like-all-my-christmases-have-come-together-the-sort-of-labour-party-i-dreamed-about

49. https://www.thejc.com/news/uk-news/corbyn-pictured-with-man-who-called-for-labour-members-to-be-able-to-question-holocaust-1.470194
50. https://labourlist.org/2019/03/siobhain-mcdonagh-links-anti-capitalism-to-antisemitism-in-labour/
51. https://twitter.com/jewdas/status/1041264401448423429

CHAPTER 8

1. https://yougov.co.uk/topics/politics/articles-reports/2019/05/30/if-every one-revealed-how-they-voted-last-week-labo
2. https://www.theguardian.com/commentisfree/2019/may/27/second-referendum-labour-corbyn-leave-remain-tories
3. https://yougov.co.uk/topics/politics/articles-reports/2019/06/07/voting-intention-brex-26-lab-20-lib-dem-20-con-18-
4. https://www.theguardian.com/politics/2019/aug/27/labour-is-the-party-of-remain-says-keir-starmer-brexit; https://www.theguardian.com/politics/2019/sep/10/tom-watson-to-break-labours-uneasy-truce-over-brexit
5. https://www.thetimes.co.uk/article/emily-thornberry-defies-jeremy-corbyn-in-push-for-remain-vote-wwzmcx6f8
6. https://www.huffingtonpost.co.uk/entry/jeremy-corbyn-westminster-security-pass_uk_5b98088de4b0511db3e6c1e6?utm_hp_ref=uk-homepage
7. https://www.thetimes.co.uk/article/mi5-head-andrew-parker-summons-jeremy-corbyn-for-facts-of-life-talk-on-terror-vwxncthlf

CHAPTER 9

1. https://www.theguardian.com/politics/2019/oct/30/lib-dems-could-win-hundreds-more-seats-in-election-says-swinson
2. https://theconversation.com/election-coverage-thanks-to-brexit-labour-had-a-media-mountain-to-climb-129099
3. https://www.theguardian.com/commentisfree/2019/dec/03/election-coverage-bbc-tories
4. https://www.theguardian.com/uk-news/2019/nov/25/labour-condemns-attacks-on-two-canvassers-in-their-70s
5. https://www.standard.co.uk/news/crime/labour-activist-in-70s-may-have-cracked-ribs-after-being-attacked-while-campaigning-in-herefor dshire-a4296331.html

6. https://www.buzzfeed.com/alexwickham/a-former-labour-mp-has-endorsed-one-of-the-most-right-wing
7. https://www.theguardian.com/commentisfree/2019/dec/06/john-major-conservative-general-election-vote-head-heart
8. https://www.bloomberg.com/news/articles/2019-11-20/corbyn-holds-johnson-to-draw-in-debate-u-k-campaign-trail
9. https://www.theguardian.com/politics/2019/nov/15/labour-full-fibre-broadband-is-the-uk-lagging-behind-other-countries
10. Ibid.; https://www.theguardian.com/commentisfree/2019/nov/17/labour-broadband-election-victories-housing-schools-hospitals
11. https://www.ft.com/content/ab3692b0-2317-11ea-92da-f0c92e957a96
12. https://www.independent.co.uk/news/world/asia/china-illness-outbreak-sars-pneumonia-sick-virus-wuhan-health-a9265506.html

CONCLUSION

1. https://bettingandgamingcouncil.com/news/chief-executive/
2. https://www.thetimes.co.uk/article/labour-mp-savages-partys-water-policy-5ksdz6zpd
3. https://wwtonline.co.uk/news/portsmouth-water-welcomes-former-mp-angela-smith-to-the-board
4. https://www.ft.com/content/00170888-ec98-4d12-ba5e-458e7bf8b5bc
5. https://newsgeneration.com/2014/04/04/pr-case-study-walmarting-across-america/
6. https://www.theguardian.com/environment/2014/nov/18/revealed-key stone-companys-pr-blitz-to-safeguard-its-backup-plan
7. https://www.theguardian.com/media/2011/jul/14/phone-hacking-rupert-murdoch
8. https://static1.squarespace.com/static/5db0ca668552dd5ab1168a91/t/5df3b3521678ca75389801cf/1576252248629/Reasons-OmPoll-13-12-2019.pdf

Acknowledgements

This was not an easy book to write. For those of us who believe that wealthy societies have the means and ability to cure their injustices, Labour's electoral rout on 12 December 2019 felt like being trapped in a horror film with no end. It had followed years of increasingly embittered political polarization which was exhausting for all involved. There was no respite, of course. I wrote much of this book during the enforced national lockdowns which followed the Covid-19 pandemic, as hundreds of thousands died across the world, economies crashed, and normal human activity was suppressed. There have been many periods of hope and optimism throughout the history of our species; this, as you will all know, was not one of them.

There are many people I'd like to thank for their help, support and advice, not least as they were often dealing with far greater stresses than my own. As ever, there are two people I would like to give special thanks to. One is my indefatigable editor, Tom Penn. Few writers have the honour of having an esteemed author as an editor – please, do read his phenomenal books. He would undoubtedly like to edit all of this out, but unfortunately he can't, but his intellect, astonishing eye for detail, far better prose than my own, empathy and, above all else, patience made this book possible. As ever, the successes are shared, but any errors are mine alone.

My agent, Andrew Gordon, took a chance on me over a decade ago, and had no rational reason to do so. I am beyond indebted to his unwavering support, his guidance, his wisdom. I wouldn't be doing what I do without them both and I am eternally grateful.

Bela Cunha did an amazing job copy-editing this at ludicrously short notice; my eternal apologies and gratitude. Allen Lane's fantastic senior editorial manager, Richard Duguid, kept all the wheels turning, just as he did for my last book. To the incredible Isabel Blake and Julie Woon: I'm in huge debt for your brilliant work publicizing the book.

George, you put up with a lot, and your unconditional love in difficult times deserves, as ever, to be properly recorded.

I've been blessed over these last few years to have the support, solidarity and love of friends whom I'm proud to have in what has been a turbulent time. Many of you have read excerpts of this book and suggested edits and changes, and I can't thank you enough. So, thank you Nick Baker, Dan Beaumont, Alex Beecroft, Jack Bond, James Butler, Shami Chakrabarti, Andrew Fisher, Becky Gardiner, Jeff Ingold, Eleanor Jones, Leah Kreitzman, Josh Lee, Clive Lewis, Debbie Linsky, Josie Long, Rory Macqueen, Kirsty Major, Leon Marshall, Joss McDonald, David Mosley, Ellie Mae O'Hagan, Tom Peters, Nick Pope, Georgie Robertson, Joe Ryle, Ash Sarkar, Ricky Power Sayeed, James Schneider, Michael Segalov, Rachel Shabi, Faiza Shaheen, Jonathan Shainin, Maeve Shearlaw, Stefan Smith, Jon Stone, Joe Todd, Michael Walker, Abi Wilkinson, Matt Zarb-Cousin.

My dad, Rob Jones, died between my previous book and this one. I owe everything to him and to my mum, Ruth Aylett, whose burning passion against injustice I inherited. We haven't won socialism yet, alas, but one day.

And finally, to the younger people in particular inspired by the last few years. Many may now feel jaded, demoralized, fed up. But nothing has given me more hope than the next generation. Whatever the failures of those older than them, I'm more convinced than ever that it will be those younger than myself who will save us all. Learn from the mistakes of the past – but never abandon your courage, determination and commitment to finally building a world free from injustice, exploitation, oppression, bigotry and violence.